Women and the Historical Enterprise in America

Women and the Historical Enterprise in America

Gender, Race,
and the Politics
of Memory,
1880–1945

Julie Des Jardins

The
University of
North Carolina
Press
Chapel Hill
and London

Manufactured in the United States of America
Set in Minion types by Keystone Typesetting, Inc.
The paper in this book meets the guidelines for
permanence and durability of the Committee on
Production Guidelines for Book Longevity of the
Council on Library Resources.

Library of Congress Cataloging-in-Publication Data
Des Jardins, Julie.
Women and the historical enterprise in America :
gender, race, and the politics of memory, 1880–1945 / by
Julie Des Jardins.
    p. cm. — (Gender & American culture)
Includes bibliographical references (p.) and index.
ISBN 0-8078-2796-7 (cloth: alk. paper)
ISBN 0-8078-5475-1 (pbk.: alk. paper)
1. Historiography—Social aspects—United States—
History. 2. Historiography—Political aspects—United
States—History. 3. Women historians—United States—
History. 4. United States—Race relations. 5. Sex role—
United States—History. 6. United States—
Historiography. 7. Memory—Social aspects—United
States—History. 8. Memory—Political aspects—United
States—History. I. Title. II. Series.
E175 .D47 2003
973'.07'2073—dc21   2003000563

cloth   07   06   05   04   03   5   4   3   2   1
paper   07   06   05   04   03   5   4   3   2   1

FOR LADY

Contents

Acknowledgments

This book was a long time in the making, and I have many people to thank for helping me bring it to completion. Through the course of research, I came in contact with librarians and archivists who generously shared their knowledge of materials and dedicated valuable time to assist me. In particular, I want to thank Peter Carini at Mount Holyoke Archives and Special Collections, Michael Jackson at the Rockefeller Library at Brown University, Amy Hague and Sherrill Redmon of the Sophia Smith Collection at Smith College, Jean Berry at the Wellesley College Archives, Sydney Roby of Special Collections at Goucher College, and the staffs at the Moorland-Spingarn Research Center at Howard University, the John Hay Library at Brown University, and the Schlesinger Library at Radcliffe College. Of course with any historical research, funding is of the essence. I would not have been able to travel to archives without the generous fellowships and scholarships granted by the Brown University graduate school, the Brown University history department, the John Nicholas Brown Center in Providence, Rhode Island, and the Schlesinger Library at Radcliffe College.

Friends and colleagues offered helpful advice on the manuscript. I want to thank Adam Nelson, Seth Schulman, Ed Rafferty, and participants in workshops at the John Nicholas Brown Center and the Conference on Historical Memory at Yale University for their insights in the early stages of drafting. Jim Patterson was an incredibly helpful reader when I presented this work as a dissertation; despite being in England on sabbatical, he pored over the completed manuscript, caught things no one else did, and offered me sage advice for continuing in the field of professional history.

About the time Bonnie Smith completed *The Gender of History*, I had the good fortune of talking with her about my project. I was not sure how I would feel about this meeting. I thought I had stumbled onto new topics and materials only to discover that she had asked similar questions about women historians well before I conceived my project. Nevertheless I was heartened that a scholar whom I had long respected thought women historians and the gender of historiography important areas of investigation. Bonnie Smith proved to be a generous scholar and encouraged my focus on twentieth-century historians and African American women in particular. That brief meeting inspired me to see the manuscript to completion.

When I eventually submitted an abstract of the project to the University of North Carolina Press, I was grateful that it fell into Kate Torrey's hands. She quickly decided that my work coincided with the topics in the Gender and American Culture Series and invited me to submit the manuscript. Throughout the publishing process she has demonstrated tremendous patience with me, an unmistakable first-time author. She has been very encouraging, as has everyone at UNC Press. I would especially like to thank Ron Maner, Stephanie Wenzel, Nancy Hewitt, and the other anonymous reviewer assigned to my manuscript. Although I was not sure what to expect, in the end I was astounded at the careful reading and substantive advice I received for revision. These reviewers turned what I assumed would be a painful ordeal into a rewarding and productive experience.

There are two people at Brown University whom I especially want to acknowledge for their dedication to me as a student and historian. Mari Jo Buhle has been a wonderful friend, and I see her as a model of all I hope to be as a historian of American women. As I grappled with my ideas for this book, she seemed to know just what feedback I needed to move on to the next stage of thinking and writing. She has never given me a piece of advice that has not been dead on, and in hindsight I am glad I listened so intently. Then there is Jack Thomas. He took more time to read and discuss drafts of this book than I deserved. Piles of other students' projects sat waiting for his careful attention, and yet he always made me feel like his only student. How he did this, I will never know, but I will certainly never forget. He convinced me that narrative, and specifically the story of *people*, is still vitally important. I will never have a knack for dramatizing people like he does, but I feel privileged to have witnessed how he thinks and hope that his influence will continue to enhance my work.

Finally, there are those people near and dear to me who were encouraging and patient in the years I was writing this book. To my precious companions from Providence—Seth and Susanne Schulman, Deb and Sterling Vernon, Harley Johnson and Amy Wagoner Johnson, and Jeff and Dana Reiser—thanks for being such wonderful friends and brilliant people. All the Des Jardins, Hardwickes, and Bowleys continue to remind me how nurturing family can be; my sister Jory and my father, Joel, also remind me that family can be great unofficial agents and fans. Of course my mother, Joy Des Jardins, the woman to whom this book is lovingly dedicated, never doubted that my days in basements of libraries and in front of computer screens would pay off. As for my husband, Christopher, I thank him or whatever force is responsible for transporting him thousands of miles to a foreign culture and a studio apartment down the street from a graduate student about to embark on her dissertation in American women's history. You, my love, have undoubtedly seen and heard it all.

Abbreviations

AAUW	American Association of University Women
ACA	Association of Collegiate Alumnae
AHA	American Historical Association
AHR	*American Historical Review*
ANA	American Negro Academy
ANHS	American Negro Historical Society
AP	Associated Publishers
ASNLH	Association for the Study of Negro Life and History
AWSA	American Woman Suffrage Association
CAW	Congress of American Women
DAR	Daughters of the American Revolution
ELF	Emma Lazarus Federation
FDMHA	Frederick Douglass Memorial Home Association
HRS	Historical Records Survey
HTM	*History Teacher's Magazine*
JACA	*Journal of the Association of Collegiate Alumnae*
JNH	*Journal of Negro History*
LWV	League of Women Voters
MVHR	*Mississippi Valley Historical Review*
NACW	National Association of Colored Women
NAWSA	National American Woman Suffrage Association
NCNW	National Council of Negro Women
NHB	*Negro History Bulletin*
NSHR	Negro Society for Historical Research
NWP	National Woman's Party
NWSA	National Woman Suffrage Association
SCD	Society of Colonial Dames
WCWA	World Center for Women's Archives
WILPF	Woman's International League for Peace and Freedom
WNIA	Women's National Indian Association
WPA	Works Projects Administration
WTUL	Women's Trade Union League

Women
and the
Historical
Enterprise
in America

Introduction
Discovering Women's Hidden History

Mercy Otis Warren, historian of the American Revolution, once remarked that men were too busy making history to be troubled with recording it themselves. She, on the other hand, a woman behind the scenes, on the sidelines, and in the background of noteworthy events, wrote *The History of the Rise, Progress, and Termination of the American Revolution* in 1805 as a leisure activity but also as her patriotic obligation. Warren would not be the last woman to answer the call to chronicle moments of national glory. Lydia Maria Child, Elizabeth Ellet, Juliette Kinzie, Frances Caulkins, Caroline Dall, and dozens of others continued where Warren left off, remembering the national past for moral instruction, civic training, and public consumption. In the nineteenth century, American women embraced their roles as the custodians of national history. They studied the past from the books they kept in home libraries and preserved family relics of bygone years, all to prepare themselves for their maternal duty to raise civic-minded children and future citizens.[1]

Conduct books, school primers, and course listings for some of the first women's colleges and finishing schools reveal that historical knowledge was considered an important piece of intellectual equipment for the well-bred woman throughout the nineteenth century. One commentator insisted that women should read history if for no other reason than to "giv[e] them a disgust to comedies and romances" and to prevent "vanity and affectation." An etiquette book in 1833 listed history as one of the subjects indispensable for preparing young ladies "for the active duties of life." Between 1830 and 1870 it became commonplace for female seminaries to offer ancient, modern, and U.S. history for these very reasons. In the 1860s Elmira Women's College offered general history, and "Felton's Historians" was required reading for Vassar College's "Classical Course." School administrators believed that Ancient Greek and American history would instill democratic ideals in young soon-to-be mothers; by the 1880s both had become prerequisites for attendance at Smith and Mount Holyoke colleges.[2]

The scarcity of male elementary and secondary educators after the Civil War prompted women to take their knowledge of history outside the home in unprecedented numbers to make it their vocation in local schoolhouses and libraries. The rising number of women history teachers was commensurate with the increase of women teachers on the whole in these years. Ever since Catharine Beecher's midcentury declaration of teaching as "woman's natural profession," Horace Mann and other advocates of the common school movement had been encouraging women to take up this public work. By 1870 three-fifths of all elementary school teachers in America were women. Fifty-seven percent of teachers for all pre-college grades were women by 1880; 65.5 percent, by 1890; and 70.1 percent, by 1900.[3] At the same time school teaching was turning into feminine work, church, state, and patriotic groups were giving history greater attention as a classroom subject and a realm of social and civic knowledge. Several New England states made curricula in U.S. history compulsory in elementary schools as early as the 1820s, but after the Civil War it became a requirement nationwide, partly in reaction to the unsettling demographic and industrial changes in postwar cities. State laws now stipulated that it was the schoolteacher's duty to use history to instill in students a "love of country[,] and to lead them into a clear understanding of the virtues which were the basis upon which was founded a republican constitution."[4]

Suddenly it appeared that the historical learning women facilitated in both the private and the public spheres had been ascribed greater social significance than ever before. Mothers, aunts, and sisters perhaps long understood that by wielding their knowledge of the past to guide the development of future citizens, they could gain public authority unachievable by other means. Nina Baym estimates that at least twenty women published history textbooks for home and school use between 1790 and 1860 and established national reputations not as "historians" per se but as dutiful educators of children. Emma Willard's position as the director of a New York seminary for girls, for example, sanctioned her writing of historical textbooks, which in turn gave her the power to shape historical discourse in the public domain where women had traditionally been kept silent. In this way the relationship between history and the woman historian was reciprocal: Just as her creation of national narratives affirmed the existence of the nation-state as an exceptional entity, history as a product of her thoughts and actions affirmed her worth as an agent of public discourse.[5]

Most women did not achieve the national influence of Willard but, rather, remained in local communities writing history for town newspapers, teaching history in elementary schools, or collecting family relics to display in town halls and historical societies. They found that their designated responsibility as custodians of the local past allowed them to perform the work of historical preservation, paid and unpaid, with authority, influence, and social acceptance. Such was the case at the former Transcendentalist community Fruitlands, where Clara Endicott Sears bought the deed to the property and saved its original structures from ruin. Mary Jeffrey Galt and Cynthia Tucker Coleman, the cofounders of the Association for the Preservation of Virginia Antiquities, also garnered support for their preservationist projects well beyond their local community, turning Jamestown Island and the Powder Magazine in Williamsburg into places of national repute.[6]

These women did not differ from the tens of thousands across the country who made up the rank and file of local preservationist groups by the late nineteenth century. The Daughters of the American Revolution (DAR) (1890) and the Society of Colonial Dames (SCD) (1891) preserved monuments and colonial vestiges on a national scale, while organizations such as the Mount Vernon Ladies' Association, the Ladies' Hermitage Association, and the Monticello-Jefferson Memorial Association maintained single homes and monuments as symbols of American values. The Dames explained in their constitution that they recovered the tangible aspects of the colonial past "to stimulate a spirit of true patriotism and a genuine love of country"; as they embarked on the twentieth century, several members even fashioned themselves as "masters" of historical pageants. Partly theatrical production, partly historical allegory, and partly patriotic propaganda, in the 1910s these popular rituals gained influence through women who served as planners, spectators, choreographers, actors, and artists— and even as symbols, for women and girls commonly dressed up as the feminine figures of Liberty and Columbia for these displays.[7]

Women outside New England were equally devoted to retrieving the past for civic purposes by the turn of the century. The United Daughters of the Confederacy and southern chapters of the DAR and SCD arose from local confederate veterans organizations following the Civil War and pressed to make their interpretations of the sectional conflict known to the rest of the country. Mildred Lewis Rutherford, historian-general of the United Daughters (1912–16), worried that northern women's versions of national events were becoming the official accounts in schoolbooks and classrooms across the country and dedicated herself to righting their historical wrongs. Women expressed similar sentiments in the West and Midwest and likewise established organizations to interpret the past as they saw it. The Native Daughters of the Golden West, like the Daughters of the Utah

Pioneers and members of dozens of analogous organizations, disseminated patriotic, albeit regionally exceptionalist, history in hopes of gaining social influence and cultural authority.[8]

Susan Pringle Frost (the historic district of Charlestown), Elizabeth Thomas Werlein (the French Quarter of New Orleans), and the Daughters of the Republic of Texas (the Alamo) were just some of the preservationists who achieved clout as civic educators at this crucial moment at the turn of the century—when fears intensified about immigrant newcomers jeopardizing American values and university men sought similar cultural authority for themselves. At a time when white, domestic women still had no formal access to the political process, preserving national sites and planning historical parades had proven an effective means for them to claim rights to the American legacy and its associated privileges. Women discovered that there was power to be gained in placing an interpretive spin on the national past.

Indeed all the manifestations of the historical enterprise—collected and written, preserved and taught, enacted and studied—had fallen into the universe of the white, middle-class domestic woman by the turn of the twentieth century. And yet for reasons to be explained, scholars have obscured her close association with the historical enterprise. Here we attempt to retrieve her from obscurity, ultimately to reveal her as an important predecessor and counterpart to women who broadened historical practice in the twentieth century. Pageant masters, domestic writers, and preservationists are not the focus of this book, but their relationship to the historical enterprise sets the tone for the plots that unfold in the following pages. These domestic women, conservative in their political outlook and nostalgic in their views on the national past, may have unwittingly paved the way for diverse groups of American women with new agendas—radicals, feminists, and race activists, among others—to engage in the public sphere, as both historians and historical heroines in the making. As professional and popular writers, librarians, archivists, and activists, many women offered new perspectives on the national past that reshaped historical practice in lasting ways. This study contains the stories of only some of these women who refined usable pasts in the early twentieth century, but they are presented as a point of departure for more thorough discussions of women, gender, race, and the distinctive relationship of all three to the historical enterprise and public memory in America.

Today we still typically refer to white men in the academy when discerning the forces responsible for the way national history has been conceived and practiced over the preceding 100 years. Historiographers have summoned Frederick Jackson Turner's "Frontier Thesis" in 1893 and his call for more "social" history as president of the American Historical Association (AHA) in 1910 as turning points in the historical field. Similarly, speeches such as Carl Becker's "Everyman His Own Historian" and Charles Beard's "History Written as an Act of Faith" have been recalled as watershed events that brought in new ideological or methodological tides—in these cases the inauguration of cultural and historical relativism. But are the ideas of academic men all we should consider? Perhaps by assuming that male scholars arbitrated all the ways Americans understood the past we give an inordinate amount of attention to the production of academic scholarship and not enough to its actual consumption among the wider populace outside the academy, where women were prolific shapers of history.

To be sure, women writers and preservationists of the late nineteenth century would not have proclaimed themselves "social" or "cultural" historians, nor would they have associated themselves with the same intellectual program as the scholars who came to identify themselves by these terms later in the twentieth century. Nonetheless I will suggest here that a good many of them pioneered social and cultural perspectives that characterized historical practice in the academy well after they were forgotten. Nina Baym maintains that women constructed forms of history before and after 1850 that were situated comfortably within a domestic tradition of writing about people's daily, social interactions. Bonnie Smith has also described women's historical writing in the last third of the nineteenth century as "encyclopedic" and "polymathic" in genre and perspective, encompassing aspects of the past beyond the male focus of political figures and military events to shed light on changing social relationships in ordinary contexts.[9]

Domestic women had no intention of pioneering the historical methodologies and perspectives that would allow future writers to question Whig interpretations of national progress or to recast historical women outside their traditional sphere; they peopled their accounts and described facets of everyday life in the past not as subversives but as dutiful mothers reminding their children of the origins of the American republic and its associated civic values. Yet by the 1910s women with different agendas were borrowing their methods, examining the past through shifting social and cultural lenses to counter the historical justifications for white, male hegemony and the scientific historian's emphasis on the political arena. In the Progressive Era in particular, women examined American groups in the everyday as a means of reforming labor conditions, race relations, exploitation of Native Americans, and immigration policy in growing industrial cities. At the same time participants in the suffrage and woman's rights movements reworked versions of the national past as a means of sparking social and political change for women in the public sphere. As new generations of women became professional historians, librarians, and archivists who recovered the hidden stories of nonwhites, non-Protestants, and women, they also debunked the myth of progress upon which former historians built the exceptional American past, present, and future. These historians rewrote the past to serve new reform agendas, yet they owed a methodological debt to earlier domestic writers and woman patriots who shared an interest in similar subjects: women and social groups in the everyday.

My case for the connection between women's production of social and cultural history in the nineteenth and twentieth centuries is difficult to make, in part because the process of historical professionalization that began in the 1870s and 1880s seemed to interrupt the continuity between historical practices in America before and afterward. Joyce Appleby, Lynn Hunt, and Margaret Jacob have written about this transitional moment when "science and history got linked together," describing it as one during which history began to take its modern form "as an organized, disciplined inquiry into the meaning of the past." Peter Novick has also explained how scienticity came to be "the hallmark of the modern and authoritative" for the new class of twentieth-century professional historians, causing former conventions of history writing to lose their appeal. I would suggest, however, that these earlier conventions did not altogether disappear; rather, they were modified in the twentieth century to match the scientific milieu of the academy.[10]

It is largely because of this scientific recasting of history that the influence of women as historians before, during, and after professionalization has been obscured, for the scientific ideal was inevitably masculine in its nature and effects. David Hollinger and Margaret Rossiter have remarked that the very language of twentieth-century scientism appropriated gender and its corresponding hierarchies, but not until recently has Bonnie Smith suggested that the recategorization of history as a science brought about its similar regendering. "The development of modern scientific methodology, epistemology, professional practice, and writing," she concludes, "has been closely tied to evolving definitions of masculinity and femininity." Indeed the authority of all women historians seemed to diminish as history shifted from a feminine realm of knowledge to a masculine field of "scientific" expertise.[11]

Women by no means stopped writing or preserving history during these years, but their influence on the nascent historical profession has been overshadowed by the focus scholars then and since have placed on the work of male standouts in the university and the implicitly gendered meanings they constructed in defining scientific history and its expert practitioners.

Professionalization, scientization, and academicization will be examined here as gendered processes to assess how women renegotiated their places in the historical enterprise in this transitional period. Only then can the field be recast to include women's role in its development and can we understand how women ultimately reinterpreted the past for their own advancement in the twentieth century.

It is certainly useful to look at the professional strategies of the few women who did succeed in becoming historians in the American university by 1945, but academicians do not reveal the entire influence of women historians or the scope of the effects of gender on historical practice. When we look outside the ivory tower, we see that women became savvy marketers and disseminators of their versions of the past on the grassroots level: in classrooms, over the airwaves, in popular markets, and for mass consumption. Often their bottom-up methods for the dissemination of social and cultural history mirrored their insightful methods of historical analysis. As marginal figures to the historical profession, many represented the pasts of Americans marginalized by race, class, ethnicity, or gender in ways that scholars have little acknowledged.

When academic production is no longer the center of focus, the continuity between nineteenth- and twentieth-century historical practice becomes more readily apparent, as does women's participation in the development of history as a professional field and medium for activist expression and social change. We see that while women did break the barriers of gender in some cases, engaging in the scholarly culture of the academy, others continued to construct narratives and preserve the artifacts of history on their own terms, giving past and present realms of female activity their due recognition. Others still took history in activist directions in the twentieth century, invoking versions of a usable past to make gains for woman suffrage, labor legislation, and heightened social equality for Americans of color and the working class. Indeed the story of women's historical work in the twentieth century no longer appears to be a simple linear narrative of progress or an account of how patriarchal regimes suppressed feminine expression. It becomes an account of individual women and groups actively employing, invoking, and preserving the past for varied and complex purposes—*despite* and *because* of their marginalized position in the historical profession.

I have singled out African American women in this study for their particularly limited access to professional credentials, for in many cases this forced them to become the most resourceful historians of the twentieth century. A small group of black, middle-class clubwomen discovered historical writing as an effective means for promoting the merits of the race, and they initially emulated white women historians in hopes of bringing social uplift to their communities. Later than white women, but by no means less substantially, they were able to articulate their past and present plight as distinct from other American women and even men of their race. They had fewer material resources and opportunities to write history, and so they came to rely more heavily on oral tradition, commemorative strategies, interdisciplinary methods, pedagogical techniques, and grassroots mobilization to shape the contours of race memory and their own legacies as black women. One need not have access to official documents, government repositories, or tenure in a university history department, they proved, to render original and empowered history of African American women, but simply the wherewithal to search for this hidden past in the most inauspicious of places.[12]

The special access of African American women to the cultural traditions and social relationships of the past had nothing to do with their female biology or any feminine proclivity to tend to the historically mistreated. What appeared to be their instinct was really just a consequence of the historical perspective they unavoidably cultivated from the margins of the academic establishment, the masculine professions, race organizations, and the male public sphere. Already distanced from structures of power, women of varying racial and cultural backgrounds found themselves in closer social proximity to the historically inarticulate and eventually articulated for them. Women may have felt like outcasts from the field of professional history, yet their outsider status allowed them to investigate the past uninhibited by the scientific mantra of the university: to examine the past only through written documents, inside "official" realms of public and political activity, and always above the fray of social advocacy. They enjoyed the flexibility to poke and prod where male historians thought it inappropriate to roam: in the pasts of the poor, the oppressed, the abused, and underprivileged. Like their historical subjects, they often understood the complexity of power because they themselves never enjoyed the luxury of taking it for granted. As many women consequently viewed the past from the bottom up, they scrutinized the layers of social relations, economic conflicts, and cultural crossroads underneath the facade of official history. Whereas men often viewed the American past superficially as one of perpetual progress, these women peeled back the layers to see it as a patterned prevailing of power. In this way women turned their marginal positions into stations of privileged historical perspective.

It would be reductive to describe all the women in this study as constructing history and influencing memory in similar ways or for similar ends. As professional scholars, feminists, race reformers, advocates for

Native Americans, and labor activists they embarked on this work for a variety of reasons and employed a unique set of techniques given their social objectives and available tools. A common link between them, however, was their ability to enable and be enabled by the practice of social and cultural history from multiple points of view. Collectively they encouraged methodological shifts away from Rankean empiricism in the twentieth century and once again toward a larger repertoire of historical lenses to shed light on the communal, private, and everyday realms of human experience—where women were better revealed. As this study tracks a different course for women in the tale of American historical practice, it also traces their increasing ability to assert themselves through historical mediums. Their works will become a lens through which to chart an intensifying activist and historical consciousness among them, yet, at the same time, to discern the different identities they sought for themselves as women with distinctive historical crosses to bear. The women introduced here took a variety of paths, but they all reclaimed the past as a way of reclaiming their present.

I

The Regendering of History, 1880–1935

Chapter 1
From Feminine Refinement to Masculine Pursuit, 1880–1920

In 1921 a writer for the *New York Evening World* asked the question, "Why was it left for women to write the most authentic histories of New York?" Several men had attempted to write authoritative histories of the great metropolis before, he noted, including the likes of William Smith and Washington Irving. Yet the accounts written by women over the preceding fifty years seemed to him the most accurate. There was Mary Louise Booth's *History of the City of New York* (1859), for example, as well as Alice Earle's *Colonial Days in Old New York* (1896), Ester Singleton's *Dutch New York* (1909), and Mrs. Schuyler Van Rensselaer's *History of the City of New York in the Seventeenth Century* (1909).[1] Of all the New York histories, however, the one that impressed him the most was *History of the City of New York: Its Origins, Rise, and Progress*, a massive, multivolume work written by "Mrs. Mary Lamb" between 1877 and 1881. Sources told him that Lamb "accomplished her labor under most discouraging conditions. . . . At her own expense she ran down important historical clues." While her dedication did not lead to instant wealth, it paid off in the long run, for her book continued to be relied on for details about New York's major figures and events. In honor of her impressive feat and lasting impact, this journalist wished to raise Lamb from the depths of obscurity to make the seemingly anonymous historian a subject of history in her own right. Unfortunately for Lamb, this correspondent for the *New York Evening World* could not recollect the past with nearly the same accuracy he attributed to her, for the woman to whom he kept referring as Mrs. Mary Lamb was really Martha J. Lamb, once the esteemed editor of the *Magazine of American History*.[2]

Lamb had stumbled onto history writing relatively late in life. As a young woman she served as a math instructor at a polytechnic institute, leaving to marry and establish an orphanage in Chicago. Eight years later she moved to New York, only to be virtually bedridden from the moment she arrived. Under doctor's care she began reading about New York's local history. Her fascination led to avid note taking and the manuscript of

History of the City of New York fourteen years later. Once the publisher A. S. Barnes introduced Lamb's two volumes to the public, reviewers overwhelmingly sang its praises: "The style fully equals that of Macaulay, or Froude," wrote one scholar. "While the theme is the most spacious and splendid in American local history, her enthusiasm for it has matched its greatness, and her treatment, on the whole, has been ample and brilliant," wrote another. One reviewer went so far as to conclude, "This woman has written the most complete history ever published of any city in the world."[3]

History of the City of New York would not be an isolated success; Lamb went on to write two other books to favorable reviews, *The Homes of America* (1879) and *Wall Street History* (1883), along with dozens of smaller historical works.[4] By 1883 she had become such an established historical authority that she was chosen to be the editor and financial manager of the *Magazine of American History*. She devoted herself tirelessly to the journal from 8:00 in the morning until 4:00 in the afternoon every day, again to the admiration of most critics. The *New York Times* reported in 1888, "Mrs. Lamb never published an uninteresting number of this periodical," and the *New York Recorder* announced that under Lamb the magazine was "more read and esteemed among those who mold the national mind than any other periodical of the day."[5] It was not long before Lamb's reputation had earned her remuneration and privileges that most women writers could only imagine. When she first researched volume 1 of *History of the City of New York*, she was said to have nearly begged for more than the $50 a month she received for it. However, when she closed her deal for volume 2, A. S. Barnes agreed to give her sole control over the disbursements for engraving and electrotyping. Two years later Funk and Wagnalls agreed to give her a relatively high percentage of the royalties for *Wall Street History*. That same year when the Historical Publication Company bought the *Magazine of American History*, Lamb and her nephew set up the new share structure of the company over which she now presided.[6]

By the time she died in 1893, Lamb had written hundreds of historical articles and essays and been inducted as an honorary member into over a dozen historical societies and associations in New England and New York. Commentators frequently remarked that Lamb had mastered the historical craft as well as any man of her day. In 1881 the women's literary club Sorosis honored her with a lavish New York reception, where she received letters of congratulation by the presidents of several historical societies, universities, and even former U.S. president Rutherford B. Hayes. In 1886 President Grover Cleveland hosted a dinner party for Lamb and invited the legendary historian George Bancroft to take part in the honors. Upon her death the *New York World* reminded readers that Lamb's histories had won her acclaim as "one of the most advanced women of the century." Another writer eulogized that she "was the one woman who has written history successfully." "Not only did she take interest in historical matters," he added, ". . . but she won respect and admiration of eminent and erudite historical scholars on both sides of the Atlantic, and came to be recognized as an authority on historical matters."[7]

The woman whom the writer for the *New York Evening World* wanted to snatch from obscurity in 1921 had in fact not always been so obscure after all. By all accounts Lamb had arrived as a respected historian in her own right. Thus this fact can only beg the question, Why was she so little known to New York journalists by 1921, only forty years after she first came to prominence as a great "lady historian"? More curious yet, Why was a journalist in 1921 so surprised to discover that at least three other women had written histories of New York since Lamb had published hers in 1877? Perhaps most baffling of all, Why would her eulogizers insist that Lamb was the *only* woman historian of influence when she died in 1893?

Certainly the reason was not the lack of women writing commercially successful or widely read histories at the time. Alice Earle and Sarah Bolton, for example, published most of their local histories and historical biographies between 1885 and 1900, albeit to far less fanfare than Lamb enjoyed before 1881. Ironically, at this time women were gathering influence as the writers of "collective biographies," compilations of historical sketches— usually of dignitaries, leaders, martyrs, and generals—that presented the public men of history as universal role models for young readers. As a genre the collective biography allowed women to disseminate their prescriptions for national manhood to mass audiences as never before, although late in the nineteenth century these prescriptions did not differ much from those of nearly 100 years earlier, when Mercy Otis Warren first recorded the history of the American Revolution. Whether Pilgrim ministers, Founding Fathers, Union soldiers, Horatio Algers, frontier pioneers, Cavalier planters, or American statesmen, great men had always made up the substance of women's nineteenth-century historical writings. Bolton, the most widely read collective biographer of the time, compiled *Lives of Poor Boys Who Became Famous* (1885), *Famous American Statesmen* (1888), and *Famous Men of Science* (1890). *Poor Boys* alone sold more than 50,000 copies in its first few years of print, much to the pleasant surprise of publisher Thomas Y. Crowell, who then contracted with Bolton to write more sketches of famous "leaders," "authors," and "givers." Through her writings she reinforced men's domain in the past as the public and noteworthy realms of politics, letters, science, commerce, and religion—and women's by omission as the unremarkable private sphere.[8]

Just as women remained anonymous in Bolton's histories, so did she as a woman historian. Whereas men such as George Bancroft and Francis Parkman had won esteem as "gentlemen historians" in the nineteenth century, women rarely enjoyed the corresponding distinction. Martha Lamb seemed to be an exception, but only for a time, for by 1921 even her reputation as a lady historian had to be recovered. In the decades after she published her books, other women wrote history prolifically and marketed it widely, though few won recognition as lady historians. Bolton's sketches of great men had turned into popular history of mass proportions, yet she never regarded herself as one of the great writers or intellects of history, a distinction she reserved for the male heroes in her books. Perhaps Bolton perceived anonymity for herself and all women custodians of the past as a necessary cross to bear; women did not make history but recounted it for the benefit of younger generations.

Bolton spent the better part of the 1880s reconstructing the lives of history's great men, yet a good number of them were not all that historic in the sense that they were still alive when she wrote about them. In fact some were, if only peripherally, part of her same Boston social circle; Ralph Waldo Emerson, Oliver Wendell Holmes, and Thomas Wentworth Higginson, for example, were men about whom she wrote but with whom she had also been socially acquainted. The familiarity with which she privately wrote of them suggests that she may have perceived herself as part of the same universe of historically significant movers and shakers. Although she kept a low profile as a woman biographer, she was prominent publicly as a moral reformer and temperance advocate. Through this feminine work Bolton had always believed that women could achieve great social influence —and eventually historical significance, it appears.[9] For not long after writing exclusively about male subjects, Bolton began inserting women into her volumes of historical heroes. Her *Successful Women* (1888), *Famous Types of Womanhood* (1892), and *Leaders among Women* (1895) promoted the traditional domestic ideal but also depicted women as agents of national progress. One of Bolton's exemplars of "famous womanhood" was Susanna Wesley, mother of theologian John Wesley, whom Bolton praised for giving her son his early religious and civic instruction. "Her courage, her submissiveness to authority, the high tone of her mind . . . were visibly repeated in the character and conduct of her son," Bolton explained. "What John Wesley would have been with an ignorant mother, it is difficult to conjecture. . . . It is a blessing to the world that Susanna Wesley ever lived."[10]

According to Bolton, John Wesley's dutiful mother did more than act as an agent of moral progress; she directed the path of a heroic man and thus changed the course of national history, much like Bolton herself hoped to do by recalling the deeds of heroines in the past for potential heroines of the future. Like *Poor Boys*, *Lives of Girls* sold more than 50,000 copies its first few years in print and went through some two dozen editions. "Better than notices of the press," Bolton reflected, "have been the scores of letters received from women in various parts of the country, telling me how my book has inspired them to try to do something in the world."[11] In the 1880s and 1890s other women authors made a career of writing about "Eminent Women," "Famous Women," and "Women Worthies." Moral reformers Frances Willard and Mary Livermore compiled over 1,500 sketches in *Women of the Century* (1893), a work undoubtedly intended to be both inspirational and prescriptive for young American girls. To no surprise, in this year of her death Martha Lamb was included among these 1,500 noteworthy women. Phoebe Hanaford's *Daughters of America* (1883), Louisa Moulton's *Our Famous Women* (1883), and Frances Willard's *Women in the Pulpit* (1889) served much the same dual functions as history and instruction on the ideal feminine character.[12]

Examined collectively, these works reveal the growing inclination of women to present their contributions to national progress as distinct from yet equal to those of remarkable men. Bolton and her contemporaries were not the first to depict historical women in this way, however. In the 1850s Elizabeth Ellet had compiled similar works about aristocratic, pioneer, and revolutionary women and had won a popular following as a historian.[13] Nina Baym suggests that such history in biographical form may have been the least defiant yet most effective way female authors could make a case for women's historical agency. In the mid-nineteenth century, women were more acceptable as subjects of biography than of history, in part because they were deemed better "objects to be contemplated rather than subjects of activity" and agents of historical change.[14]

By the 1890s the market for these works had reached mass proportions; along with collective biographers such as Bolton, several popular writers of colonial history shifted their emphasis from Founding Fathers, male soldiers, and heads of households to ordinary women turned role models in early American society. Alice Earle and Anne Wharton, perhaps the most prolific female writers on the colonial era, considered the exploration of the domestic experiences of women in the colonies and the early republic as necessary aspects of their work. In *Through Colonial Doorways* (1893), Wharton insisted that "to read of councils, congresses, and battles is not enough: men and women wish to know something more intimate and personal of the life of the past."[15] Likewise in this passage from *Colonial Days and Dames* (1894), Wharton sought to reveal the private women behind publicly renowned men: "Although Mary Washington and Abiah

Franklin are chiefly known to later generations as the mothers of great sons," she prefaced, "it is evident that both of these women were possessed of strong character and distinct individuality. Firmness, moderation, and deep religious sentiment were leading traits of Mrs. Washington; while Mrs. Franklin, thrifty and hard-working, having at two-and-twenty undertaken Josiah Franklin with his brood of little children, which her own contribution of ten augmented to the goodly number of sixteen, still found time, to reflect upon theological questions."[16]

The commitment of Earle and Wharton to revealing the domestic woman was evident in their contributions to Scribner's six-book series Women of Colonial and Revolutionary Times. Accompanying biographies by Catherine Schuyler, Eliza Pinckney, Maud Goodwin, and Alice Brown, Earle's *Margaret Winthrop* (1895) and Wharton's *Martha Washington* (1897) proposed to shed new light on the invisible women behind historically noteworthy men. "Women have been short shrifted in historical accounts and therefore this will be something slightly new," Wharton prefaced. "The story of Martha Washington's life has not been an easy one to tell, so largely has she, as a distinct personality, been overshadowed by the greater importance of the figure that had stood beside her."[17] Wharton hoped to place the legacy of this "woman worthy" into the popular consciousness and, at the same time, to fill in gaps left by traditional political narratives with vivid details of daily domestic life. Similarly, in *Through Colonial Doorways* she recalled the domestic rituals that took place concurrently with more frequently recorded political events. As President Washington attended elaborate ceremonials in his honor, Martha, Wharton recounted, was "detained at home . . . putting her household in order, and shipping china, cut glass, silver-ware, and linen from Mount Vernon to the capital." No longer trivial details, these domestic tasks behind the scenes, Wharton argued, added to Washington's hospitality and diplomatic success. Thus they rightly found themselves in the foreground of her narrative, as political and military campaigns slipped into the backdrop.[18]

Throughout the nineteenth century, domestic historians had found woman worthies—queens, first ladies, actresses, saints, and martyrs—the most deserving of historical attention. Yet Earle and Wharton often abandoned the focus on exceptional individuals to examine unexceptional women in the collective and everyday. Earle's *Colonial Dames and Good Wives* (1895) and *Homelife in Colonial Days* (1898) and Wharton's *Colonial Days and Dames* and *A Last Century Maid* (1896) revealed ordinary women rather than exceptional and typically male individuals. "I give a description of a group of women . . . rather than an account of some special dame of dignity or note," Earle explained in *Colonial Dames*. Calling one group

"The Boston Neighbors," she maintained that their interactions with one another revealed "a picture of the social life of women" more successfully than if she discussed single figures in isolation. Detailing common "courtship and marriage customs," "sports and diversions," "holidays and festivals," "girls occupations," and "kitchen firesides," she offered a descriptive and layered view of social and cultural life suddenly peopled by heroic yet regular women.[19]

Again, as much as these works were intended to serve as history, they also served as civic primers; their glimpses into the lives of ordinary "dames" revealed an idealized view of feminine character to young female readers. The *New York Times* called the collective series of Scribner's biographies "a valuable element in the education of the American girl."[20] Yet even close inspection does not easily reveal which lessons about gender its women contributors wanted to prescribe. Alice Earle was perhaps the most indecisive. In *Colonial Dames* she championed the Victorian ideals of maternal piety and feminine deference at the same time she introduced embryonic versions of the twentieth-century "new woman"—self-sufficient, independent, politically invested, and even sexual—as a heroic model of femininity. Included in her cast of characters were "women of affairs," "colonial adventuresses," and "Dame Margaret Brent . . . the first woman in America to demand suffrage." She lamented that Brent, "a clear-cut, unusual, and forceful figure of the seventeenth century . . . vanishe[d] out of history, in a thoroughly feminine role, that of mourning sweetheart," for it was her role as a political activist—outside the domestic sphere—that made her the model heroine in Earle's eyes.[21]

Her broad set of criteria for defining noble womanhood in the colonies suggests that Earle was unsure about what the ideal of femininity should be as the twentieth century approached. She argued that the historical impact of women in the private sphere was significant, for this was where they had arbitrated the mores for all American citizens. Ultimately she looked to women's traditional roles in the home for solutions to the social disconnectedness of the new industrial order, but also to argue for their valuation in the public sphere. Thus she rightfully maintained, for example, that women in preindustrial society managed to work in the public marketplace and yet still be considered "good wives." By using history to reinforce Victorian domesticity yet also to recommend more expansive public roles for women, Earle seems to have been torn between the values of older and modern times. Yet even if she never recognized it explicitly, her choice of historical vantage points—on groups of women and their ordinary social interactions—enabled her to render an empowered perspective of women that would have activist applications for historians to follow.

By the 1890s Sarah Bolton and Alice Earle were proudly acknowledging American women as public and historical figures in ways that Lamb could never have claimed in the 1870s and 1880s, yet neither enjoyed Lamb's same renown as a lady historian. The reasons for this are still not easily explained. Like Lamb, Bolton and Earle had established reputations writing fiction, poems, and children's stories before moving on to careers in history. They were also the descendants of soldiers in the American Revolution, a genealogical connection that Lamb exploited to claim special access to the colonial past of New York fifteen years before Earle did the same in 1896. Lamb had been the first historian of the SCD (as well as its founder), but Earle's lineage also earned her a similar place as national historian in both the SCD and the DAR. The credentials of these women were virtually the same, so why was Lamb remembered in the 1890s as "the only successful woman historian"?

The answer may lie less in the women themselves than in their timing. All three believed that their family bloodlines gave them special access to the American past and that as domestic women they had the moral authority to disseminate their renditions of this past in the public domain. Lamb, Earle, and Bolton were all devoted mothers and philanthropists, yet it seems that these domestic duties enhanced Lamb's historical authority to a greater extent in the 1870s and 1880s than Bolton's or Earle's did ten and twenty years later. Commentators regarded Lamb's activities as a historian and moral reformer as complementary and believed that she had struck the perfect balance as both a fact-finding chronicler and a literary domestic woman. One praised her as a meticulous historian as well as "a hard worker in other fields besides the one in which she has gained honor and renown." Indeed her membership in twenty-seven learned and historical societies and her tireless devotion to charitable organizations were not perceived as a detraction from her historical work but, rather, as validation of the veracity of her claims. One writer for the *Springfield Republican* even hoped that Lamb's "industry, patience and devotion" would inspire all "cultivated New England women" to write their own town or local histories.[22]

The balance struck by Lamb by 1880 did not earn the same favor fifteen years later, when Bolton and Earle were their most prolific. In fact, by then Lamb's own accomplishments as a lady historian would lose luster next to the blinding truth thought to radiate from the new breed of university historian, who sought recognition not as a literary figure or moralist but as a scholar in a specialized field of social science. University men felt a greater need to be affirmed as historical "experts" and sought scientific criteria through which to identify themselves as authoritative interpreters of the past. In the aftermath of Charles Darwin, Karl Popper and other secular theorists encouraged this trend toward positivist history. American historians in particular became increasingly obsessed with the scientific methods of Leopold von Ranke that had already reshaped ideas on the nature of historical inquiry in German universities. As American graduate schools became refashioned spaces of scholarly production rather than intellectual consumption, producers of original, "scientific" historical research insisted on turning the university into their protected fortress. Building on Newtonian notions of universality and the Enlightenment belief in the human ability to know truth, professional historians with university training in archival method began to claim sole rights to knowledge of the past.[23]

In the ideal conditions the scientific historian was thought able to detach himself from all his psychological, familial, and cultural contexts, rendering his historical judgment devoid of personal bias. Peter Novick claims that *objectivity* became the most revered trait of the new scientific historian, thought achievable when fostered in the disinterested setting of the university. The purest form of scientific neutrality, objectivity became the aspiration of the new professional historian, and yet remarkably, in terms of gender it was hardly a neutral concept. The professional establishment often considered women who wrote history as unobjective by nature, sometimes even parochial and compromising of historical accuracy for dramatic effect. Having little access to seminar training in the university, some of the most enthusiastic women "antiquarians" were thought ill equipped to acquire scientific facticity to the extent of the trained academician. By virtue of their traditional roles as local, familial, and community historians, they were deemed unable to take on the omniscient perspective of national political systems that scientific objectivity entailed.[24]

As scientific history turned increasingly disinterested in perspective during the 1880s, it became political, though not politicized, in content. Taken from German models, it was a recounting of past politics rather than the romantic reminiscence of the Victorian era, with particular stress placed on the development of the constitutional government and legal apparatus of the nation-state. In this period of southern Reconstruction, political turmoil, and urban growth, such emphases were not without immediate application; constitutional and political historians believed their narratives could induce national cohesion if democratic institutions seemed rooted in history.[25]

As they constructed narratives about the political progress of the nation-state, scholars came to privilege certain historical facts over others, namely those culled from documents deemed official: state and court records, legal papers, or anything stamped with a government seal. It followed that as official sources delimited the research methodologies of professional historians, these men in turn fetishized the *written* document and the apparatus associated with its production. Professors of graduate seminars in turn-of-the-century history departments versed students in the particulars of epigraphy, papermaking, handwriting, seals, and watermarks, along with the criteria against which to test the authorial authenticity of these written forms.[26] One professional guidebook was typical of the new scientific turn, instructing aspiring historians to use only "deeds, contracts, charters, privileges, court decisions"—none of which provided much insight into the agency of women or of history's other non–property holders and legal nonentities. The historian's reverence for the "official" had a devastating effect on the reconstruction of women's "unofficial" past experience. The constitutional and legal documents of the Western world, unlike the diaries and letters mined by domestic writers, contained little explicit evidence of women as holders of property or in positions of official capacity, yet these records piqued the interest of academic historians the most. The domestic lives of women, children, and family in local settings were not of interest to scholars who looked to public and formally political arenas for actions central to national progress.[27]

Whereas the romantic historians of the nineteenth century once interpreted utterances in letters and memoirs as transparent representations of historical truth, now they were regarded as tainted sources by virtue of their private nature. Scientific historians highlighted male figures as the most integral to national plots, not unlike Francis Parkman and other male historians earlier in the nineteenth century. Now, however, they were devoid of romantic characterizations. Revolutionary war generals, politicians, chiefs of state, and the Founding Fathers were not flesh-and-blood men but stoic figures who carried out the official business of the national past. Although largely stripped of his foibles and family life, the white Western male retained his status as the prototypical historical subject, and the masculine remained the "universal signifier" in scientific narratives of the past.[28]

This preference for official figures and source materials diminished women's role in the past, but it also reduced their competency as historical investigators. "Scientific impersonality," a desired goal of the legitimate scholar, was thought achievable through the relocation of historical research into official spaces that were less emotionally charged than the domestic spaces women typically occupied. Already in Europe Ranke had defined the new brand of historical training as a distinctly male right of passage, the ability to unearth historical truth as a measure of virility, and the "historical laboratory"—the seminar room or research archive—as masculine space. Certainly this was a departure from accepted thought in the nineteenth century, when women of refinement had filled parlors and public lecture halls, common arenas of historical learning. Martha Lamb, for example, wrote histories in her New York apartment and also attended public lectures as both an audience member and an invited speaker.[29] Now German-trained historians would insist that such venues promoted a superficial understanding of trivial topics, and that the most profound learning could take place only within the exclusively male confines of the historical laboratory.[30]

Ranke's notions were prohibitive to the woman researcher, who was often denied admission into these spaces or access to bureaucratic positions that would put her in closer proximity to official documents. They were particularly devastating for Alice Earle, who had long prided herself on her ability to dig for historical truth in other places. The personal testimonials she gathered for books such as *Colonial Dames and Good Wives* were now deemed worthless to her scientific counterparts, who regarded her years of searching in family attics as a waste of time. As a civic-minded, middle-class woman, she was once content to write about colonial domesticity within the suburban sanctity of her Brooklyn Heights home. A thirty-nine-year-old mother of four when she wrote her first history, she did not initially see any conflict between her domestic situation and her ability to interpret the national past. The balance she struck between roles as mother and writer differed little from Lamb's or most women authors' earlier in the nineteenth century; in fact the moral wisdom they cultivated from the domestic hearth was thought to give them authority as commentators on the national character. Unfortunately, scholars no longer believed that the national character was bred in the private sphere alone. Women lost their historical authority once they were perceived to occupy a place so distant from the public and political seats of action.[31]

As scholarly men applied scientific criteria to national history, Earle appeared less the lady historian than the lady scribbler, a fate Martha Lamb escaped just in the nick of time. In fact, when Lamb sought government documents to write papers in the 1880s, officials respected her work and happily gave her "admittance to the inner precincts of the State Department at Washington."[32] Fifteen years later, however, Earle did not feel nearly as revered. As she researched her book *Colonial Days in Old New York*, she exhausted the sources at the American Antiquarian Society and the Long Island Historical Rooms and proceeded to the New York Hall of Records. She described the ambience of the government repository as unwelcoming—and masculine. "Flanked by scores of spittoons . . . errand boys, messengers, aged porters, [and] young attorneys," who exchanged papers with "mechanical rapidity," Earle felt lost in a bureaucratic sea of men and documents, and in the end no one would help her find the historical evidence she was looking for.[33]

Amateurism vs. Professionalism: A Crisis of Identity

As a middle-class mother and the daughter-in-law of prominent revolutionary patriots, Earle felt a sense of mission to educate others about the American legacy. Her activities in patriotic historical societies and her writing of colonial history were supposed to remind her children of their heritage and to teach all children of the heroic origins of the nation. Her colonial histories embodied the personalism of Elizabeth Ellet's *The Women of the Revolution* in 1850; often they sounded impressionistic, informal, and even gossipy, yet her civic-minded purpose justified her familiar, didactic tone. Her maternal sensibilities gave her special access to the familial, private, and tactile aspects of the colonial past. As a chronicler with a distinctly female voice, she made little apology for her intimate connection to her subject material and in fact admitted in *Child Life in Colonial Days* (1899) that her motivation to write on the topic derived from "affectionate interest, not from scientific interest."[34]

Nevertheless, now, on the eve of the twentieth century, her claim seemed somewhat disingenuous. While she continued to write in a traditionally domestic style, she was also seeking professional status characteristic of the modern new woman and affirmation as a scientific historical scholar. Biographer Susan Williams maintains that Earle's commitment to a professional career as a historian was total. Unlike earlier domestic writers, she played an active part in negotiating her contracts with publishers and insisted on complete control over artwork, photography, design specifications, and royalty arrangements. Moreover, in academic circles she was compelled to explain that she employed the "scientific" methods of university professionals when the need arose. Already in 1896 she claimed to write her "histories inductively from facts by the most approved scientific processes." Her desire to be the affectionate mother yet also the scientific scholar suggests that Earle was in transition much like her historical subjects, seeking legitimacy as a domestic writer of the Victorian age yet also as a public historian of the modern era. Unfortunately for her the two identities were increasingly at odds with each other, as the scientific historian became more entrenched in a position of authority.[35]

In search of expert status, new practitioners in the field of professional history had not only defined their scholarly output as scientific but also as the antithesis of what they differentiated as amateur writing. "Amateurism" in the historical field was not yet a concept with fully adapted meaning, but professionals gave it definition as they fashioned their personas as experts, creating dualistic notions of professionalism and amateurism that fell, respectively, along masculine and feminine discursive poles: the objective and biased, scientific and literary, official and personal, restrained and emotive, intellectual and superficial, political and social, empirical and intuitive, trained and untrained, meticulous and imprecise, rare and mundane, omniscient and parochial, scholarly and pedagogical, high and low—and of course, male and female. Often these polarities proved false, as women exhibited an ability to write the most rigorous masculine and male-centered history. Nonetheless, the widespread belief in their veracity created real adverse conditions for women seeking status as expert interpreters of the past.[36]

The construction of historical amateurism is essential to any understanding of the work of women as historians in these years of professionalization. Bonnie Smith rightly insists that "in so disavowing the historiographic past of amateurism, one takes a stand on the side of professionalism, which in its procedures, practices, methodology, writing, fantasies, and organization has built historical science out of gender by privileging male over female."[37] Her recognition of the gendering of professionalization has been a first step toward reclaiming a more complete picture of women's role in the development of historical practice. However, it is also clear that the connected processes of scientization and academicization also helped to transform the tone, content, methods, and style of scholarship in the nascent field of professional history, as well as the persona of the historian, in easily discernible ways.

Certainly by the turn of the century, male historians continued to write "romantic" history, just as a handful of female professional historians produced scholarship in the new scientific tradition. Nonetheless, the fact that women's access to academic training was so much more limited than men's gave amateurism just that much more of a feminine connotation. Scholars in the twentieth-century academy regarded the Victorian narratives of women such as Clara Waters and Elizabeth Ellet as cultural trivia rather than viable history, which appeased the appetite of an untrained readership (often assumed female) for superficial details about the everyday fashions, habits, and personal travails of royalty and mythical figures. By the turn of the century the male scholar of history had come to delineate a function for his historical narratives that was completely different from that of American women's narratives; whereas women's amateur accounts served as allegory, parable, or civic lesson that straddled the divide between history and fiction, men's scholarship was the strictest form of objective truth—and thus the purest form of history. Reducing domestic history and other women's genres to religious moralizing, uncritical patriotism, and voyeurism, the male scholar insisted that his scientific narratives served the nobler purpose of exposing truth.[38]

Seeking further validation as a scientific investigator, the male academic historian held up his work as a purified written form, which unlike lesser literary productions was uninfluenced by market forces or individual interests. At this time when historians such as Sarah Bolton and Alice Earle were turning profits in the marketplace, defining scientific history in this way marked the gender of historical amateurism even further as feminine. Prolific domestic writers were now construed as quintessential amateurs by virtue of their profitable subject matter, and yet ironically as popular historians they rarely reaped many of the proceeds they generated for book publishers. Earle, for one, wrote six commercially successful books under Charles Scribner's Sons only to fall out over a cash advance that she was promised but never received. Likewise Frances Victor, a popular historian of the Northwest, earned "less than a copyist in the City Hall would be paid" for the books she wrote for Hubert Howe Bancroft's Pacific Coast History Series. Even so, the marketability of their books made these women appear financially driven in the eyes of the disinterested scholar who claimed to write in the name of truth over money.[39]

In these subtle ways scientific historians assigned gender to amateurism, forcing the once authoritative woman historian to assume an ambiguous status between amateur and expert by 1900. Such was especially the case for Frances Victor, initially a serial fictionist who came to applaud the new scientific age of truth-seeking and tried to transform herself from a storyteller into a serious research historian. Novels did have their uses, she explained, as the "dessert after meals—the comedy after the heavy drama of real events." However, now she believed that the novel's long-term effect on its predominately female readership was to "warp the judgment and pervert the conscience." History, she maintained, could be as romantic as fiction, but its faithfulness to real life made it more enriching for both writer and reader.[40] Attempting to fashion herself as the quintessential historical expert—a hard, fast researcher, not a pedagogue—she essentially relinquished her second marriage and domestic life for a life of historical investigation. Unlike popular historians, Victor insisted that she turned up truth more than she turned out profit. "None have more completely lost sight of their own pecuniary interests than I have," she boasted, "my work and not my income having always been first on my mind." True enough, she turned down monetary offers from living Oregon pioneers who authorized her writing of their personal biographies. Far too preoccupied with the affirmation of historical scholars, she doled out unsolicited criticism to academic editors in the effort to portray herself as an unquestioned professional insider.[41]

Victor was sure that her meticulous archival methods made her histories more accurate than others written about the Northwest. To an editor of Oregon history she promoted her latest manuscript as the product of research equal to any professional scholar's: "I take pride in feeling that my work was done with a thoroughness which, while it provoked opposition in some quarters, makes it superior to most original histories," she wrote. "In particular, I endeavored to rescue from oblivion, if only by the merest mention, the names of Oregon pioneers. . . . I give a history of the missions —which the missionaries themselves never have done—and I settle forever the question as to motive and deed of Dr. Whitman in his journey east. It makes a strong and interesting book."[42]

Victor did gain recognition as somewhat of an authority among select circles. Professor E. G. Bourne cited her findings in his own research, and she was called on to review a regional biography for the *American Historical Review* (*AHR*), then under J. Franklin Jameson's editorship. In the eyes of most other university historians, however, she never truly achieved scholarly status. The fact remained that she had never received the formal university training deemed necessary to conduct serious archival research. Never able to shed her original designation as a serial fictionist, she continued to be recognized more commonly for her adventure stories, travel narratives, and social columns in San Francisco newspapers than for her attempts at rigorous historical research. Victor would wax and wane in essays about the differences between history and literature, yet to the academician her versatile pen made her a lady scribbler, not a serious historical scholar.[43]

Straddling the line between professional and amateur, Victor found herself pleading with academics to fund and review her work while she did research for Bancroft's Pacific Coast History Series. Unfortunately, her fears that the position might compromise her autonomous reputation as a historian proved warranted. She claimed to work "six days a week from sun-up until sundown," but her designation as a mere researcher afforded her a minimum amount of pay and no formal acknowledgment of her original work. Without academic credentials she could hardly expect better, however, especially given Bancroft's own intensifying penchant for scientific method. In 1893 at the Columbian Exposition in Chicago she tried to have the last word, proudly displaying her name on the spine of the four Pacific Coast histories she claimed to have authored.[44]

Victor's ambiguous legacy shows how the rise of professional culture undermined the work and status of the woman historian trying to eke out a living in these years. Likewise Delilah Beasley, an African American club-woman, was a historian in search of scholarly affirmation that never came. A nurse turned personal masseuse, she moved west with a client and eventually was drawn to the research that resulted in the race history *The Negro Trail Blazers of California* (1919). In total, Beasley spent eight years requesting access to the papers of pioneer families and private citizens' personal libraries, often to compensate for her lack of access to university archives. She called on Professor Charles Edwards Chapman of Berkeley to obtain some of the state's Spanish archives and asked the curator at the Bancroft Library to verify the names and dates of her historical subjects. Nonetheless, scholars generally criticized Beasley's overlaudatory, uncritical tone in her final manuscript. They believed that her attention to the good deeds of California heroines—temperance workers, clubwomen, and pious wives of state officials—compromised the scholarly merit of her work, as did her frequent use of oral testimony in lieu of written documents.[45]

During most of the years Victor and Beasley were trying to establish themselves as expert historians of the West, Alice Earle was suffering a similar fate on the other side of the country. In some respects she resembled the university scholar; she sustained membership in a professional history organization (the AHA) and had been asked as a "learned antiquarian" to assert her expert opinion in reviews for *Dial* magazine. Still, many academicians believed her social and cultural perspectives of women, children, and community life unsuitable subjects for scientific scrutiny. Moreover, while she indicated her sources, she never adopted the practice of scientific notation or other conventions that served as proof of scholarly training. Earle died having written eighteen books and dozens of historical articles, but her prolificacy never won her the esteem of scholars, who in the end considered her works showpieces for the bookcases of women and children rather than serious historical texts. Her fate suggests that scientific historians did not denounce domestic writers outright; their writings, though unfit for scholarly consideration, still held pedagogical value elsewhere—for juvenile and immigrant audiences.[46]

Academic historians insisted that credible history required credentials and access that Victor, Beasley, and Earle did not possess, yet all three wanted professional recognition just the same. By the turn of the century dozens of women had embraced the field's emphasis on political, legal, and official themes. This was understandable given their desire to be affirmed scientific scholars, yet it also proved ironic since these were the public realms into which they possessed no personal right of entry. As Bonnie Smith has recently explained, the new male scientific historian installed sexual difference into the core of professional identity, and he installed it at the "nexus of science and politics." The woman historian found herself in a double bind: To acquire professional status, she had to accept the scientific criteria of the university historian as well as his political shift in emphasis, and yet this redirection became one of the greatest justifications for the disfranchised woman's eventual fall from historical authority.[47]

Perhaps the greater irony was that the tenets of scientific history, as they invalidated nearly all women historians, became the scientific historian's means for reifying the memory of Martha Lamb—if only for a brief time. Upon her death, scholars maintained that what made Lamb a superior historian was that she did not write history like a woman. The *Boston Transcript* reported that Lamb wrote "with a calm and discriminating judgment"; unlike Earle's books, Lamb's *History of the City of New York* contained hard facts and detailed footnotes that could be scientifically confirmed.[48] A journalist for the *New York Graphic* summed up what differentiated Lamb from the breed of woman amateur that followed:

> Mrs. Lamb holds and worthly [*sic*] fills a position most important and res[p]onsible. She is the editor of the *Magazine of American History*. Not a magazine, mind you, of pretty little rhymes, of delectable love stories and fashion articles, all so dear to the feminine heart, but a magazine of hard, solid, immovable facts! Honestly now, do you know among all your dear five friends, a woman who does not hate facts and look upon them as her natural enemy? Mrs. Lamb is the exception that proves the rule, and the almost phenomenal growth of the magazine since her graceful, womanly form filled the editorial chair tells forcibly that she not only loves facts but knows perfectly well how to manage them.[49]

Today most would agree that Lamb's history of New York holds up as an impressive piece of writing and research; however, it did not differ much from the works women historians wrote decades later in virtual anonymity. Notes Lamb left confirmed that her sources were often the same inventories, diaries, and personal recollections that Earle used for her histories of colonial women and family life. Lamb quantified many of her historical claims and backed them up with extensive footnotes; however, she, too, believed it important to flesh out her male and female figures as human beings who endured the trials of daily life. In later years she explained that her goal was not to be the neutral, fact-obsessed social scientist nor the overly emotive literary woman. "I was expected to infuse life and color into every paragraph," she recalled, "and to hit the happy medium between the dull repetition of details and the indulgence of fancy. . . . I had undertaken to introduce biographical sketches and family history into the narrative of public affairs, *which no American historian had hitherto attempted.*" Yet this was not the accomplishment for which university historians remembered her by 1900, if they remembered her at all.[50]

By 1921 scholarly and popular memory of Lamb's histories had started to fade, hence the attempt to recover her work in the *Evening World*. However, for a brief time in the late nineteenth century she enjoyed a better reception as a woman historian; she wrote history before the professional turn was complete, and thus did not suffer the stigma male scholars placed on the "amateur" women who followed. In the tributes written about her immediately before and after her death, there was not a single mention of her status as an amateur or a professional; most often she was described simply as a "writer of history" and a gifted one at that. In 1882 the *Baltimore American* had declared her "the most industrious, as well as distinguished of workers in the field she had chosen," indifferent to the distinctions that scientific historians were soon to make.[51] Looking back on her career, many professional admirers concluded that in some ways she was a scientific historian waiting for the new age of history writing to be formally declared. Now, with more hindsight, it might be more accurate to say that Lamb enjoyed the perks of falling comfortably into two traditions of history: a domestic one that had not yet fully declined, and a scientific one that was just coming into prominence. Lamb wrote her histories just as her meticulous style was coming into vogue in the academic world but while she still maintained moral authority as a Victorian woman of letters.[52]

Women in the Masculine World of Academic History

Lamb, Victor, Earle, and Beasley never acquired the training or credentials of university historians; by 1900, however, there was a handful of women (eight with doctorate degrees) deemed qualified to research and write scientific history. Katharine Coman of the University of Michigan, for example, had become an economic historian at Wellesley College and in many respects became Alice Earle's professional antithesis. Groomed for empirical research under Professor Charles Kendall Adams, her first article, "Wages and Prices in England, 1261–1702," debuted in the *Journal of Political Economy* in 1893 to the rave reviews of male scholars. Coman supplemented her historical text with tables and charts of data extracted from the same sorts of legal rolls and bursar records Earle occasionally consulted when writing about her colonial subjects. However, it was Coman's quantitative analysis, put in terms of "depreciation," "fluctuation," and "average prices," that scholars preferred over Earle's qualitative descriptions of colonial women's homes and personal possessions. In 1903 Coman became one of the first contributors to the *Economic Historical Review*, solidifying her place as one of the pioneers of economic history.[53]

Several other women standouts earned reputations as scientific historians at Bryn Mawr College, the first and for a time the only women's college in the country that offered a Ph.D. in history. In the first decades of the twentieth century, professors there adhered closely to new scientific tenets, requiring graduate students to demonstrate a mastery of six different fields, including historical bibliography and criticism. Typically, on exams they asked students to give an account of political events, to evaluate the outcomes of great wars and the regimes of great men, or to describe and compare the evolution of systems of government in America, Great Britain, and Western Europe. Not unlike the men at Johns Hopkins or Harvard, one Bryn Mawr graduate student had to classify historical source materials, evaluate the factuality of documents, and chart the progress of the "science" of paleography. "Sketch the history of the French Archives since 1789," one examiner requested, "or of the records of the central government of England in medieval and modern times." Another examiner asked her to "explain the science of diplomatics" and to describe the problems a researcher encounters "in the determination of a particular fact."[54]

Bryn Mawr and other women's colleges graduated a number of eventual professional historians, yet it was perhaps Mount Holyoke College that underwent the most dramatic transformation, from a small division of seminary learning to a center of specialized training and scholarly production. Like departments at Wellesley and Vassar, its offerings in history were limited in the late nineteenth century, and its instructors were better trained as educators than researchers. Nonetheless, by 1890 the faculty had redirected the historical curriculum away from religious, moralistic themes and toward constitutional history and political economy in America and abroad. One instructor designed a modern seminar on European historical theorists and required students to use the campus library to conduct original research.[55] By 1923 the faculty had instituted an honors program in which students worked closely with faculty mentors to write theses in American, medieval, ancient, Russian, and Asian history. By the 1930s *Historians and the Writing of History* was one of the more than thirty course offerings in the department, giving advanced students further training in historical technique and interpretation. As a result of this expanded curriculum, approximately 900 students majored in history at Mount Holyoke between 1900 and 1939. Twenty-nine of them went on to earn Ph.D.'s in history, nearly 10 percent of the total number awarded to women in American universities in these years.[56]

One can trace Mount Holyoke's scientific turn to 1900, when Mary Woolley, a former master's student under J. Franklin Jameson at Brown University, became president of the college and brought with her a new philosophy that transformed Mount Holyoke into a research institution. One historian on the faculty remembered that "Miss Woolley started out right away with a definite intention of breaking with the past completely. . . . Christian womanhood in her mind was all right but its importance was immediately taken over by the conception of scholarship . . . and scholarship just as good as any men's college offered a man."[57] Woolley's first major hire in the history department was Nellie Neilson, a Bryn Mawr doctoral student already considered one of the most promising authorities in medieval English history. Shortly after her arrival, Woolley packed the department with more women bearing doctoral credentials and research agendas, including Bertha Putnam (1908) and Viola Barnes (1919), scholars who had received their Ph.D.'s at Columbia and Yale, respectively.[58] Barnes became best known for her work in American colonial history, and Putnam for her systematic classification of the legal and economic documents of British medieval history. Reviewers described critically her *Early Treatises on the Practice of the Justices of the Peace in the Fifteenth and Sixteenth Centuries* as overly footnoted and cross-referenced, yet no one disputed its scholarly nature or the high degree of training and research it required.[59]

Indeed the scholars of Mount Holyoke seemed to have a keen understanding of how the American historical field had evolved, where it was going, and their place in its development. In an unpublished history of the department, Neilson explained that "when several members of the present department came into office, a new conception of the aims of historical study was being added to the old. There came, in part from German Universities, the stress on historical investigation of the political, constitutional, and economic development of countries, and with it came the need for a detailed study of historical sources, of languages, bibliography, and the like as tools of history."[60]

Neilson's summary of the scientific times emerged from a privileged perspective at the profession's academic core; from the onset of her career she enjoyed the professional acceptance of male peers, publishing in major historical journals and sitting on important organizational committees. She received full professor status at Mount Holyoke only three years after being hired and thereafter served on committees and executive councils for the AHA, the Medieval Academy, and the medieval journal *Speculum*. Her success had much to do with the fact that her professional climb occurred in the female-centered environment of Mount Holyoke, where Woolley gave her the freedom to research subjects at will, to attend scholarly meetings at home and abroad, and to remain active on professional commit-tees.[61] To be sure, she accepted, if not embraced, the new scientific predilec-tion for political, constitutional, and diplomatic history and became a prominent academician in her own right, rejoicing that history was no longer "the praise of ladies dead and lovely knights" so commonly evoked by domestic women. Her colleague Viola Barnes agreed that the new em-phasis on empirical research was a positive step forward for women histo-rians and that any attempt to return to earlier modes of history would be "like asking scientists to return to the 19th century thought before the atom was split and when doctors still bled people."[62] The shift toward scientism did not strip Neilson and Barnes of historical authority but empowered them to participate in political and constitutional discourses once deemed outside their appropriate realm of interest.

Of course most women in the academy felt differently as historians who would never achieve the same professional acclaim. The younger academic historian Margaret Judson, a Mount Holyoke undergraduate before train-ing at Radcliffe, discovered in her case that it was not enough to write the same sort of history and employ the same methods as her male peers. "Many historians seemed surprised that a woman historian wrote upon constitutional and political ideas and had done research in legal sources," she recalled, and in the end this surprise manifested as unfair treatment.[63] Her perceptions suggest that the scientific ideal did not always promote similar outcomes for men and women trained in scientific settings, and most women historians who worked in coeducational colleges and univer-sities agreed. The gender biases women encountered in these institutions were not merely the consequence of historical scientism but also the reflec-tion of widespread attitudes in the entire academy. Male professors resisted working with female students, citing studies that claimed to prove em-pirically that women were incapable of the same intellectual training as men and that they undertook it at risk to their reproductive health. Har-vard medical professor Edward Clarke asserted these biologically deter-mined notions to open ears in university departments, perhaps in reaction to fears that women graduates would threaten social norms to which American society had grown accustomed.[64]

Women academicians suffered gender biases in all fields, but there is evidence that sexism was particularly acute in history departments, where male scholars distinguished their discipline above all others in the social sciences as fiercely masculine. The fact that few women were entering history departments at the turn of the century was not due to the lack of women entering colleges and universities or the social sciences generally. By 1910 almost 40 percent of the total undergraduate population in American institutions of higher learning was female, increasing to 47 percent the following decade. As more schools in the West and Midwest turned coeducational or opened women's campuses, female enrollments in many of them began to exceed male enrollments. Once considered well outside women's proper sphere, colleges and universities were gradually becoming acceptable public spaces for women to refine their skills for private life, particularly in the fields of "domestic science" and pedagogy. Career literature of the Association of Collegiate Alumnae (ACA) indicates that for the small percentage of women going into postcollegiate study at the turn of the century, the fields of medicine, law, and the ministry were more attractive than academia. As for the few who did move on to academic careers, they tended to gravitate toward the natural sciences or the feminized sectors of education, librarianship, social work, nursing, and home economics —not history.[65]

By 1904 more than 450 American colleges offered history courses in varying specializations. Institutions that admitted female students reported that history was a popular field of study, second only to English as a discipline in which women sought master's degrees. However, their interest in history tapered off at the doctoral level, despite the fact that the number of positions in professional history had swelled. Kate Everest Levi was the first woman to earn a doctoral degree in history in 1893; only seven more women had joined her by 1900, twenty-two by 1905, and forty-eight by 1915.[66] In 1897 the AHA began compiling its annual lists of history dissertations completed and in progress in American universities. They reveal first and foremost that men far outnumbered women in doctoral programs and that the ratios did not change much between 1897 and the 1930s. In 1913, for example, only 37 of 309 dissertations in progress were the works of women, a disproportionate number of whom were studying at Cornell, Yale, and the Universities of Wisconsin and Chicago. Women were especially underrepresented in ancient and medieval history (two women to twenty-five men), subfields that required meticulous translation of documents. Women wrote in the greatest proportion on subjects in American history and specifically on localized topics for which they had greater access to archival materials (nineteen women). Included among these projects were Katharine Gallagher's "Life of Bishop Kemper" and Margaret Morriss's "Maryland under the Royal Government," studies deemed appropriately scientific by virtue of their male and political subject matter.[67]

Bryn Mawr, Radcliffe, Cornell, Yale, Columbia, and the University of Pennsylvania started granting Ph.D.'s in history to women in the early twentieth century, and soon land-grant and coeducational schools in the West and Midwest began attracting female students to their programs.

Women with doctorate degrees in hand found positions in the greatest volume at the Sister Schools in the East—Smith, Wellesley, Vassar, Bryn Mawr, and Mount Holyoke in particular—where administrators were committed to hiring women scholars. The number of prominent female faculty at these schools tapered off after 1920, however, as administrators perceived that male scholars would give their history departments heightened prestige. At the same time the presence of female faculty steadily increased at land-grant colleges, where lower salaries and heavy teaching loads caused male faculty to leave, often for posts vacated by women in the East. In regional terms, women were apt to have better success finding positions at western institutions, where faculties were generally less distinguished and endowments were low. Agnes Wergeland and Laura White, for example, left New England and later became history department chairs at the University of Wyoming. Similarly, Maria Sanford was asked to leave Swarthmore College in the 1880s only to rejuvenate her academic career at the University of Minnesota, where administrators eventually named a residence hall in her honor.[68]

The earliest graduate historical seminars in American universities resembled the masculine ideal as conceived by Ranke earlier in the nineteenth century, although women found ways to infiltrate them. Frederick Jackson Turner permitted students Emma Helen Blair and Louise Phelps Kellogg into his graduate courses at the University of Wisconsin, only to overwhelm them with male-centered narratives and themes. At the University of Michigan, Charles Kendall Adams conducted seminars attended by future historians Lucy Salmon, Alice Freeman Palmer, Mary Sheldon Barnes, and Katharine Coman, although he admitted to conceding to their presence with only "polite toleration."[69] Throughout the 1890s women took part in the graduate seminars J. Franklin Jameson convened at Brown University, although there were rarely more than one or two women in attendance at any given session.[70] A student took the following minutes in one of his seminars in 1898; invited speaker and Harvard professor Albert Bushnell Hart reinforced the masculine biases of academic history as he delivered "A Chase after Manuscripts":

The manuscripts, the chase after which Dr. Hart described, in a very interesting manner[,] were those of Salmon P. Chase.

. . . Mr. Chase early in his public career became impressed with the idea that the records of his life would be of value; accordingly he preserved his papers with great care. He also kept with more or less regularity, Journals, at first written by himself but afterward dictated—His letters he preserved to the number of about 5000.

At the beginning of his pursuit after these manuscripts Dr. Hart wrote to Secretary Chase's daughter, Mrs. Kate Chase Sprague[,] but received no answer. He also communicated with her sister, Mrs. Hoyt, . . . he discovered some material but of no great quantity. . . .

Dr. Hart next determined to attack the matter more systematically, and accordingly went to Washington and interviewed Mrs. Kate Chase Sprague (who, he believed, was the only woman who ever had political influence). From her he learned that certain papers of Mr. Chase's were in possession of a certain deposit company, where they had been for twenty years. It turned out there were two trunks of them. . . .

In 1894, the daughter of [a] Mr. Hamlin, after writing to Dr. Hart that there were no papers of Mr. Chase in their possession later wrote that she believed she had discovered what he was looking for. . . . In the first [trunk] there was little of value, but the second contained a mass of valuable papers.

Dr. Hart read to the meeting, and passed around for inspection a number of letters to Mr. Chase; among these letters from John Brown (of Harper's Ferry fame), Horace Greeley, . . . John G. Whittier, President Lincoln, General Grant, etc. etc.

In closing Dr. Hart wished to impress it upon every American that it was his duty to preserve the papers of public men.[71]

One can only surmise how Gertrude Kimball, the one female graduate student at this seminar, internalized the masculine messages of Hart's lecture. She was told that the only roles women played in the process of constructing history were as human safety deposit boxes waiting for the qualified male historian to redeem the documents and properly interpret their meaning. Once more the life stories of political men were deemed historically significant, and the correspondences between political men about official business were the only fruitful source materials. Kimball may have questioned where she stood as a woman scholar in the historical process. Yet in the end she adhered to the conventions she was taught, writing male-centered accounts of New England trade in the eighteenth century.[72]

Kimball's experience suggests that while women had found ways to enter the academic "laboratories" of the scientific historian, their presence did little to change the undertones of sexism cultivated there. Like men in other professions at the turn of the century, male historians organized academic fraternities that remained closed to women. Jameson organized one such group called the Convivium Historicum, which convened annually after 1917 at a resort in the Connecticut woods. His "history club," social as much as it was professional or intellectual, was more exclusively male than the university seminar. Much like any saloon or gentleman's club frequented outside the university, it provided a setting where the male scholar could "talk shop" and build networks of associates outside the purview of female colleagues.[73]

The private writings of women historians through the 1930s confirm that the "old boys' club" was alive and well in academic history and that the attitudes of male historians reflected larger conceptions of women's place in the professions and society. Margaret Judson, for example, resented the way her male preliminary examiners treated her as a graduate student at Radcliffe College. "As a gracious gesture the professors had arranged that tea be served before the exam, and as a woman of course I was asked to pour," she recalled. "Three times Professor Haskins handed his cup of tea back to me saying, 'Weaker please Miss Judson.' "[74] Arguably, the deference Judson was expected to demonstrate had as much to do with her age and lesser status as a graduate student as it did with her gender. Nevertheless, her memory of failed attempts to study in the Harvard libraries reveals a more clear-cut instance of an academic culture of chauvinism: "The stacks in the Widener Library were closed to women after six o'clock because the authorities claimed women students might be raped in these narrow, long, often deserted dark corridors. . . . When given permission to work in the stacks of the Harvard Law Library, it was granted only if I entered by the *back* door. Otherwise, the head librarian, obviously not desiring to have women researching in his male bastion, might see the woman and forbid further research there."[75]

Judson continued to go to the Harvard libraries despite her grudging reception, for these male bastions did in fact have superior research materials. She likewise encouraged her junior and senior history majors to leave campus for the libraries at Rutgers when she became an instructor at the New Jersey College for Women.[76] Scholars such as Judson resented the old boys' club mentality in academic history, but it was an attitude that had thrived undisturbed for some time. It was fostered not only in university history departments and fraternities but also in the professional organizations academic men established in the late nineteenth and early twentieth centuries, including the AHA. In 1884 Johns Hopkins professor Henry Baxter Adams collaborated with other prominent university scholars to establish the organization, the purpose of which was to lend legitimacy to the budding discipline of academic history by making conspicuous a definable community dedicated to the consolidation of scholarly methods and standards. Adams recognized that the only way to earn national recognition for the infant organization was initially to open it to a broad-based membership, and thus he welcomed older patrician historians, business-men, secondary school teachers, and enthusiasts to become members along with university-trained specialists. In the first annual report of AHA pro-ceedings, he even insisted that there was "nothing in the Constitution of the American Historical Association to prevent the admission of women into the Association upon the same qualifications as those required of men."[77]

Nonetheless, despite Adams's seeming openness toward women and nonacademic members in these early years, the executive members of the AHA, all of whom were male, laid the groundwork for the professional, scholarly identity the organization would assume for the next sixty years. In 1884 no woman appeared on the AHA's list of original members, and the board invited only four women out of 120 guests to its first annual meeting. The following year the dues-paying membership of the AHA increased to 287, yet Katharine Coman, Lucy Salmon, and Martha Lamb were the only women listed as attendees at the annual meeting. Indeed, Lamb, who was being honored with a lifetime membership, recalled sitting on the speakers' platform alongside Bancroft, Adams, and Jameson at the third annual meeting, not a single other woman in sight.[78]

In 1886 the female AHA membership increased to a dozen historians and educators affiliated with patriotic organizations, local historical so-cieties, and social science departments of women's colleges. Lucy Salmon, the most active woman member in these formative years, created a stir with the publication of the critically acclaimed "History of the Appointing Power of the President" in the first volume of the *Papers of the American Historical Association*. It was based on a master's thesis she had written at the University of Michigan under Charles Kendall Adams, a man who did not think that women were "suitable for seminar work" but witnessed Salmon excel in his courses as both an undergraduate and a graduate student nonetheless. Like so many of the first women academics, Salmon bided her time as a high school teacher until she could find the resources to return to graduate study. After receiving her master's degree, she returned yet again to teaching but left when offered a scholarship to Bryn Mawr College. There she replaced the patronizing mentoring of Adams for the downright demeaning deportment of Woodrow Wilson, a professor who according to Salmon had only grudgingly directed her research. Despite the lack of positive male mentoring she managed to produce a work of political history that men in and outside the academy found intellectually rigorous and worthy of the AHA's first publication. One U.S. senator even described it as "the best thing that had ever been written on the subject."[79]

Salmon would eventually have a commanding presence in the AHA, but she would remain an atypical case; collectively women's representation in the general membership continued to be lower than men's. Attendance tallies at annual meetings reflected the ambivalent attitude of the male leadership toward women members into the twentieth century. Although more than 100 women had finally attended annual meetings by 1900, nearly all were passive observers or wives of male organizers and presenters. Despite his initial claims, Henry Baxter Adams shared this ambivalence, recognizing the need for women's indirect participation yet at the same time curtailing their numbers and influence. Once regretful that women were underrepresented at one annual meeting, he admitted that it was "a mistake to exclude them from the dinner in the evening" and that all meeting participants should be invited the next time. On the other hand, in 1897 he was reluctant to invite another woman to accompany Lucy Salmon on the Committee of Seven, a body of investigators of pedagogical practices, insisting "that one woman is enough!"[80]

After 1900, individual women members did start to gain acknowledgment for their scholarship. Louise Phelps Kellogg received the AHA's prestigious Justin Winsor Prize in 1903, followed by Annie Abel in 1906 and Mary Williams in 1914. Similarly, Louise Fargo Brown won the Herbert Baxter Prize in European history in 1911. However, at annual meetings Lucy Salmon continued to be the only professional woman historian scheduled to speak with regularity. In 1903, 1905, and 1907 only four other women participated with her as invited speakers, compared with dozens of male historians and archivists, and at subsequent meetings women did not present papers at all.[81] By the 1910s, women had established a small presence on committees, although this was mainly on pedagogical committees. American Revolution historian Susan Kingsbury secured a place on the General Committee in 1912, and Lois Mathews, historian and dean of women at the University of Wisconsin, was a member of the Nominations Committee in 1914. Salmon was the first female executive board member in 1915, followed by Ruth Putnam, a candidate without scholarly credentials but one for whom Salmon rigorously lobbied. After Putnam, Mary Williams (Goucher), Nellie Neilson (Mount Holyoke), and Elizabeth Donnan (Wellesley) followed suit. Still, while individual standouts made some headway on committees, women failed to achieve a collective presence in the AHA in the early twentieth century. Despite making up almost one-fifth of the total membership, women only occupied 5 percent of leadership positions by 1920.[82]

In hindsight the appointee system for choosing the rotating AHA executive members may have had much to do with the disproportionate representation of women on committees. Instead of accepting nominations from the floor, the president pro tem nominated a committee of three, which in turn selected a slate of officers who were elected unanimously until the committee of three became an elected body in 1916. Despite the democratic changes, men continued to choose male colleagues to occupy seats of influence, further relegating women members to the peripheries of AHA business.[83] Male members on the program committee proved all-powerful in determining the nature of topics presented at annual meetings and published in the AHA *Papers*; their subjects of choice often revolved around the male figures who orchestrated the nation's political and consti-tutional past. "Town and Country Government in the English Colonies" and the "Founding Fathers of New Haven" were two papers given at the first annual meeting that set the tone for succeeding years. The presidential addresses delivered at annual meetings also focused on male topics and the male-omniscient historian. In the 1890s, for example, James Angell offered "The Inadequate Recognition of Diplomatists by Historians" and George Fisher presented "The Function of the Historian as a Judge of Historic Persons."[84]

Indeed, sexist politics played out subtly at annual meeting sessions and turned much less subtle once official business ended and scheduled social activities began. For young men this down time at the meetings provided opportunities to collaborate with more established historians and to ex-pand their professional network to other regions of the country. But for women scholars the scheduled social activities only underscored feelings of professional isolation and institutional marginalization and set them in a national context. Between paper sessions men received invitations to "smokers" held at all-male faculty clubs, while women attended teas and receptions hosted by faculty wives. In 1905 an Honorary Committee of Ladies headed by J. Franklin Jameson's wife greeted the women attendees of the annual meeting in Baltimore, while their male colleagues gathered at the exclusive Arundel Club. Similarly in 1907, male attendees of the meet-ing in Madison, Wisconsin, went to a "smoking and conversation room" at the University Club while their women colleagues searched on maps for the "headquarters for women" at an off-campus location.[85]

The AHA propagated its masculine research agenda and professional culture beyond the confines of its annual meetings in 1895 when it estab-lished the scholarly journal the *American Historical Review*. Intended to be more scientific than its forebear, the *Magazine of American History*, which folded after Martha Lamb's death, its male editors continued to print articles and primary documents almost exclusively by and about men. Whereas Lamb once wielded a weighty editorial hand, the *AHR* offered women scholars few opportunities to display their historical acumen. Jac-queline Goggin calculates that women authored 3 percent of all *AHR* articles printed between 1895 and 1940, even though they comprised between 15 and 20 percent of the AHA dues-paying membership in these years. She believes that the skewed ratios can be attributed to the evaluation process for submissions, which unlike in later years was not anonymous. In 1897 Nellie Neilson's "Boon Services on the Estates of Ramsey Abbey" became the first woman's submission accepted to the journal, printed under the gender-neutral name N. Neilson. Later that year Mary Woolley contributed "The Development of the Love of Romantic Scenery in America," a topic that would have more than likely been considered inappropriate for the serious academic historian but was acceptable for Woolley, a historian turned college administrator.[86]

AHR editors showed little appreciation for women's submissions of original research, yet women did occasionally contribute to the journal as book reviewers, suggesting that they were not altogether disregarded as arbiters of standards in the field. Women's college historians Katharine Coman, Nellie Neilson, and Lucy Salmon wrote reviews for the *AHR* during its first three decades of publication, as did regional experts Louise Phelps Kellogg, Annie Abel, and Ella Lonn. Popular historians outside the academy sold too many books in these years to be ignored, and thus *AHR* editors felt compelled to include reviews of works by Ruth Putnam and Alice Earle more frequently than those by any woman academic.[87] Typically editors called on women to review these popular works, as was the case for the first woman-authored review in 1895. Lucy Salmon was assigned to critique Ruth Putnam's compilation of documents on William of Orange, and she judged the historian according to the scientific standards of her university colleagues. She praised Putnam's "historical instinct" and her facile ability to develop figures instead of "pigeonholing" them into "'heroes' and 'villains,' 'angels' and 'demons.'" Salmon nevertheless suggested that Putnam's analytic acumen left something to be desired. The political backdrop behind the portraiture of William the Silent was "confused and unsatisfactory," she concluded. While she privately appreciated Putnam's contributions to European history, on the pages of the *AHR* she maintained a tenor of academic criticalness, perhaps as a means of professional survival.[88]

It appeared that Salmon was content to uphold the standards of academic science even when they undermined the efforts of other women. Indeed, few of her colleagues agitated openly about the sexism they experienced in the profession, but that is not to say that it went unnoticed. Mary Williams, for one, voiced resentment over her inability to influence AHA committees to the degree of men with equal or lesser credentials. Previously a standout graduate student at Stanford and winner of the Winsor

Prize for her doctoral research on American isthmian diplomacy, she became a professor at Goucher College and wrote several important books on Latin American history. She confided to colleague James Robertson in 1919 that all she wanted was a " 'square deal'—but the woman who is so unfortunate as to have specialized in history largely asks in vain."[89] When she urged her female colleagues to protest the segregated practices of the AHA, few rose to the occasion. Most first-generation university historians chose instead to do what Salmon and Neilson had done: to emulate the male scientific historian in the hopes that professional validation would eventually come.

For some women historians this meant making active lifestyle choices to create personas deemed more or less commensurate with their professional identities as research scholars. Mary Williams, Nellie Neilson, Bessie Pierce, Viola Barnes, Elizabeth Donnan, Dorothy Stimson, and Ella Lonn, for instance, never married or had children, perhaps to leave more time for writing and research. It had been made abundantly clear to them that scholarly productivity was the sole ingredient for professional success in the modern research university, but there were drawbacks to their strategy. Liberating as single status could be, it also left women historians open to closer scrutiny; members of the university community attributed their unfeminine appearances and lifestyles to their spinsterhood. Faculty at Vassar criticized Lucy Salmon, for example, for dressing in culottes instead of the traditional feminine attire of most faculty wives and students. Likewise at Goucher College, students perceived Katharine Gallagher as an eccentric character because her English bulldogs were her only known family and she pampered them like children. The Wellesley College press paid special attention to independent spirit Elizabeth Kendall, who, like Gallagher, was a dog lover and took her Irish terrier Jack on her research trips to the Far East. One colleague even referred to Kendall as desexed, "a gypsy and as such a gentleman." She, like many women scholars, suffered the paradox of being both "invisible and extravisible" at the same time.[90]

Marriage trends among women historians were somewhat consistent with those for all women in the academy at the turn of the century. Between 1875 and 1924, 75 percent of female doctorate holders remained unmarried. This percentage decreased sharply, however, as the separatist lifestyles of the first generation of women graduates appealed less to second- and third-generation women, who attempted to combine marriage and career more frequently. Caroline Ware, for example, a student of Lucy Salmon's from 1917 to 1920, insisted that her combining marriage and academic life "could be difficult to manage" but certainly did not make her exceptional by the time she was teaching at Vassar in the late 1920s and

1930s: "I never thought, in terms of making the choice, that I could not have a career if I married, or I could not marry if I had I career." Likewise, Elisabeth Dexter, yet another historian of this later generation, decided to marry, have an academic career, and even write the history of women in careers in 1924 (*Colonial Women of Affairs*). Already married with children when she embarked on graduate study, Dexter and her husband earned their doctoral degrees the same day and went on to teach together at Skidmore College.[91]

Despite these general trends toward combining marriage and career, however, women historians still continued to marry less frequently than their male colleagues, and most who published with regularity rejected roles as wives and mothers, happily or not, to devote more time to academic research. Departmental records from Mount Holyoke and Wellesley Colleges as late as the 1930s indicate that women historians generally left their departments when they married rather than suffer the stigmatization of being seen as too domestic to produce rigorous scholarship.[92] Nevertheless, at these same women's colleges a sizable percentage of the history faculty lived with other women in Boston marriages. At Wellesley, for example, Katharine Coman lived with English professor Katharine Bates and both of their mothers. "It was a thing that was very common in those days," Viola Barnes recalled at Mount Holyoke. "They practically all, because of living conditions, low salaries and everything, lived in twos." These were certainly considerations when Lucy Salmon decided to live in a small home off the Vassar campus with librarian Adelaide Underhill and when Wells College historians Frances Relf and Louise Loomis took up residence together, for their alternative was to live without privacy in a faculty dorm.[93]

By choosing lifestyles deemed unfeminine (i.e., independent or single), women historians only partially shed the domestic stigma that made them appear to be lesser scholars. Studies conducted by the ACA (later the American Association of University Women [AAUW]) confirmed that sex stereotyping persisted in the academy regardless; though men generally conceded women's adeptness at the undergraduate levels, they believed they surpassed women as researchers once they moved up the graduate and professional ranks. Responses of male professors to a questionnaire in 1924 indicated that the inferior status of women in the university had much to do with men's assumptions about women's natural abilities; men characterized women as inherently better teachers than scholars, less driven, less intellectually engaged, and good at work "involving much drudgery" and social guidance of students. When asked if they would give preference to a man over a woman candidate of equal merit, their overwhelming response was "Yes."[94]

As men questioned women's abilities to produce rigorous scholarship, they compounded women's inability to secure fellowships, take leaves to conduct research, and eventually publish original work. Because publications were the gauge by which scholars of the twentieth-century academy increasingly were measured when considered for promotions, this cycle of nonproduction accounted in large part for women's lesser status in the academy. Goucher historian Ella Lonn confirmed for the AAUW that most academic departments did not seek fellowship money for women. Similarly, in a study of women who earned doctorate degrees between 1877 and 1930, more than 90 percent of the respondents claimed never to have received fellowships in graduate school or research sabbaticals afterward. Researchers for the *Journal of the Association of Collegiate Alumnae* (*JACA*) and the AAUW corroborated in the 1910s and 1920s that gender biases against all women researchers, including historians, caused them not only to receive low pay but also to have disproportionate teaching and administrative burdens, forcing them to linger on the lower rungs of the academic promotional ladder. Whereas the role of the historical pedagogue afforded women a heightened degree of cultural authority in the nineteenth century, in the scientific academy it remained second in status to the role of the research scholar.[95]

Whether women understood the biases against them and gravitated toward pedagogy or, in the end, pedagogy found them, almost six times as many women with doctorates went into teaching rather than research of any kind before 1930, further fueling the conjecture that women must be better educators than research scholars. One study calculated that 40 percent of female college faculty with doctoral degrees at this time taught secondary school at some point in their professional development. Given women's traditional roles as history pedagogues in the home, the percentage was likely even higher for professional women historians; between 1900 and 1930 their career paths were typically characterized by tenures at high schools, normal schools, and women's academies where teaching was the priority. Even Mary Williams, who was particularly successful in securing fellowships and sabbaticals, claimed that she researched her books as an "extra-academic activity" during her free time from teaching.[96]

Administrators burdened women historians with additional classroom responsibilities, but with the steady increase of female students they also assigned women faculty new "social" duties that encroached on their private time. Administrators at coeducational and women's colleges assigned female faculty to tasks as dorm mothers, guidance counselors, and student chaperones on the basis that they were instinctively more nurturing than men. Leona Gabel and Margaret Gale Scott both contended with these responsibilities as women's deans in addition to their history teaching at Smith in the 1930s. Alice Freeman Palmer and Lois Mathews relinquished their careers as historians at Wellesley and Wisconsin altogether when they realized that their administrative positions required full-time attention. Many of these women were also imposed upon to do "departmental housework"; cleaning, filing, and stenography were considered their natural preserve. Bessie Pierce and Frances Gillespie, for example, found themselves organizing class schedules and enrollment records at the University of Chicago, while male colleagues were exempt from such duties. While chairs at Wellesley and Mount Holyoke eventually acknowledged the disproportionate burdens they placed on women scholars and hired clerical assistants, most coeducational department chairs remained content to draw divisions of labor along traditional gender lines.[97]

AAUW and other studies confirm that heavy teaching schedules hampered the scholarly production of women professors in quantifiable ways. One-third of women who received Ph.D.'s in the social sciences before 1925 published nothing other than their dissertations as professional scholars, and 17 percent of those who published did not describe the work as research. The numbers appear even worse for women who earned history doctorates between 1926 and 1935. Although 18 percent of all doctoral degrees in history were awarded to women in these years, women produced only 13 percent of books and 7 percent of articles published by this professional cohort as a whole. Similar percentages held for the women who were asked to review books or whose books were reviewed in historical journals. As late as the 1930s, women historians continued to be about half as productive as men overall.[98]

Women historians performed extracurricular duties fearing that to do otherwise might cost them their faculty positions. Nevertheless, in private several expressed frustration at the extent to which these tasks distracted them from their research. C. Mildred Thompson characterized her work at Vassar as "one-third academic" and "two-thirds executive." Her colleague Lucy Salmon agreed, finally rejecting "corridor duty" in the student dorms altogether on the grounds that it was not her obligation as a hired faculty member. Already overburdened by a heavy teaching load, she protested to administrators: "I have a hundred and seventy names on my list. . . . I am trying to do the work of two . . . and this has meant no time for writing papers or going to educational meetings." In a similar act of defiance Elizabeth Donnan left her post as dean at Rollins College to devote more time to research at Wellesley, but her situation improved little. Likewise Dorothy Stimson stepped away from her joint position as history professor and dean of women at Transylvania College, which still required her to teach class an average of ten to twelve hours per week. "I had felt that I was running a marriage bureau," she recalled of her dean responsibilities. "I preferred the academic work and not the social work." She transferred to Goucher College in 1921, only to discover that her appointment was contingent on performing duties as dean yet again. Finally in 1947 she resigned as dean to finish her book *Scientists and Amateurs: A History of the Royal Society*. After nearly three decades she could finally be the historical scholar she always intended to be.[99]

Some male historians were unabashed in expressing their belief that departmental house and social work was the natural preserve of female colleagues. Others showed better intentions, albeit subtly promoting sexism just the same. As academic advisers, for example, some would counsel women students to apply exclusively to secondary and normal schools to ensure their best chances of employment, paying no mind to the fact that in these positions heavy teaching loads were imminent but scholarly advancement was not. Margaret Judson claimed that her adviser's recommendations were completely different for his male students; upon his suggestion, she took a job at a women's college, sealing her fate in a career with few opportunities for advancement. In the 1920s and 1930s, professors Arthur Schlesinger, Merle Curti, William E. Dodd, and Carl Russell Fish mentored women for careers in research, and Evarts Greene of the University of Illinois was a vocal advocate for awarding female colleagues positions in the field's professional organizations. Unfortunately, what these few men did for women on an individual basis paled in comparison with the effects of sexism in academic history on the whole.[100]

Letters of recommendation reveal that when promoting women students for jobs in other departments, male professors frequently touted candidates' personal appearance rather than their ability to produce original research. In a letter of recommendation, Mary Williams's adviser at Stanford thought it helpful to add, "She is rather above the average in height, slender with a distinctly Swedish or Norwegian face, strong features, a little bit nervous in appearance at first, but really with good control of herself." This sort of commentary was typical in the 1880s, when the *New York Graphic* described Martha Lamb as "amiable, affable and gracious, blithe as a bird . . . [with] a handsome, gentle face." Before the professional turn this description of Lamb's exterior confirmed her internal virtue and, by association, her historical authority. In the masculine university, however, it served to do the opposite. Just as women's journals and diaries no longer presented transparent truths to the scientific historian, neither did women's feminine traits, moral or physical. Their womanly features now turned them into objects to be judged, undermining their search for professional affirmation. Thus when Frederic Paxson at the University of Wisconsin assured Katharine Gallagher's future employers that "her appearance is good & her personality is vigor-ous and pleasing," he may have unwittingly compromised her legitimacy as a serious university scholar.[101]

Well intentioned or not, the praise of individual men did little to secure women research posts or professional advancement on the whole. Whereas newly hired men could generally expect promotion to a full professorship within several years, women such as the University of Chicago's Bessie Pierce were less fortunate.[102] Pierce proved to be a productive historian, publishing several acclaimed monographs and in 1936 becoming the first female AHA council member from a coeducational school. Nevertheless she stagnated as an associate professor at Chicago for fourteen years, well beyond the point of promotion for her less prolific male colleagues. Compared with other women at Chicago, Pierce was fortunate. Frances Gillespie was a faculty member for twenty-seven years (1921–48) and never received tenure, and Shirley Farr, who taught in the department for eighteen years (1915–33), never advanced beyond the level of instructor.[103] Such professional obstacles were certainly not lost on women historians themselves. In 1930 an untenured instructor lamented the fate of women in the profession: "I consider that women with Ph.D. degrees in history are handicapped as regards securing positions congenial and suitable to their training," she concluded. "Opportunities where they can teach advanced work in history are very few. Furthermore, the positions in women's colleges (undergraduate) are about the only positions open to them. There the work is too heavy to allow much time for research, and it is not of a very advanced nature compared with opportunities open to men in graduate faculties. Men may combine graduate courses with their research. Women are mainly concerned with teaching undergraduate history. I would not advise a Ph.D. in history for women."[104]

This commentary echoed the truths understood by the majority of women historians, including an ambitious and promising scholar named Isabel Abbott. After attending Brown University as an undergraduate, she received a master's degree and went on to Bryn Mawr for her Ph.D. in British constitutional and economic history in 1924. She was plagued by financial hardships early on. Her adviser Howard Gray continually tried to find scholarships for her at Bryn Mawr; but the women's college awarded no assistantships, and Abbott never benefited from its modest research fellowships. To make ends meet, she took a temporary teaching position at the University of Minnesota before even embarking on her graduate examinations. She applied for permanent positions at reputable women's colleges, but administrators were reluctant to hire a candidate with incomplete credentials. Gray wrote glowing letters of recommendation to Wellesley and Connecticut Colleges and renewed Abbott's status every year at the Bryn Mawr employment bureau, but again to no avail. In a contemplative moment of hindsight she wrote Pembroke dean Margaret Morriss, "You once told me that it would be wiser to get my degree before I began teaching even if I had to go into debt for it—and you were right."[105]

Abbott considered herself lucky when she was finally hired as an assistant professor at Rockford Seminary in Illinois, but her early struggles merely snowballed as she strove for promotion. At one stage she found herself teaching a full load of classes, writing her thesis, and preparing for her preliminary exams at the same time. "I am heartily sick of working on the thesis summers without making much progress and then losing during the year the little progress made because I am unable to continue amidst the thousand and one demands made on one's time in a small college such as Rockford," she complained to her adviser.[106] She managed to string together a rough draft of her thesis in 1936 but never found the time to convert it into a book. An opportunity to publish did eventually come in 1942, when the AAUW awarded her with a fellowship to complete an article for *Speculum*. This, however, would be the extent of her scholarly productivity aside from several reviews she would write for the *AHR* in following decades. In the end her thesis never made it to publication. With one article to her name she remained entrenched at Rockford, where she enjoyed her students but resented the low salary and exhausting schedule. She was not promoted to full professor until 1948 and was awarded her first paid research sabbatical in 1949, twenty-five years after she first set out to become an academic historian.[107]

In 1943 William Hesseltine and Louis Kaplan published a study in the *Journal of Higher Education* on women's progress in the field of academic history through the 1930s. They determined that only 334 women successfully earned Ph.D. degrees between 1882 and 1935, compared with the 2,055 total degrees conferred. Although the number of women doctorates was steadily increasing, women continued to be marginalized in the field on all counts. As late as 1939 the majority of women in academic employment remained clustered in women's colleges, and a disproportionate number settled for work in normal colleges, teaching colleges, and high schools. Although men increasingly secured senior positions in coeducational and women's colleges, no woman yet had been employed in the history department of a men's college.[108] In summing up the results of the study, its authors were not ambiguous about the professional gains of the woman historian in the early twentieth century:

The list of distinguished women scholars is not long; the record of the average woman who persevered in academic study until she attained the doctorate is not impressive. She has seldom held high or responsible positions in the teaching profession, and she has not proved a productive scholar.... The teaching of history and historical research are activities in which men engage in greater numbers than women. Women who took the Ph.D. in history hold poorer positions, are more likely to be unemployed, and are less likely to do research than men. Moreover, the historical profession awards less recognition to its women members.[109]

Hesseltine and Kaplan based their conclusions on the statistics that they as conscientious social scientists carefully compiled during the first decades of the historical profession. Nonetheless, while they certainly corroborated Abbott's experience, their numbers did not reveal the entire story. Indeed no one could contest the fact that the proportion of women to men in the upper echelons of the historical profession remained low or that the masculine culture of the academy made it considerably more difficult for women to achieve highly in the field. However, the study failed to mention that over the years women historians had honed strategies to mitigate the impact of gender bias in the field, if not to combat it directly. In fact some women eventually organized themselves into a collective force to be reckoned with in both history departments and professional organizations, lobbying successfully to elect Nellie Neilson the president of the AHA in 1943, the same year Hesseltine and Kaplan's article appeared in the *Journal of Higher Education*.

Thus while gender bias posed a formidable obstacle to their professional development, women historians still found ways to influence professional practices and politics. The inability to secure funds for research remained a critical problem for women in the historical field, and yet some individuals succeeded in this regard. In the case of thirty-year-old Annie Abel, for example, a full-tuition graduate scholarship in 1903 permitted her to leave her post as a teacher at a Kansas high school to earn a Ph.D. at Yale.[110] She continued to win monetary prizes to supplement her salaries at Goucher and Smith, including a travel grant from the AAUW in 1925 and a two-year grant from the Social Science Research Council in 1928, which helped her to complete *Chardon's Journal at Fort Clark*. Mary Williams was able to travel throughout Latin America on her Social Science Research Council and AAUW grants and during a partially paid sabbatical completed her manuscript "History of the Latin American People and Their Politics." Goucher colleague Dorothy Stimson advanced her stagnant career after winning the prestigious Guggenheim Memorial Foundation Fellowship in 1929; it provided a needed respite from administrative duties and gave her the means to research a book on ecclesiasticism and scientific thought in seventeenth-century England.[111]

It is important to point out that Stimson, Williams, and Abel were extraordinarily successful scholars—but also, not coincidentally, faculty at women's colleges. Administrators generally gave their research agendas greater support in these institutions, a fact borne out through a questionnaire distributed to women historians in the Northeast in 1931. Those at women's colleges generally taught no more than nine to twelve hours per week, a heavy workload by today's standards but certainly not unreasonable when compared with men's hours at the time. However, at Hunter and Skidmore Colleges, coeducational institutions where the ratio of male to female faculty was higher, women consistently reported assignments of up to fifteen hours per week, leaving almost no time for research or other career-enhancing activities.[112] Between 1900 and 1920 Smith, Wells, Vassar, and Wellesley established sabbatical policies to enhance the scholarly production of female faculty. The first paid leaves Katharine Coman earned at Wellesley, for example, allowed her to complete a series of English history textbooks with colleague Elizabeth Kendall in 1899 and 1902. During her third sabbatical she collected data on peasant farmers in Hawaii and the South, produced two critically acclaimed articles, and began writing her best-known study, *Industrial History of the United States* (1905). Another sabbatical in 1908 allowed her to research *Economic Beginnings of the Far West*, and another leave in 1913 freed her to travel to Europe to study the history of social insurance, research she would have published had she not died in 1915 before completing the project.[113]

In the following decades Wellesley continued to support prolific producers of scholarship—Julia Orvis and Elizabeth Donnan, for example—who in turn mentored students in the practice of hands-on archival research. At Smith College administrators also promoted research by scheduling classes only three days a week, giving students and faculty time for independent work and discovery.[114] At Mount Holyoke Mary Woolley implemented similar policies in addition to capping teaching hours and hiring research assistants for senior faculty. Viola Barnes appreciated that she "would work her head off to help you get a fellowship." In 1927 nearly half the history department, including Neilson and Putnam, took sabbaticals in Europe, again an indication that the sister schools took professional research seriously.[115] The ACA also pitched in with money for its historian members at women's colleges to do specialized research in their respective fields. The Alice Freeman Palmer Fellowship, named in honor of the historian turned women's college administrator, allowed Bertha Putnam to investigate topics regarding fourteenth-century England. In 1914 Louise Fargo Brown, at the time only an instructor at Wellesley, used the Palmer to conduct the research that secured her promotion. By 1913 the *JACA* reported awarding more scholarships to women in history than in any other field, and historians continued to be well represented in following years.[116]

Before long, students of pioneer academicians began to build on the small gains in women's funding made before them. In 1920 and 1921 Wellesley women paid tribute to Elizabeth Kendall and Katharine Coman by establishing chairs in their names. At Vassar, Adelaide Underhill collaborated with students to establish the Lucy Salmon Fund for Research for women writing monographs for publication. Soon women in coeducational institutions followed suit. In 1924 Shirley Farr established a fellowship for women to conduct research in the repositories of Washington, D.C., and Florence Porter Robinson, a scholar who only found employment as a home economics teacher, left money to the University of Wisconsin to create a history chair for a woman of promise.[117]

Modest as they might seem, these gestures on the part of a few women historians suggest that they took charge of their professional destinies and even paved the way for new generations of women scholars in the field. Abbott's struggles in academic history were common, but we see that they do not represent all that formally trained women historians achieved in the early twentieth century. Taking the practice of history outside the domestic sphere by 1900, first-generation academic historians emulated the women recast in the histories of domestic writers, suggesting that to some degree Alice Earle and others like her may have helped to shift social attitudes and pave the way for women to move into public work in the academy and elsewhere. From here the reputations established by women such as Coman, Neilson, and Salmon opened public avenues of historical research for women in government institutions and other social science fields, where a reverence for social neutrality no longer applied. Indeed, what amazingly came to pass was women's redefining of the social function of scientific history and regendering of the scientific historian, both because of and despite the gender biases of the academy. To appreciate these developments fully, however, the university cannot serve as a focal point but merely as a point of departure. A broader historical perspective is needed to blur the distinctions between history and other disciplines—as well as academic and nonacademic domains—in cases where women straddled these divides to give history socially progressive applications.

Chapter 2
Social Activism and Interdisciplinarity in Writing and Teaching, 1910–1935

Isabel Abbott's career-long search for job security, research sabbaticals, and professional recognition was typical of the experiences of many women historians in the early twentieth century. Academic chauvinism prevented her from achieving professional success to the same degree as male peers. Yet as unfortunate as her situation turned, we cannot simply conclude that Abbott viewed her career unilaterally as a failure, nor can we assume that her experience, while common, was universal. Abbott, like other women of the university, was frustrated by her pedagogical burdens, but she also found a semblance of power and influence through them. The designation of women as instinctual educators both hindered and enhanced their ability to shape historical discourse, for while they generally enjoyed fewer opportunities for research in the academy, they often discovered that their positions in the nation's elementary and secondary classrooms afforded them greater influence over the formulation of popular memory. In this chapter we explore this other side of the pedagogical role. While some women continued to view their teaching responsibilities as inhibiting, others sought to legitimate historical teaching as an area of specialized expertise. In this way they negotiated old and new historical practices and came to terms with the gendered shifts that accompanied them.

Nonetheless, the tenets of academic history also began to change in favor of women—particularly for those who never endeared themselves to the pursuit of political subjects or scientific objectivity defined as social neutrality. We have seen thus far that the notion of academic scientism initially precluded the writing of history with social reform in mind, but more women than men continued to write history for this purpose after the turn of the century, especially at women's colleges. Although the academy stopped short of becoming an environment conducive to the writing of women's or minority history, by the 1910s a small cohort of academic men and women did seek to balance scientific objectivity with social advocacy and even questioned the omniscience of the scientific historian. The heightened ideological discord in history departments over questions of historical relativism and the social function of academic research presented pockets of opportunity for progressive-minded women to take their investigations into uncharted directions, including the history of immigration, African Americans, Native Americans, women's work, and other topics formerly omitted from the historical record.

Social advocacy won a handful of boisterous proponents, but it never gained general approval as an acceptable endeavor for the university historian. Thus while some women folded social agendas into their research in history departments, others left to work in social science disciplines more receptive to the use of scholarship for advocacy. Then there were those women who left the academy altogether in search of environments where the writing of history about women, nonwhites, and the working class brought about legislative change. Uninhibited by the conventional attitudes of male social scientists, these defectors recast the pursuit of social advocacy as an endeavor that need not conflict with the pursuit of objective truth. They insisted that scientific historians could—and perhaps even should—depict the past in ways that inspired social change. In the process they confirmed that women reformers could, in fact, be tenacious scientific scholars and anticipated the sensibilities of social historians later in the twentieth century.

The Regendering of Scientific History

The fact that women alumnae and retired scholars sponsored more research by the 1910s suggests that many women had adopted the "publish or perish" mentality for themselves—and yet, surprisingly, not always at the expense of pedagogical excellence. Scholars such as Katharine Coman and Mary Williams developed national reputations for their rigorous research as well as their writings on classroom technique. Validation of women in both roles had also been made easier in part by Mary Sheldon Barnes, a graduate of classical study at the University of Michigan in 1874 who went on to cultivate her skills in normal school classrooms and Wellesley College before joining her husband Earl Barnes at Stanford in 1892. Her groundbreaking works *Studies in General History* (1885), *Studies in American History* (1891), and *Studies in Historical Method* (1896) helped affirm the history teacher as a pedagogical "expert" by deeming the teaching of history a "scientific" endeavor. Barnes introduced the "source method" to American classrooms and introduced critical thinking as a necessary component of elementary and secondary history curricula. She insisted that history teachers be more than just babysitters and facilitators of rote memorization, but trained analysts of primary sources and instigators of creative and elevated thought about the past.[1]

After Barnes died in 1898, her Michigan classmate Lucy Salmon built on her pedagogical research and forged ahead in new directions. The founder of the Association of History Teachers of the Middle States and Maryland (1906), she eventually developed programs for teachers at the elementary, secondary, and collegiate levels after observing pedagogical methods abroad. Interestingly, Salmon's recognition of the importance of teaching to her professional development did not come all at once; it was part of a gradual intellectual process that began after the acclaim for her political research of the 1880s had subsided and her entrenched life as a teacher of women began. Like other women, Salmon protested her additional teaching responsibilities but never questioned the importance of competent classroom instruction. Ultimately she took advantage of her extensive experience with students to shape the content of history textbooks and bring forth recommendations to the AHA for secondary and college curricula. The rewards she would come to feel as an educator suggest that this role, although at times in conflict with the role of scholar, was not always marginal even if consistently defined as feminine. Salmon's redefinition as a pedagogue-scholar eventually, though not uniformly, revealed the interrelatedness of teaching and research to the rest of the academic community, despite the gendered meanings attributed to each function.

Men continued to be better represented on most AHA committees, but female members like Salmon spoke about pedagogical issues with an air of uncontested authority through the 1910s, 1920s, and 1930s. Many conducted research for AHA subcommittees on teaching, Salmon being the first for the Committee of Seven in 1897. In 1903 she and Lilian Johnson were the only female speakers on the annual meeting program; both, not surprisingly, were scheduled to speak on the study and teaching of history in the South. By the 1910s, however, more women secondary teachers and normal school instructors joined Salmon at annual meetings, lending their expert opinions on historical education in American schools.[2] AHA women also came to exert considerable influence over educators outside the organization with the first printing of *History Teacher's Magazine* (*HTM*) (1909). The magazine was described by its editors as a "clearinghouse of ideas and ideals in the profession of history teaching," and dozens of female contributors provided curricula and suggestions for making history courses engaging and age appropriate. In "Letters to the Editor" teachers across the country found their voices as pedagogical experts in grade school and undergraduate classrooms. Mary Williams submitted regular bibliographies of suggested texts for classroom use, while Mildred Thompson and Lucy Salmon printed minutes of regional meetings of history teachers' associations, drawing women pedagogues into closer connection with their professional community. Educators across the country came to appreciate the magazine's practical classroom advice but also the legitimacy it lent to history teaching as a field of expertise. By 1911 the journal's subscription roster listed 1,100 more teachers than the total membership of the AHA itself.[3]

Women historians used their presumed predilection for teaching to their advantage, but again, gender biases posed limits to their influence in the university. Ironically the research of Mary Barnes may have helped make this the case. A faculty member at Stanford when she published *Studies in Historical Method*, she had hoped to assert her feminine authority in regard to teaching but also to affirm her scholarly status. She and her graduate students ran empirical tests to determine the schoolchild's memory and comprehension of historical time, detail, and causality. For one experiment they recounted to children between eight and fifteen years of age a short story and then asked what details interested them most. Barnes cataloged these responses and quantified them in terms of age and gender. According to her team of women the data were conclusive that boys had more "historical curiosity" overall, for they seemed to excel in making "legitimate and critical inference." Girls, they concluded, seemed more interested in the emotions of historical characters, details to which one hoped future mothers would be sensitive.[4]

Barnes insisted that scientific methods confirmed the accuracy of her gender-biased conclusions. Unfortunately she may have reinforced what male historians already believed about the nature of history and the gender of its practitioners versus its pedagogues. In the decades after her research, academics continued to perpetuate gendered assumptions that divided the realms of teaching and research—and social advocacy and historical objectivity by extension. Although historical pedagogy was becoming increasingly scientific to observers such as Barnes, the consensus was still that teachers, like social advocates, were nurturers by nature and thus decidedly feminine. As greater numbers of women were admitted into social science programs at Chicago, Yale, Stanford, Brown, Columbia, and the University of Pennsylvania, their male colleagues were quick to distinguish academic social science as a realm of masculine expertise and education and applied social science as feminine forms of philanthropic fieldwork.

More adamantly than other social scientists, historians insisted that taking strong positions on social issues jeopardized their authority as objective scholars. Peter Novick confirms that in the early twentieth century, "with the development of new, autonomous, policy-oriented social science disciplines, there was a migration out of history on the part of those of more activist inclination." Thus women historians, particularly in coeducational colleges and universities, found themselves having to choose topics of research carefully if they hoped to establish themselves as objective scholars. *AHR* dissertation lists in the 1910s reveal that more women than men initially investigated areas of reform and activism as graduate students, with topics such as "organized rebellion," "antislavery movements," "religious persecution," and "Indian policy" topping the lists. Yet, interestingly, the majority of women who went on to pursue professional history careers did not continue to write on such controversial topics or discontinued the practice as university historians. In the end they found it prudent to investigate great men, democratic institutions, and political systems to ground their claims as objective observers. Women in coeducational institutions not only avoided activism as a subject of scholarly inquiry but also relegated their extracurricular reform activities to outside the university or curtailed them completely.[5]

Helen Sumner Woodbury, Grace Hebard, and Maria Sanford were exceptions as scholars at western state universities who participated in labor and community reform in the early twentieth century. They resembled to a greater degree their colleagues at women's colleges in the Northeast, where a tradition of social reform had lingered since these institutions were founded in the late nineteenth century. Initially it was the pull of social responsibility that brought the first generations of students to women's colleges. Administrators had long encouraged quasi-public projects in labor, sanitation, school and prison reform, and settlement work in the name of "social housekeeping" and maternal duty. Second- and third-generation students and faculty continued in this vein and participated more openly in reform activities in the twentieth century, despite the position of social neutrality taken by the historical establishment. Sheltered from the gender biases of coeducational environments, historians at women's colleges were largely unaffected by denouncements of their feminine reform agenda. Most took the stance of Helen Thompson Woolley, a social scientist who argued that so long as science was increasingly employed to direct social reform, it made sense that reform set the agenda for social science. In her mind the divide in the university between scholarly resolve and social conscience was arbitrary, more a consequence of disciplinary politics than of any inherent truth.[6]

Armed with a similar philosophy, students and faculty at women's colleges often gravitated toward woman's rights work and hands-on service projects with immigrants and the urban poor, only finding after the turn of the century that they risked marginalization in social science disciplines defined as theoretical, politically neutral, and socially objective.[7] As a graduate student at Vassar, Caroline Ware recalled that this marriage of scholarly pursuits and social service seemed natural to her women professors; knowledge of the past, she was taught, became the "prelude to responsible social action." Thus Mary Williams, Lucy Salmon, Viola Barnes, and Louise Fargo Brown, for example, used their influence in the field of academic history to better conditions for their female colleagues, while Katharine Coman and Ella Lonn revealed commitments to women immigrant laborers through their historical research and extracurricular activities with settlements and workers' collectives.[8] Emily Hickman and Dorothy Stimson, also educators of college women, were advocates for women's political rights, eventually serving with Viola Barnes as historical consultants for the Women's Centennial Congress in 1940. While Mary Williams and Lucy Salmon were involved in more radical feminist and suffrage organizations, other historians, such as Louise Phelps Kellogg, acted as advisers to conservative groups like the Woman's Christian Temperance Union and the General Federation of Women's Clubs. Goucher's Katharine Gallagher was not particularly outspoken on politics or feminism, but she gave lectures to women's groups about historical figures like Anne Hutchinson ("The First Feminist") and Susan B. Anthony ("The Dauntless Warrior"), subjects she rarely broached in regular university courses. Meanwhile, colleague Ella Lonn lectured before the Maryland Women's Business and Professional Club, the Daughters of the Confederacy, and the Woman's International League for Peace and Freedom (WILPF).[9]

For the Goucher faculty, women became engrossing topics of history, and history became an effective instrument for furthering women's causes. Remarkably, their participation in feminist groups outside the college seemed to create little conflict with their production of history within it, which continued to be male centered. Mary Williams still advocated for the staunchest scientific history and chose research topics that resembled those of male scholars, including Anglo-American isthmian diplomacy, Latin American politics, and male figureheads such as Dom Pedro the Magnanimous. She taught the typical courses, American Territorial Expansion and Constitutional Government, and served with male colleagues on the editorial board of the *Hispanic-American Historical Review* and AHA committees. Yet at the same time she remained an active member of the National Woman's Party (NWP), the AAUW, and the WILPF. She agitated for protective labor legislation for women and for the promotion of women scholars, but no feminist rhetoric ever made its way into her historical publications.

Similarly Louise Fargo Brown and Louise Phelps Kellogg won prestigious AHA awards for their monographs on great men in politics, while they remained active in the AAUW and lobbied to elect more female colleagues to AHA executive committees.[10]

In hindsight, this decision to write about historical men while fighting for professional women might have been strategic, if not always deliberate. By emulating the practices of male scholars, women set out to prove that they could embody the traits of the objective professional even as they continued to be feminine educators and social reformers. The range of activities in which they participated indicates that the scientific ideal of objectivity hindered them professionally but did not quash their social convictions or dissuade them from organizing collectively as women. The balance they struck between scholarly and activist personas could at times appear contradictory, but it speaks to their determination to be both good scholars and effective advocates and their crafty negotiation of both roles.

Fortunately, striking this balance became easier as prominent men joined them in stretching the definitions of scientific history to include "social" content—and advocacy. Already traces of discontent with the narrow parameters of the field persisted in muted forms, as various camps of historians perceived political, constitutional, and military subjects as insufficient for understanding important aspects of the nation's past. In his 1910 AHA presidential address, Frederick Jackson Turner urged his professional colleagues to consider the "*social* forces in American history," and others quickly followed with like-minded pleas. Harry Elmer Barnes of Smith College proposed that historians consider "man's multiform activities as a member of changing and developing social groups and cultural complexes," and Harvard's Arthur Schlesinger advocated a similar turn to social and cultural perspectives in his monumental work *New Viewpoints in American History*.[11]

Scholars have since classified these male historians loosely as "New Historians," although one would be hard pressed to determine a consistent logic or ideology common to all represented by the term. As Ernst Breisach has clarified, "The calls for a New History became calls for a historiography variously characterized as cultural, social, encompassing, total, integrated, or synthetic." Regardless of the subtle differences among them, all New Historians redirected their efforts away from the political topics of men who consolidated the field back in the 1880s, and several even questioned the very function of the research they produced in the academy. Peter Novick explains that the tension between advocacy and objectivity was thought to exist "among political scientists, sociologists, and economists—not historians," but this reverence for neutrality was not uncontested in the historical establishment for long. For within the wide-ranging group of New Historians emerged the most identifiable and programmatic faction of them all: the "Progressive historians."[12]

Under the same scientific rubric as their conservative colleagues, Columbia men Charles Beard, Carl Becker, and James Harvey Robinson promoted this Progressive history, which as the term suggests, reflected a belief in social progress and perfectibility in the modern age. Whereas other scientific historians perceived conflict between social activism and the writing of objective history, Progressive historians waved their reformist banners unapologetically, insisting that history could and should be written to promote social betterment in the present day. Beard, the most reform-minded, demonstrated that scientific method could be employed toward ends other than patriotic hero-worship; his groundbreaking *Economic Interpretation of the Constitution of the United States* (1913) deflated the Founding Fathers by revealing their underlying economic motives for political power. Beard and the Progressive historians maintained that a hidden truth existed behind the jingoistic bravado of former national accounts. As the ultimate scientific scholars, they unmasked the power dynamics that drove American society in the past and propelled it to its state of social inequality in modern times.[13]

Progressive historians began their investigations with the negative assumption that modernity had created strained social relationships in U.S. society. But their research was also driven by the positive assumption that "progress" was a natural course of events, provided the historian expose and reform points of conflict. The different agenda Progressive historians brought to their research caused them to look under new rocks to discover historical truth. James Harvey Robinson insisted that at this moment of increased industrialization and social conflict, historical emphasis on monarchs, aristocrats, and elite political men seemed inappropriate. He urged instead that the historian bring the masses to the forefront as subjects and agents of historical narratives and that economic motivations and social relationships of American groups be taken into account when diagnosing the ills of the present industrial order. With a critical eye on relationships of power in the past, Progressive historians necessarily studied the plight of immigrants, westerners, Native Americans, religious minorities, the working class, African Americans, and even women—albeit to a limited extent. These groups seemed finally to occupy an important place on the contested historical terrain.[14]

The Progressive historians' rationalization for presentist, reform-minded research validated women historians who had long engaged in the work of social reform. Many had already been revising, reinterpreting, and

reappropriating the tenets of scientific history to create their own render-
ings of the past, and now in the Progressive milieu new cohorts of professional scholars were claiming that such historical perspectives could be
scientific, given the methods used to achieve them. Having combined scientific research and reform activities since her arrival at Wellesley in 1880,
Katharine Coman had been the consummate Progressive historian well
before men like Beard, Becker, or Robinson gave the term any import. At the
same time she wrote history, she worked tirelessly for Denison Settlement,
workers' collectives, and seamstress clubs established to create better wages
and sanitary conditions for women workers. Also a devoted pedagogue, she
created programs in which she lectured in the classroom on the plight of
American laborers, while she developed fieldwork assignments in Boston
settlements. Coman's mixing of intellectual and applied activities was quintessentially Progressive in its desired outcome but only gained acceptance
outside the women's college once her male colleagues declared the Progressive age of history writing nearly twenty years later.[15]

Indeed the Progressive agenda, with its activist bent and social and
economic focus, resonated with women whose work had long transgressed
the boundaries of history and other social science departments in the ivory
tower. Coman, for one, discovered that her interest in a range of social
subjects called for a redefinition and broadening of her academic identity.
In the end she fashioned herself both a historian and an economist, who
moved between academic departments to write the labor history of exploited American peoples. Susan Kingsbury was another Boston-based
historian who discovered that interdisciplinarity best matched her social
reform agenda. Formally trained in American Revolutionary history, she
taught economics at Simmons College and social economy at Bryn Mawr,
all the while serving as research director of the Women's Educational and
Industrial Union of Boston. University of Chicago professor Edith Abbott,
like Coman and Kingsbury, was a social scientist whose scholarly and
reform agendas made her work difficult to classify in disciplinary terms.
She traveled from one social science department to another, writing labor,
economic, women's, and immigrant studies that straddled the increasingly
ambiguous divide between history, sociology, economics, and political
economy. Eventually her belief in the natural connections between the
social and the economic, academic and applied, found expression and
institutional support in Chicago's School of Civics and Philanthropy,
which she developed with other women social scientists of the university.[16]

The integration of thought and action that became the hallmark of the
social service curriculum at Chicago was not something that Abbott had
immediately embraced. In fact, when she originally arrived as a graduate

student in Chicago, her intention was to prepare strictly for a career of scholarship, not social reform. Early in her studies she avoided the reformers at Chicago outright; while Jane Addams offered Philanthropy and Social Work in the extension school, Abbott took a formal course load in economics, political science, and law instead, fulfilling her requirements for a doctoral degree in economics only three years after enrolling in the graduate program.

Nevertheless, the group of women who made up Chicago's social reform community had a conspicuous presence in Abbott's life and ultimately changed the way she viewed her work as a social scientist. Her younger sister Grace had traveled with her to the city from their home in rural Nebraska and immersed herself in settlement work just as Abbott began her courses at the university. Grace became a reformer of national repute and had a powerful influence on her sister, as did Sophonisba "Nisba" Breckinridge, then a young assistant professor in the Department of Household Administration. Breckinridge had earned the distinction of being the university's first doctorate degree holder in both the economics and political science department and the jurisprudence department, yet as a woman she was unable to enter these male precincts as a full-fledged faculty member. As Abbott's graduate mentor she became a powerful role model and, in time, a close friend and professional collaborator. She inspired Abbott to substantiate a claim she boldly made to a roomful of graduate students in 1903: that women had done the "work of the world while men were doing the fighting and hunting." Abbott finally investigated her claims in 1905, when she secured a secretaryship with the Boston Women's Trade Union League (WTUL). This was her first experience conducting academic research in a reform community, Katharine Coman's Denison Settlement, but it would not be her last. She worked on studies in women's labor for the *Journal of Political Economy* and the Carnegie Institute, and with a fellowship from the ACA she left the United States to take courses with renowned social scientists Beatrice and Sydney Webb at the London School of Economics.[17]

The Webbs taught from the premise that social science should be applied toward the human condition and that all the social science disciplines provided valuable methods for investigation. Abbott sharpened her skills of observation, data collection, hypothesis formulation, experimentation, and verification under their tutelage, but she also learned to attach these methods to a social philosophy optimistic about the ability of science to shape the social environment. The Webbs and the Fabian Socialists with whom she worked at St. Hilda's Settlement in London only reinforced Abbott's growing faith in social science as an instrument of reform. When she returned to the United States in 1908, a position was waiting for her at Wellesley, but to Coman's disappointment Abbott chose to put her new social philosophy into practice as director of social research in Chicago's School of Civics and Philanthropy.[18]

Now a full-time resident of Jane Addams's Hull House, Abbott could plainly see the necessity for her social science methods outside the university. The day she moved in, she recalled her West Side neighborhood as "part of a vast city wilderness." "The streets were atrocious—badly paved or not paved, rarely cleaned or never cleaned. . . . The tenements, many of them wooden shacks that had been built on the prairie before the 'Great Fire,' were beyond description; and there were sweatshops and 'home finishing' on every side of us as we came and went." Witnessing the city from this insider perspective and with new ideological direction, Abbott was no longer detached from the social and physical ills of the city; she viewed herself as one who shared in its problems but also as a scientist with the moral responsibility to be part of its solutions.[19]

Active in the worlds of both academic and applied social science, Abbott finally completed her investigation of Breckinridge's claim about women in labor. Her *Women in Industry: A Study in American Economic History* (1910) did not prove conclusively that men had only hunted and fought through the course of history, but much more important to current labor debates it revealed women's long and varied history of physical labor and how it led to their exploitation in the modern industrial order. Abbott conceded that "it might well seem academic and impractical to deal only with [the woman laborer's] past," but she also insisted that this history would "throw some light on present-day problems," specifically the contested issues of minimum wages, maximum hours, and protective legislation. At the same time she also anticipated the skepticism of academic social scientists, insisting that her reform goals in no way diminished the credibility of her historical data. She supplemented her text with an impressive appendix of statistical tables on women's wages and employment that took her students years to collect and tabulate.[20] Abbott was ever cognizant of the fact that she defied the precedent set by male economic historians, who considered the sphere of public, productive labor to be exclusively male throughout the American past. She proved differently, tracing the fluid divisions of labor among early agriculturists through sweated trades and woman-dominated industries to the present. In the introduction to *Women in Industry*, Breckinridge acknowledged her colleague's unprecedented perspective on women and labor in the academic world. Indeed, Abbott's reinterpretation of the woman's relationship to the family wage and her changing fate in a producerist-turned-consumerist economy lent insight into her present economic and social struggles in ways university scholars and settlement workers had never before achieved.[21]

Abbott argued that scientific empiricism could be a woman's instrument for social change and academic research her method of choice for reform. Mary Roberts Smith's *Chinese Immigration* (1909) and Mary Beard's *Women's Work in Municipalities* (1915), written just before and after Abbott's *Women in Industry*, respectively, were the sort of scientifically researched, reform-minded histories women felt increasingly compelled to write in the Progressive years—labors of scholarship but also outpourings of moral and social responsibility.[22] By the 1910s a handful of academic historians were able to write about women and immigrants with the additional support of other social science departments, but others were forced to turn outside the university altogether. A strong tradition of women's social science and reform already thrived in urban settlements and gathered momentum in newly established government agencies. Publications produced for the U.S. Labor Department's Children's Bureau, the National Consumer's League, and the U.S. Woman's Bureau were activist works similar in empirical content and tone to academic studies such as *Women in Industry*. Katharine Coman ("The Negro as Peasant Farmer" [1903]), Helen Sumner Woodbury ("History of Women in Industry in the United States" [1910]), and Mary Beard (*A Short History of the American Labor Movement* [1920]) were just a few research historians who wrote for government agencies in the Progressive Era.[23]

Outside the academy these women felt less pressure to assume a pretense of social neutrality, as the very purpose of their studies was to make historically informed judgments for proceeding with municipal and social policy. University of Wisconsin economic historian Helen Sumner Woodbury found that she struck the right balance for her in turning to government work. Through the course of her university career she had collaborated on textbooks and specialized studies with such notable scholars as Richard Ely and John Commons, and by all accounts she had achieved enviable success compared with her female peers. Yet as she eventually explained to Commons, her research for the Children's Bureau (1913–18) allowed her to leave the relative "drudgery and obscurity" she experienced in the shadows of her prominent academic mentors to establish herself as a scholar with deeper social purpose.[24]

The academic establishment on the whole continued to view women as philanthropic fieldworkers rather than skilled social scientists, but male directors of independent research institutions received university women with greater enthusiasm. It was Frances Gardiner, for example, director of the Department for Historical Research at the Carnegie Institute, who encouraged Edith Abbott to continue her research of women's labor in 1906, paying her $100 a month to compile more data for *Women in Industry*.[25] J. Franklin Jameson, Gardiner's successor, did little to promote women faculty as a professor at Brown or at the University of Chicago, but at the Carnegie Institute he hired academic historians Louise Fargo Brown, Helen Catterall, and Elizabeth Donnan, who served him well as historical researchers. Donnan compiled four volumes of *Documents Illustrative of the History of the Slave Trade to America* (1926–35), and in 1929 Catterall completed the important work *Judicial Cases Concerning American Slavery and the Negro*.[26] Jameson not only sponsored publications in race history, but he employed Ruth Anna Fisher, an African American woman, as the institute's resident agent in England. Fisher was a graduate of Oberlin College and the London School of Economics and formerly taught at the Tuskegee Institute. She became an expert on European archival materials and a respected representative of the Carnegie Institute. When Jameson stepped down from his directorship to become the chief of the Division of Manuscripts at the Library of Congress, Fisher followed him there and stayed in the division for the next thirty years.[27]

While nonacademic institutions benefited from the exodus of women such as Fisher from university departments, women in return obtained the freedom to investigate areas of the past long ignored by the academic establishment, including the untapped field of Native American history. University presses accepted monographs on slavery and urban poverty with increasing frequency, but the historical abuses of Indians continued to receive only marginal attention at regional presses. Fortunately government agencies compensated for the lack of academic support by providing women with access to archival evidence and funds to publish their findings on Native American topics. Frances Victor proved as early as the 1890s that one need not have academic credentials to seek government sponsorship for these projects. Frustrated by the rejection of university presses and her menial compensation at the Bancroft Library, she finally turned to the Oregon state legislature, which hired her to write *The Early Indian Wars of Oregon* (1894).[28]

Nearly twenty years after Victor, Annie Abel also turned to government agencies for sponsorship of Native American research. Her doctoral thesis at Yale was a Winsor Award–winning study on Indian consolidation west of the Mississippi, yet as a professional historian she failed to generate funding for more research in the field. Spending weekends in 1910 in the records room of the Indian office in Washington, she finally uncovered shocking evidence of the U.S. government's abusive Indian policy in California, but no university press would publish her findings. Her fortunes changed in 1912 when the U.S. Bureau of Indian Affairs hired her as its official historian and granted her the resources to compile the letters of Indian agent James S. Calhoun and complete her long-awaited research on Indians in the Civil War, *The Slaveholding Indians* (1915–25).[29]

The U.S. Bureau of Indian Affairs created opportunities for Abel that never would have materialized through the academic community, and they ultimately established her among scholars and popular audiences alike as an authority on Native Americans. Twenty years later an Oklahoma native named Angie Debo followed a professional path similar to Abel's as a historian of Americans Indians. Like Abel she grew up on the western plains and earned her academic credentials in fits and starts. Formal schooling was not offered past the ninth grade in her rural community, and Debo was forced to teach school in neighboring counties to contribute to her family's necessities. Nevertheless she gradually saved for college and in 1915 completed her bachelor's degree at the University of Oklahoma. After more financial setbacks she eventually paid her way through graduate school at the University of Chicago. There she was seduced by the reform impulse that had drawn Abbott fifteen years earlier and would shape her history for decades to come.

When Debo embarked on graduate coursework in history, both Abbott and Breckinridge were writing prolifically in other departments on immigrant life and conveying to students their newfound understanding of racial, ethnic, and cultural differences in the city itself. Their Progressive mission left a lasting impression on the soon-to-be historian of the Native American West. Debo left Chicago, as one biographer phrased it, "never waver[ing] in her belief that historical understanding could lead to more intelligent policy making in the present and future." Along with Chicago's women reformers, Latin American historian James Fred Rippy left a lasting impression on Debo in her graduate years. Inspired by his teachings on U.S. imperialism abroad, she eventually sought to investigate what she called the "real imperialism" on American soil—on Indian reservations and tribal homelands. Debo went on to teach at West Texas State Teachers College before going back to the University of Oklahoma to earn her Ph.D. in the early 1930s. Her mentor there was Edward Everett Dale, a former student of frontier scholar Frederick Jackson Turner. Little did Dale anticipate the havoc his student would wreak among his colleagues, most of whom still paid reverence to Turner's heroic view of white conquest in the American West.[30]

After she graduated, Debo was frustrated by her inability to secure a permanent academic position, and she settled instead for curatorial work at the Panhandle-Plains Historical Museum before publishing her dissertation, *The Rise and Fall of the Choctaw Republic* (1934), with the University of Oklahoma Press. Like Abel's graduate research, Debo's earned her a prestigious history award, the AHA's John H. Dunning Prize, in 1934. Still, academic work or solicitations from academic presses would never come easily. She used the $200 she received with the Dunning Prize to pay off her life insurance premium and spent the next five years in virtual poverty as she sought a publisher for *And Still the Waters Run*, a historical exposé of the U.S. government's exploitation of the Five Civilized Tribes. She eventually saw the manuscript published in 1940, but by this time she had taken out a loan against her life insurance policy and turned in desperation to the Works Projects Administration (WPA) for employment. The day after Macmillan rejected her manuscript on the Creek Indians (later published as *The Road to Disappearance* [1941]), she secured a job as director of the Federal Writers' Project in Oklahoma. Debo admitted that work on the WPA state guides series could be frustrating; her staff of untrained writers and editors often negated the Native American struggle or any blame on the part of white land speculators for having caused it. For the time being, however, the job paid the bills and put her in a better position to fashion a career as an independent scholar of Native American history.[31]

Debo—and Abel and Abbott before her—took advantage of new opportunities open to women researchers outside the academy in the early twentieth century. In so doing they moved the Progressive agenda forward, writing history that complemented social activism for women, immigrants, Native Americans, and the industrial working class. Without question their research influenced the content of national narratives, but they stopped short of shifting the consensus view of the past in the collective American mind. For while women researchers recounted their versions of the past in universities and government agencies, middle-class domestic women in the DAR and the SCD were continuing to leave a different imprint on national memory. Unlike Progressive scholars, these patriotic women found mounting strength in their numbers; by 1933 there were nearly 12,000 Dames and 160,000 Daughters nationwide.[32] The DAR, the SCD, and analogous groups were not motivated to perform the work of history for liberal reform, nor did they assume that industrial modernity could accommodate social progress. Whereas Progressives scrutinized the past to expose the deeply rooted origins of America's ethnic, cultural, and socioeconomic divisions, rank-and-file preservationist groups generally viewed celebratory accounts of the national past less critically, nostalgic for an idealized vision of America before the modern age. As Protestant wives, mothers, and educators, the Daughters and Dames instilled patriotism in the next generation of Americans by remembering their forefathers but forgetting nearly everyone else.

Indeed, many of these women's familial legacies were intimately tied to the buildings and districts they preserved for posterity. By organizational decree the SCD insisted that its membership "be composed entirely of women who are descended in their own right from some ancestor of worthy life who came to reside in an American colony prior to 1750" and played a role "in the founding of a commonwealth, or of an institution which has survived and developed into importance." The somewhat less exclusive Daughters needed only to prove that they "descended from a man or a woman who with unfailing loyalty to the cause of American independence, served as a sailor, a soldier or civil officer in one of the several Colonies or States, . . . or as a recognized patriot, or rendered material aid thereto." Once authenticated, the bloodlines of patriot women gave them special access to the colonial past and the moral authority to foster American values through the relics they preserved from a more idyllic time.[33]

For these Daughters and Dames the present moment of increased immigration, rural populism, and rampant unionism was certainly less than ideal. Michael Kammen describes the "Colonial Revival" seen in the work of the DAR and the SCD as a yearning for psychological anchors amidst cultural and spiritual crisis. Women had been preservationists, educators, antique collectors, genealogists, popular writers, and historians throughout the nineteenth century, but now this work took on a heightened sense of social urgency. Historical biographers such as Sarah Bolton, Alice Earle, and Anne Wharton—women with genealogical ties to colonial New England—helped relieve the cultural tensions of modernity with popular versions of simple, ordered life and strong community and family values in the colonial past.[34] In the process, they also established a well-defined group of authentic Americans, unified by the bonds of "interest," "taste and habit," and "blood," that did not include Indians, slaves, or non-Protestants.[35] Aside from the few "red bloods" who appeared only sporadically in her narratives as "uncivilized" and troublesome house servants, Earle's whitewashed memory rendered colonies that were ethnically, racially, and religiously homogeneous. Her cultural authority derived from hereditary connection to exceptional early Americans, but she also referred to colonial women fondly as "our great-grandmothers," suggesting that she assumed her readership to be of similar Anglo-Saxon stock.[36]

Earle's filiopietism functioned like that of all women patriots who uncomfortably straddled the Victorian and modern eras; it reflected a desire to retain former influence as a guardian of civic virtue but also a new bid for social power amidst the encroachments of modernity. According to James Lindgren, the personalism women cultivated as custodians of local and family history served as an effective counterweight to the impersonal (and masculine) market economy of the twentieth century. The nostalgia of the Daughters and Dames was not theirs alone but indicative of a larger "anti-modernism" taking root in sectors of white, Protestant America.[37] Antimodernism was not a monolithic ideology but, rather, a multifaceted response to what had gone wrong in capitalist culture. T. J. Jackson Lears has described it as a bourgeois reaction to "over-civilization" in consumerist urban centers. Converts to aesthetic and intellectual movements in Arts and Crafts, Orientalism, and medieval folklore, for example, hoped to set American society aright by reviving its preindustrial, producerist ethic. In other circles, including most white women's preservationist groups, antimodernism took on a distinctively nativist undertone, as it became less a critique of capitalist materialism than an assessment of the deterioration of community under the capitalist system. They believed that recent surges in immigration led to further social atomization and the destruction of values once shared among a homogeneous citizenry. Thus they reminisced of a simpler time—but specifically one devoid of nonwhites, non-Protestants, and the social tensions they were thought to have brought to modern American life.[38]

Given these beliefs, the historical projects of the DAR and the SCD were necessarily expansive but excluded many women. The Daughters decided in 1894, for example, that black applicants, even when technically eligible, were not "personally acceptable" for admittance into the organization. Both the Daughters and the Dames took intolerant stances on immigration and pacifist activity and championed the Anglo-Saxonist ideas of eugenicists, social Darwinists, and antiradical groups. The Daughters attributed the dissemination of leftist writings to foreign groups that infiltrated national borders for the purpose of spreading "anti-American" propaganda. In their thinking, the preservation of U.S. history—and colonial history in particular—went hand in hand with lobbying for the mandatory draft or war nursing on the front lines: all became matters of national defense.[39]

After World War I, scholars and women patriots alike reacted to international tensions by transforming history lessons in elementary and secondary schools into a form of civic indoctrination. In state after state, officials questioned public school history teachers—most of whom were women—about whether they had ever been active in the promotion of German, Communist, or "anti-American" propaganda; "disloyal in word, deed, or manner to nation or state"; or "passive or indifferent with reference to patriotism." Authors of history textbooks omitted references to the

Chinese, Japanese, Italian, and Jewish immigrants to America, and in several states Quaker and pacifist educators were simply dismissed from teaching positions altogether. Women suffered the brunt of this paranoid censorship, yet ironically mothers and wives in preservationist and patriotic societies were some of the strongest advocates of racial and ethnic nationalism.[40]

Patriotic women had long employed history as a means of civic education for their own children, but now it was also an instrument of "Americanization" for the nation's growing foreign contingent. Not surprisingly, much of this history perpetuated the Anglocentric hero-worship Progressives such as Abbott, Coman, and Mary Beard hoped to eliminate. In 1921, for example, the national DAR published *The Beginnings of America*, a reader written at the level of an American-born first grader. It recounted to newly arrived immigrants the origins of the nation, rooting authentic Americanness in the cultural inheritances of the English colonists.[41] The Dames also published history primers for immigrant children and offered scholarships to student writers of patriotic historical essays. In the 1920s the Dames' national committee on patriotic service sponsored the showing of the motion picture *The Making of an American* in schools and social settlements. State chapters such as the Illinois SCD were particularly active in immigrant neighborhoods. Despite Jane Addams's often conflicting prescriptions for education, the Dames taught U.S. history courses in Chicago settlements and worked with the Newberry Library and the Immigration Protection League to distribute civic primers to children and parents. The historian of the Connecticut SCD summed up what she hoped to achieve through this educational work in immigrant districts: "Americanization is the whole aim. . . . We hope to see our future founded upon the best of the past."[42]

Her intentions reveal the conflicting agendas for which white women employed history in the early twentieth century. Whereas Progressives identified the origins of difference between women, immigrants, and the working class ultimately to accommodate cultural diversity in the modern age, the Daughters and Dames hoped to eliminate the appearance of difference to promote a monolithic American culture and ease immigrant acculturation. In this sense the latter were not so different from most university scholars, for only after 1920 did a select few investigate the lessons of patriotic groups in the name of cultural tolerance. Again, several women found themselves in the center of these developments. In 1926 University of Chicago historian Bessie Pierce addressed cultural and ethnic diversity in history texts most directly in her comprehensive study *Public Opinion and the Teaching of History in the United States*. Claiming to assess the "propagandist influences on textbook-making exerted by religious, patriotic, racial, and other organized groups," Pierce identified in particular the historical agendas of southerners, Irish, Catholics, and race purists, who, along with the Daughters and Dames, censored "un-American" topics in texts and classrooms. She brought into high relief the scientific assumption that history was unfettered by current political preoccupations and cultural attitudes. Choices of omission in American texts were deliberate, but by exposing the motivations behind the selective narration of the past, she hoped to promote a culturally diverse national narrative for the future.[43]

Pierce's research finally drew attention to issues other academic women historians had been addressing in lectures, studies, and articles of smaller scale. Unfortunately her work did little to change the view of patriotic groups about how national history should function in the years ahead. Robert Dorman contends that by the end of the 1920s the Daughters, Dames, and other white Americans—nativists, Klansmen, drys, fundamentalists, and "Middletowners" among them—still clung nostalgically to a history that excluded nonwhites, non-Protestants, immigrants, the poor, and other "inauthentic" Americans. Even worse, they resorted to "intrusive legislation, coercive vigilance, and even violence" to keep their mythical history intact. Indeed, women such as Alice Earle had been part of this group self-defined as "one-hundred percent American," and membership had privileges that her descendants were not ready to relinquish. She never achieved high status in academic circles, but no scientific scholar could strip her of the historical authority her family tree provided. Perhaps Bessie Pierce, a scholar who never benefited from lineage or academic promotion, had less to lose by revealing patriotic history for what it was: the story of the victors in American society.[44]

Eventually even Lucy Salmon, author of the definitive history of the appointing power of the president, saw little to gain by keeping focused on the Founding Fathers and the powerful men who followed. Her conversion to new methods and perspectives reflected the Progressive impulse already embodied in Coman and Abbott, but it was also something more. Salmon, the quintessential chronicler of political history, was not immune to the gender biases that compromised the status of all women in the university. Although she established a scholarly reputation within the male bastions of the university and the AHA, her inherent secondary status led her to question and even expand the fundamental tenets of scientific history in ways no one else could claim. Through her perspective as a woman, she was able to pave a unique path toward cultural tolerance and relativism, eventually making her way into the uncharted realm of historical modernism.

The Transformation of Lucy Salmon

Whereas Katharine Coman had already begun her career in the 1880s with a proto-Progressive research agenda, her contemporary Lucy Salmon developed into a Progressive reformer, an interdisciplinary scholar, and a feminist activist more gradually—but with no less impact in the historical field. Her career-launching "History of the Appointing Power of the President" was the staunchest sort of male-centered, civic-minded scholarship, but she stopped short of proclaiming patriotism the primary function of American history. In fact, by the time she wrote her report for the AHA Committee of Seven in 1899, she had already concluded that those who taught history for this purpose "glorif[ied] the past at the possible expense of truth," yet she conceded that this was nearly impossible to combat. Later in her corrective work *What Is Modern History* (1917), she would attribute the nativist paranoia of patriotic groups to the prevailing ignorance of ethnic history in American schools. The history of the United States and of humankind itself, she argued, was a story of racial and ethnic admixture. "How can we deal with the melting pot in America unless we know that the races have always mingled and intermingled?" she asked fellow historians. Despite her colleagues' increasing interest in eugenicist theories, she refused to heed their warnings of a looming "racial abyss." "I have always felt," she countered, "that our great strength as a nation has come from the mingling of the many races."[45]

Salmon's call for a diverse national narrative indicates a drastic transformation in her ideas about the function of national history and the role of the professional historian since her early years in the field. She criticized not only her colleagues in university history departments but also elementary and secondary schoolteachers, who she felt were more commanding influences on young American minds. Ironically, in the 1880s she had rejected a career of high school teaching in search of more prestige as a university scholar. By the 1890s, however, she had become one of the greatest champions of historical educators and had taken more interest than her male university colleagues in nonacademic publics. She seemed, in fact, to move back and forth between audiences with relative ease, taking advantage of the reputation her political histories had earned her among university men yet also the authority she had achieved in secondary classrooms through her writings as a woman pedagogue.

Bessie Pierce undoubtedly relied on this same dual authority as an academic scholar with access to the classroom when she set out to write *Public Opinion and the Teaching of History* in 1926. As the Progressive agenda found greater acceptance (or at least tolerance) in the academy, the traditionally feminine role of the pedagogue grew in influence, if not in stature. The woman history teacher could unabashedly employ her lessons in the classroom to raise social consciousness and even stimulate political action, and Salmon was partially responsible for this becoming the case. In time she believed it was a scholar's responsibility to work with academic and nonacademic groups to promote historical learning of social value and called for a closer connection between primary, secondary, and tertiary institutions and the communities they serviced. Although she started her career at Vassar living in the women's dorm, Salmon eventually moved off campus to a small house in Poughkeepsie to become a "member of the community"—a responsibility she lamented too few academicians cared to fulfill. Her next objective was to instill a regard for the larger community in Vassar history students. "What can you do in your home community to promote public interest in favor of civil service reform / an independent judiciary / personal responsibility for the conduct of public affairs?" she asked on a course exam in 1913. For the remainder of her teaching career such questions were commonplace; like so many of her colleagues at women's colleges, she came to view no inherent tension between historical learning and community action and would insist that the professional historian had an obligation to find these broader applications for her scholarly work.[46]

Some of Salmon's male colleagues, including Vassar president James Monroe Taylor, believed that her choice to write so prolifically on historical pedagogy sank her further into the feminine role of the nonscholar. Of course Salmon would not see things this way; her interest in teaching technique did not come from a feminine need to nurture but an intellectual yearning to see and use the past in new ways. Just as she broadened her methods as an educator, she expanded the scope of her research to include subjects beyond party politics and politicians, a development that likely stemmed from her daily interactions with college women. She had grown to resent having to recount the history of public men as a way to inspire civic virtue in female students, especially when they were not expected to become anything other than domestic women after graduation. At Vassar she introduced courses like those that mentor Charles Kendall Adams offered at Michigan, but she strayed from his focus on political men and official documents and even discarded his preference for the formal "seminar room" to conduct class in the comfortable setting of the parlor of the women's dorm. Her relocation of historical learning outside the "history laboratory" was like her relocation of historical research outside the official repository. Both adjustments became necessary to make history relevant for women, but also to make women relevant to history.[47]

In these seminars Salmon drew women into active participation with the national past by interpreting female realms of activity—outside the formal political sphere—as important facets of American history. There was little by way of scholarly material for Salmon to assign on women in the 1890s, so she created classroom materials and exercises. By the 1910s Edith Abbott and Katharine Coman had published studies on the history of women's work, and Helen Campbell and Helen Sumner Woodbury had given serious scholarly attention to the racial and ethnically feminized work of domestic service.[48] Nevertheless, with less fanfare Salmon had set this research agenda long before, publishing *Domestic Service* (1897) as historical scholarship but also pedagogical experiment. Vassar students, never more than passive readers of history texts in other classes, became Salmon's fieldworkers for this project, sending out questionnaires to white women to find out the ages, skills, and compensation of their hired help. Their results revealed that attitudes toward domestics had a history just like any political party or movement, and one need not be a professional historian to chart them. Unfortunately, male colleagues criticized *Domestic Service* as ahistorical and unscholarly compared with Salmon's previous research in political history. One reviewer for *Nation* believed that the attention she gave to such a degraded topic as domestic servants was simply "unworthy of her talents." Anticipating similar reactions to the second of her domestic studies, *Progress in the Household* (1906), she supplied a preemptive rejoinder: "To the economists . . . it doubtless seemed unreasonable that one who had apparently always been connected with work of history should meddle with economics; to the historians, it probably seemed apostasy to wander, even for a moment, from the path of history, *Ergo mea apologia*."[49]

Salmon's defense did not signal the end of her wayward turn. She continued to profess expanded coverage and interdisciplinary approaches to women in the past until her death in 1927. Many factors contributed to Salmon's change of heart in regard to historical methods and subject matter, not the least of which was her increasingly antagonistic relationship with male administrators and colleagues. Yet it was perhaps a sabbatical to Europe in 1899 that became the catalyst for her complete intellectual redirection. Taken amidst mounting controversy and depression over departmental politics, Salmon's two-year tour of the continent was not a search for official documents but a personal soul-searching and epiphany about viewing material culture as a window to the past. As she explored the excavations of Corfu as a mere tourist, she realized that there was a rich history to place and culture that could not be extracted through written documents alone. Indeed the very architecture and layout of city streets could reveal a textured past if the historian remained open to the possibility. She confided in a letter to Adelaide Underhill that as she proceeded through Europe, she realized her work had "been absolutely lacking on the side of the relation of monumental and literary historical evidence" but that this was going to change.[50]

When she returned to Vassar in 1901, she was newly inspired to explore the physical substance of daily life—not only to enhance history already written, but to bring women into active participation with history as its worthy interpreters and agents. In "Some Principles in the Teaching of History" (1902) she implored educators to equip themselves with an interdisciplinary frame of mind as well as an expanded set of source materials beyond the written document, including the "physical, linguistic, social, and monumental." The following year she insisted in front of an audience of New Orleans teachers that history could not only be found in "domestic and civic architecture" or in "the names of towns," but within the very pages of a history textbook provided the observer ask the right questions: "why the book is divided into chapters, why the page has a margin . . . why the book has illustrations." Clues to the cultural past came in an infinite array of sizes and forms and were accessible to anyone—scholar or layperson, man or woman—who had an inclination to find them.[51]

Here Salmon's interests in pedagogy and interdisciplinarity fused to promote women implicitly as historical subjects, agents, and experts. She called for an expanding repertoire of historical theaters, source materials, and perspectives in the classroom, drawing women's past experience out from obscurity as a most fortuitous consequence. Despite critics' claims that they were groundless, even whimsical, her ideas found solid application in classrooms of women. "Show how the city of Poughkeepsie could be used as historical material if all literary records of the place had perished," she requested on an exam in 1907. "How far can you unify your work in history with other subjects?" she asked on another in 1924. Her books *The Newspaper and the Historian* (1923) and *The Newspaper and Authority* (1923) were largely the culmination of ideas that came out of the exercises she assigned over the years. By asking students to see the newspaper as a historical source and a cultural relic, she showed that she had grown in new directions since her professional coming of age in the 1870s. Taught initially to respect the methodological and disciplinary boundaries of scientific history, she eventually problematized the rigid use of select documents and in the process opened the door for others to retrieve the past experience of women and other historical castaways.[52]

Of course she would not abandon her historical lens on legal, political, or constitutional topics altogether; rather, she repositioned and expanded it to refract multiple perspectives of her former subject material. Likening history to a human body, Salmon perceived government and politics not as the whole of history but merely as its skeleton. The "subfields" of economics—production, commerce, manual labor, and communication— became history's organs, arteries, muscles, and nerves, respectively; the masses studied in sociology became its flesh; the professions and literature, its brain; art and aesthetics, its form and color; psychology and philosophy, its mind; and ethics and religion, its soul. In "The Curriculum" (1922) she sought to eliminate disciplinary distinctions altogether, describing "the artificial division into separate water-tight compartments of all the different subjects . . . [as] arbitrary, artificial, and unreasonable." Salmon's resounding message to anyone who would listen was *connectedness*, not merely between academic disciplines but between teacher and scholar, academy and community, politics and culture, and men and women past and present.[53]

Women social scientists sang her praises for giving serious attention to subjects once deemed beyond the scope of scholarly inquiry. University of Chicago dean Marion Talbot lauded her efforts to make domestic servants more than "a topic of conversation of gossip" but a "subject for scientific investigation and study."[54] However, it was also no surprise that as Salmon looked beyond the battlefield and the congressional floor for history in everyday activities and objects, her publications found themselves in journals such as *Boston Cooking School Magazine* and the *Craftsman* alongside pieces by occasional weekend writers. Editors of academic journals like the *Yale Review* remained uninterested in her attempts to find "History in a Backyard" or in such inauspicious places as "Main Street" and "The Kitchen Sink." To their reasoning her jaunts into the junkyards of history lacked the intellectual gravity expected from professional scholars. Salmon's examinations of domestic life and material objects were hardly visionary, they thought; in fact, she seemed to cross the line back into historical amateurism —that ambiguous space where Alice Earle, antiquarian collectors, and other women observers of culture had since been relegated. These editors seemed not to notice that from behind Salmon's commonplace artifacts ordinary women in history made a rare yet timely appearance.[55]

In the end Salmon's redefinition as a historian came at the expense of her academic reputation. At Vassar James Monroe Taylor questioned her methods and found little value in her focus on subjects outside the accepted scientific scope of her male colleagues. He nearly replaced her with a younger male historian, someone who in his estimation would teach "the fact side of history" instead of wasting time with historical ambiguities. Little did he know that her study of objects was hardly old-fashioned but a sign of the modernist impulse to come.[56]

Only after Salmon died did her experiments in the field of history leave a more lasting impression on academic women. Adelaide Underhill made sure that the ideas Salmon privately formulated about history found expression in the posthumous works *Why Is History Rewritten?* (1929) and *Historical Material* (1933).[57] Already, however, her impact could be felt by the next generation of women at the Seven Sister schools, especially former Vassar students turned professional historians, such as Dorothy Stimson, Julia Orvis, and Eloise Ellery. Caroline Ware was another student profoundly changed by the experience. Though she had the fortune of training under Frederick Jackson Turner in his final years of teaching, Ware also got just "under the wire" to work with Salmon, who in the end left the more lasting impression: "[Salmon] was a funny, big, heavy woman with a deep voice, and a sort of indirect way of saying very direct things, or a direct way of saying indirect things," she fondly recalled.

> But she had us looking at sources, she had us recognizing that people were people. . . . She had us study laundry lists, what did that tell, you know, about how people dressed and lived. . . . Once you had been raised by Miss Salmon that way, you couldn't function in any other terms. You couldn't just learn or teach what the book said. . . . I can't see a textbook as an instrument of college teaching—I wouldn't go near a textbook with a ten-foot pole. . . . If you were a Lucy Salmon product, you couldn't see a textbook for the dust.[58]

For Ware, history could no longer be consigned to a textbook, nor its significance relegated to the classroom. Her mentor's insistence that "knowledge existed to be used" only reinforced her family upbringing in civil service and her later decisions as a professional scholar. After she completed her doctoral work at Radcliffe in 1925, Ware returned to Vassar as a member of the faculty; in 1934 she left to become a consumer advocate under the New Deal administration. She returned to academia once again as a professor of history at Sarah Lawrence College, but she spent most of her remaining career at Howard University (1942–61), where she turned history into a vehicle for racial tolerance and understanding. Living in Washington, D.C., she continued to serve on commissions to amend the Food and Drug Act, regulate health insurance, and debate consumer price controls. She went on to compile *Labor Education in the University* in 1946 while teaching in a Bryn Mawr summer school program for working-class women. Like so much of her research, the study grew out of her double role as a scholar and a social advocate.[59]

Ware was not alone in extending Salmon's message about historical methods and applications. Viola Barnes, also originally a political historian, echoed Salmon's pleas for usable history and interdisciplinarity in the late 1920s and 1930s at Mount Holyoke and even saw these ideas reflected in a new course curriculum. Although still a strong proponent of scientific method, she criticized her colleagues for fragmenting the American experience into subdisciplinary compartments and picked up Salmon's cause to integrate "the threads" of American history. Barnes vowed to make *people* "the terminals of whatever was happening" in the national past and developed the first integrated college major in "American Culture." "You must study them ["the people"] and see from all angles," she explained, but

> you couldn't do it if everything was siphoned off into threads. It was like a knitted thing that was in separate yarn and not together. . . . You wouldn't have a thread of history and a thread of economics and a thread of philosophy, and a thread of political science and so on. But you took the culture of the people and you took it as a blend, not like a pie where you have several little pieces, as you do in the interdepartmental major. A cake is what I'm taking about. . . . That's the major. It's American culture, it's American people.[60]

Mixed metaphors aside, Salmon's influence on this synthetic vision was unmistakable; the disparate threads of the American past could indeed be woven together into a connected study of American culture. Better yet, Salmon had already provided Barnes with the recipe for this historical cake she envisioned. Provided the observer did not search for the past only in written documents or solely within the formal political sphere, the various ingredients—women, nonwhites, and other marginal groups—would come to the surface but also blend together into a thing called American culture. This model of historical investigation was both intellectually pleasing and emotionally compelling for the next generation of women in the university. Yet after Salmon's death analytic tools, investigative practices, and conceptual categories of knowledge in nearly all the social science fields, including history, continued to be gendered in such a way as to limit the extent to which women could integrate methods and material. Not unlike historians, sociologists and economists suffered masculine bias that resulted from their fields' professional consolidation. The politics of disciplinarity stifled their ability to collaborate between departments or to experiment with interdisciplinary methodologies, just as they had for scientific historians. As successful as Barnes had been in institutionalizing Salmon's integrative approach to history, Salmon still had powerful detractors in most research universities and social science departments.[61]

Women did not find conditions conducive to the study of women or American culture in history, sociology, or economics departments, but anthropology was a social science that proved an important exception. As a discipline it had developed along a different course; from the outset women had played an active role in establishing its institutional premise and defining its epistemologies. Alice Fletcher, Elsie Clews Parsons, and later, Ruth Benedict and Margaret Mead stood out as key figures in the developing field, shaping its practices to legitimate women as both subjects and investigators of the past. These social scientists created their own investigative authority as "participant observers," roles that often ensured them better access to private rituals and cultural meanings than the distanced historian would have. They demonstrated that women could do more than occupy niches of expertise in a scientific field; they could drive a field's methodological approach and even dictate its activist agenda.[62]

With its different path to maturity, anthropology may have been the most instrumental of the burgeoning social sciences in the development of women's history in the twentieth century. As a field of inquiry it expanded the arsenal of historical source materials, gave new focus to the female experience through time and cultures, and introduced the historian to new frameworks through which to view women's roles in the past. Most important, anthropologists provided evidence of cultural and historical relativism, which, historians of women would discover, could counter assumptions about the essential nature of women's roles in the past and present. The concept of cultural relativism eventually provided a functional analytic framework for Progressive women historians, allowing them to explore women in the past without universalizing the female experience within the Western paradigm of separate spheres.

Anthropologists were able to achieve their unique perspectives of culture by observing peoples other social scientists ignored, particularly Native Americans. Moreover, unlike historians, anthropologists studied the native past unapologetically to address present social injustices and to shed light on assumptions of biological sexism that determined gender roles in Western culture. Alice Fletcher was one such anthropologist who undertook the study of Indian women both to learn about the native past and to seek a "historical solution of 'the woman question.'" Through the study of "primitive" cultures she and her female colleagues postulated the existence of matrilineal and matriarchal social units in the past and questioned what their implications would be for the current social organization of the sexes.

Matilda Stevenson's investigation of the Pueblos in the 1890s and Frances Densmore's study of the Chippewa in 1910 revealed women in roles of social power that were inimical to traditional views about the nature of sexual hierarchies in "civilized" culture.[63]

As anthropologists challenged Western notions of separate spheres, they lent credence to the idea that gender roles were socially constituted throughout American history. In 1913 Elsie Clews Parsons maintained in *The Old-Fashioned Woman* that the power dynamics between the sexes were uneven, fluctuating, and relative from one society to the next. Building on the work of her mentor Franz Boas, who had already questioned long-held assumptions of biological determinism and cultural evolution, she challenged traditional faith in the progress of American society and the differentiated gender roles that were thought to have occurred as an inevitable consequence. A woman of independent means with an interest in oral culture, she would eventually help pioneer the field of academic folklore and sponsor the work of Zora Neale Hurston, another Boas protégé who in the late 1920s and 1930s observed hoodoo practices of southern blacks and women's role in the transmission of their oral culture. The same year Hurston published her study of black folklore *Mules and Men* (1935), Margaret Mead carried Parsons's and Boas's logic to its furthest conclusion, postulating the complete malleability of sexual nature and submitting it to culture in *Sex and Temperament in Three Primitive Societies* (1935). These studies of women anthropologists initiated the university community to the idea that women had been figures of power in other times, places, and cultural contexts, despite their conspicuous absence in the documented evidence of the Western world.[64]

Although these ideas might have seemed a drastic departure from the worldview of most academic historians, they did resonate within sectors of the profession already embroiled in debates over cultural and historical relativism. As early as the 1910s, William E. Dodd promoted Karl Lamprecht's "Kulturgeschichte" in the United States, and after World War I Carl Becker and Charles Beard showed leanings in the relativist direction. The writings of Italian theorist Benedetto Croce inspired both Progressive scholars to think critically about the nature of historical perspective and objectivity. Becker finally articulated his thoughts in the essays "Detachment and Writing of History" (1910) and "Everyman His Own Historian" (1935), and Beard publicized the debate over relativism with his 1933 AHA presidential address, "History Written as an Act of Faith." These prominent men were influential but also part of a larger trend. Other historians had also begun to question the claims of empirical science, to revise tenets of Rankean historicism, and even to accept relativist history to varying degrees by 1930. Peter

Novick contends that relativism soon "flowered not just as a methodological imperative, but as a moral and intellectual posture," and "factualist objectivity . . . gave way in the interwar years to an emphasis on 'point of view.' "[65]

Perhaps of all the academic historians practicing in the 1930s, Caroline Ware summarized these developments best, for they were not unanticipated by her mentor Lucy Salmon years earlier. "The adoption of a cultural approach by historians may, indeed, be regarded as a cultural phenomenon in itself," she wrote. "It is the obvious product of a society with an increasingly collectivist base, in which specialization of function, with its fragmentation of experience, has been carried to the point where there can be no illusion that the experience of the individual constitutes a microcosm of the whole." It appears that what few were willing to accept about Salmon's work in the 1910s was becoming increasingly engaged by the 1930s. Academic historians were entertaining not only the practice of cultural history but also the relativism that made Salmon's forays into the everyday life of women as compelling as the formalized study of exceptional men.[66]

The Nonestablishmentarianism of Mary Beard

It is ironic but not altogether surprising that the handful of male scholars who embraced relativist points of view by the 1930s have received most of the attention in recent historiographical studies. Bonnie Smith and Nicholas Adams remind us that James Harvey Robinson, often credited alongside Beard and Becker as a pioneer of New History, did not even consider relinquishing his historical positivism until sometime after 1914— long after Salmon had questioned the omniscience of the scientific historian.[67] Salmon seemed to take historical relativism for granted, as did Mary Beard when she framed her activist histories of women in the 1930s. An independent writer, Beard had long viewed the social inaction of university historians not as reverence for scientific objectivity but, rather, as a sign of social exclusivity, elitist apathy, and civic irresponsibility. Her disdain for the arrogance of university scholars grew so intense that she refused to be associated with them, celebrating her unaffiliated status even as she remained happily married to one of the academy's most revered figures. But even Charles Beard eventually distanced himself from the academic establishment, resigning from Columbia in protest of dismissals of antiwar faculty in 1917. He then organized New York's Training School for Public Service, and the following year he joined Thorstein Veblen, John Dewey, and Robinson to launch the New School of Social Research, where he planned to accomplish what his wife had made her life's work: to generate historical research for the purpose of social reform.[68]

An ardent nonestablishment historian, Mary Beard was likely responsible for her husband's relativist turn before he formally declared it to the AHA in 1933. She explained in *On Understanding Women* (1931) that when determining historical truth, "everything seems to depend upon the historian—the locus in time and space, the mere detail of birth, affiliations of class, and the predilections of sheer uncritical emotions." Two years later, in *America through Women's Eyes*, she credited cultural anthropologists for inspiring her fluid view of historical perspective. To her relief, they called for the "integration of knowledge" as an alternative to the "specialism" of professional historians. "In the light of this wider and deeper understanding of the course of culture and civilization," she exulted, "all the divisions of thought, so assiduously cultivated by specialists—such as economics, politics, war, art, literature, education and feminism—are being dissolved as independent entities." Calling for connectedness, Beard continued where Salmon left off, engaging all social and cultural disciplines but stressing the connection between anthropological epistemology and broader perspectives of women's "long history" from the primitive to the present. The "better memory" of anthropologists, she argued, reveals that woman did more than contribute to the development of civilization but actually "launched civilization as her primordial urge." "The original woman now appears," she rejoiced, "not as Evil Genius but as Creative Good."[69]

On Understanding Women was Beard's first call for a broader view of the feminine past. "Written history, compiled mainly by men, though not always, has been fragmentary," she wrote, ". . . and the pattern of conceptual thought about women has been derived from partial history and partial experience." For women to receive their historical due, "the narrative of history must be reopened, must be widened to take in the whole course of civilisation as well as war, politics, gossip and economics . . . in relation to the total process." Once historians stopped conceiving of culture as "collections of commodities in a basket called history," they would see that "everything is related to everything else: religion to philosophy, philosophy to commerce and war, war to politics, politics to religion, women to religion, philosophy, war, commerce and politics, and men to religion, philosophy, war, commerce and politics. Here are revealed the actions and reactions of social forces molding both the sexes."[70] Thus just as Salmon had quietly done already, Beard employed knowledge from other social and cultural theorists to shatter the disciplinary boundaries prohibiting a more rounded view of women's history. She insisted on "integrating all the aspects of life" in the past, "widening the range of interest to the very borders of culture and deepening its roots in the substance of history."[71]

Ironically Salmon and Beard came to the same conclusions from very different origins. Salmon was a university historian whose reformism grew out of disillusionment with the academy, while Beard was a Progressive reformer who turned to historical scholarship as a social corrective. Long before Charles became a commanding academician, Mary and her husband were already committed to alleviating the socioeconomic inequalities they attributed to laissez-faire politics and unbridled capitalist greed. As newlyweds they had traveled to England and become intimately acquainted with the activist community at Ruskin Hall and the leading figures of the country's militant feminist and labor movements. When they returned to New York in 1902 (roughly when Salmon returned rejuvenated from Europe), they were newly committed to the "revolt against formalism" and Progressive social reform. Mary became a mother but continued to organize for the WTUL and the Shirtwaist Strike of 1909. She joined the suffrage movement but sought the vote less as a symbol of gender equality than as a means to equip working-class women with a political voice on labor issues. Though initially active in the National American Woman Suffrage Association (NAWSA), she relinquished her leadership role to commit more fully to the cause of workingwomen and other victims of the capitalist system.[72]

Her determination to expand the reach of democratic institutions to all Americans was evident in the series of history textbooks she wrote with Charles over the next thirty years (*American Citizenship* [1914], *The History of the United States* [1921], *The Rise of American Civilization* [1927], and *The American Spirit* [1942]). True to the Beards' social agenda, these texts highlighted the historical plights of the socially, politically, and economically underprivileged and underrepresented in other academic studies: industrial workers, religious minorities, African Americans, and occasionally women. Mary considered herself the impetus behind the nontraditional perspectives and expansive cultural themes in their textbooks, including *The Rise of American Civilization* in 1927. "Reviewers often imply that the whole product is [Charles's] in spite of the fact that he had never written on cultural themes before," she confided privately after its publication. "I drudged on the work for three years and especially since the cultural side was my hunch." Her emphasis on culture and its relative nature made sense, given what she hoped to accomplish. American history had to be viewed through a broad cultural lens to allow a plurality of perspectives, she figured; otherwise it would perpetuate the worship of its self-proclaimed victors.[73]

Like Katharine Coman and Edith Abbott, Mary Beard had a commitment to women, the laboring class, and urban reform that led her to write general texts and then eventually works of women's social history. Keeping true to her intent to see "America through women's eyes," Beard believed that Mary Chesnut became as good an informant on the Civil War period as any military man, and her *Diary from Dixie* as good a source as any official record of the time. Nineteenth-century domestic historian Elizabeth Ellet became one of Beard's cultural consultants on the everyday lives of women during the American Revolution, but Mercy Otis Warren, herself a witness to the Revolution, was perhaps an even more authoritative expert. Beard lent equal credence to the works of social scientist Alice Clark and domestic writer Alice Earle in recounting the lives of colonial women. The fact that the former was a scholar and the latter was not was of no consequence, since in Beard's mind, academic credentials said less about one's abilities as a historian than about being indoctrinated in a masculine worldview.[74]

Her approach to history, while unacademic in one sense, was nonetheless unmistakably grounded in the empirical method that trained social scientists could provide. One can surmise that Charles was an enormous influence in this regard, but Mary also looked to women social scientists and reformers for guidance. Edith Abbott's research, for example, served as much of the foundational evidence for chapter 4 of *America through Women's Eyes*, "Machine Industry and Plantation." Likewise Beard cited the various studies of Abbott's colleagues, including University of Chicago sociologist Anna Spencer and Hull House social scientists Jane Addams, Florence Kelley, and Alice Hamilton, who provided some of the only historical data available on the work conditions of immigrant girls. One social scientist in particular, Charlotte Perkins Gilman, had left an impression on Beard since her college years at DePauw University in the 1890s, for Gilman provided anthropological perspectives of the past to challenge gender roles much like Beard would attempt thirty years later.[75]

A proponent of sociologist Lester Ward's "gynecocentric" theories on the origins of modern society, Gilman proposed that over time men had hindered women's natural potential to develop and prosper. In *Women and Economics* (1898) she traced women's economic autonomy from primitive cultures and argued that ultimately the distinctive attributes of men and women together created civilized culture.[76] She would go on to write more polemical works from this interdisciplinary perspective, including *Human Work* (1904), *The Man-Made World; or, Our Androcentric Culture* (1911), and *The Home* (1910). In the last work she turned the domestic institution into an object of historical analysis, showing that social attitudes about women's ties to the hearth had outlived their practical purpose. "In all this long period of progress the moving world had carried with it the unmoving home," she lamented, "the man free, the woman confined; the man specializing in a thousand industries, the woman still limited to her domestic functions." As woman gradually proved her economic worth outside the home in venues such as the labor force and the marketplace, Gilman believed that domestic mythology lost its application. The longer memory of anthropologists, both she and Beard agreed, allowed this more complete view of women's work to surface.[77]

Gilman reverted to the distant past to prescribe a wider range of public roles for women in the future. Sociologist Anna Spencer did the same fifteen years later, focusing her historical lens on primitive times to reveal women's contributions to human civilization. In *Woman's Share in Social Culture* (1913) she argued that women's appearance as "a 'silent partner' in the building of the outer temples of thought and action during the ages when she has been denied the tools of self-expression in art and science, in literature and politics, is no proof that her contribution has been small even in these lines." The reason for women's scant recognition, in Spencer's mind, was the narrow focus of the male historian. Her objective was thus to lift the woman "as chief laborer of primitive life" from the shadows of obscurity "caused by exclusive homage of great individuals." She framed her relativist ideas in terms of "environmental change," which over time created "new forms of social organization" and consequently a "changing feminine ideal." What especially appealed to Beard was Spencer's attempt to create a new metanarrative of women's history, one that invoked the primitive as an ideal moment in women's past, when material interests and industrial culture did not obscure their social value.[78]

Because Spencer was a sociologist and Gilman a radical activist, professional historians paid little to no attention to their historical theories on women. Yet perhaps for these reasons they had grabbed the attention of Mary Beard early in her reform career. Indeed, some of the most innovative thinking in regard to women's relative role in history had come from the camp of social reformers who searched for ways to improve labor conditions for women and immigrant poor. Jane Addams, for example, also looked to the distant past to prescribe more empowered social roles for twentieth-century women. Her inauspicious book *The Long Road of Woman's Memory* (1916) anticipated some of Beard's later writings by questioning the presumably static nature of historical memory itself. It was not some simple unchanging process of cognition, she explained, but a complex and continued reappropriation of cultural meanings through generations. Memory was not a transparent representation of the past but, rather, a transmuted version that "soften[ed] its harshness and beautif[ied] its barrenness." Women's memory over expanses of time had functioned in contradictory ways to preserve but also to challenge social convention, and it was the latter function on which Addams concentrated, arguing that women could regain control of memory's interpretive reins to wield it consciously "as a selective agency in social organization."[79]

Critical of the individualistic mindset of modern war-torn society, Spencer, Addams, and Mary Beard looked to primitive cultures and gynecocentric origins for models of a more collective, humane, and socially equitable ideal—and in the process marked this ideal as essentially feminine. Spencer called for a "spiritualizing of maternal function," while Beard implored women to return to their primitive roles as "life-givers." Their invocation of the historically feminine roles of nurturer, civilizer, and mediator as modern antidotes for war made sense given the international climate in which they professed their ideas. Addams wrote *The Long Road* on the eve of U.S. intervention in World War I, and Beard wrote two of her women's histories during the interwar years and then another, *Woman as Force in History* (1946), immediately following the hostilities of World War II, when tensions between Cold War powers were escalating to uncomfortable fruition. As leaders in the international peace movement, Addams and Beard believed that women were an indispensable part of the peace process as cultural mediators; their long history in pacifism was now, more than ever, essential cultural knowledge for men and women trying to exist in a modern world.[80]

Indeed Addams, Gilman, and Spencer gave precedent to Beard's activist intentions for women's history, and yet in the 1930s her ideas still gained only lukewarm acceptance in the university. Scholars were not ready to acknowledge a full curriculum of her long history, but she fleshed out the logistics of such a program anyway in the hope that a women's college would pioneer it and win converts. Written for the AAUW, her fifty-page syllabus, *A Changing Political Economy as It Affects Women* (1934), was organized according to the premise that there were connections between women's far-ranging historical roles and their present potential to achieve "creative citizenship." First and foremost, she urged, women educators must consider the ramifications of teaching male-centered history exclusively: "Let us try to imagine what it would be like to know nothing of even men's past," she proposed. "Women alone are supposed to be able to manage without knowing themselves; with knowing men only. The result is that university women, like all other women, face the world insufficiently equipped to do much more than complain about sex discriminations in a 'man's world.'" Like her forthcoming book *Woman as Force in History*, Beard's syllabus historicized the roots of feminists' preoccupation with sex equality and called for a broader study of women in history, in terms of both time and disciplinary framework. In addition to reading the works of anthropological theorists, who she claimed were "almost unanimous in their belief that the female of the species launched civilization," she called for students to engage in the research of social history. "It reveals woman always at the center of action and of thought," she explained, "helping to shape military and political policies of [the] time, even as they affect herself."[81]

Beard's call for women's learning did not fall completely on deaf ears. Four years after Beard published her syllabus, Isabel Abbott, still a fledgling economic historian at Rockford College, was inspired to examine women in long history in a course called Women in the Middle Ages. On the final exam she asked students to use class readings to conjecture about gender relations in medieval Europe. One student gave the question considerable thought:

> *The Goodman of Paris* . . . is of great value in studying the position of women in *the middle ages*. It is a book of instructions written by a husband, age 60, at his wife's request. The wife is but 15 years old, revealing again the fact that marriage was arranged, usually for financial reasons. . . . The book *deals* with religious and moral instruction, how to care for the household, manage the servants, prepare the food. . . . The emphasis put on wifely obedience is a very interesting part of the book. . . .
>
> Another very important source of material for me is the *Paston Letters*. This series of family letters written in England during the fifteenth century is very interesting. There are many letters written by women, a large share of them by Margaret Paston. . . . It reveals that women were able to read and write—at least the women of the better class. Margaret Paston carried on her husband's business for him during his frequent absences—she collected rents, heard complaints, bought provisions. She was even able to give good advice to her husband's son concerning business affairs. . . . Economic Documents and Records reveal interesting bits of information. There are court records which reveal that women owned property, engaged in trade [such] as ale making + baking, + similar pieces of information. . . . I also think I should do more with economic documents and things of that sort in order to find out more about the extent to which women participated in trade and in general try to find out more about women of the lower classes. Most of my material so far has been on noble women or upper middle class.[82]

The response suggests that Abbott encouraged her students to redefine history to include customs and social relationships that pervaded women's everyday lives. One might also conjecture that she understood what Beard and Salmon had been alleging in terms of source materials: that the past could be revealed in sources deemed "unhistorical"—literature, letters, household inventories, and other "unofficial" writings—as well as "official" documents read in alternative ways. Yet just as it appeared that Abbott had been converted, her comments on the exam reveal an incomplete acceptance of Beard's ideas. "The historian does not use the term 'document' in this sense, but in a narrower one," she penciled in the margin. "For him a document is an original official paper, not literary or other some source material." Indeed this response suggests that a shift to new historical methods and paradigms was not occurring uniformly. It would take a long time for a scientifically trained historian like Abbott to reconceive historical practice so completely, even, as Beard argued, if such shifts validated her as a historical agent as much as they did a woman practitioner. Nevertheless, Abbott's student seemed well on her way.

Perhaps faculty were closer to achieving Beard's plan for women's learning at Goucher College, where historians welcomed innovations in historical teaching for women. Professors Ella Lonn and Mary Williams expressed opinions regularly on the subject for *Historical Outlook* (formerly the *HTM* until 1916), and fellow colleague Dorothy Stimson set out to prove that scientific history, in the most literal sense, could be taught and mastered by women. Having written a dissertation titled "The Gradual Acceptance of the Copernican Theory of the Universe," she created a History of Science course in an effort to dispel notions that women were averse to science and that history and science were unrelated.[83] In the 1920s and 1930s Williams also expanded the department's offerings with History of the Woman Movement in the United States, a course that required the reading of texts by feminists Charlotte Perkins Gilman, Ellen Key, and Olive Schreiner. The administration eventually discontinued the course "on the grounds of its content," to Williams's disappointment. She complained to the school president, "Some of my department colleagues think it too sociological for the Department of History. . . . Others seem to think it a course on the history of woman suffrage, with special stress on the 'shrieking sisterhood,'—the militants." While Williams embraced Mary Beard's interdisciplinary vision for women's history, others still refused to believe that such material was history at all.[84]

The acceptance of Beard's social and cultural history of women was not yet complete, but there were reasons for optimism. The same year she published her syllabus, the *Washington Post* announced the AHA annual meeting with a headline that read, "Larger Place for Women in Histories of Future Seen by Prominent Writers: Tendency toward Social and Cultural Phases Are Cited."[85] Indeed, this reporter was not wrong in linking increased historical attention on women to historians' more frequent engagement of social and cultural perspectives. On the other hand, what was reported as news may really have been old habit refashioned in new garb. I have argued here that women's exploration of the social and cultural past was innovative and characteristic of future developments in the profession of history. Nevertheless we have also seen a degree of continuity between women's historical writing and teaching in the nineteenth and twentieth centuries, for domestic writers such as Ellet and Earle explored the cultural and social interactions of groups in daily life decades before Mary Beard did the same. In the twentieth century, Progressive historians recast these historical explorations into a scientific mold, employing empirical methods and losing much of the personalism characteristic of feminine history before the professional turn. The interdisciplinarity promoted by women in the Progressive Era allowed them to expand their investigations beyond the political realm of white elites to include Americans of color, the working class, and women. With heightened legitimacy, they sought to reweave their recovered versions of the past into the fabric of popular memory.

II
Perspectives from the Professional, Social, and Geographic Margins

Chapter 3
Women Regionalists and Intercultural Brokers

The same year Isabel Abbott offered her course in medieval women's history, graduate student Julia Cherry Spruill was reading private accounts and literary sources—to determine women's underlying social role not in medieval Europe but, rather, in the colonial South. Unlike Abbott, who was trained by Bryn Mawr's great constitutional and economic historians, Spruill studied at the Institute for Research in Social Science at the University of North Carolina, where social scientists other than historians encouraged her exploration of women's lives in the past. She combed official court orders, wills, inventories, and other legal documents for her dissertation turned book, *Women's Life and Work in the Southern Colonies* (1938). Yet it was the personal correspondence and diaries of women themselves that gave her the most insight into social attitudes about gender roles in colonial southern society. They offered Spruill a deeper layer of historical understanding than did court documents alone, for according to her female informants the stigma placed on their sexual transgressions frequently overrode any legal sanctions against them. This fact was not borne out in court decrees but confirmed in the " 'ladies' morality books" she relied on for reading between the lines of legal records. Spruill did examine deeds and wills like other scientific historians but in alternative ways. They provided insight into the significance colonial society placed on girls' education, for instance, by allowing her to compare the proportions of money parents left male and female children for school tuition. The social attitudes Spruill sought to recover were elusive and rarely quantifiable, but she believed that their potent influence on colonial society made them worth the great lengths she went to in order to speculate about them.[1]

Forty years earlier Spruill may have had to endure the same criticism Salmon received for *Domestic Service*, a subject academics deemed "unworthy of her talents." Yet in 1938 *Women's Life and Work in the Southern Colonies* courted favorable academic reviews. Such forays into the everyday practices of unexceptional people were gaining acceptance in university history departments, a trend made evident by a panel of prominent scholars who prepared papers on the cultural approach to history at the AHA annual meeting in 1939. In her introductory remarks to the panel papers, Caroline Ware charted the recent leanings of scientific historians toward perspectives that revealed new evidence of "hidden" and unexceptional pasts:

> Both the course of events and the findings of various social sciences made increasingly clear the inadequacy of all treatments of the past which dealt only with the articulate groups. As economists examined social situations by reference to statistical series which reflected mass behavior; as sociologists undertook to probe the experience of inarticulate social groups; as psychologists revealed something of the nature of man in his social relationships; and as the new techniques of mass expression and communication sucked all parts of the society within their orbit, historians were inevitably forced to face the question of how the masses had lived and thought and reacted in the past. They began to realize that whereas they had considerable information about rulers and how they exercised their power, they had little or none about the ruled and how they had responded. They knew something of the literary and artistic high lights, but little of the mass culture from which these high lights stood out. However little they knew about Shakespeare, they knew less about his audiences. Least of all did they know the manner of living and the processes of change which affected the multitude. They had, on the whole, assumed that the texture of social life in any time and place was more or less of a piece—that the experiences, attitudes, thoughts, and values which found record were representative of those which went unrecorded.[2]

Ware's call for interdisciplinary investigations of mass culture sounded remarkably like the ideas of cultural historians later in the twentieth century. Indeed, she looked forward to new investigations of the traditionally "inarticulate"—nonwhites, the working class, and women—as legitimate subjects and agents of history. Male cultural historians also appreciated the implications of this new perspective, yet perhaps as a woman she stood at a better vantage point from which to evaluate the cultural past of the historical profession itself. Looking back at the rise of "scientific historians," she determined that "the terms in which they shaped their questions and presented their data were still largely determined by their own social outlook." "They were members of the academic fraternity," she explained, ". . . as professionals, they enjoyed a measure of prestige and security; they moved across class lines with an ease denied to other social groups; they associated, directly or indirectly, with those who wielded political power, but themselves rarely shouldered the responsibilities of active political life." The privileged positioning of these gentlemen "provided the windows through which they looked on the past as well as on the present," Ware decided, nailing shut the coffin of the neutral, omniscient historian once and for all.[3]

Ware was a professional scholar from a prominent family of Harvard men who made up past generations of the fraternity to which she referred, and yet her insights came from someone who viewed power from the point of view of an outsider. Despite her privileged beginnings she gravitated to the fringes of her professional fellowship and soon came to identify with others on the fringes of American society. As a woman scholar and intellectual mentor to African American students at Howard University, she understood somewhat better what it felt like to be marginalized by gender and social prejudice. The same could certainly be said of other women who wrote about groups outside the northeastern establishment. Spruill, for example, a southern woman who wrote regional history about unexceptional women, would likely never have earned a reputation outside the South without the sponsorship of Harvard professor Arthur Schlesinger. Even with his commendation, her research was virtually ignored by academics until social historians reinvigorated interest in it in the early 1970s.[4] Angie Debo was another historian marginalized by gender and geographic location, but perhaps even more so by her controversial research on Native Americans. Her banishment to the outer reaches of the historical profession was quickened by her insistence on exposing the racial and cultural provocations that shattered the myth of the Turnerian West.

Our designation of these regional scholars as marginal is rarely simple; in this chapter we acknowledge the margins as sites of disempowerment and limitation but also as spaces of opportunity, experimentation, and perspective for women historians. Much like Ware, Debo found that the margins could be a vantage point from which to expose power dynamics between elites and nonelites in the American past. One biographer has admiringly described Debo as an "intercultural broker" whose "intimate knowledge of disappointment and economic hardship predisposed [her] to affiliate with the less fortunate" in both American history and society.[5] I agree, but I also argue that the role of intercultural broker was one to which many women historians were predisposed in the twentieth century. As custodians of local, regional, race, and ethnic history, they redefined the margins of the historical establishment as spaces of privileged perspective on the social and cultural past. The positive reaction to Spruill's history of southern women had much to do with the heightened receptivity of social

and cultural history in the university by the 1930s. However, women outside the academy and on its peripheries were integral to this development.
In many ways Spruill's survey of women did not differ from the local,
family, and regional stories women had been writing long before history
was deemed a science or an academic discipline. Just as diaries and home
inventories revealed the life of the southern woman to Spruill, they had
revealed the life of the New England woman to Alice Earle nearly fifty years
earlier and Elizabeth Ellet fifty years before that.

When we view women's production of history from the margins and
outside the historical establishment, the emergence of social and cultural
perspectives in the 1930s no longer looks like a shift into uncharted waters
but a resurfacing of a tradition of history started and perpetuated by
women. In recent years Anne Firor Scott has attempted to amplify the
"unheard voices" of women historians of the South and acknowledge the
special perspective they brought to historical practice in the early twentieth
century.[6] We, too, look to some of these women; however, we concentrate
on women historians in the West, due to their greater neglect. The early
twentieth century saw an explosion of western histories that show the
extent to which women invoked the Indian legacy in their social and political commentaries of the Depression and interwar years. Regardless of region, women both west and south wrote of their own pasts as they unveiled
other cultures in American history. Few were formally recognized historians, but here we assess their work as historians and intercultural brokers
whose perspectives of power allowed them to see the past in new ways.

Women Regionalists: Finding Culture
outside the Academic Establishment

Spruill's study was not the first examination of women's or social
history to come out of North Carolina's Institute of Social Science Research. Fifteen years before the publication of *Women's Life and Work*,
Genevieve McMillan had written a master's thesis titled "History of Higher
Education of Women in the South," and in 1937 classmate Guion Griffis
Johnson published *Ante-Bellum North Carolina: A Social History*. The
likely champion of these graduate projects was institute director Howard
Odum, a social scientist whose own research indicated his commitment to
the forgotten southern past. Like Edith Abbott and the Progressive historians in the industrial North, he employed scientific method ultimately to
improve the human condition but turned his attention to the impover-
ished rural South. His studies of black folk culture dovetailed with his
students' projects in southern women's history and derived from a similar

desire to understand the balance between humans, nature, and culture—between "social forces" and "common traditions."[7] Spruill maintained that her goal in *Women's Life and Work* was not to present an idealized image of the chivalrous planter but "to find out as much as possible about the everyday life of women, their function in the settlement colonies, their homes and domestic occupations, their social life and recreations, the aims and methods of their education, their participation in affairs outside the home, and the manner in which they were regarded by the law and by society in general." She and Odum focused on different social groups, women and slaves, respectively, yet both chose to study people whose experiences had been formerly obscured by historians with sectional allegiances, patriotic and academic agendas, or racist and chauvinist worldviews. Together they revealed a pluralistic culture stripped of stereotypes and sentimentality that belied the monolithic myth of the plantation South.[8]

Colleague Guion Griffis Johnson took a similar tack in *Ante-Bellum North Carolina*, writing on rural life, sports, religion, education, ceremonies, provincialism, and class structure while paying particular attention to housewifery, child rearing, and the daily rituals of women.[9] Her emphases were nearly identical to Alice Earle's in her histories of colonial New England forty years earlier, but Johnson's were couched in the language of social science and designed to meet a different social agenda. Whereas Earle nostalgically wrote history from an entrenched place of domestic authority, Johnson hoped to present a previously unexplored southern past from a position of newfound scholarly clout. Anne Firor Scott explains that women such as Spruill and Johnson studied the private, "unofficial" aspects of southern women's lives as historians who identified with the illegitimacy that continued to mark their topics of research in the historical establishment. Their feelings of physical, professional, and intellectual isolation led them to write history on and about the margins—in this case the everyday lives of southern women as women of the South themselves.[10]

Unfortunately, while Spruill and Johnson lent fresh perspective to southern history, they, like most women educated in the South, remained in marginal positions as instructors at normal schools and southern women's colleges. Such was the case for Julia Flisch, an AHA member and one of the first academic historians of southern social history. After graduating from the Lucy Cobb Institute in Georgia, she was denied admission to the University of Georgia on account of her sex. She spent years teaching at the Georgia State College for Women before receiving a master's degree from Wisconsin in 1906. Her article "The Common People of the Old South" was published in the AHA annual papers in 1908, but to little fanfare in academic circles. Her story is regrettably like Virginia Gearhart Gray's nearly a generation later. Gray, too, joined the AHA while working in relative obscurity as a substitute teacher at Sophie Newcomb College. It was not a coincidence that the handful of women historians of the South who did rise to greater professional prominence did not train or forge early careers in the region. Goucher professor Ella Lonn, for example, was a respected historian of the Civil War South but earned her doctorate degree at the University of Pennsylvania. Marjorie Mendenhall, a protégé of Arthur Schlesinger, wrote "History of Agriculture in South Carolina, 1790–1860" as her dissertation but built her career at Radcliffe and Vassar Colleges. Gray, like Lonn and Mendenhall, went north initially to write her Ph.D. thesis at the University of Wisconsin but settled in the South after graduate school. Thus despite the fact that "The Southern Woman, 1840–1860" (1927) was one of the first academic works in southern women's history, the academic Northeast hardly noticed it.[11]

These historians in the South did not differ from women in the Mid- and Far West isolated by physical distance from the historical establishment. On the other hand, historians turned department chairs, such as Laura White and Agnes Wergeland (Wyoming), discovered that the distance afforded them opportunities denied them in the East. It is doubtful that their colleague Grace Hebard would have ever secured a position in New England like her senior post at the University of Wyoming. Male scholars questioned the validity of her doctoral credentials, which she received in absentia through correspondence courses at Illinois Wesleyan University in the 1890s. She went back to school to earn this degree after working as an engineer in the U.S. Surveyor's Office, more proof to her detractors that she was a dabbler rather than a serious research historian. Nevertheless, at Wyoming Hebard's previous vocation was a nonissue; she became a celebrated fixture in the department and a prolific writer of western history.[12]

Once women historians settled into institutions outside the Northeast, many enjoyed the freedom to experiment with new methods and subject material without fear of professional reprisal. In closer proximity to sources in uncharted areas of research, many even pioneered subfields in Native American, cultural, and ethnic history. University of Chicago graduate students Rachel Eaton and Catharine Cleveland, for example, went to the Far West in the 1910s to research their dissertations in social and cultural history. Eaton spent the remainder of her career at small colleges in the western states, where she gathered primary evidence for her Native American studies, including *Domestic Science among the Primitive Cher-*

okees and *John Ross and the Cherokee Indians* (1914). Cleveland's dissertation turned book, *The Great Revival in the West* (1916), turned attention from Protestant New England to the role of religion in building communities on the western frontier. Describing the "jerking, barking, and rolling" that took place at the western revival camp meetings, Cleveland painted a democratized portrait of evangelical spirituality that revealed the West as a distinctive and significant setting in U.S. history. University of Chicago historian William E. Dodd, later the academic mentor of Angie Debo, drew attention to Cleveland's study of revivals by agreeing to write its introduction: "Miss Cleveland has shown clearly the religious 'destitution' of the frontier. . . . The author certainly presents in the following pages, the best, and I believe, the only scientific account of this important movement."[13]

Dodd was rare in his commitment to regional subjects, let alone to women historians like Cleveland. The more common fate of women regionalists was that of Julia Flisch, who as a card-carrying AHA member attested that the organization defined national history in regionally exclusive ways. The *AHR* rarely published the works of women who wrote on topics originating outside the political Northeast, in stark contrast to the *Mississippi Valley Historical Review* (*MVHR*) (1914) and the *Journal of Southern History* (1934), which accepted submissions of women's local racial and ethnic research with regularity.[14] In 1935 women authored or edited nearly one-fourth of the articles on the *Journal of Southern History* annual list and 15 percent of the books it reviewed. These percentages were substantially higher than those for the *AHR* and disproportionately high considering the ratios of women in academic history departments overall.[15] Mississippi Valley Historical Association president Solon Buck begged to know in 1923 why writers and teachers of American history seemed solely preoccupied with "the local history of New England and Virginia and so little of the history of our own states," especially when the "first Americans" continued to occupy the western plains, about which so much history remained unwritten.[16] Certainly women regional historians furthered Buck's agenda. Annie Abel wrote pieces on Native Americans in the West with regularity for the *MVHR*, and Ella Lonn was a frequent contributor to the *Journal of Southern History* and the *MVHR*, earning enough clout to become the first woman president of the Southern Historical Association. Western historian Louise Phelps Kellogg reviewed over twenty-five books for the *MVHR* between 1914 and 1929 and in 1935 became the president of the Mississippi Valley Historical Association. By then, women made up 20 percent of the Executive Council of the Southern History Association and 33 percent of the program commentators at its annual meeting.[17]

The welcome reception of women as members of regional organizations and as contributors to their journals had much to do with the fact that regional history was often the local history to which they had access. Because regional editors were less committed to national narratives, they left the door open for women without formal training or academic affiliation to submit pieces on topics near and dear to them. Thus the *MVHR* published Helen Broshar's "First Push Westward of Albany Traders" (1920) and Dorothy Dondore's "Points of Contact between History and Literature in the Mississippi Valley" (1924), pieces that the *AHR* would have likely refused. Jane Berry's "Indian Policy of Spain in the Southwest" (1917) and Hallie Farmer's "The Economic Background of Frontier Populism" (1924) were also typical of submissions by women to the journal in the Progressive years, regardless of their academic training or affiliation. The *MVHR* embraced research in Indian, immigrant, and Populist history, subfields in which women anthropologists and sociologists had long shown interest as local observers of social groups. Unlike the *AHR*, which began in the 1890s, these regional organizations and journals came of age in the 1920s and 1930s, once social and cultural history, and folk history to a degree, had won greater acceptance in the historical profession.[18]

Regional publishers welcomed women's research through the 1920s, and in the 1930s the trend continued as New Deal agencies recruited women to conduct historical research on an unprecedented scale. The Roosevelt administration allocated federal funds to establish the Historic American Buildings Survey and the Historical Records Survey (HRS), both of which hired out-of-work preservationists and untrained women to perform the work of history.[19] First conceived by DAR genealogist Jean Stephenson in 1930, the HRS consolidated the nation's local source materials for the purposes of preservation, education, and expediting future research. The HRS was part of the Federal Writers' Project and was eventually subsumed under the Records and Research Section of the Division of Women's and Professional Projects of the WPA. Its employees created finding aids and other reference works for county archives and the nation's manuscript collections, but they also served as regional historians in effect, writing sketches of towns, counties, landmarks, and churches for the WPA state guidebook series.[20]

The HRS became the greatest catalyst for the production of local history the nation has ever seen, and women were its indispensable rank and file. Mothers, wives, and professional women who would never have had the opportunity to become acquainted with the nation's historical documents were now becoming trained historians and archivists. The number of women who worked for the HRS in its years of existence (1935–42) is unknown, but it is probable that the project mobilized hundreds, if not thousands, of women to labor in historical archives.[21] It is also likely that women university historians flocked to the HRS in greater numbers than their male counterparts, since relatively few full professors were forced to look for work during the Depression, but lower-level lecturers and instructors—many of whom were women—needed viable employment alternatives. Margaret Shelburne Eliot was appointed the national supervisor of the manuscripts project of the HRS, and unemployed historians Angie Debo and Juanita Brooks became state directors of the Oklahoma and Utah surveys. Laid off from her full professorship in 1932, Kathleen Bruce also turned to the HRS in 1938 and became state director in Virginia. One of the greatest acquisitions of the WPA during the Depression was unemployed anthropologist Zora Neale Hurston, whose work in African American communities in rural Florida continues to be consulted by scholars of race and cultural theory today.[22]

Newly organized case papers, payrolls, court minutes, church attendance rolls, miscellaneous dockets, and tax records revealed facets of the lives of ordinary Americans that were previously obscured from the historian's field of vision. Women HRS workers compiled, classified, indexed, edited, and published these government and church records to make source materials widely accessible for an up-and-coming generation of cultural historians, an accomplishment not lost on pioneer urban historian Constance Green. In 1940 she announced to fellow AHA members that they had "the outstanding achievements of WPA writers and workers on the HRS" to thank for paving new avenues in the field of cultural history. Their efforts demonstrated "the feasibility of enlisting the aid of the professional and untrained" in building this emergent field, for "the story of how American people have lived as individuals and as communities must be told by details" they collectively made available for scholarly research. In a nutshell, WPA women allowed historians to depart from "top down" models of political and diplomatic history to examine, in Green's words, "American life from the bottom up."[23]

Her approach to the past was a departure from the scientific mantra of university historians in the 1870s and 1880s, but so was the role she envisioned for women in the emerging field of cultural history. Women's interest in bottom-up methods was not entirely new; Progressives had already employed them when writing labor and immigrant history in the 1910s and 1920s. But now workers for the WPA fleshed out the historical lives of everyday women as revealed through personal writings and folk relics. As the WPA director in Utah, historian Juanita Brooks collected more than 450 diaries and journals of Mormon women for the Library of Congress and the Utah Historical Society, contributing in significant ways to the recovery of a feminine frontier.[24] Hurston also applied a bottom-up philosophy to recapture the African American folk past for the WPA. "The Negro farthest down," she insisted, generated "the greatest cultural wealth of the continent." No longer interested in "high" culture, she studied the everyday customs of her hometown of Eatonville and other Everglade communities for *The WPA Guide to Florida* (1939) and "The Florida Negro." Her bottom-up approach necessitated more than the search for material relics. The Negro farthest down did not own much of material value but carried the invaluable possession of memory. Hurston listened to spoken stories and acknowledged their profound influence on southern culture. Perhaps because she herself had been raised with these same oral-aural traditions and was a noted storyteller of Eatonville life in her own right, Hurston could see the value of folklore better than other academicians. One biographer describes her as "a living representative of the southern folk idiom" who at the same time observed it as a distanced social scientist.[25]

Only after Hurston's WPA colleagues compiled oral histories of African American slaves in the 1930s did academic historians truly entertain the use of oral evidence for the otherwise unrecoverable pasts of American women and people of color. As they studied the social and economic communalism of Native American and folk cultures with renewed appreciation, pockets of regionalist scholars came to recognize materials women had long relied on locally—oral testimony, folk songs, and material relics—as legitimate historical sources. Hurston's and Green's methodologies may have appeared new, a reflection of the cultural radicalism of the late Harlem Renaissance and regionalist movement of the Depression years. Yet their belief that nonwritten forms of local history held valuable cultural knowledge echoed the thoughts of Mary Sheldon Barnes almost fifty years earlier in her *Studies in Historical Method*. An unorthodox pedagogue at the time, Barnes implored other women to develop skills of observation in young history students not by assigning them rote history texts or facsimiles of official documents but, rather, by letting them get their hands dirty in the physical evidence of history in their communities. Her "source method" called for the collection of objects in local repositories where children could interact with them and exercise their historical imaginations:

> [They] should contain Indian relics, pictures of native Indians, photographs of historic sites and buildings, all the historic maps of the locality, . . . old costumes and uniforms, old dishes, utensils, tools, coins, stamps, and portraits,—everything, in short, which serves as a material

link between then and now. There, too, should be found the files of local newspapers, made as complete as possible, and as soon as possible firmly bound. Letters, diaries, manuscripts, which have local historical value should be collected and bound. . . . All the literature that has gathered about the place should also be gotten together,—any poems, novels, biographies, which celebrated the place of its citizens.[26]

Again, concepts that seemed new to the historical profession by 1940 were actually contiguous with a tradition of history women had established in the nineteenth century and that Salmon had taken in new directions in the 1900s. Green and Hurston represented a brand of scholar that was professional, but also a longer line of women localists for whom "culture" had always been an interest. They were not different from earlier generations of women who had pushed for the collection of local relics to construct a cultural history; this old objective was merely made easier by the systematic consolidation of historical sources in the 1930s and 1940s.

Finding Women's Place in Western History and Historiography

Outside the academy, local lore and relics were customary elements of women's research repertoire, and this was particularly true for women who lacked the written documents to write histories of the American West. Delilah Beasley had relied heavily on oral testimony for her history of African American Californians, as did Frances Victor when writing her histories of Native Americans in the Pacific states. In the 1930s and 1940s Grace Hebard, Juanita Brooks, Angie Debo, and Mari Sandoz became experts at finding the hidden pasts of western women and native groups whose lives were irretrievable through traditional records alone. The bottom-up approach they brought to social and Native American history may have acquired new cachet in select academic circles by 1940, yet it was an approach that they necessarily had refined earlier as women who wrote from and about the margins.

These women shaped a tradition of western history distinctive for its bottom-up recovery of unwritten pasts, but others had revealed a multitude of hidden Wests long before the regionalist impulse of the Depression years. Nineteenth-century protoethnographers Mary Eastman (1850s) and Susan Wallace (1880s) wrote historical works on native groups in the American Southwest and Northern Mexico. Their stories of expansion and empire romanticized the Spanish Southwest much the same way the accounts of male historians did the frontier, but Eastman and Wallace also provided some of the first glimpses of the region's prehistoric native cultures and alternatives to the Anglocentric views of civilization that dominated American historiography.[27] Several decades later in the 1880s and 1890s, western women found an enthusiastic readership for their historical works just as there had been for the colonial revivalist texts of Alice Earle and Anne Wharton in the Northeast. Elizabeth Custer, Martha Summerhayes, Alice Baldwin, and dozens of wives and daughters of military men and pioneers historicized their experiences at wilderness outposts. Their writings, coupled with the Native American studies of Mary Austin, Alice Fletcher, and other regional scholars, merely scratch the surface of historical texts women authored about the West in the early twentieth century.[28]

Indeed, dozens of professional and amateur women historians have left western accounts to posterity, only to have them classified as memoirs, adventure stories, captivity narratives, travel accounts, anthropological studies, and serial fiction—not as contributions to the canon of western history.[29] Their lack of recognition as historians suggests that while women in the West benefited from greater literary opportunities in the twentieth century, western history in particular developed into a staunchly masculine field, in both content and perspective. The virile identity of the historical West speaks primarily to the influence of Frederick Jackson Turner, whose essay "The Significance of the Frontier in American History" (1893) defined the West as a masculine geographic, mythic, and historical space. After Turner introduced his Frontier Thesis, other historians and fictionists embellished his depictions of the West as a site of rugged individualism and accepted his definition of westward expansion as a uniquely male right of passage, paying little heed to the women who also made the trek to the frontier. Glenda Riley maintains that in his writings Turner continued to "subsume women under the generic category 'men'" without apprehension, sheer irony given his mentoring of Emma Helen Blair and Louise Phelps Kellogg, two of the most highly regarded western historians of the early twentieth century. He always told his students to view the past through present concerns, and yet, as Riley notes, "the contemporary significance of such issues as women's rights and roles escaped him."[30]

Perhaps unwittingly, Turner and generations of historians he influenced concealed women's roles in settling the frontier and crafting its history. Only recently have scholars mined western women's nineteenth- and twentieth-century writings for their unique historical perspectives and discovered that they understood the West as a space of physical grit and social struggle, as a complex cultural crossroads that belied the region's existence as myth. As Peggy Pascoe explains, women historians of the West became intercultural brokers whose own experiences of discrimination and hardship led them to a clearer understanding of the contradictions in the Turnerian fiction of the frontier as a democratic site of opportunity. As mothers, wives, missionaries, teachers, anthropologists, and ethnographers, they were in a position to depict the West as a settled, demilitarized community, not simply a contested empire. Churches, schools, family, domesticity, daily ritual, and survival became central points of focus, as women represented Native Americans and themselves as agents of frontier life.[31]

Women's narratives about the West did not function like the colonial revivalist texts back east in one important respect: They went to great lengths to affirm the femininity that women of refinement in the South and Northeast took fewer pains to defend. They often invoked childhood memories to defuse accusations that the West was uncivilized terrain where women toiled like men and interacted with savages, often refashioning a distinctive, yet respectable brand of western womanhood in the process. In *Path Breaking: An Autobiographical History of the Equal Suffrage Movement in Pacific Coast States* (1914) Abigail Duniway depicted the frontier as a space of social liberation for men and women alike but also noted the exceptional opportunities the West provided nineteenth-century women in terms of formal political power. Rolling into one the mythical personas of the western pioneer and the eastern lady of gentility, she attempted to create historical significance for a new historical type: the western woman, who until then had suffered relative obscurity in the national record.[32]

In this way the historical projects of women in the East and the West were necessarily different. Yet in a broader sense western women employed history much the same way Alice Earle invoked memories of New England life: as a means of moral and civic education. In fact, a long line of women historians found the West better suited to performing civic work. As far back as the mid-nineteenth century Elizabeth Ellet had stirred the patriotic imagination with an account of virtuous women transplanted, *Pioneer Women of the West* (1852), but the most influential book in this respect came under the authority of a man, *Woman on the American Frontier* (1876) by William Fowler. It, too, romanticized the white woman in the West as a heroic "civilizer" of natives, not different from the idealized role women carved out for themselves as educators of immigrants in eastern cities.[33]

Whether inspired by Ellet, Fowler, or just an ingrained sense of feminine obligation, women did travel west in the nineteenth century to perform the work of "evangelical ethnology," and as missionaries on reservations they made national history part of their repertoire of civic lessons designed to acculturate Indians to American life. The Women's National Indian Association (WNIA) taught history on western reservations with seemingly benevolent intentions, much the same way the DAR did in immigrant neighborhoods back east. History served as a vehicle through which to teach the English language along with legal concepts and civic practices. Missionary women believed such knowledge to be a necessary accoutrement of the civilized American citizen, but also the necessary equipment for Native Americans to defend their rights and families from government exploitation. In this sense the work of WNIA women was paradoxical to say the least: They taught Indians the white man's history (often the story of their own demise) to lift them from poverty and despair white expansionists created for them.[34]

The University of Wyoming's Grace Hebard also thought history an essential component of civic training in the West. Her Ph.D. thesis, "Immigration: Its Relation to Citizenship," addressed the issue in reference to newcomers to the Northeast, but soon she looked to history to perform the same acculturative work among Native American populations. By 1916 she had fashioned herself a full-fledged "instructor of Americanization," but unlike her eastern counterparts she found the story of the western pioneers a better educational tool and a more authentically American tale.[35] Instead of locating American identity in colonial New England, she took her cues from Turner, rooting it in the western frontier. Her patriots were not the Founding Fathers but the Brave Pioneers—Father De Smet, Kit Carson, and Marcus Whitman, among a cast of other white adventurers. Her best-known book, *The Pathbreakers from River to Ocean: The Story of the Great West from the Time of Coronado to the Present* (1911), reiterated her notion that genuine models of heroism were formed through rites of passage on the frontier: "No territory or period of history so abounds in heroic deeds, daring adventures, and hazardous enterprises which have directly served to bring about civilization as the region known as the Great West." Her commitment to patriotic education through history was also evident in the textbooks she wrote for the Wyoming Department of Education. Her *History and Government of Wyoming*, for example, reissued throughout the 1910s and 1920s, located the American legacy in the goal of manifest destiny: "The 'red-man' waged continual war against the settlers and yielded to advanced civilization very stubbornly," she wrote, only in the end to celebrate the white man and the prevailing of his civilized culture.[36]

Hebard's *Pathbreakers*, like colleague Agnes Laut's *Pathfinders of the West* (1904), glorified frontiersmen as quintessentially American heroes and, like the accounts of male writers, polarized the West into the savage world of the Indian and the soon-to-be-civilized world of the white man. Yet at the same time there were women writers busily scripting a different tale: the West as a complex site of cultural admixing and social conflict. Brigitte Georgi-Findlay has examined hundreds of women's frontier accounts and concluded that as historical texts many accurately presented the West as contested terrain between cultures, classes, ethnicities, and genders. As observers with more ambiguous forms of power, these women were better positioned to commentate on nuanced social relationships between men and women, Indians and whites. The assimilation of Indians was hardly a measure of progress or an intended function for their historical narratives; rather, it was portrayed as an aggressive assertion of white, capitalist power.[37] Angie Debo and Mari Sandoz, authors of some of these histories, identified with Progressive historians rather than women of the WNIA. They, too, shared a disdain for classist privilege and capitalist exploitation, whether committed against industrial laborers or Native Americans. Just as Abbott and Salmon had rejected the patriotic lessons of the DAR and the SCD, Debo and Sandoz objected to narratives of white conquest over Native Americans and offered historical accounts with a nearly reverse denouement. They questioned the moral righteousness of national history as a celebratory tale of predestined westward expansion, choosing instead to write revisionist tales of exploitation and moral decay. Their objective was not to make the extermination of Native Americans an accepted or static part of the canon but, rather, to incite change in social attitudes and land allotment policies, much the same way Abbott and Beard had worked to reform labor laws in the industrial East.[38]

There are some useful parallels to draw here between the Progressive historians of the Northeast and regional historians of the West, but Robert Dorman cautions that there were also important differences. He agrees that while Debo and Sandoz also focused on historical conflict, class polarization, and the oligarchic forces of capitalism in their narratives, their choice of historical lens was fundamentally different. They not only "watched American history unfold from the Indians' reverse perspective, from the other side of the cultural-racial line," he insists, but they substituted the "upward-tending narratives" of Progressives with ones that carried a brutally frank message: Westward expansion was not social progress but exploitation—even worse, the decimation of once autonomous native cultures. By the 1930s progressive liberalism was increasingly mainstream in academic circles, yet Sandoz and Debo rejected this posture for a cultural radicalism that condemned the social and economic hierarchies liberals left intact.[39]

In this important respect these western women identified with a smaller cadre of American regionalists—including university press editor Joseph Brandt and Howard Odum, among others—who engaged folk and native perspectives to challenge social structures and even to neutralize "the acids of modernity" as they perceived them. This radical brand of regionalism in the 1920s and 1930s was vastly different from the sectionalism of the Daughters of the Confederacy or the Native Sons of the Golden West; no longer the source of romantic claims to genuine American identity, "region" was now a national concept, less a site of exceptional or inevitable Americanness than of class consolidation and cultural pluralism. Through the perspectives of African Americans and Native Americans, radical intellectuals and artists revealed the Cavalier South and the Rugged West as little more than figments of the white historian's imagination. Debo, for one, now believed that the individualism made heroic in Turnerian narratives of manifest destiny held little promise as a model for the future. The "progress" Turner once charted through westward expansion seemed to come to a near standstill with the onset of the Depression, so she looked to reveal the West for what it really was: a site of endless exploitation and struggle for racial, social, and economic supremacy.[40]

Thankfully for Debo, Joseph Brandt, formerly the founder of the University of Oklahoma Press, published her *Rise and Fall of the Choctaw Republic* in 1934 and proved instrumental in eventually publishing *And Still the Waters Run: The Betrayal of the Five Civilized Tribes* with Princeton University Press in 1940. Dorman describes *Rise and Fall of the Choctaw Republic* as the prototypical "depression-era parable" that told of "the systematic exploitation of the powerless by the powerful, of the 'common man' by 'economic royalists.'" Debo's rendition of western expansion was not about "the progress of the empire" but, rather, about the human toll of domestic imperialism. In essence, Debo offered the Native American perspective and flipped the Turnerian paradigm on its head. The Indian republics, once parts of a larger utopian society, were now as she saw them, "forced to accept the perilous gift of American citizenship," along with the "wilderness of civilization" that white settlers brought with them to the West.[41]

Indeed the case can be made for Debo's connection to the Progressive project and more specifically to the radical regionalism of the 1920s and 1930s described by Dorman. On the other hand, the social and professional marginalization she experienced as a woman sets her apart from other Progressive and radical men. Her lack of professional standing intruded upon her writing of history, perhaps in ways that gave her a more layered understanding of relationships of power in the American West. Thus without dismissing the connections already made, consider Debo, Mari Sandoz, and others soon to be introduced as integral contributors to a longer-standing tradition of women writers of Native American history about which little has been written. Debo unearthed some of the first documented evidence of Indian exploitation, but she was hardly the first woman to recount her discoveries in a sympathetic light or to link them to forms of power that infringed on her as a woman. As early as 1829, for example, Lydia Maria Child invoked history as a weapon for the native cause; her book *The First Settlers of New England* served as the plea of a Christian woman turned historian to prevent the passing of the Indian Removal Act of 1830. It seemed fitting that she, a Victorian matriarch, should protect Indians from further exploitation—as fitting as it became for her to write for the antislavery and woman's rights movements in later decades. Like many women reformers who tried on hats as historians in the nineteenth century, Child realized that history was an effective medium through which to universalize claims to natural rights. Of course the very act of rewriting the past was empowering in itself, for it turned her into an assertive agent of public discourse.[42]

Fifty years later, New England journalist Helen Hunt Jackson also assumed a protective stance toward Native Americans that led to her writing of history. She became aware of the travails of the Indians after attending the lecture of a Ponca chief in Boston in 1879. He spoke of his people's suffering under U.S. policies that stripped them of their ancestral lands, motivating Jackson to look through the records available on the subject at the Astor Library in New York. She found enough material to draft a historical manuscript that substantiated the Ponca's claims.[43] In a letter to writer/reformer Caroline Dall she expressed her intentions for the book she would soon write: "The points I want brought out in the notices of my book—are 1st that the Indians 'right of occupancy' was a right recognized by all nations . . . 2d that the Indians['] massacres of whites in the early days were almost without exception, either *instigated* or *hired* by the English[,] French, or Amer[ican] commanders—or they were the result of the provision put in *all* our early treaties that if white intruders crossed the Indian lines 'The Indians may punish him [*sic*] as they see fit!' "[44] Jackson's *A Century of Dishonor* (1881) became a scathing indictment of the U.S. government's "murder, outrage, robbery, and wrongs" against displaced native tribes. Four days before her death, she sent copies of the book at her own expense to President Grover Cleveland and the members of Congress. Her appeal undoubtedly played a part in the passing of the Dawes Act in 1887. Bound in red cloth, her books were embossed with Benjamin Franklin's famous words, "Look upon your hands! They are stained with the blood of your relations."[45]

In accordance with the new Dawes legislation, anthropologist Alice Fletcher took part in parceling land allotments to the Omaha, Winnebago, and Nez Percé, only to bear witness to new forms of exploitation. The

Dawes Act promoted the republican ideal of individual farm ownership at the cost of tribal culture and autonomy, and Fletcher responded by replacing Jackson's moralistic pleas with scientific ethnographies that generated academic interest in the Indian cause once again. The Peabody Museum published her works on Native American music, oral culture, and ritual ceremonies, but she also submitted pieces to popular journals like *Century Magazine* in hopes of reaching a broader audience of sympathizers. To Fletcher, social activism and history writing went hand in hand, just as they did for Progressive women back east. Her studies revealed Native Americans as "civilized" self-sustaining peoples, further underscoring the devastation wreaked by white expansionist policy.[46]

Biographer Valerie Mathes describes Jackson as a modern muckraker, not a Victorian driven by the evangelical fervor of the WNIA.[47] Frances Victor perceived her role in much the same light as she wrote *The Early Indian Wars of Oregon* a decade later: "Fiction and sentimentalism on the one hand, and vengeful hatred on the other, have perverted the truth of history," she decided. To make amends, she, too, assumed the role of undercover historical investigator, claiming to dig deeper for truth than professional historians and government officials. Following Jackson's and Victor's efforts in the late nineteenth century, women historians of the West built on this tradition of exposé, recovering the pasts of Native Americans for social change. Annie Abel spent weekends in the dusty records of the Indian Office in Washington in the 1910s, only to uncover evidence of a federal Indian policy in California that duplicated the slavelike system of the old Spanish.[48] Mary Austin was less a muckraker than a tireless advocate, but she also wrote history to bring attention to the Pueblos of the Southwest, starting with *The Land of Little Rain* in 1903 and *The American Rhythm* a decade later. Had she been writing in a university, colleagues might have shunned her disciplinary schizophrenia, for she was writing history, ethnography, folklore, and anthropology all rolled into one. Of course like Abbott and other cross-disciplinary social scientists, she recognized that her subject defied specialized attention, especially since her primary goal was to present Indian history and culture any way that would pique interest: "How many letters of commendation to editors . . . how many times I have done it up in jewelers cotton for Women's Clubs, or ripped up in its interest the modest complacency of University professors," she recalled in later years, for it would be another two decades before academic regionalists finally followed her lead and deemed Southwest Indians worthy of scholarly attention.[49]

Austin's campaign would leave a lasting impression on women in succeeding generations, including some with professional credentials and respected reputations in the academy. Rachel Eaton, Annie Abel, and Emma Helen Blair were just three of the scholars determined to alter social attitudes and native policy through the writing of history in the 1910s and 1920s, and unlike the writers who preceded them, they enjoyed access to government records and grants. Abel's three-volume study *The Slaveholding Indians* (1915, 1919, 1925), the first articulation of the Five Civilized Tribes' interests during the Civil War, would never have been written had she not been hired by the Bureau of Indian Affairs.[50] Likewise Blair received federal money to compile *The Indian Tribes of the Upper Mississippi Valley and Region of the Great Lakes* (1911). Initially conceived of as a collection of military and political history, Blair read between the lines of the correspondence of military men to put together a study of Indian subsistence strategies, amusements, creation myths, superstitions, and spiritual rituals—an unintended source of social and cultural history.[51]

As compilers and editors of primary source materials, Abel and Blair suddenly made the unofficial history of native groups accessible to other historians and readers at large. Their ability to use government documents was novel, as were their social and cultural readings of them, yet their retrieval of hidden truths had been the goal of women for some time. Contemporary historiographers might reasonably classify these women as professionals, social scientists, and academicians, in distinction to moral reformers, amateurs, or antiquarians of the nineteenth century; but without the interruption of professionalization, a longer tradition of women writers surfaces that includes Child, Jackson, and others committed to Indian reform. Blair's intentions for Indian history in 1911 sounded strikingly similar to Child's in 1829. "I have endeavored to round out and unify the subject as presented in the documents here published," she prefaced in *The Indian Tribes of the Upper Mississippi Valley and Region of the Great Lakes*,

and to place before the reader a more accurate and lifelike view of aboriginal life and character than is usually entertained by readers who know the Indian mainly through newspaper and magazine 'stories,' novels, and 'Wild West shows.' My work on these volumes will be well repaid if those who read them gain a clearer realization that the Indian is in reality very much the same kind of being that his white brother would have been if put in the red man's place; and that we all, whether red, black, brown, yellow, or white, belong to one great human race, the work of one Creator.[52]

By the end of the 1920s, women historians were taking advantage of a growing mound of cultural sources and an increasing penchant for bottom-up perspectives to make their case for Native Americans more convincing. Flora Seymour, a member of the Board of Indian Commissioners, wrote *The Story of the Red Man* (1929) with the expressed intent of finding the native voice: "In the records we catch a glimpse of him here and there. . . . We can only guess how he would have told the story. What would he have said of the Spaniard who came for gold and jewels. . . . Unfortunately he had no written language, no historian to leave to future ages his version of the tale." Conceding these limitations, Seymour compensated for earlier histories written exclusively with official documents, rendering a sensitive account of cultural mutuality and racial admixture between white man and red man on the western frontier. "We like to forget the Indian origin of the American citizen whom we call 'Mexican,' and the undoubted Mexican mixture in the southwestern Indian whom we speak of as 'full-blood,'" she noted. "But the facts of history are not with us in this." Indeed she showed that the Southwest consisted of a racial mix of mestizos, mulattos, "zambos," and "coyotes" interacting to shape the hybrid cultures of the real American West.[53]

Seymour's shifting perspective brought Turner's racial assumptions about westward progress and, as she termed it, "the odd process we call civilization" into high relief. Yet perhaps her most distinctive contribution to western history was her acknowledgment of Indian women as cultural agents on the frontier. Aside from the occasional folkloric reference to Sacajawea, native women formerly received no attention in the narratives of white historians, who described the historical West as a space of white male supremacy, red male savagery, or white feminine civility. Seymour balanced the polarized frontier with depictions of family life, marriage, child rearing, and feminine work and peopled the wilderness with native mothers, daughters, wives, and heroines: Catherine of Detroit, Queen Ester of the French Indian Montour family, the mixed blood Susette La Flesche, and the outspoken activist Sarah Winnemucca, who wrote her own western memoir, *Life among the Paiutes*, in 1883. Seymour did not minimize the physical strength or social influence of these native women, particularly not Queen Ester, who "dashed out the brains of sixteen captives." Nor, remarkably, did she sentimentalize the memory of the white women commonly cast by western writers as demure civilizers of the savage West. She included Eliza Spalding and Narcissa Whitman, wives of government officials, in her portrait of the frontier but as unremarkable figures who fell prey, like Indians, to violence and disease.[54]

Seymour's work unveiled a native culture that women localists had long observed and that a handful of academic regionalists had finally engaged by 1930. Four years later such studies even caused Grace Hebard, the prolific writer of white conquest narratives, to rethink her approach to western history. Already in the late 1910s she had begun to show a timely redirection as a historian, writing about the first white women in Wyoming and revisiting the state's first suffragists. Her more radical revolt from Turner did not occur, however, until she completed three decades of research for a book called *Sacajawea* (1934).[55] To this point male western historians had shown little interest in Sacajawea aside from her secondary role as a guide for the Lewis and Clark expedition. Now Hebard proposed that the Indian woman was essential to the mission and even suggested that her historical anonymity was self-imposed:

> If the objection is raised that no effort was made by Sacajawea to proclaim herself to the world as the guide of the expedition, this is easily answered. Although Sacajawea, as a matter of fact, willingly told her story both to whites and Indians when they asked her about it, she was naturally not inclined to boast of an exploit which, by bringing the first white men into the territory of her people, eventually destroyed their hunting grounds and brought an end to their freedom. In other words, that which might be regarded as worthy of great praise among the whites, would be bitterly condemned by the Indians, and naturally she did not care to court such unpopularity.[56]

Hebard searched for evidence "in the field" to make a case for Sacajawea's historical significance, traveling to various Indian reservations and transcribing testimony from pioneers, soldiers, scouts, and native folklorists as to her identity and previous whereabouts. Like Hurston, she insisted that oral evidence was key, for it gave her special access to an "insider story" unknowable through written documents alone. "Although the Indians have no written history," she prefaced, "their memories are trained to a remarkable degree to retain tribal history; and Indian verbal testimony is, therefore, as much to be relied upon as the writings of any other race." This philosophy was a drastic departure for Hebard, who confessed earlier in her career to being little interested in this "insider story," let alone the use of oral testimony to secure it. She nevertheless anticipated the criticisms of scientific historians and tried to make her oral evidence appear as authoritative as possible. Not just any interpreter, but a government official and his transcriber accompanied her to interviews for the book, and to ensure accuracy two Shoshone witnesses corroborated that the questions had been accurately translated. "No hearsay evidence was accepted," Hebard pledged, "and every effort was made to prevent collusion."[57] Unfortunately her disclaimers failed to win over male critics, many of whom believed the testimonies to be nothing more than gossip designed to render an over-laudatory interpretation of the less than extraordinary native woman.

Western historian Bernard DeVoto harshly concluded that Sacajawea "received what in the United States counts as canonization if not deification," and that "Grace Hebard's *Sacajawea* [wa]s in some degree a product of this mawkishness."[58]

In spite of her critics, Hebard appeared to accept the Native American woman as an integral occupant of the western historical landscape, though she never shed her presumptions about this landscape as masculine terrain. In the end she still largely adhered to the Turnerian formula despite herself; while she described her project as the earnest "search for authentic historical material which would enable her to rescue Sacajawea from the semi-oblivion into which her name had fallen," she largely made the case for her subject's rescue by associating her with men of stature. For this reason the title *Sacajawea* was somewhat of a ruse, for in setting up these associations, Hebard did not even mention the title character until fifty pages into the narrative, and then only briefly as Lewis, Clark, and company referred to her: "the wife of Charbonneau," "our interpreter," "the interpreter's wife," or sometimes just "Janey." In Hebard's mind the story drew to a logical close only after she established "conclusively that the central figure of the volume was in reality the famous guide of the Lewis and Clark expedition, and that she was the mother of Baptiste and the foster mother of Bazil." Although Hebard succeeded in rescuing Sacajawea from anonymity, the native woman only existed in relation to noteworthy men.[59]

Hebard's conversion to Indian-centered history was far from complete, but more successful attempts immediately followed. Just as *Sacajawea* was being published, Angie Debo was putting the finishing touches on the dissertation turned published manuscript *The Rise and Fall of the Choctaw Republic*. Like Seymour's *Story of the Red Man*, Debo's work engaged the native perspective and brought women to the foreground. But she challenged more directly white scholars such as Hebard who unknowingly imposed their own ideas about proper gender roles when evaluating the civility of Indian cultures. According to Debo, white scholars perceived an "unequal division of labor between the sexes, where women performed the drudgery and the men occupied themselves in such pleasurable occupations as hunting and fishing." She countered, explaining that the ways Choctaw men and women divided up tasks in no way reflected the hierarchical structuring of gender or work witnessed in most Western cultures. They assigned completely different value to feminine responsibilities, and women served as helpmeets alongside husbands in battle, a task deemed most honorable in Choctaw society.[60]

Debo revealed Native American gender roles, when examined from other than the white historian's typical point of view, as complementary, not unequal, and here she echoed the conclusions of Alice Fletcher, Elsie Clews Parsons, and so many of anthropology's women pioneers. She also buttressed the claim Beard made that same year that the "better memory" of anthropology shed flattering light on women's past. *The Rise and Fall of the Choctaw Republic* blurred the line between history and anthropology and in fact offered insights into the native state of mind that have since been characterized as "ethnohistory." In later years Debo explained that her decision to study the native lore and mentality occurred after she had prepared for a Greek history course at West Texas College. If scholars studied the myths and legends of the Greeks to understand how they defined themselves as a people, she wondered, then why could the same logic not hold to understand how Native Americans defined themselves? Indeed she raised the question at an isolating moment as she eked out a living at an obscure women's college, but the methodologies for answering it were likely influenced by decades of exposure to the ideas of kindred spirits: women localists, anthropologists, social scientists, and other marginalized colleagues who had cultivated bottom-up approaches.[61]

In 1936 Debo searched for a publisher for her most controversial history yet, *And Still the Waters Run: The Betrayal of the Five Civilized Tribes*. Like histories already written by women, it uncovered damning evidence of the government's deliberate exploitation of Indians and the Dawes commission's misappropriations of lands; but its indictment of prominent Oklahoma families made it a hot potato that publishers were reluctant to handle. Researching the book nearly fifty years after Jackson first combed the Astor Library, Debo was shocked to find that what she uncovered was unknown to historians and the public at large:

> When I was at the University, I had courses in Oklahoma history, but those courses never mentioned the things I was uncovering. . . . I would go up to the basement of the old Interior Building and there were bundles in tied red tape . . . and I would untie those bundles and I would take notes. I began to find out more things and they got worse all the time. . . . All these white people came in with their anti-Indian feelings. I went back home with my notes. Nineteen thirty-six was the worst summer we had. . . . While I was typing [?] were running streams down my face and body. When I would write a chapter I would read it to my mother. She would say nobody will ever publish that book. But I went ahead and wrote it and I submitted *And Still the Waters Run* to the University of Oklahoma Press.[62]

The University of Oklahoma Press initially expressed interest in the manuscript but pulled out of negotiations in fear of the reaction it would incite.

Joseph Brandt eventually agreed to publish it at Princeton in 1940, and while it was met by the overwhelmingly favorable reviews of scholars, it never landed an academic job for Angie Debo.[63]

Released on the eve of U.S. involvement in World War II, *And Still the Waters Run* lamented the decimation of an Indian culture that could, if preserved, serve as a blueprint for peace amidst intensifying global hostilities. Mari Sandoz similarly predicted that the white assault on Native American culture would breed a domestic form of Nazism if it had not already. The simpler communitarianism of her Indian subjects held the key to alleviating fascist oppression abroad and a comparable form of imperialist dominance at home. In 1942 she presented the world of the Oglala leader Crazy Horse in a biography bearing his name. Through the anthropological exploration of social taboos, gender roles, kinship structures, and daily ritual, she made a convincing case for his people's cultural superiority over the bellicose white man. She shed the stereotype of Rousseauian innocence so often attributed to Indians to cast them instead as true "civilizers" of the West. Her measure of civilization was not capitalist profit but participatory democracy, and in Sioux culture she found the purest form of representative government and self-regulation. Just as Debo had looked to the Choctaw (and Frances Densmore to the Chippewa and Margaret Mead to the Samoans), Sandoz looked to the Sioux to commentate on the current state of racial and gender relations in American society, upending Darwinist hierarchies in the process. In effect, she readjusted the white historian's traditional lens, refracting aspects of Sioux culture that best accentuated the injustices of U.S. society by contrast.[64]

Sandoz had a difficult time marketing this socially conscious work as legitimate history, but this was not a new problem. The masculine meanings Turner and company attributed to the West continued to shape perceptions of western history in the popular mind, ironically while such ideas were losing resonance among radical regionalists. Sandoz's biography of her father, *Old Jules* (1935), was like *Crazy Horse* in that it, too, did not match publishers' expectations for western history or literature. By depicting her father as the abusive man that he was and the West as the terrain that bred his hostility, she rendered a "biography of community" that was too honest to perpetuate the myth of the West to which publishers had grown accustomed. Dorothee Kocks rightly observes that *Old Jules*, like *Crazy Horse*, threatened the very definitions of western history by making "ludicrous the idea of democracy for which his region so often was made to stand." Frustrated by their inability to classify this biography, publishers threw up their hands in resignation; one even suggested that Sandoz fictionalize the account before Little, Brown finally printed it as written in 1935.[65]

Sandoz had a contentious relationship with publishers and fared even worse with academics. Scholars of history resented her novelistic style, and she herself admitted that portions of *Old Jules* and *Crazy Horse* were imagined figments of what she called "felt history." Biographer Helen Stauffer claims that Sandoz had heard the oral tales of Native Americans from such a young age that she had virtually absorbed them subconsciously. Thus she often invented dialogue for her historical characters, not to do injustice to the facts, which she knew better than most, but to invoke a more vivid portrait that would stir the modern reader into an active relationship with the past. Like Frances Victor and Grace Hebard, Sandoz relied on the methods of professional historians but also on visits to the places she wrote about to render the most accurate accounts of people and events. She wrote *The Battle of Little Bighorn* (1966) after weeks of camping out at the site of the contest, for only then could she feel as though she "had stalked very close to the spirit of this fierce, handsome, brown-haired war chief" named Crazy Horse. Unfortunately she never saw this final history in print. It was published posthumously, and even then the pains Sandoz took to collect evidence did not dislodge the piece from the ambiguous place critics designated between categories of history and belle lettres.[66]

In the effort to write western history on her own terms, Sandoz walked a path that many women writers had traveled already, though she stopped short of reaching total obscurity. Her experience in the end was eerily close to Angie Debo's; both women reinterpreted the western past from the margins of the historical establishment and suffered professionally for their questioning of the Turnerian paradigm, even though male scholars were beginning to do the same. Aside from a few in tribal schools and libraries, Oklahoma educators ostracized Debo for writing false history, while publishers accused Sandoz of not writing history at all. Their depictions of the historical West as dystopia defied the academic consensus view of the frontier as a site of democratic progress. Yet as bold as their assertions were, they took solace in the knowledge that they drew their evidence from a most reliable source: in this case the well of personal memory. Their girlhood experiences belied the myth that democracy and prosperity grew out of westward expansion. As children both women endured bouts of hunger and hard physical labor; in a West of supposed opportunity, neither could afford to maintain regular attendance in school and suffered physical and emotional toil to keep their families intact. Sandoz endured range wars between cattlemen and homesteaders, paternal beatings, and even blindness from overexposure to blizzard conditions on the Nebraska plains. Her questioning of the mythical West in the end grew out of the privileged perspective of nonprivilege. The West as she knew it was not a space of civilized progress but a site of social and economic politics that designated her family as immigrant outsiders and Native Americans as obstacles to white aspirations.[67]

Sandoz and Debo may have resented their reception in the historical establishment, yet remarkably both understood their professional struggles as consequences of their personal pasts and perspectives of power. In 1940 Sandoz reflected on her rough-and-tumble, hand-to-mouth childhood on the western plains, concluding in the end that it brought greater moral purpose to her writing of history: "The underprivileged child, if he becomes a writer, is interested in social justice and in the destruction of discrimination between economic levels, between nationalist levels, between color levels, and so on." Debo had already come to similar conclusions in graduate school, when she took mentor Edward Everett Dale to task for his unquestioning acceptance of the Turnerian paradigm. "His philosophy may be summed up in one word," she quipped, "*Progress.*" On the other hand, she could hardly blame him for his interpretation of the western past; he took on "the viewpoint of the American pioneer" because he was the legendary figure nearly personified. A former range rider and Oklahoma homesteader, Dale embodied a western "Horatio Alger hero" in a life that, unlike Debo's, read "like an American saga." He had encouraged Debo to explore Native American history and even to pursue the suspicions that became the damning research for *And Still the Waters Run*, yet he never fully relinquished his glorified view of the West as a hotbed of democracy, heroism, and unwavering progress.[68]

In the meantime his student suffered personal and professional backlashes, a fate that she eventually accepted as the price for telling the truth. Once she discovered it, she insisted that she "had the same obligation to correct abuses as any other citizen." Sandoz, too, declared that she had "a stern obligation to avoid any word or implication that might encourage human injustice."[69] Their common sentiments may have isolated them from professional historians at the time, but with broader perspective they appear kindred spirits to a longer line of women historians that persisted even after Debo published *And Still the Waters Run*. Historian Juanita Brooks, for instance, faced religious expulsion for exposing the Mormon Church's role in the Mountain Meadows Massacre of 1857. A devout Mormon who grew up near Salt Lake City, she published her findings despite warnings of repercussions from family and friends. Indeed Brooks worried that she would be excommunicated from the church much the same way Fawn Brodie had been for writing the defamatory biography of Mormon leader Joseph Smith, *No Man Knows My History* (1945). On the other hand, her evidence of the abuses against Native Americans was too irrefutable to ignore. Thus just as Debo searched for a willing publisher for *And Still the Waters Run*, Brooks waited years before Stanford University Press published *The Mountain Meadows Massacre* in 1950. To no surprise she was denounced a "dissenter" by the Mormon Church, yet like Brodie, Sandoz, and Debo, she chose personal ostracism to silence. "Nothing but the truth is good enough for the Church to which I belong," she justified. "God does not expect me to lie in his name."[70]

After brief acclaim as award-winning writers, Sandoz (recipient of the literary prize of the *Atlantic Monthly*) and Debo (recipient of the Dunning Prize of the AHA) would spend the better part of their forties and later appealing to publishers to print their works, almost always to no avail. Single women with no other source of support, both suffered deep economic hardship as a result. Debo was reacquainted with the "starving times" of her childhood, while the divorced Sandoz claimed to get so used to being hungry that she could predict when collapses would come. Honest to the point of controversy—and hunger—these women remembered the West in ways the historical establishment was not yet ready to accept. Their stories were not designed to celebrate the white man's conquering of the West but to admonish his ruthless decimation of Native American culture. They became the translators for voices previously unheard by chroniclers of the West, in this sense occupying the role of intercultural broker for Native Americans but also for themselves as women. Their position on the geographic fringes of the national landscape and the professional fringes of the historical establishment provided them with a special perspective that cast them off from the western canon and rooted them in a distinctive tradition of women's western history.[71]

Chapter 4
African American Woman's Historical Consciousness

In the Progressive Era, Debo, Abbott, Beard, and dozens of women in and outside the academy explored the past struggles of Native Americans, immigrants, and workingwomen and found that the margins—physical and professional—could be a privileged place from which to view the past. From here women acquired perspectives of power to which professional men were too close to gain much perspective at all. This being the case for white women, African American women were even better situated to lend original historical insight. The institutional chauvinism of the academy inhibited the work and promotion of all women historians, but its coupling with scientific racism devastated the prospect of historical careers for women of color, who did not appear on the academic scene until the 1940s. Nonetheless, their compounded experience of race and gender became the impetus for experimenting with an expansive arsenal of sources and methods to recover the unexplored subjectivity of the African American woman in history.

The physical and professional margins became spaces of perspective for Debo and Sandoz, as did the social margins for Zora Neale Hurston, a woman of color who not only thrived from the peripheries of academic social science but also turned black folk into her cultural vantage point for social critique. Her formal study of culture started when Barnard founder Annie Meyer offered her a scholarship to become the only black student at the college. Hurston began collecting folklore under the auspices of the anthropology department in 1927, when most social scientists were still reluctant to consider such research legitimate scholarship. No American university had yet established a folklore department; Howard Odum and Guy Johnson studied Negro songs in the South, but only Hurston commentated on them as an inside informant who understood their subtle meanings to blacks and assimilated the behavioral processes that produced them. White Mississippian Newbell Niles Puckett masqueraded as a hoo-doo doctor to write *Folk Beliefs of the Southern Negro* (1926), only to pathologize the black personality in his final assessments. Hurston, by contrast, was connected to her subject emotionally and intellectually and observed without aesthetic superiority or self-consciousness. "Her racially different folk culture was tolerated by whites as a primitive mode of apprehending experience," writes biographer Robert Hemenway, "yet she knew there was nothing primitive about it. . . . She had known both written and oral traditions, had participated in American civilization at the levels of both 'high' and 'low' culture, and her commitment to folklore as a field of study was an inchoate challenge to the cultural imperialism that could declare these vertical judgments."[1]

Carla Peterson, a scholar of nineteenth-century African American women writers, believes that the social margins did indeed become "a space that they could call home"—where "the incarcerated could escape and perhaps even return, the gaze of their wardens; undo the dominant culture's definitions of such binary oppositions as order/disorder, normal/abnormal, harmless/dangerous; break down those boundaries separating the one from the Other." At the same time, however, she cautions us not to overestimate the perspective liminality provided black women; while their distance from the core of the historical establishment was liberating in one sense, in another it prevented most from articulating how their historical plight continued to haunt them in the present. The margins have not only been " 'pure' spaces of 'radical openness and possibility,' " she explains, but "sites of repression and sites of resistance . . . often uncomfortable places . . . sources of horrifying pain, generators of unspeakable terrors." In this study of African American women historians two and three generations later, we, too, view this social space as both empowering and stifling. It is because of this dual functionality that the margins interest us as complex sites of discursive production.[2]

Because the women discussed here had less access to academic credentials or historical authority than white women, some set out with a new strategy for articulating their past struggles, constructing social, cultural, and folk history as a means of empowerment. This was possible only when they viewed their own hidden legacies as distinct from those of African American men or white women, and this did not happen at once. In some respects twentieth-century clubwomen turned historians ignored the valuable lessons of the women who preceded them—Sojourner Truth and Frances Ellen Watkins Harper, for instance—who had already made a case for the historical distinctiveness of African American women through written and nonwritten forms other than formal history. In the years of Reconstruction they participated in woman's rights and political debates, but unlike most organized feminists and race men, they made pleas for all humanity regardless of sex, race, class, or political affiliation—a sign that they understood that their complex burdens defied historical generality. Despite these astute observations of nineteenth-century women, most African American writers and commemorators in the twentieth century revised history as part of a project of "race uplift" that they shared with men and that often emulated the strategies of white women. Anna Cooper proved to be an exception, for she argued in the 1890s that white and male historians buttressed their own social standing through histories that reduced black women to second-class citizens, second-class African Americans, and even second-class females. It would take some time before her understanding of historical uniqueness was shared once again by women who had the means to articulate, publish, and disseminate black women's history in the twentieth century.[3]

Reconstructing Race Memory and Regendering the Race Historian, 1880–1920s

The first uses of written history by African American men and women as a method of race uplift were intermittent, which is understandable given their limited opportunities to read, write, or finance the distribution of printed texts.[4] Nonetheless, in the nineteenth century they formed a handful of literary and historical societies, reading rooms, lyceums, and small libraries with the goal of increasing literacy and historical knowledge of the race. The Gilbert Lyceum of Philadelphia, for example, admitted both men and women as early as 1841. Other groups, such as the Female Literary Societies of Philadelphia (1831), New York (1836), Rochester (1833), and Buffalo (1837); the Minerva Literary Association in Philadelphia (1834); and the Ohio Ladies Education Society (1840s), consisted strictly of black women. Like the middle-class literary organizations of white women, these associations defined a historical canon for the "respectable" man or woman of the race through prescriptions of proper subject material.[5]

Fifty years later the Boston Society for the Collection of Negro Folklore and the American Negro Historical Society (ANHS) in Philadelphia grew out of an increasingly urgent sense that the preservation of the African American past was essential for waging social battles in the present. Its members were prominent middle-class blacks who collected "relics, literature and historical facts relative to the Negro race."[6] Women were indispensable rank-and-file members of the ANHS and similar organizations. The Washington-based Bethel Literary and Historical Association (1881), for example, maintained women on its executive board and as organizers, fund-raisers, and public lecturers. Bethel provided a venue for prominent race men such as Frederick Douglass to promote race uplift, but club-women Fannie Jackson Coppin and Hallie Brown also spoke on the African American in history. In 1900 Ella Elbert even broached the subject of women's exploitation in the field of domestic service to an audience at the Metropolitan A.M.E. Church. By 1892 the Bethel membership had elected club leader Mary Church Terrell president of the organization, a sign that female members had achieved some parity in the Reconstruction years of race reform.[7]

At this juncture race workers were not yet defining racial progress in Afrocentric terms—in history texts or elsewhere. Until the Harlem Renaissance of the 1910s and 1920s, most race historians employed a strategy one can loosely describe as emulation, modeling their narratives on those of white historians to legitimate their claims to social equality. Much of this early history was compensatory in tone, at least to the modern sensibility. Black figures were often shaped into an Anglo mold and inserted into familiar patriotic accounts as worthy historical heroes. Nevertheless, Peterson warns that these texts, while seemingly emulative, "cannot be dismissed as a mere aping of the dominant discourse . . . [or] simply a version of Foucauldian 'counterdiscourse.'" A complex discursive hybridity occurred; the race narrative of the Reconstruction years "borrow[ed] the vocabulary and categories of the dominant discourse," but it also "disrupted it and 'challenged its boundaries,'" she insists, to perform what Henry Louis Gates has described as a "black double-voicedness."[8] Peterson is not referring to late nineteenth-century race histories exclusively, but certainly they, too, were strategically appropriative and radical in their ability to take from familiar narratives to undermine the racial status quo. Early works such as William C. Nell's *Colored Patriots of the American Revolution* (1855) and James Guthrie's *Campfires of the Afro-American; or, the colored man as a patriot, soldier, sailor, and hero, in the cause of free America* (1899) were demonstrative in this respect.[9]

By the twentieth century the first literate, middle-class African American women writers followed suit with similar patriotic tropes and compensatory storylines. Mary Curtis's *The Black Soldier: The Colored Boys of the United States Army* (1915) and Laura Wilkes's *Missing Pages in American History, Revealing the Services of Negroes in the Early Wars in the United States of America* (1919) were typical in their seemingly emulative function.[10] They also remind us that the goal of race uplift through the lionization of past figures was one that middle-class men and women shared going into the twentieth century. However, a slightly different dynamic between male and female race workers started to take shape in the 1890s, as the latter were demoted to secondary roles as historians and commemorators. Learned men such as Alain Locke and W. E. B. Du Bois, first-generation race scholars, adhered to the mantra of academic scientism and its gendered subtext; they validated their status as intellectuals by distancing themselves from women race workers who lacked formal academic credentials. Like the first generation of white social scientists who separated themselves from women social workers, these men created figurative and literal divides between thinkers and doers, trained and untrained, and professional and amateur of the race, setting themselves apart from women as interpreters of history and eventually as historical agents.

The gendered politics of professionalization were at work once again, only this time in the ranks of men and women who would launch the New Negro History Movement later in the twentieth century. Certainly this was the case in the ANHS, much to the frustration of its women members. Clubwomen Gertrude Mossell, Fannie Jackson Coppin, and Frances Ellen Watkins Harper belonged to this elite society, but their right of entry had not come easily. The granting of membership status to women had been unresolved until Harper broached the subject at an Emancipation Proclamation celebration in 1898. By 1903 women had won the right to be members, though no more than seven (about one-eighth of the total membership) at once.[11] Male members soon touted themselves as the historical experts and acquisitions specialists of the organization, and women as their less learned brigade of community organizers and collection custodians. Jacob White and his wife were indicative of this new dynamic; as secretary of many Philadelphia race organizations, he kept a massive collection of organizational minutes, programs, and memorabilia, while she quietly compiled these records behind the scenes into an organized collection for the ANHS. For the fifteen years after the society disbanded, the wife of founding member Matthew Anderson saw to the maintenance of formerly donated materials. Similarly the widow of William Still maintained his Underground Railroad Collection after his death and deposited it in a respected archive. These wives occupied necessary roles as collection custodians, and yet their negligible status in the ANHS is verified by the fact that their first names never appeared in the organizational records.[12]

Women's struggle for acceptance in the ANHS reflected a growing penchant for formal training and financial independence among the membership. A similar differentiation between men and women occurred not only in Philadelphia but also in Washington after Frederick Douglass's death in 1895. Race workers organized a memorial committee to plan proper honors for the activist, transforming him into a symbol of the best in African American manhood. There were memorials and school closings across the city, and soon commemorators in other cities followed suit. Organizations such as the Pen and Pencil Club, the Liberal Culture Society of Chicago, the Republican League, and the Douglass Commemorative Society initiated new traditions of banquets, expositions, and ceremonies in loving memory. Race workers in his hometown of Rochester, New York, erected a monument and commissioned a commemorative biography of the local legend. Almost immediately Douglass had become the symbol of race uplift for all African Americans seeking racial justice and social betterment.[13]

The fact that Douglass was held up as the preeminent historical role model for African American boys and girls alike suggests that "uplift" was initially a rallying cry not particular to sex but to class, for it characterized the larger race project taken on by nearly all middle-class African Americans by 1900. Nonetheless, men and women would come to remember him through different means, due in no small part to the widening gap between African American men and women in political, economic, and professional terms. These gender schisms could be seen, for example, in the homage paid Douglass by husband and wife Nathan and Gertrude Mossell. One of the first successful African American physicians in the country, Nathan Mossell relied on his newfound wealth and reputation as a medical professional to open the Frederick Douglass Memorial Hospital in 1895. Gertrude Mossell, on the other hand, was a dutiful mother, clubwoman, and local educator who disseminated information about Douglass through the local institutions where she volunteered and served as head of the Douglass Memorial Hospital Women's Auxiliary.[14]

Prominent race men, unlike their wives, controlled the financial resources to erect buildings, publish bibliographies, and commemorate Douglass in conspicuous ways that infiltrated public spaces occupied by blacks and whites alike. In 1907, for example, Daniel Murray, the first professional African American archivist at the Library of Congress, was the likely force behind a congressional bibliography of Douglass's written works. His was followed by a bibliography compiled by the wealthy bibliophile Arthur Schomburg, whose Douglass memorabilia included over 179 published writings, speeches, and biographies by and about the legendary man.[15] In stark contrast to these gestures of wealthy men, women race reformers generally promoted Douglass's memory through a hands-on approach, writing in local newspapers and planning memorials in the schools, churches, and institutions that served the African American community directly. Terrell, the first president of the National Association of Colored Women (NACW), initiated these activities in 1897 when she introduced a resolution to the District of Columbia school board to formalize Douglass Day in the public schools. Washington schoolteacher Emma

Merritt pushed Terrell's cause, publishing articles in the *Voice of the Negro* that made pleas to recognize Douglass's birthday as a national holiday. Fellow schoolteacher Laura Wilkes, meanwhile, secured the funds to print and reprint her children's book, *The Story of Frederick Douglass*, in 1899. Like so many historical biographies by white women at the turn of the century, hers was a moralistic piece composed to inspire children to virtuous citizenship. Responsible citizens were good for the country, she argued, but even better for the race. As a woman educator this message was hers to convey.[16]

African American clubwomen embraced the work of commemoration as mothers and educators, recognizing that the white women of the DAR and the SCD had already earned much cultural authority doing the same. The NACW seized the opportunity to become sole custodian of Douglass's Cedar Hill estate in 1916 when male executors of the Frederick Douglass Memorial Home Association (FDMHA) expressed to NACW president Mary Talbert that they were no longer willing to raise funds to maintain the property. Talbert turned over a check for half of the outstanding mortgage and interest, hoping that the NACW's preservation of Cedar Hill would demonstrate black women's ability to contribute to national progress, but more urgently to the Negro race.[17] In 1917 the *Crisis* spread the word that the NACW urged "all patriotic, race-loving Negroes to . . . save and restore the home in the manner that the white women saved the home of George Washington." "We realize that today is the psychological moment for us as women to show our true worth," Talbert wrote, "and prove that the Negro woman of today measures up to those strong, sainted women of our race who passed through the fire of slavery and its galling remembrances."[18]

Nannie Burroughs, Mary McLeod Bethune, Hallie Brown, Maggie Walker, and other prominent club leaders volunteered for the first Cedar Hill subcommittees of the NACW, only to discover that the project would require more time and money than initially estimated. The cost of the complete restoration of the home was $15,000, and unlike most of the men formerly on the FDMHA board of trustees, NACW women had few connections to corporate sponsors or financial resources of their own. They nonetheless began doing what they knew best, mobilizing on the grassroots level through fund-raisers and educational programs at schools, clubs, and churches throughout the District of Columbia environs.[19] Financial reports indicate that their local campaigns were successful; from improvements of the roof, window screens, and weather-beaten fixtures to beautification of the grounds and roads leading to the home, the women spared no expense in renovating Cedar Hill to reflect the definitive progress of the Negro—but also their own progress as effective workers for the race. Their efforts suggest that African American clubwomen felt they had much to prove and authority to redeem, and indeed race men in the District of Columbia took notice, seeking them out to promote the grassroots projects of the New Negro History Movement later in the 1920s.[20]

The Douglass commemorations confirm that twentieth-century clubwomen emulated white women as writers, teachers, and popularizers of patriotic history to win social legitimacy for the race. Some New England women even made similar claims to the American colonial legacy, joining black men to establish the Society of the Descendants of Early New England Negroes. Like the Daughters and Dames, the Descendants traced their bloodlines to patriots who lived before 1800 and provided documented proof of the fact. Chapter rolls indicate that women occupied executive positions in the society and were genealogists as meticulous as white women in the DAR or SCD. Indeed, they hoped their efforts would earn them a respected place in national memory. Unfortunately they did little to bring about a recasting of black men or women as cultural outsiders in the national record, as white historians continued to write racially exclusive accounts of the American past.[21]

Race women still oddly made use of white models for race uplift, despite the conflicting proclivities of white historians. Terrell, for example, planned NACW commemorations of white women who embodied the maternal benevolence she idealized for black womanhood. In 1906 her figure of choice was the fallen Susan B. Anthony: "There are so many recorded, indisputable facts which show the incredible amount of work she performed in behalf of my oppressed race as well as her own handicapped sex," she asserted on the pages of the *Voice of the Negro*, imposing upon her readership a virtual amnesia over the last forty years of Anthony's activist career. After 1869 Anthony formally broke with Douglass and race sympathizers in the Republican Party to dedicate herself full time to the suffrage activities of white women. Nevertheless, Anthony's inaction regarding the racist policies of the organized suffrage movement was of no interest to Terrell, who used her memory for emulative purposes anyway. For that matter, antislavery author Harriet Beecher Stowe proved equally functional. In 1911 Terrell organized a series of activities in honor of the white woman's centennial birthday and even raised funds to establish a fellowship for African American girls in her name.[22]

That Terrell commemorated white women to inspire African American girls may appear misdirected, but she feared that nineteenth-century black women, most of whom were victims of slavery and a distorted historical record, were not yet inspiring themselves. This is not because women slaves did not previously try to inspire; several had shown interest in reshaping their personal stories for public consumption even as slavery persisted as an institution, and with the help of literate sponsors they published accounts of their experiences in bondage. Questions of authorship make them flawed sources, but they were sincere attempts to set forth the black woman's experience as distinct from that of white women and black men.[23] Harriet Jacobs, most notably, offered restrained glimpses of the sexual predation she endured as a female slave. Yet by the turn of the century middle-class women like Terrell wanted to disassociate from painful slave narratives such as Jacobs's. The sexual stereotypes African American women still encountered were residual distortions of black women's victimization under slavery. With an eye toward achieving respectability, Terrell would not be alone in constructing accounts of the past that stripped African American womanhood of the sexuality Truth, Jacobs, and others revealed and defended as they had fought to establish their personhood in the nineteenth century.[24]

African American clubwomen followed the lead of white women once again in the twentieth century, writing histories that presented figures as upstanding matriarchs devoid of sexuality. They observed that various historical forms—particularly the war memoir and the club movement history—had already served white women well as mediums that chronicled their benevolent deeds and justified the extension of their moral influence in the public sphere. Mary Livermore and Annie Wittenmyer, for example, earned recognition for themselves and all white benevolence workers with their memoirs of Civil War nursing (*My Story of the War* [1887] and *Under the Guns: A Woman's Reminiscence of the Civil War* [1895]). As narratives of maternal self-sacrifice they garnered public support that allowed both women to further their reform careers in temperance and woman suffrage and chronicle their personal and collective accomplishments yet again in *History of the Woman's Temperance Crusade* (1878) and *The Story of My Life* (1897).[25] African American women were officially restricted from war nursing, yet several served anyway and historicized their experiences in search of the same high regard. Susan King Taylor's *Reminiscences of My Life in Camp* (1902) brought perspective to the struggles of African American Civil War soldiers, but also to African American women's pedagogical roles before and after the war. In *Two Colored Women with the Expeditionary Forces* (1920), Addie Hunton and Kathryn Johnson recalled the kinder treatment they received from the French during World War I than from their own white countrymen and -women. Unlike the war histories of race historians in the nineteenth century, their account revealed both war front and home front as raced as well as gendered. These patriotic women gave of themselves despite the bigotry of white military officials and the hostile reactions to their conducting of benevolent work deemed appropriate for white women only.[26]

These war memoirs certainly shed new light on white and masculine military history, and soon African American women sought recognition on the domestic front, publishing official histories of their clubs and social movements after 1900. Jennie Croly had already provided an archetype of clubwomen's history by documenting the founding of the first white women's literary clubs in *Sorosis: Its Origins and History* (1886) and *History of the Woman's Club Movement in America* (1898).[27] African American women followed suit with chronicles such as *A History of the Club Movement among the Colored Women of the United States of America* (1902) and Elizabeth Davis's ambitious *Lifting as They Climb* (1933). These accounts resembled white institutional histories in form, style, and tone and emphasized black club leaders' status as moral, accomplished reformers, just as white histories had extolled the virtues of white women, with much success.[28]

Like the club movement history or the war memoir, the collective biography was another form that historians—both black and white, male and female—found effective for raising historical consciousness by the turn of the century. Male authors discovered that these group composites could highlight race achievement as no history had done before, and female writers quickly added to this genre as authors of religious race history. Susan Shorter, for example, highlighted the roles of women in organized religion in *Heroines of African Methodism* (1891). That the church offered black women their first opportunities to create historical discourse and to celebrate female figures was not coincidental, for the same held true for white women earlier in the nineteenth century when they first sought entry into realms of public activity.[29]

A few men saw the value in accompanying volumes about great Negro men with virtuous Negro women. Lawson A. Scruggs and Alphus Majors contributed to this corpus of biographies with *Women of Distinction* (1893) and *Noted Negro Women* (1893), as did Benjamin Brawley with *Women of Achievement* (1919) under the auspices of the Woman's American Baptist Home Mission Society.[30] Like Sarah Bolton, Frances Willard, and Mary Livermore, compilers of white women's biographies, Majors intended his *Noted Negro Women* to "give inspiration to the girls of present and future generations" and to serve as a manual of proper womanly behavior. Many of the figures he highlighted were club and temperance workers such as Josephine Silone Yates, a "pious," "self-sacrificing," "sainted" mother and wife. He similarly praised Sarah Dudley, a Christian temperance advocate and foreign missionary; Phillis Wheatley, an exemplar of "perfect docility"; and Zelia Page, a noble "friend of the poor." Included among his cast was

African queen Anna Zinga, notable less for her cultural roots than her conversion to European Christianity. Like Mary Terrell, Majors affirmed the accomplishments of his women worthies by comparing them to white women of renown, even heralding entertainer Flora Batson as "the colored Jenny Lind."[31]

Terrell's sentiments were not different from those of other race historians who looked to white models of heroism and womanhood for inspiration, but the strategy was hardly uniform. Only one year after Majors published his book, Philadelphia clubwoman Gertrude Mossell departed from this well-rehearsed, emulative approach to compile *The Work of the Afro-American Woman*. Also a collection of biographies, it expanded the historical view of feminine realms of activity beyond the church and home into sectors of productive labor and proto-professional activity. Mossell paid homage to the white Victorian ideal, yet she proposed that the black woman's ability to adhere to feminine duties despite the most adverse historical conditions made her the better exemplar of noble womanhood. Perhaps she had Majors in mind when she graciously, though perhaps disingenuously, conceded that "the men of the race, in most instances, have been generous, doing all in their power to allow women of the race to rise with them." Nonetheless, she was clear in wanting to offer a historical corrective. Race historians must give the labors of the African American woman new attention, she explained, just as Annie Meyer had "garner[ed] up the grain from the harvest field of labor of our Anglo-American sisters" three years earlier in *Woman's Work in America*. The African American woman soldier, physician, missionary, and artist were, as Mossell portrayed them, participants in the "civilization" and "uplift" of the race. Unlike Terrell, Mossell did not forget the women authors of slave narratives in the nineteenth century. Her bibliography cited their works as historical sources alongside those of social scientists.[32]

Mossell's consciousness of women's historical legacy as distinct and noteworthy was rare but not entirely unprecedented by 1894. Like Sojourner Truth and others earlier in the nineteenth century, Anna Cooper formally had acknowledged the differing pasts of African American men and women just two years before Mossell published her history of women's work. A learned scholar and Washington high school teacher, Cooper had long pondered the problem of women in race history from a pedagogical perspective. When looking back into the African American past, she argued, one could detect

> a real and special influence of woman. An influence subtle and often involuntary, an influence so infinitely interwoven in, so intricately inter-

penetrated by the masculine influence of the time that it is often difficult to extricate the delicate meshes and analyze and identify the closely clinging fibers. And yet without this influence—so long as woman sat with bandaged eyes and manacled hands, fast bound in the clamps of ignorance and inaction, the world of thought moved in its orbit like revolutions of the moon; with one face, the man's face always out, so that the spectator could not distinguish whether it is the prevalence or sphere.

"Religion, science, art, economics, have all needed the feminine flavor," she continued, "and literature, the expression of what is permanent and best in all of these, may be guarded at any time to measure the strength of the feminine ingredient."[33]

It is remarkable how closely Cooper's ideas anticipated Lucy Salmon's in 1900 but especially Mary Beard's in the 1930s. Conceivably her compounded burden of race and gender caused her to be contemplative of the historical legacy of black women and the harmful effects of masculine history much earlier. Her groundbreaking *Voice from the South* (1892) lent a historical voice to African American women that was separate and distinct. She reasoned that just as race intellectuals did not expect white historians to have the perspective to "put themselves in the dark man's place, neither should the dark man be wholly expected fully and adequately to reproduce the exact Voice of the Black Woman." This task she assigned to the black woman herself as part of her larger objective of "re-training the race." Any attempts to teach or lift up African Americans would be inadequate, she insisted, until they all acquired an appreciation for the cultural and historical worth of black women.[34]

A Voice from the South raised new questions about women's role in race memory, many of which women revisited in the July 1904 edition of the *Voice of the Negro*. Prominent club leaders, including Terrell, submitted pieces to this issue that assessed the social standing of the African American woman since the Civil War.[35] Several cast doubt on what was by now a well-rehearsed metanarrative of race progress, concluding that the trajectories of men and women were so uneven that the history of the race was really two separate stories with very different outcomes. Men and women did not enjoy the same social status past or present, several pointed out, in large part because they had vastly different historical crosses to bear. In "Not Color But Character," Nannie Burroughs argued, in essence, that black men were as guilty as white men for perpetuating the racialized ideology of "noble womanhood" over time; they, too, raised white women up as ideals of femininity at the black woman's expense. "White men offer more protection to their prostitutes than many black men offer to their best women," Burroughs lamented, attributing this in no small part to the black man's historical amnesia when it came to the trials and tribulations of black women. Like Burroughs, Addie Hunton implicated distortions of historical memory for the black woman's current social and economic struggles in "Negro Womanhood Defended." Sexual violence inflicted on the black woman in the past led to her continued stigmatization in the present, she explained. If history were set right, her "double burden of excessive maternal care and physical toil" would be seen anew as obstacles overcome that made her "more chastened and purified," not depraved or hypersexed as whites often presupposed.[36]

Regrettably, the contributors to the *Voice of the Negro* called for a more thorough investigation of black women's history at a time when the academy offered scholars, white or black, no incentive to give the subject attention. In 1904 scientific racism was pervasive in American colleges and history departments; few professional practitioners were African American or produced scholarship that portrayed race relations in a sympathetic light. Even worse, colleges and universities across the country, though particularly in the South, instituted openly racist policies that encouraged the production of Anglo-Saxonist scholarship and denied students of color access to archival collections for research. Few works by African Americans found their way into mainstream historical journals or were accepted at historical conferences. With the exception of W. E. B. Du Bois, it would be years before African American scholars published articles in the *AHR*.[37] African American men steadily received more degrees in the social sciences in the twentieth century, but relative to white men even their numbers were insignificant: Only fourteen had earned doctorate degrees in history or the history of education by 1940. Although more African American women than men entered undergraduate programs by the 1920s, no woman earned a Ph.D. in history in these years. This is not altogether surprising considering that the majority of white women who received Ph.D.'s in history were partly or fully educated at women's colleges and that almost all African American women college graduates were relegated to coeducational institutions.[38]

History departments did not welcome African American women, but African American women also proved unreceptive to careers in history. Lucy Diggs Slowe, dean of women at Howard University in the 1920s and 1930s, observed that her students were intensely interested in history as undergraduates but that this tapered off in their graduate years. In 1931 well over one-third of her undergraduate students took history courses, more than double the number taking sociology and five times more than the number taking economics. Although several women went on to write master's theses in history, none made history a career, electing instead to enter social science fields more conducive to community reform.[39] Like other Howard undergraduates, Sadie Mossell (Alexander) majored in history but shifted focus as a graduate student at the University of Pennsylvania. In 1922 historian Carter Woodson wrote dean Herman Ames asking if Mossell would be interested in conducting research for the Association for the Study of Negro Life and History (ASNLH). Ames confirmed that Mossell had "an excellent foundation in both Modern European and American History" and that he "kn[e]w of no one to recommend better fitted for the position." Yet by this time Mossell had long withdrawn from history to earn her Ph.D. in economics. The historical field simply did not appeal to this educated woman of color, who, in her rare position, thought her energies more productively spent in a field with activist potential for the race.[40]

Finding Women's Distinctive Place in the History of the Renaissance

Of course, the absence of African American women in academic history departments never stopped them from investigating race history on their own as independent researchers. Delilah Beasley, for one, insisted that she analyzed archival material with the same rigor for her *Negro Trail Blazers of California* as did credentialed scholars, even if critics failed to agree. A woman more successful in this regard was Oklahoma schoolteacher Drusilla Houston, who drew from early scientific studies of primitive cultures to write one of the first race histories with an *originist* or Pan-African interpretation. Poring over library books on the Egyptian, Arab, and Indian worlds in search of civility among nonwhite peoples in the distant past, her *Wonderful Ethiopians of the Ancient Cushite Empire* (1926) argued that Africans, not white Europeans, were the true originators of civilized culture.[41] Her ideas intrigued race scholars insofar as they removed the focus from the white man in history and cast doubt on his version of the formation of racial hierarchies over time. As early as 1904, ANHS president Robert Adger had complained that white historians were guilty not only of ignoring the Negro in history but also of intentionally distorting his memory. Houston's account offered a corrective, but a belated one, for she made assumptions that African American intellectuals such as Adger had come to question by the time her book appeared in 1926. Although she offered a fresh perspective on the black man's historical legacy, she did not evaluate his accomplishments according to criteria of his own making, using the same definition of civilization as white historians to define racial progress.[42]

In this important sense her conclusions brought little relief to African American bibliophiles who by the 1910s and 1920s looked to evaluate race history on their own terms. Book collector Arthur Schomburg, for instance, suggested that the best way to start recasting race history was to gather historical and literary works written by authors of African descent and to make them available to researchers who would reassess race accomplishment according to Negroes themselves. Schomburg was not a professionally trained historian, but like most in his bibliophile circles he was partial to the empirical standards that had come to define history as a scientific discipline in the academy. "The blatant Caucasian racialist with his theories and assumptions of race superiority and dominance has in turn bred his Ethiopian counterpart," he asserted, "—the rash and rabid amateur who has glibly tried to prove half the world's geniuses to have been Negroes and to trace the pedigree of nineteenth-century Americans from the Queen of Sheba." These sentiments were undoubtedly directed at historians like Houston who, armed with library cards and vivid imaginations, had come to create a compensatory race history not wholly unlike accounts that had come before it. He urged instead that historians apply the rigorous methodology of trained scholars to replace "the vagaries of rhetoric and propaganda" with a "systematic and scientific" approach to fact-finding in the past.[43]

Schomburg articulated his thoughts about race history during an intense period of cultural production known as the Harlem Renaissance, when race intellectuals, historians included, diverted their attention from the improvement ideology of race workers to an authentic Negro folk culture on its own terms. The purpose of race history was no longer to ease the black man's assimilation into white culture, but to make him feel at ease with, even empowered by, his own cultural past. Reproduced in Alain Locke's *The New Negro* (1925), Schomburg's essay "The Negro Digs up His Past" made the first plea to historians expressly for new scholarship: "The American Negro must remake his past in order to make his future," he urged. "Though it is orthodox to think of America as the one country where it is unnecessary to have a past, what is a luxury for the nation as a whole becomes a prime social necessity for the Negro. For him, a group tradition must supply compensation for persecution, and pride of race the antidote for prejudice." Schomburg explained that the American identity shaped in white history relied on the exclusion of the black experience for definition. Describing the compensatory history of the nineteenth century as "over-corrective" and the historical biographies of "eminent" race men as "over-laudatory," he proposed that historians relinquish Caucasian models of individual heroism in which "Negroes of attainment and genius" are "unfairly disassociated from the group," advocating instead a focus on the collective heritage of Negroes over time and national boundaries.[44]

Equipped with university training and a new philosophy toward history, collectors in the ANHS teamed up with Schomburg and merged with a small but growing number of academic social scientists to create a circuit of collecting clubs and intellectual societies that thrived through the Harlem Renaissance years. The American Negro Academy (ANA) (1897), the Committee of Twelve (1904), the Negro Society for Historical Research (NSHR) (1911), and eventually the ASNLH (1915) were inspired by the efforts of the ANHS. The membership of the ANA included Howard professors Kelly Miller and Alain Locke alongside established collectors Arthur Schomburg and John Cromwell, while the Committee of Twelve, another decisively exclusive band of intelligentsia, relied on the scholarly status of Booker T. Washington and W. E. B. Du Bois to lend weight to its historical studies. These new societies shed any preoccupation with race assimilationism for a redefinition of historical progress on the Negro's own terms—at least the terms of the educated Negro male. Women, untrained in the science of historical interpretation, were absent from the rolls of these organizations.[45]

Curiously, one woman stood as an exceptional, albeit peripheral member of this elite circle of bibliophiles. Ella Elbert was an avid collector of Negro history and literature who kept in close contact with members of the ANHS and the NSHR. Her acceptance among male intellectuals was perhaps attributable to her status as a highly educated reformer yet also as a woman of means. She earned the distinction of being the second African American woman to graduate from Wellesley College in 1888, pursuing the study of history and eventually attaining a master's degree in political science; but she was also married to the highly successful Samuel Elbert, believed to be the only African American practitioner of medicine in Wilmington, Delaware, in 1900. In addition to her participation in Washington-area women's and alumnae clubs, Elbert became a lecturing member of the Bethel Literary and Historical Association and an instructor of history, civil government, and economics in the Normal Department at Howard University, hence her rare perspective of historical learning. Like few others, she witnessed first-hand that students, especially women, had access to few materials that offered them a sense of historical identity. She purchased Robert Adger's personal book collection some time after 1904, hoping one day to make it available to female students.[46]

Elbert, for the time being, remained more active in women's clubs than collecting circles, in effect embracing the feminine role of community educator over that of race intellectual. Her male colleagues, on the other hand, considered their scholarly status essential to their claims as experts on the Negro past and touted themselves as learned men of national stature rather than as local grassroots activists. Their preoccupation with status was warranted, given the public acceptance of racist history written in the name of social science. Southern revisionists and nationalists such as E. Merton Coulter, John Burgess, John Fiske, William Archibald Dunning, James Shouler, and Ulrich Bonnell Phillips argued the innate inferiority of African Americans as a race and found a warm reception in history departments everywhere, particularly the South. Progressive historians were more sympathetic to the plight of African Americans than were other academics, but their preoccupation with the economic causes of slavery did little to revise the legacy of race relations in the present. Indeed, race bibliophiles had much ground to cover if they hoped to create an empowered history of commanding influence.[47] While Schomburg approved of the scholarly agenda of his colleagues, he also acknowledged the need to compensate for the academy's focus on the economics of slavery and the politics of Reconstruction. Scholarship so narrowly defined, he warned, would derail the ANA's professed goal to disseminate social and cultural knowledge of the Negro to a wide cross section of the American public, women and children included.[48]

Ultimately, Schomburg's reasoning led him to establish the NSHR, an organization that invited a broader range of members and topics of research. Its members intended to use their rare acquisitions to produce publications for lay audiences, and several revealed a sincere interest in the history of black women. In 1912 Jack Thorne published "A Plea for Social Justice for the Negro Woman," an indication that he perceived righting the historical wrongs against women as part of the larger goal of vindication for the race. Despite its more widespread ambitions, however, the NSHR remained in the end as insular as the ANA and the Committee of Twelve, failing to make the sources it amassed accessible to women, children, and researchers in the African American community. In effect, it continued to be a cadre of well-intentioned but exclusive race men who were willing to engage women as historical subjects but never completely as historical practitioners.[49]

Learned men with credentials and wealth came to be known as the shapers of race history during the Harlem Renaissance, yet it could be argued that African American women best put their ideas about history to practice. Narratives of emulation no longer appealed to male race scholars by the 1920s, but they were even less constructive for the black women who had since taken up Anna Cooper's call to reveal their historical legacy as race and gender distinct. Decades before Schomburg proposed that the Negro "dig up his past," Cooper had already made pleas for less sentimentalized depictions of the real social and economic conditions weathered by black women uniquely. The domestic ideal mythologized by white historians was a framework unbefitting a new black women's history, given the burdens black women still bore as a result of distorted, one-sided race memory. Jerena Lee, Nancy Prince, and Sojourner Truth had entered the public sphere unprotected as domestics, seamstresses, and waged laborers; they experienced indignities—but also economic independence—that middle-class white women had never known. Cooper challenged African American women to remember these aspects of their collective past, to reject the ideals of white womanhood, to acknowledge their secondary status in race reform, and to create a black women's history that also measured accomplishment on its own terms. She spoke to laboring women but also to those who had since joined the ranks of the black elite; though they no longer suffered the same economic hardships, they experienced gender and racial discrimination in organizations of men and white women who were ignorant of their historical obstacles overcome.[50]

By the turn of the century, African American women had met Cooper's call for a distinctive history in fits and starts. Gertrude Mossell, Susan King Taylor, and a handful of others published works before 1920 that revealed aspects of the black female experience in one sense or another but not as completely as Cooper had envisioned. Nevertheless, in the 1920s several clubwomen, failing institutional support, followed in Beasley's and Houston's footsteps and forged ahead as independent writers. Often their works were collective biographies of middle-class women of relative privilege, but they also introduced an increasing number of race heroines who embodied traits better suited to combat their historical circumstances as breadwinners and productive laborers. Hallie Brown's *Homespun Heroines* (1926) and Sadie Daniel's *Women Builders* (1931), for example, described community reformers, educators, and self-sufficient wage earners whose domestic lives did not receive top billing. As a clubwoman herself Brown paid an inordinate amount of attention to organizational work over productive labor as the locus of female accomplishment. On the other hand, she found inspiration in the entrepreneurialism of C. J. Walker, a businesswoman who sought economic prosperity for the entire African American community:

Madam Walker was one of those whole-souled Christian characters that saw in the development of a larger business but another avenue and opportunity to serve her race. She realized that the great need of her time, and this is equally as true to-day, was avenues of honorable employment for developing young manhood and womanhood of the race. Keen of observation, she noted that millions of dollars were spent by our people annually for toilet requisites, that nearly all of these millions were going to the man who did not help colored charities or employ colored boys and girls. Madam Walker realized that in this as well as other fields the Negro could make jobs for himself by establishing his own institutions and patronizing them and thus bring his dollars to his own pockets.[51]

Like Brown, Sadie Daniel acknowledged the economic savoir faire of this remarkable woman. Yet she also pointed out that this asset made Walker a heroine markedly different from white social workers and philanthropists of her day. Walker the "woman builder" focused on education, health care, and the creation of jobs in the African American community for laboring and professional classes alike, without the moral judgments of white philanthropists and social reformers. She seemed to appreciate more fully than the white domestic woman that economic self-sufficiency was the key to social uplift, and this distinguished her as a wholly different model of ideal womanhood. Daniel's portraits of Maggie Lena Walker, Mary McLeod Bethune, and other upstanding black women revealed self-assured builders of "educational, financial, and social institutions" such as the Independent Order of Saint Luke and the Phillis Wheatley Association. Focusing on accomplishment in the secular sector to a greater extent than the race biographers who preceded her, Daniel maintained that this was where black women exhibited economic pragmatism, pedagogical prowess, and enlightened community action.[52]

Because Daniel wrote about women who were still alive, *Women Builders* may not have been construed as history in the traditional sense. Nevertheless, she characterized her book as history in the making, celebrating her heroines for "the enlightenment and improvement of their race." With greater hindsight one might argue that Daniel was indeed making history literally and in more ways than one. Her record provided evidence of women builders that scholars have since expanded on in the twenty-first century to describe and historicize a distinctive tradition of "womanist" reform. Alice Walker first coined the term as a descriptor for black women's niche in predominantly white feminist culture, yet Elsa Barkley Brown and others have since described womanism as an activist sensibility more encompassing than white feminism. Whether called "women builders" or "womanists," Daniel's race reformers focused on economic autonomy and broad community action, setting them apart from white reformers or feminists within a distinctive historical legacy.[53]

Daniel laid a groundwork on which later historians could build, but there were more immediate benefits to come out of her models of feminine achievement. They provided ammunition against the distorted but long-perpetuated memory of promiscuous sexuality that still haunted African American women as Daniel wrote in 1931.[54] Remnants of these sexual fantasies had lingered in the American mind through Reconstruction, and women authors for the next fifty years remained silent about the personal lives of their historical heroines so as not to add fuel to the flame. Scholars who continue to note this tendency in African American women's writings attribute it to a number of other factors—the pain that gets relived with memories of sexual violence certainly topping the list. Darlene Clark Hine and Deborah Gray White lament that in their concerted efforts to portray themselves and all black women as upstanding public figures, these writers have made it difficult to sustain a resonant black women's history for the twenty-first century. "Scarred by the negative images and the adversarial relationships they traditionally had with public institutions," White explains, "black women have proven reluctant to let go of any material that might reveal their private selves."[55] Most scholars agree, however, that the care with which women related the personal lives and private personas of their historical figures was a logical strategy, for they lived in a sexist society that defined feminine virtue in racial terms.[56]

Such caution was initially necessary, but it may have finally outlasted its purpose as more race fiction and biography circulated that sensitized readers to the African American woman's historical plight. This fact was no more apparent than when Mary Church Terrell sought a publisher for her autobiography in 1932. Her working title for the piece, "The Long Rocky Road" (later "The Confessions of a Colored Woman"), seemed inappropriate, given her rosy portrait of a life that resembled the easy affluence of a well-to-do white woman. After several rejections from publishers, Terrell took her manuscript to a literary critic who offered this candid advice:

You haven't been able to place your manuscript, there may be several reasons for this. In the first place, it seems to me that your very sense of justice has been something of a drawback, for although you deal with a number of the slights imposed upon you and other people of your race, you have to a certain extent glossed over the difficulties that confronted you. As you say on page 368, you "have given the bitter with the sweet—the sweet predominating", but I am sure that we would not accuse a person of your tolerance, of ingratitude if you revealed more of the dark side of your life. . . .

If you had done more with the obstacles in your way, we might appreciate your successes to an even greater extent, and of course we might have an even better idea of what you and your race are up against. ... You see, so many honors have come your way and they stand out so distinctly in the course of your book, that it is possible that white readers might envy you and say that colored people can win out if they try as hard as you.[57]

The reaction that this critic warned Terrell not to elicit may have been the one she hoped to achieve. It was her last intention to disclose the pain in negotiating a white world, and as a light-skinned, middle-class, educated woman, her struggles were undoubtedly less substantial than those of the majority of black women. Deborah Gray White maintains that Terrell successfully passed for white when comfort and convenience demanded it, often traveling in "whites only" railway cars and eating at white restaurants. At the same time, unpublished letters revealed that Terrell felt the liability of race in ways she would not publicly admit. On lecture circuits she entered through the back doors of halls and stayed with friends to avoid segregated accommodations. Any resentment she might have had, however, she never articulated in her published writings, fearing that such admissions would undermine her ability to break down racial stereotypes. What better way to argue for equality, she thought, than to recall those times when whites took her for one of their own.[58]

Nevertheless, by portraying herself as untouched by defamation or indignity, Terrell left the impression that all black women could overcome obstacles of race to be women of refinement. The fact that her manuscript told a story of progress without setback made it little different from most of the race biographies that preceded it. Though Terrell made adjustments before Ransdell Publishers printed the finished manuscript in 1940, she was still somewhat cautious in relating personal and private travails. Her new title, A Colored Woman in a White World, was telling of the social strife black women faced in American society. Yet her account was largely the story of a public woman who made little mention of her role as a wife, a mother of three children who died shortly after birth, or as a woman who felt the color of her skin in economic or social terms. She tried to obliterate the stigma of racial inferiority by ignoring its potency for harm, coming close to dismissing the obstacles faced by black women altogether. White suggests that Terrell's mentality was pervasive in the club movement circles in which she traversed; there the mantra "the personal is political" did not yet register or resonate. In fact just the opposite was true: The political became personal—even charged—though NACW leaders hid such personality conflicts behind a unified facade.[59]

Terrell was familiar with the cultural project of the Harlem Renaissance, yet in the end she whitewashed her past to legitimate her claims to a prominent place in history. Her silence on the grittier details of her life may have imparted better than words that black women continued to be stigmatized in ways men and whites could not appreciate. By the time Terrell published her autobiography in 1940, African American men had made significant headway recasting their history in the professional field. Since the 1910s and 1920s dozens had published scholarly research that focused on the African American male for the *Journal of Negro History* (*JNH*) and the Associated Publishers, both established by Harvard-trained historian Carter Woodson. In stark contrast, African American women had barely made progress in the university; only one had earned a Ph.D. in history by 1940. At Howard University women were beginning to produce master's theses in race history, but most reflected the academy's overwhelming preoccupation with slavery and in no way highlighted the experiences of women in particular.[60]

The climate was still not right in history departments to introduce a black women's social or cultural history, but that is not to say that these fields remained unexplored, for they were of inherent interest to women who deserted history for disciplines less hostile to race activism. Just as Progressive women employed the tools of a range of social science fields to uncover the lives of women, laborers, and immigrant groups, Zora Neale Hurston took advantage of this heightened penchant for interdisciplinarity to forge some of the first substantive academic research on African American women. Hurston was a noteworthy novelist but also a WPA field-worker, historian, anthropologist, and folklorist, and her many hats lent her unprecedented flexibility and perspective. Like Progressive women, she took full advantage of her position in the academy to achieve scholarly legitimacy for her historical subjects. She commented on Negro folk culture with an air of authority and a pretense of neutrality, but she also had an appreciation of the larger social applications of her findings.[61]

A student of pioneer anthropologists Ruth Benedict and Franz Boas ("Papa Franz," as she affectionately called him), her scholarly credentials won her the respect of other academic historians, but she never relied solely on the academy's affirmation to earn her living. She traveled to the South under the auspices of the Columbia anthropology department but also the WPA and the ASNLH, and thus she was never bound by the disciplinary politics or cultural assumptions of the university. Hurston's intimate knowledge of Negro culture suited her to the role of "translator" for white and scholarly audiences. At the same time, she fulfilled the anthropological role of participant-observer to perfection. Her childhood background gave her special access to her subject material, but her academic training gave her the lexicon for its scientific translation: "From the earliest rocking of my cradle, I had known about the capers Brer Rabbit is apt to cut and what the Squinch Owl says from the house top," she recalled in the 1940s, "but it was fitting me like a tight chemise. I couldn't see it for wearing it. It was only when I was off in college, away from my native surroundings, that I could see myself like somebody else and stand off and look at my garment. Then I had to have the spy-glass of Anthropology to look through at that."[62] Robert Hemenway credits Boas with giving Hurston a "taxonomy for her childhood memories." Indeed, Boas rehearsed her in rigorous methodology and insisted she obtain accurate texts of folktales and songs. Her intuition about folk *style*, however, could never be learned in an institutional setting; it grew out of her upbringing and the greater ease with which her subjects conversed with her than with academic outsiders.[63]

In her autobiography *Dust Tracks on a Road* (1942), Hurston minimized the role of racial prejudice in forging her literary and scholarly careers, refusing, in her words, to be part of "the sobbing school of Negrohood." Unlike Terrell, however, her reason for rejecting the victim role went hand in hand with her intellectual project, which was to celebrate, not to forget, Negro folk culture past and present. As Hurston saw it, this culture was a source of pride, but so was the charge of maintaining it, and this task had traditionally been relegated to women. In her compilation of folktales, *Mules and Men* (1935), Hurston's attention to folk culture necessarily extended to women as its primary preservers and agents. Historically the Negro woman's lack of access to reading, writing, or material sources meant that she resorted to nonwritten forms such as song and folktale to transmit race history and culture from one generation to the next. Hurston recognized that these nonwritten forms became essential cultural clues to the history of African American people, but also to the African American woman's distinctive subjectivity in the past.[64]

Hurston was not the only social scientist who listened to spoken words to recover the Negro woman in history. In 1929 Ophelia Settle Egypt, a graduate student under Charles Johnson at the Social Science Institute at Fisk University, interviewed 100 former slaves in western Tennessee to compile an "autobiographical account of Negro ex-slaves." The titles she gave the oral histories reveal her primary intent to keep slaves' subjectivities intact: "My Mother Was the Smartest Black Woman in Eden," "Father Gave Her to His White People after the War," "I Can't Forgive Her, The Way She Used to Beat Us." She built a convincing defense for her use of oral testimony in what became the "Unwritten History of Slavery":

Much had been written about the slavery system as an aspect of the economic order. Little as yet has been written about the system as a moral order . . . [how] sentiments, habits, and conduct are fashioned and channeled as one lives within that framework. . . .

The [interviews] herein made available, reveal some of the personal experiences of the slaves in the declining days of the institution. They tell what the slaves saw and remembered; how they, themselves, or others whom they know lived through the drudgery of menial work and the fear of the impending precarious world; how the slaves met their basic needs of sex, hunger and rest, within the very narrow confines of the system. They represent essentially the memories of childhood experiences, and provide, in a measure, a personal history of the social world as recreated and dramatized by these slaves in course of the telling. Taken as a whole, these autobiographies constitute a fabric of individual memories, which shed interesting light on the mentality of the slave.[65]

Egypt rejected the scientific assumption that her project should prove empirically the truth of the testimonies given. She qualified that "the merit of these documents lies not so much in the accurate recording of the historical events, as in the realistic fabrication of the experiential world of the persons themselves." Unlike her document-obsessed peers in history departments, she was far more interested in the slave's perceived reality, her rendition of truth in personal memory.[66]

Egypt's examination of black oral history would be a rare occurrence in the American university. Nevertheless, by the 1940s several African American women had come into their own as professional interpreters, if not yet as legitimate subjects of academic history. Merze Tate (Radcliffe, 1941), Lula Johnson (Iowa State, 1941), Margaret Nelson Powley (Columbia, 1940s), Elsie Lewis (1940s), and Helen Edmonds (Ohio State, 1947) were a few of the first to earn Ph.D.'s in history. Yet of these women, Edmonds was the only one to write a dissertation on an African American subject, "The Negro Fusion Politics in North Carolina." Fearful of professional repercussions, she insisted that her colleagues not typecast her as a race historian but, rather, as a scholar of American history broadly. Like the white women who entered history departments before her, she proceeded within the establishment cautiously, having better insight into the politics of race, gender, and promotion as a woman who could take nothing for granted. It is likely that Edmonds, like Caroline Ware, viewed the male historians she worked alongside as a privileged fraternity. But for now she used her perspective of power to master the male historian's professional rules, not to shed light on the subtle ways he dismissed her past, as Debo had for

Native Americans and Hurston had for African Americans in the South. For now, the writing of race history was a luxury that only men could afford. Anna Cooper articulated this fact in 1892, Terrell subconsciously confirmed it in 1940, and the first African American women historians in the academy eventually recognized it for themselves.[67]

But again we must emphasize that what prevailed in the academy did not always prevail in the popular consciousness. Just as we argued that white women's shaping of historical memory could not be fully assessed from inside the academy, this holds doubly true for African American women, whose historical projects almost always left direct impressions on audiences in the schools, clubs, churches, and libraries of their local communities. Delilah Beasley, Anna Cooper, Drusilla Houston, and others highlighted here are proof that the story of the African American woman's role as twentieth-century historian did not begin in the 1940s, but earlier. When viewed from outside the academy, through a lens focused on the grassroots campaigns of the New Negro History Movement, the African American woman's role in shaping race memory is no longer secondary, but vital.

III
Constructing Usable Pasts

Chapter 5
Womanist Consciousness and New Negro History

Men such as Carter Woodson, Benjamin Brawley, Benjamin Quarles, and Charles Wesley enjoyed newfound authority as chroniclers of race history in the twentieth century, while African American women remained trapped in a cycle of someone else's making. More of them sought professional status as historians revising the distorted past, and yet the past continued to be used against them, hindering their professional status and historical authority. Some turned to other social science disciplines instead of surrendering to the whims of institutional history. Others took the road traveled by Lucy Salmon and Bessie Pierce and sought authority as historical pedagogues. The fact that African American women turned to teaching was borne out in 1931, when Lucy Slowe confirmed that nearly 90 percent of her female graduates at Howard pursued careers in education. Elementary and secondary teaching had long been designated feminine fields in American society, and this was particularly the case in African American communities.[1]

Stripped of the authority to construct race history, African American pedagogues still influenced how the writings of men shaped historical consciousness. By the early 1940s, Marion Thompson Wright, Marion Cuthbert, and Edna Colson had written dissertations at Columbia University that examined the historical education of elementary, secondary, and college students and prescribed new curricula in race history.[2] Classmate Marie Carpenter's *The Treatment of the Negro in American History School Textbooks* (1941) resembled Pierce's research of texts in the 1920s; it, too, addressed the problem of selective omission—in this case of African Americans—from historical narratives taught to children. Formerly a teacher at the Dunbar High School in Washington, Carpenter knew firsthand that textbooks were silent in regard to African Americans, but to make her point to scientific scholars, she compared the treatment of African Americans and whites in eighty-six commonly used high school texts and quantified the treatment of each. As predicted, the Negro had been virtually ignored since emancipation as an important participant in national affairs. Carpenter insisted that a return to compensatory narratives was not the solution for the skewed coverage, recommending instead that teachers pressure publishers to print more history authored from the Negro point of view.[3]

Unfortunately, by the time Carpenter published her findings, the problem had no longer been the lack of written material about the Negro, but its lack of accessibility to young readers. Male race scholars had already written prolifically, and yet as an educator Carpenter could see that this history had not filtered down to shape the popular consciousness of the African American community to any great extent. Her colleagues at Columbia employed empirical methods to evaluate race historiography but, unlike male scholars, also used their findings to direct the course of historical learning at the grassroots level—in this case the African American classroom. Their interest in the production of history outside the university may have been piqued in the 1910s and 1920s by kindred spirit Lucy Salmon but also by the grassroots artists, writers, and historians of the Harlem Renaissance who reaffirmed Negro culture past and present. Clubwomen also continued to convene in organizations to cultivate their distinctive womanist ideology of reform. Accounting for the complexity of factors that came together to create their unique place in American society, these African American women had a vision for social change that cut across gender, age, or socioeconomic status; the whole community was the target of their efforts to promote race uplift and eventually race history.

The New Negro History Movement of the twentieth century has been billed as an effort of learned race men exclusively, despite the fact that women revised race history and incorporated it into their arsenal of womanist strategies to educate children, church congregations, and community groups. We will attempt to understand how the New Negro History Movement evolved into such a masculine entity, but only to retrieve women's special place in it. Just as we viewed the work of women academics and regionalists in light of gender, our assessment of the New Negro History Movement must also take gender into account, for masculine notions of scientism influenced the identity male race scholars sought for themselves and impeded women's authority as historians. African American women's collective position on the margins of the historical profession, outside the university, on the lower rungs of social power, and in the trenches of race reform gave them fresh perspective on history and memory that white women and black men did not possess. As we chip away at the gendered construction of professional and nonprofessional, scientific and amateur historians, African American women's projects as teachers, clubwomen, and librarians suddenly surface as effective vehicles of empowered race history and social change.

Finding Women's Niche in the New Negro History Movement

In 1936 Mary McLeod Bethune, founder of the Bethune-Cookman Institute and leader in the African American women's club movement, became the only woman executive member of the ASNLH, the preeminent agency of New Negro history in the twentieth century. Looking back, she remarked that the black woman "ha[d] not always been permitted a place in front ranks where she could show her face and make her voice heard with effect. . . . The part she played in the progress of the race ha[d] been of necessity, to a certain extent, subtle and indirect."[4] Indeed her statement holds a high degree of truth if taken as a commentary on her role in the shaping of race memory in the twentieth century. As disseminators, popularizers, researchers, and catalogers in the back rooms of new archives of black history, black women held the keys to the past to unlock the shackles of racial prejudice. Nevertheless, Carter Woodson, the man and mind behind the ASNLH, did not immediately recognize their essential role in developing the field of black history; in the beginning his desire to legitimate race history as a scholarly field caused him to disregard women's abilities to advance it. Only after a decade of assessment would he realize that in their social duty to children and community, women could impart historical ideas and shape collective memory in ways male historians could never achieve alone.

When Woodson and his associates first created the ASNLH at a Chicago Young Men's Christian Association in 1915, they considered it a social imperative to establish an agency that combated pseudoscientific racism as it produced affirmative race history. Outside the academy, films such as *Birth of a Nation* (1915) played to large audiences, and the Ku Klux Klan gained influence in the South and Midwest, its national membership peaking at 5 million by the following decade. Inside the academy, history had become a formal academic discipline, institutionalized with professional publications, organizations, and modes of credentialization at the same time its practitioners were applying ideas of Anglo-Saxon supremacy to the study of race relations in the past. With these developments, Woodson feared that the Negro was becoming "a negligible factor in the thought of the world." "The need of the hour was not to write books from the scant materials available," he insisted, "but to collect and preserve sufficient data of all sorts on the Negro to enable scientifically trained men to produce treatises based upon the whole truth."[5]

Few men were in a better position than Woodson to make a place for New Negro history in the academic establishment. He was one of the first-generation race scholars trained in that very milieu, earning a master's degree from the University of Chicago in 1907 and his doctorate in American history from Harvard in 1912. Trained in the positivist tradition of the German school, he understood and, in fact, believed in the merits of empirical method and the ability to determine an objective and accurate truth. At the same time, scholars of the Progressive school had convinced him that history could be a tool for social change. He differentiated amateur race historians of the nineteenth century from twentieth-century professionals like himself, describing the former as "agitators for the abolition of slavery and for the recognition of Negroes as citizens" and the latter as men committed to social change but less dependent on "agitation and propaganda." Woodson spent years teaching at African American secondary and tertiary institutions, including West Virginia Institute and Howard University. Nevertheless, his inability to be recognized elsewhere underscored his belief that blackness denied him participation in historical dialogues of the scholarly elite. To gain validation for himself and his race, he would have to apply his training to a race-conscious brand of activist history, one that competed with the prevalent discourses of the white academy and society at large.[6]

Woodson is generally recognized as the man responsible for taking up the project of New Negro history where amateur race bibliophiles left off, making scientific its methodologies and content and institutionalizing its practice within a formal network of organizations and publications headquartered in Washington. Along with the ASNLH, he established the *JNH* in 1916 and the Associated Publishers (AP) in 1922; they printed articles and books by African American historians that were often rebuffed at mainstream presses. The AP grew to be a stock company bought into by several prominent race men, yet Woodson insisted on serving as executive director and lead editor of all publications. While he avoided academic affiliations, he welcomed the support of white academicians, appointing to the executive board Albert Bushnell Hart, Robert E. Park, Franz Boas, E. A. Hooton, William E. Dodd, Arthur Schlesinger, Evarts Greene, and Carl Russell Fish. Though not all were historians, every white scholar involved in the ASNLH was a social scientist committed to liberal scholarship and the pursuit of New Negro history. Frederic Bancroft even supplied funds to award yearly prizes in the growing field.[7]

Woodson became a master at courting prominent white philanthropists to fund the training of African American researchers.[8] Nevertheless, to keep his financial backing, he was pressured to present AP publications as authoritative historical sources produced by highly trained research scholars. His focus on professional scholarship, in time, had a deleterious effect on African American women, who were almost always excluded from the press's operations before 1930. Woodson recalled how he "looked around for young men of ability and encouraged them to prepare themselves for historical research," but he made no mention of young women, perhaps because so few had been admitted to graduate departments in the social sciences in these years and there were absolutely none in the field of history. It was hardly coincidental that of the fourteen African American men who received doctorates in history or the history of education before 1940, eight would work directly with Woodson and be propelled into national prominence through their dealings with the ASNLH.[9]

Woodson's preference for men was not due to a shortage of women who volunteered to be researchers. A whole team of women, for example, joined Zora Neale Hurston in Florida to serve as data collectors for her *JNH* studies. Woodson referred to these female workers as "investigators," in clear distinction from his formally trained male "historians." Archivists Ruth Anna Fisher and Irene Wright were indispensable to the New Negro history effort, collecting documents on people of African descent in Europe and Spanish America. Yet women's influence in the ASNLH rarely advanced past the level of field research. Membership rolls indicate that personnel turned over frequently, but women did not fill executive positions until Mary McLeod Bethune became president in 1936.[10]

To what degree Woodson edited the work of women contributors is not known. However, it is clear that he wielded a strong editorial hand in every issue that went to press and more than likely refined the occasional local, family, and education histories submitted to the journal by uncredentialed women. Woodson himself wrote many *JNH* book reviews, revealing in no uncertain terms his preference for the work of professional scholars who wrote on masculine topics. Delilah Beasley, for example, received the worst condemnation from Woodson when he reviewed her *Negro Trail Blazers of California*. She claimed to apply the most rigorous research methods to the material she unearthed in the personal collections of California residents. Yet Woodson insisted that the text, which lacked a detailed bibliography and scientific footnoting, was amateur in tone and irredeemable as a useful historical text. "Judged from the point of view of the scientific investigator, the work is neither a popular nor a documented account," he decided. "When one considers the numerous valuable facts in the book, however, he must regret that the author did not write the work under the direction of some one well grounded in English composition. As it is, it is so much a hodge-podge that one is inclined to weep like the minister who felt that his congregation consisted of too many to be lost but not enough to be saved."[11]

Woodson resented that women like Beasley made scholarly claims for their works, for they only seemed to undermine his efforts to legitimate the field of Negro history. Schoolteacher Laura Wilkes, a paying member of the ASNLH, was especially vocal about what appeared to her to be his categorical rejection of women contributors; the last straw was his refusal to review her *Missing Pages in Negro History*, a work she went to great lengths to research:

> It has come to my knowledge that by the historical societies of the other race, the writings of *members* received favorable, or unfavorable treatment as merited, in publications issued by them.
>
> I have been until lately in good standing in the society you edit for; I submitted my work to you as soon as it came from the press and yet for some reason it has *not* received the *courtesy*, I had every right to expect for it. . . . There must be some reason for your attitude, toward one who as a *member* of the society had a *right* to public consideration. It would not have been a *favor*, but a *right*. . . . I wanted to tell you that I felt you had not given me as a person who has done the work I have, my just deserts. I feel as your colaborer, for (I have directly researched five hundred teachers) since July 1st 1921 on this subject that *equity* as a member of the society demanded something different. . . .
>
> Only this Mr. Woodson, when the next *woman* appears on the horizon, if she is working in *your* field, let the world know it, if her work is done well, judged by your standard *say so* if not show her *how it* can be bettered. This will be her *right* if she pays her dues. *She is one of you.*[12]

To Wilkes, Woodson's rejection came off as pompous chauvinism rather than academic snobbery. Yet it is likely that his response to her book had more to do with the lack of academic credentials backing it, for he proved more than willing to review the books of professional women historians, who in the early years of the *JNH* were few and predominantly white. In 1920, for example, he reviewed Ella Lonn's *Reconstruction in Louisiana* (1918) with much praise: "Miss Lonn's book is an exhibition of the true scholarly spirit," he wrote. "All the[se] facts are put together in a logical manner and show that the author is not only gifted with keen analytical powers, but is also endowed with a peculiar faculty for organizing and marshalling facts." Likewise, Elizabeth Donnan's volumes of *Documents Illustrative of the History of the Slave Trade to America* and other compilations of primary documents *JNH* reviewers judged approvingly as "objective" works that demonstrated unbiased empirical method. That Woodson took less issue with women than their inability to bring scholarly status to New Negro history is perhaps best confirmed by his relationship with Zora Neale Hurston. Her anthropological studies always received commendation in the *JNH*, but rarely without a listing of her academic credentials: "She is regarded as a novelist, but at the same time she is more of an anthropologist," Woodson assured readers, "being trained at Barnard College of Columbia University, where she came under the influence of Dr. Franz Boas."[13]

The ASNLH sponsored Hurston's research in the Florida Everglades, but not without the intervention of some prominent scholars. Woodson initially considered funding the more established Alain Locke instead, but Boas's involvement (and perhaps the financial backing of Elsie Clews Persons) won Hurston a grant for six months of research. Her intentions were to proceed through the South collecting African American songs, tales, and superstitions through oral interviews. At the time, southern black folklore was relatively untapped as a field of investigation; Philadelphia scholar Arthur Huff Fauset and white writer John Chandler Harris had published the only folk studies of notice when Hurston entered the picture. As a black native of the South, she was anxious to bring new insight to the field, but Woodson often chided her for letting her interest in storytelling take precedence over archival research. Like white academic historians, Woodson was obsessed with the written word; he could not understand why Hurston needed a tape recorder to document black history, nor did he trust her use of personal memory as historical evidence. The relationship between sponsor and "ASNLH investigator" grew strained; as Hurston lingered in the South collecting interviews, Woodson threatened to cut off her funding unless she performed the necessary work in historical documents. In 1927 she capitulated, submitting to the *JNH* an uninspired transcription of records from a seventeenth-century black settlement in St. Augustine.[14]

More African American women scholars filled the pages of the *JNH* in following years, but it is important to note that the percentage who were professional historians remained proportionately low. Although contributors such as Hurston, Jessie Parkhurst, and Dorothy Porter wrote articles grounded in historical themes, by training they were anthropologists, sociologists, and archivists—not historians. The fact remained that black women looked to social science disciplines other than history to supply models of cultural relativism and paradigms more conducive to race reform. In the end their disciplinary breadth enhanced their historical coverage of topics in the *JNH* in ways unseen in the *AHR* and other professional publications. In "Cudjo's Own Story of the Last African Slaver," for example, Woodson finally allowed Hurston to demonstrate the value of oral interviews. She claimed that her subject, Cudjo, a man in his late nineties, was the last living slave to come to America by ship in 1859. His interview revealed a rare glimpse of tribal warfare before the white man brought him to America, but also the terror and sadness he felt as a man taken from his home. Hurston's piece supplied nuggets of a single slave's subjective experience that could never be found or even inferred through the legal sources upon which scholars of slavery (including ASNLH historians) had become so dependent in recent years.[15]

Another innovative piece, Jessie Parkhurst's sociological study "The Role of the Black Mammy in the Plantation Household," exposed the origins of race and gender stereotypes more effectively than the most liberal race studies of professional historians. Parkhurst referred to the Black Mammy for the first time as an imaginary figure of movies and print, not a mainstay of plantation culture, and she described the idealization of the mammy as the by-product of the southern white man's search for aristocratic status.[16] Parkhurst integrated African American women into the male-centered subject material that first defined New Negro history in the 1910s, as did Howard librarian Dorothy Porter, who in 1931 submitted an article on Sarah Parker Remond to the *JNH* that revealed a woman other than Sojourner Truth as a champion of abolition: "Seventy years ago, the name of Sarah Parker Remond was well known on at least two continents to many thousands of persons who were interested in the movement for the abolition of slavery," she wrote. "A free Negro woman of remarkable ability and intellect, she was one of the few lecturers of her sex and race who, during the Garrisonian era, could command the attention of lords and mayors, as well as that of thousands of laymen, in behalf of the oppressed Negro slave."[17]

By virtue of their interest in reform and labor activism, women *JNH* contributors also produced original studies in the fields of labor and social history. The first full-length sociological study written by a woman was Elizabeth Ross Haynes's "Negroes in Domestic Service" in October 1923, a by-product of Haynes's master's degree research in political science and her labors as domestic service secretary for the U.S. Employment Service. It was not the first *JNH* article about women, but it was one of the first to examine the plight of the married African American laborer. Haynes brought this formerly unrepresented group to the fore, shedding light on the dire economic consequences of the dual roles of mother and breadwinner in recent American history.[18] Haynes's article on laboring women may have been the inspiration for a piece submitted to the journal shortly afterward, "The Negro Washer Woman: A Vanishing Figure," written by Woodson himself. His steadily growing interest in such topics suggests that he was beginning to recognize women past and present as integral to his race history project.[19]

Hurston, Porter, and Parkhurst explored the past through new social and cultural lenses that Woodson found appealing, but in the 1920s the place of women in the New Negro History Movement became more pronounced in other ways as the ASNLH leadership witnessed their ability to popularize history in African American communities. The male trustees of the FDMHA had already learned that women made excellent community organizers and promoters, and in the late 1920s Woodson became equally convinced. Although he appeared to be obsessed with the scholarly status of the ASNLH to the disadvantage of women historians, achieving the approval of academics was never the intended end in itself. Such affirmation was merely a first step toward disseminating race history on a mass scale, for Woodson's close associations with the ANA and the NSHR had taught him that a balance between the scholarly and the popular must be struck to create meaningful change in social attitudes.

The growing number of uncredentialed women authors publishing successfully—Drusilla Houston, Delilah Beasley, Hallie Brown, and Sadie Daniel, among others—led Woodson to recognize that the work of the ASNLH need not be limited to the production of scientific scholarship but could include accessible forms of popular race history.[20] He never completely relinquished his preference for the research of professional scholars, but in the 1920s he tempered his stance on what the ASNLH would accept for publication and with increasing frequency and qualification printed the works of women amateurs. Often in the form of eyewitness accounts and collections of oral and family histories, such works contributed, in Woodson's mind, to the New Negro history project by appeasing the preferences of lay readers for local, celebratory, and uncomplicated stories. In 1922 E. C. Williams, a reviewer for the *JNH*, reevaluated Elizabeth Ross Haynes's collective biography *Unsung Heroes* (1921) and praised its author for writing it "in a language and style suited to young readers." Reviewing Addie Hunton and Katherine Johnson's *Two Colored Women with the American Expeditionary Forces*, Woodson himself conceded that the authors made "no pretense to scientific treatment" in their account of Negroes in World War I, but that this was excusable; as a "beautiful story" of women recounting their own personal experiences, it had value and the ability to resonate with the public.[21]

Wearing the hats of teachers, community reformers, and preservationists of family history, women became contributors to the *JNH* with grow-

ing regularity. Anna Bustill Smith, for example, received a favorable response to her request to submit a genealogical record of her prominent
Philadelphia family in 1925, an unlikely outcome had she submitted the
piece earlier. Clubwomen Leila Amos Pendleton, Alice Dunbar-Nelson,
and Mary McLeod Bethune wrote for the journal not as scholars but as
upstanding women looking at how far the race had come and could go in
the future.[22] Not coincidentally, a large percentage of articles women submitted were progress narratives of institutions of learning, as they found
that education history and pedagogy were areas in which they could exhibit uncontested expertise. In 1917 Mary Church Terrell highlighted the
educators at Washington's Dunbar High School, including among them
the first woman principal, Anna Cooper. Grace Hays Johnson, a teacher at
Bennett College, contributed a piece in 1937 that prescribed ways to incorporate themes in Negro history into general humanities curricula. Mary
McLeod Bethune relied on her same unquestioned authority as an educator in "The Adaptation of the History of the Negro to the Capacity of a
Child": "Great efforts are being made to provide materials . . . in order that
there may be a larger knowledge of and greater appreciation for the background and contribution the races have made to the cultures around the
world," Bethune remarked. Only now, she insisted, "youth need[ed] this
story in its own language."[23]

As Woodson was discovering, women's ability to write, teach, and popularize history for the masses was the key to the progress of the New Negro
project in the twentieth century. He increasingly envisioned the *JNH* as a
source for the kind of social and cultural history in which women showed
interest and aptitude, and it was only a matter of time before women
enjoyed roles as authors and subjects of *JNH* articles more often than in
any other major historical publication in the country. Jacqueline Goggin
has calculated that the *JNH* published more articles about women prior to
the 1950s than the *Journal of Southern History*, the *AHR*, and the *MVHR*
combined. Better yet, women in these years authored more than double the
number of articles in the *JNH* than in any of the other three professional
journals. Women contributors who were trained historians tended to be
white, an indication that academic history remained closed to black
women. Regardless, women's influence on the social content of race history
was undeniable.[24]

Allowing women to wield influence in his publications, Woodson had
demonstrated open-mindedness that unfortunately did not always carry
over to other aspects of his ASNLH directorship. His stubbornness over
some of the finer points of administration caused white backers to donate
money to other projects.[25] This loss of support did not necessarily spell an

end to the association, however. It appeared that white philanthropists had done little to disperse race history to African Americans in the first place. An assessment of *JNH* circulation between 1915 and 1925 revealed that subscriptions in African American communities were low. Only 300 libraries subscribed to the journal, and most were in accredited universities where few students of color were admitted; 75 of the libraries were in southern schools for white students exclusively. The time was right to look for new avenues of support in the African American community and to women in particular—first for money, then to popularize race history on a grander scale.[26]

On paper, women did not appear to be the wealthy sponsors Woodson needed. In 1928, for example, only two of the association's forty-nine donors of $25 or more were women. White philanthropists from the Julius Rosenwald Fund, the Laura Spelman Memorial Foundation, and the Phelps-Stokes Fund had been largely responsible for the sums of money to support ASNLH scholarship, followed in generosity by individuals such as Jesse Moorland and Arthur Schomburg. But records of individual donations may not have told the complete story, for budget figures at the end of the decade also indicated a countertrend. The bulk of ASNLH funds came not from white philanthropists, scholars, or the membership fees of prominent race men and *JNH* readers, but from contributions in the African American community—gathered primarily through school, library, and club drives organized by women. Although women appeared insignificant as individual financial supporters, they carried strength in their numbers and certainly in their social roles as mothers, educators, and community organizers.[27]

Woodson could not ignore the ability of women to influence and mobilize a massive population base through grassroots campaigns. The network of African American women's clubs had grown larger in the twentieth century, as had the number of African American women teachers in elementary and secondary schools throughout the country. The ASNLH was as eager to take advantage of the energies of both constituencies as women were to incorporate New Negro history into their programs and lesson plans. Elementary school principal Maria Baldwin scraped together annual ASNLH membership dues in order to keep abreast of the latest research for pedagogical purposes. Similarly, Janie Porter Barret, head of the Virginia Industrial School for Colored Girls, attended ASNLH meetings and conferences and wrote Woodson expressing support for all that he attempted to do to rewrite the Negro past: "I think so highly of the valuable work your organization is doing," she assured him. "You are making a distinct contribution to American history, for no complete history could be written of this country without these facts you are giving us."[28]

Women's enthusiasm for the history of the ASNLH did not suddenly manifest in the late 1920s; even as Woodson insisted on writing scientific history, his call to unearth unused evidence about the Negro brought amateur women historians and preservationists out of the woodwork. By 1929 the ASNLH had collected more than 2,500 manuscripts, and by 1941 it housed more than 5,000 items in the Library of Congress. Although the exact amount is unknown, it is certain that women, inspired by Woodson's attempt to rewrite the African American legacy, gave much of this material. Woodson appeared to be the first historian interested in seeing the family relics they had been holding onto for years. Writer and widow Alice Dunbar-Nelson thus offered the ASNLH several of her husband's poems and unpublished manuscripts, while another woman donated her great-grandfather's bill of sale from when Thomas Jefferson sold him to James Madison. In 1924 a Philadelphia woman wrote Woodson expressing interest in setting up interviews with African American Civil War veterans in order to get their experiences down on paper while they were still alive.[29] African American women were not alone in answering Woodson's call for documents. A female relative of Civil War hero Thomas Wentworth Higginson sent the ASNLH letters written by African American soldiers under his command, while the daughters of James S. Rogers, a white captain in Company F of Higginson's regiment, offered testimonials of African American soldiers' experiences. One daughter told of her intentions to write her own cultural history with these materials: "Not only are there letters of decided interest but they contain the words of many of the songs of that particular locality. . . . It had been my plan to make a series of articles detailing the humor, pathos and music of the Negro soldier of '63 as I know him through those letters."[30]

White women helped to fill in the gaps of Woodson's empowered race history, while several African American women sought to revise it altogether. Laura Deitz Howard, for example, in 1928 insisted that her father, a poor man, should receive recognition for inventing the elevated railroad. As evidence she provided a citation from the *Scientific American* in 1865 in which Frederick Douglass gave her father the credit for the patent. West Virginia schoolteacher Leota Clair culled information about the pioneers of education in her state and proposed preparing something for publication. Another Baltimore woman submitted the information she had gathered over the years concerning the discrimination of African Americans on steamboats and was heartened to find that Woodson thought it "of historical value," despite the fact that most of her data came from the testimony of her mother, not from official documents.[31] Reports on the association's annual history conferences listed dozens of African American women as attendees and winners of prizes for historical research and collections. In 1924 former ANHS member Gertrude Mossell attended the spring conference in Philadelphia to witness a college woman receive honors for the best collection of Negro folklore. Although she never enjoyed the same attention as a custodian of memory, Mossell could take stock in knowing that race men now found value in this important work.[32]

With increasing confidence in their abilities to contribute to the New Negro history project, African American women began writing Woodson with an eye toward collaboration. One of the most ambitious projects was proposed in 1922 by Booker T. Washington's widow, Margaret Washington, a yearly contributor to the ASNLH research fund and president of the International Council of Women of the Darker Races. "We are trying now to get every one interested in putting into our schools Negro History and Negro Literature," she wrote Woodson. "We have decided in addition to this to get this Negro History and Literature into all schools for Negroes. We have formed ourselves, eighteen or twenty, into a body for studying Negro History and Literature, and particularly that which refers to the women of the race. . . . We are trying to get other women from Africa, the Islands, India and other countries of the dark races. . . . I also want you to make me out a course of study in Negro History and Literature."[33] Seeking similar assistance from the ASNLH, Nettie Ashbury, president of the Federation of Colored Women's Organizations in Washington State, proposed a local radio program on Negro history, while Mary Talbert invited Woodson to speak at the national NACW convention about Afrocentric history. Florida Ridley Ruffin, president of the Society of the Descendants of Early New England Negroes, shed her preoccupations with Revolutionary bloodlines to offer Woodson secretarial reports of New England organizations, old deeds, tax receipts, letters, and scrapbooks of her parents and other free blacks. Now with the enthusiastic support of black clubwomen across the country, Woodson's empowered race history could be disseminated on a scale his executive board could never achieve alone.[34]

It was not long before state and local ASNLH branches run primarily by women spread the word about Woodson's empowered race history. Initially the branches were intended to serve as collection bureaus of historical materials: "old newspapers, books out of print, receipts, manumission papers, deeds, wills, and the like, bearing on the past of the Negro." But now Woodson urged women volunteers to create history themselves, "to undertake actual research into the local history of persons who have achieved something worth while," and to serve as historical educators in local schools, clubs, and churches.[35] The branch system mobilized women most successfully when the ASNLH instituted its first Negro History Week in 1926. On the national level, Woodson appointed Helen Whiting assistant supervisor of Negro education. Mary McLeod Bethune, Jessie Parkhurst, and children's author Jane Shackleford prepared teaching kits for local ASNLH branches, departments of education, city school districts, principals, librarians, and teachers that contained posters, biographies, pamphlets, and lists of books for suggested reading on the Negro past.[36] The effective funneling down of this national campaign was evident from Washington to Los Angeles, where branch librarian Miriam Matthews was inspired to plan her own Negro History Week activities:

> As a member of the Association for the Study of Negro Life and History, I was impressed with Dr. Carter G. Woodson's campaign, initiated in 1926, for the celebration of Negro History Week during the second week in February. Since there was no activity in Los Angeles, not even a single notice in any of the Negro newspapers, I decided in 1929 to try to stir up some interest here. First I wrote articles for the local Negro press, announcing the February dates for the celebration, explaining the program, and the use of special Negro History Week kits which could be ordered from the Association. . . . Stressing the importance of everyone knowing something about Negro history, I published reviews of books on the subject which could be borrowed from local branch libraries, and also featured reviews on the subject at the Helen Hunt Jackson Library Book Club, which I organized in 1929. Rare books and pamphlets on the Negro were borrowed from collectors for library exhibitions; also art produced by Negro artists. I gave talks on Negro history and race relations to school classes and community organizations, both black and white, in various parts of the city.[37]

The first Negro History Week proved so successful that it continued to be observed in following years by school districts in major cities, thanks largely to women educators. Vivian Cook, a junior high school principal and Negro History Week chairman in Baltimore, was just one of thousands of frontline soldiers in the campaign to promote race history. She and her committee members created extensive lesson plans, radio spots, museum exhibits, library displays, and publicity to educate the community about the African American past. Not surprisingly, her volunteers were also mothers and women educators in the local Baltimore environs.[38]

By 1930 the ASNLH had successfully added a pedagogical component to its program in New Negro history. Field agents implemented lesson plans on the local level and ran sessions at every annual meeting devoted specifically to teaching in elementary and secondary schools. The ASNLH mailed instructional aids to teachers and cooperated with local school districts to create courses and textbooks for serious and truthful learning about the Negro. In cities where branches did not exist, a national committee under educator Susie Quander served as a liaison between grassroots volunteers and the headquarters in Washington. She was also the force behind the Nation-Wide Sustaining Member Campaign, a membership drive that increased the number of women in the ASNLH by charging a mere $1.00 annual fee. Any profits lost on membership fees were more than compensated for through the earnest fund-raising of new women members in their local communities.[39]

Negro History Week and its associated programs promoted race history like never before, yet by 1936 Mary McLeod Bethune, the newly appointed president of the ASNLH, believed more needed to be done to keep the African American past in the national consciousness year-round. During her fourteen-year tenure as president, her priority was making the scholarly work of the association even more accessible to lay readers, especially children, but this could not be achieved through Negro History Week alone. In 1937 the ASNLH created the *Negro History Bulletin* (*NHB*), a reader issued every month that elementary and secondary schools were in session. It contained pictures and short passages suited to younger readers, and while the interpretations of history in the *JNH* and the *NHB* were essentially the same, the different format and pedagogical tenor of the latter lent itself to highlighting the work of women more often than did the *JNH*.[40] Jane Shackleford's *Child's Story of the Negro* (1938), for example, received praise in the *NHB* as a book "written by an experienced teacher, a woman who understands children and speaks their language." Helen Whiting's *Negro Folk Tales* (1938) and *Negro Art, Music, and Rhyme* (1938) were similarly extolled by reviewers now proudly associating women writers with the AP label. Within five years of the *NHB*'s first printing, its editorial board and writing staff were made up almost entirely of women writers and educators.[41]

NHB contributors reverted to older methods of nineteenth-century race historians, often highlighting eminent African Americans as positive role models for young readers. Now, however, lists of notables included heroic women more frequently than in the *JNH*. In the October 1941 issue, for instance, seven female and two male contributors wrote as many biographical sketches on notable women as on men.[42] Many of these submissions had a revisionist tone and even criticized white institutions once emulated in race narratives. In 1943 one contributor examined women's patriotic organizations in "Negro Women Eligible to be Daughters of the American Revolution." Lamenting that the DAR's brand of patriotism had become virtually synonymous with racism, this writer questioned how the organization could exclude women of color who were eligible members. "It is supposed to be composed of persons known to be the lineal descendants of those who served in the army and navy of the American Revolution . . . [yet] hundreds of Negro women who are descendants of soldiers who followed George Washington in that war can never penetrate that sphere." The author of this biting commentary was not a woman denied membership, but Carter Woodson himself.[43]

Indeed, by the 1940s Woodson's inclusion of women in the New Negro history project seemed nearly complete. In 1945 he submitted "The Negro Historian of Our Times" to the *NHB*, a piece that acknowledged women as special contributors to the African American historical canon. Praising writers of juvenile history who "rendered the public a great service," he singled out *NHB* contributors Shackleford and Whiting and ASNLH members Elise Derricotte, Jessie Roy, Geneva Turner, and Chicago public school teacher Madeline Morgan. Maud Cuney Hare's cultural history, *Negro Musicians and their Music* (1936), set her apart in Woodson's eyes as one of "the most distinguished of her race." His tribute to men and women alike was accompanied by "The Rise of the Negro Historian," a piece fittingly written by yet another woman, ASNLH member Helen Boardman.[44]

The juxtaposition of these two articles was symbolic; it mirrored the successful complement of men and women in the *NHB* but also in the work of New Negro history more broadly. Bethune's appointment to the executive board was also symbolic of the gradual feminizing of tactics to promote Negro history by the 1930s. She applauded the men of the ASNLH for applying scientific technique to Negro history. However, she also agreed with Woodson that "knowledge or information in and of itself is not power, is not progress." "We must have the popularizer to stand between the masses whose knowledge of things is indefinite and the research worker whose knowledge is authoritative."[45] In no uncertain terms, Bethune placed key objectives of the ASNLH squarely in the hands of the female "popularizer" of race history. An educator, clubwoman, mother, and organizer, she redefined race history as more than an academic exercise, but a tool for change in the African American community.

The Woman Librarian and New Negro History

ASNLH publications were not the only sources of New Negro history in the early twentieth century. Bibliophiles in the ANA, the NSHR, and the Negro Book Collectors Exchange donated their personal collections to public institutions so that they could be used by new generations of students and history writers. With the urging of sociologist Kelly Miller, Jesse Moorland agreed to sell his private collection to Howard University in 1914. Carl van Vechten donated the James Weldon Johnson Collection at Yale; Henry Slaughter sold his private materials to Atlanta University; and Arthur Schomburg sold his collection of books, newspapers, and prints to the Harlem branch of the New York Public Library in 1925. More than 30,000 donated items made their way to Fisk University and Tuskegee and Hampton Institutes in the early 1940s, and by 1945 Arthur Spingarn had supplemented Moorland's original donation at Howard with his own literary collection, turning the Moorland-Spingarn Research Center into one of the biggest race archives in the country.[46]

Men such as Spingarn and Moorland understood that race history could not be written until source materials by and about the Negro had been collected, consolidated, and indexed for easier use. *Accessibility* was the key factor in reclaiming the past, and bibliographies of race materials became the valued tools of the Negro historian. In 1905 W. E. B. Du Bois published *A Select Bibliography of the Negro American*, followed the next year by a list of government holdings on the Negro likely compiled by African American congressional librarian Daniel Murray. Monroe Work, director of the Tuskegee Institute's Department of Records and Research, compiled the *Negro Year Book* (1912) and *A Bibliography of the Negro in Africa and America* (1928). Meanwhile popular distributors made race reference works like *Afro-American Encyclopedia* (1895), *Who's Who of the Colored Race* (1915), *The National Cyclopedia of the Colored Race* (1919), and *Who's Who in Colored America* (1927–40) widely accessible to the public.[47]

With these reference works in circulation, the lay reader enjoyed access to more historical information than ever before, and yet the pasts of African American women continued to remain largely a mystery. This was ironic considering the extent to which women made the materials in race bibliographies available to others in the early twentieth century. Amy Spingarn, Dorothy West, and Dorothy Peterson, among others, gave generously to the Johnson Collection at Yale, and Ella Smith Elbert finally donated her collection to Wellesley College in 1938. Her alma mater received the titles she had purchased from Robert Adger at her fiftieth college reunion, in addition to hundreds of items she had collected since. Her later acquisitions—titles written by polemicist Anna Cooper and memoirs of women slaves Harriet Jacobs, Chloe Spear, and Jerena Lee—reflected a heightened feminist consciousness since her college days.[48] Archives at Radcliffe and Smith would eventually surpass Wellesley's in size, but for now Elbert's gift was unprecedented at a women's college. She hoped that the books would "be of real value to both graduate and undergraduate students of history

and economics and help towards a more intelligent and unbiased understanding, not only of the past, but also of some of the present day problems
that confront our country." Indeed, Wellesley professor Elizabeth Donnan,
now a preeminent scholar of slave history, eagerly awaited the arrival of her
materials for further research. Fittingly, a plate inscribed with the name of
Katharine Coman, Elbert's mentor in the 1880s, was affixed to the inside
cover of every book in the collection.[49]

With the exception of Elbert, few donors placed items where women
researchers had easy access to them, but this does not mean that women
played no part in the reinterpretation of race history to come from Negro
collections. The organizing, indexing, maintaining, and disseminating of
these materials fell almost exclusively into the hands of women library and
archival professionals, who served as collection custodians and experts on
the information they contained. While African American women continued to be deterred from careers in academic history, many trained in
the growing field of librarianship and in so doing shaped race history in
equally important ways. Educator Elise Johnson McDougald anticipated
the significant role black women librarians would occupy in the twentieth
century when she contributed "The Task of New Negro Womanhood" to
Alain Locke's *The New Negro* in 1925. "Comparatively new are opportunities in the field of trained library work for the Negro woman," she
wrote. "Once trained, the Negro Woman librarian will scatter such opportunities across the country."[50] Indeed she was correct in predicting that
women librarians would create opportunities, although not to the extent
that they created them for African Americans outside the library field.
Vivian Harsh, for example, assembled one of the most extensive collections
of Negro history and literature as head librarian at the George Cleveland
Hall branch of the Chicago Public Library, attracting to it Zora Neale
Hurston, Langston Hughes, Richard Wright, and members of the community at large. Her lecture forums provided venues for engaging new discourse about race memory and fostering race pride in individuals who
never realized that such a rich cultural legacy existed.[51]

The broad social agenda black women brought to the public library was
not entirely without precedent; white women discovered in the latter half
of the nineteenth century that library work, like preservation or reform
work, afforded them a high degree of cultural authority. Moreover, public
and branch libraries were growing at a feverish rate. In 1896 there were only
971 public libraries in the country that held more than 1,000 volumes, but
that number increased to 2,283 by 1903 and 3,562 by 1913. During those
same years library work grew decidedly feminine. The first woman librarian was hired in the United States in 1852, and already by 1878 two-

thirds of the library workforce was female. By 1910 women made up 78.5 percent of library workers, and nearly 90 percent by 1920. Dee Garrison suggests that this feminization had much to do with the seeming domestic and pedagogical responsibilities that became attached to library work in the Progressive period; like the teacher or settlement worker, the librarian became the proselytizer of moral and social uplift in industrializing cities, "the guardian of the thought-life of the people," children and immigrants in particular. Indeed, librarians became important rank-and-file social reformers who provided non-English-speaking patrons the opportunity to read texts deemed appropriate and uplifting. Nonetheless, Garrison cautions that the legacy of the white woman librarian also be viewed in light of the cultural biases that informed her work, for "the building of public libraries," she writes, "was motivated by a fear of egalitarianism and upheaval from below as much as by a desire for democratic extension of education."[52] The first African American women librarians, in sharp contrast, worried less about revolt from below; library work to them was not a mode of Americanization or moral suasion but of race pride and uplift.

When McDougald submitted her ideas on women librarians and Schomburg offered his thoughts on historical collecting to *The New Negro*, there is no telling whether they realized the intertwined nature of their subjects. Yet as New Negro history inspired the African American, librarianship became a vehicle through which growing ranks of African American women promoted New Negro history. Again, women's relationship to the New Negro project was not immediately apparent. All African Americans were denied access to library work until 1900, when the first man of color graduated from a library service program, and black schools of library service did not come into being until Hampton Institute opened one in 1925. Daniel Murray broke an important color barrier with his appointment as librarian and curator of the Negro collection at the Library of Congress, yet by the time he retired in 1922, African American women still had not entered the field. High school librarian Virginia Proctor Powell Florence, the first African American woman to earn formal credentials, finished her studies in 1923 yet did not receive a degree until the University of Pittsburgh awarded it retroactively in 1931.[53] The fact that Florence was even admitted to library school was impressive enough; applicants younger than twenty but older than thirty-five years were discouraged from programs altogether, as were women without college degrees. In the case of many African American applicants, a high school diploma, a strong pedagogical background, and high entrance exam scores usually had to suffice. Nella Larsen's two semesters in library school included courses on reference work, headings, classification, current events, indexing, and bibliography, subjects that put her in good stead to determine the makeup and organization of future race collections.[54]

Virginia Lacy Jones recalled the discriminatory practices of the library program she enrolled in at the University of Illinois in 1936, but she found that as time wore on, she was not alone as a black woman with training in research archives. After working in relative isolation as head librarian at Louisville Municipal College, she became a catalog librarian at Atlanta University, where she came in contact with dozens of African American women from university libraries and associations. Eliza Atkins Gleason, dean of Atlanta University Library School, Susan Dart Butler, and a handful of others proved that librarianship was a field in which black women could not only succeed but also excel in positions of influence and eventually educate the public on race history.[55] As early as 1922 the American Library Association had reported the need for more women of color in the nation's growing number of minority libraries, and it dedicated a conference in 1931 to the question of special recruitment. In 1920 there were only 22 African American women in such institutions, but by 1930 the number had increased to 210.[56] In 1937 the Columbia Civic Library Association published a study that revealed the extent to which African American women embraced opportunities in library science. Of the 123 graduates of Hampton Institute Library School, all but nine were women. And of the 181 degrees in all library science programs awarded to African Americans by 1936, over 90 percent went to women.[57]

To be sure, in the twentieth century, librarianship remained a field predominated by women, regardless of race; by 1930 90.3 percent of all librarians were female, about 17 for every 1,000 professional women in America. On the other hand, these numbers do not reveal the deeper qualitative effects of librarianship in African American communities compared with elsewhere. As a field of professional advancement and a vehicle of social reform, library work was arguably more attractive for black women, since they did not have the same opportunities in other feminine fields. After World War I, libraries suffered an exodus of white women enticed by increased pay in journalism, clerical work, and sales—sectors that remained closed to black women.[58] Marilyn Nelson argues that unlike white women or black men in library work, black women made the most of the positions open to them, fostering a womanist consciousness, a "humanist vision of community," that funneled down and radiated outward in the years of the Harlem Renaissance.[59]

Whereas most African American male graduates of library schools occupied positions at large research archives and academic institutions, women looked to service their local communities directly. The few women at academic libraries worked exclusively with students of color at normal schools, junior colleges, and industrial and agricultural schools, while the majority of other women took jobs at high schools, middle schools, and public and branch libraries in major cities and the rural South, where access to materials had long been an obstacle. Eliza Atkins Gleason, the first African American to earn a doctorate in library science (University of Chicago, 1940), wrote her dissertation, "The Southern Negro and the Public Library," in an earnest attempt to expand resources where they were most desperately lacking. Miriam Matthews wrote her master's thesis, "Library Activities in the Field of Race Relations" (1927), at Berkeley and then served minority patrons at the Vernon and Watts branches of the Los Angeles Public Library. These women were typical in that they were more concerned with opening channels of education at the grassroots level, where children made up the brunt of the patronage, than with facilitating advanced academic research.[60]

By the 1930s, black women had carved out authoritative niches in public and branch libraries as guardians of culture and arbiters of juvenile literature. But whereas white librarians had once removed titles from shelves deemed "un-American" or of low moral value, black women now chose books for their children's departments for the purpose of race empowerment.[61] Charlemae Rollins of the Chicago Public Library had been a storyteller since 1926 and collaborated with colleague Augusta Baker on a bibliography of acceptable children's titles called *We Build Together* (1941). Baker, a former schoolteacher and librarian at the Countee Cullen Branch of the New York Public Library, insisted that the history children read today would affect race- and self-perception in the future. She recalled the miserable state of historical education for children when she first came to the library in 1937: "With the exception of one school in the area, where the principal was a black woman, there was little interest in the subject on the part of the schools, teachers, parents—and librarians." Her solution was to promote the acquisition of children's books that depicted African American historical figures in a positive and undistorted light. The James Weldon Johnson Memorial collection she created in 1939 consisted only of titles that met her strict criteria of historical accuracy and social value, without the caricatured portrayals typical under the program of Americanization that had previously dominated the branch library system.[62]

Black women quickly proved their worth as branch librarians, and by the 1930s and 1940s several had also shaped the library collections of the country's largest Negro archives. Foremost of the academic race repositories, the Moorland-Spingarn Research Center boasted an almost entirely female support and administrative staff that included curator and eventual director Dorothy Porter.[63] Although she did not originally set out to create a clearinghouse of race history, Porter's broad knowledge of sources and commitment to collecting, organizing, and maintaining them would make her a vital contributor to race history in the twentieth century. Born in 1905, she was raised in New Jersey and went to Minor Normal School in Washington before transferring to Howard in 1926. After graduating in 1928, she enrolled in the library science school at Columbia and received a B.L.S. in 1931 and an M.L.S. in 1932. Already familiar with the Howard collections from her days as an undergraduate library aide, Porter expressed interest in expanding the collection and was hired as curator of the Moorland Foundation materials. Her master's thesis, "Negro Writers before 1830," was an expansive project that required the unearthing of previously unknown or underutilized sources. It served as a preview of the broad-based bibliographic work for which she became so well known by historical researchers and writers during the next forty years.[64]

Porter had an uncommon intuition about where to search for clues to black culture and history, perhaps because she had such an extensive knowledge of both around the world. In the early 1940s she left Howard to pursue a master's degree at Radcliffe and worked with Harvard faculty in the fields of social and intellectual history, foreign policy, and diplomacy in America, Europe, and Africa. Her research in an eclectic mix of fields led her to speculate about the political, social, and cultural significance of people of African descent outside American borders. From Cambridge she wrote to Howard dean Rayford Logan: "Why have not white and Negro students selected topics on the subject? . . . Is it that they are unaware of the subject matter or is it that the materials which would give them the information are not available or perhaps unknown to them?" She returned to Howard convinced it was the latter and began collecting information on the Negro in "science, art, music, religion, diplomacy, [and] military tactics," particularly in the underexplored regions of Latin America.[65]

The race collection Porter inherited at Howard in 1932 had grown to be one of the largest in the country, and yet little effort had been made to make it accessible to researchers. Porter was the first to impose a comprehensive system of organization on these materials, starting first with the 1,650 items of Lewis Tappan that had been left disorganized since their donation in 1875 and proceeding to Moorland's collection of prints and books. She restored all the books in the collection and by 1938 had entered more than 20,000 items in the card catalog.[66] The Moorland Collection was impressive, but Porter insisted that it still lacked "material written by the Negro before 1850; anti-slavery periodicals; [and] present day publications." She kept an eye out for reasonably priced acquisitions through private book dealers, and her arduous work paid off as she acquired a keen sense about what written materials existed for research on the Negro past.[67]

Porter's staff was made up predominantly of women archivists, filers, and assistants committed to the broad promotion of race history. Yet as employees of a private university, they catered to the whims of faculty more often than to the needs of the larger African American community. For this reason one could argue that the womanist tradition described by Nelson came to fuller fruition at the Schomburg Center in Harlem. Like academic repositories, the Schomburg Center became home to materials from which scholarly history could be written. Yet unlike Atlanta or Howard Universities, the center made materials available to students and patrons with no formal academic affiliations. Schomburg's decision to place his collection in a branch library is telling of his hope to advance popular education from the start; indeed, the branch system in New York had been devised not long before strictly for the purpose of making books accessible to a greater number of patrons. In theory, branch librarians were more than collection custodians. As Garrison suggests, they were "apostles of culture" who engaged in "library extension work" for the benefit of the entire community. This was particularly true of the women at the Schomburg Center; in addition to maintaining race materials, they planned an extensive calendar of programs to advance the culture and history of the Negro.[68]

Most Schomburg women were members of neighborhood reform and educational groups that discovered that the library's materials helped immeasurably to extend the cultural learning they had already been advocating. Sadie Delaney, for example, was hired at the Harlem branch in 1920 but was also affiliated with parent teacher groups, the Young Men's Christian Association, the National Council of Negro Women (NCNW), and the advisory board of the National Association for the Advancement of Colored People. In her four-year tenure at the library, she created a Negro collection and organized the first African art exhibit for the public. In a 1923 article "The Library: A Factor in Negro Education," she conceded that the branch was underfunded but succeeded better than any other institution in providing "background to the Negro who has a desire to know his race history." She organized a book lover's club to promote further use of library collections, a concept that only gained momentum after she left the branch to pioneer the field of bibliotherapy at the U.S. Veterans Administration.[69] Like Delaney, colleague Regina Andrews developed cultural programs in the Harlem community, serving on the board of the American Council for Nationalities Service, the National Urban League, and the Harlem Experimental Theater. Creator of a program called "Family Night at the Library," she also scheduled programs on Negro history and culture that she extended when she became the first African American to head the 115th Street branch library in 1938.[70]

Librarians such as Delaney and Andrews were the life force of the branch and had been since its inception. Colleague and head librarian Ernestine Rose was also instrumental as the facilitator of the purchase of Schomburg's collection in 1925. It was her hope that his materials would better service the particular needs of the Harlem community, which in the years since she started at the branch had shifted from being predominantly Jewish and Spanish to almost exclusively African American. Rose believed that the branch's materials as well as its personnel should reflect the neighborhood's changing racial makeup. "One of the services which the colored assistants render the library," she maintained, "is the knowledge of neighborhood affairs and people which they gain far more quickly than the members of the alien race."[71] She was quoted further in the *Library Quarterly*: "We have here in Harlem the greatest negro city in the world—approximately 175,000 colored inhabitants. There should be available for these people and for those who have their interests at heart the most interesting and complete collection that can be formed. These books will foster the interest of the children and young folk in the history of their own race and inspire them to develop their own talents. The collection should be available equally to scholars, the man in the street and to school children of all races."[72]

In 1936 Rose reported happily that the Schomburg Center had become a community space where more and more people convened to study Negro history and culture. Whereas fewer than 100 people a month used its collections in the late 1920s, by 1938 it was common to see more than 1,000 monthly visitors. Indeed, Rose had set a new precedent in running a research archive, making historical materials accessible to people with no claims to specialized or scholarly expertise. Logs of the groups coming to the reference department indicate that people both from Harlem and outside the community were taking tours and conducting research. The George Washington Carver Society, the Ladies Library Club, the African Student Association, Harlem Hospital sociology students, and various Bible and vocational groups were listed on attendance roles in the 1930s and 1940s, as were white women from Sarah Lawrence, Mount Holyoke, and Barnard Colleges.[73] This open-door policy could be frustrating to professional scholars who came to the center to do research without distraction. As one Schomburg librarian explained, "I don't feel however, that we can refuse such [nonprofessional] groups as this helps more than we realize to make for better un[d]erstanding and race relations and certainly for more interest in the Negro generally, as most people have no idea of the vast amount of material on this subject and what the Negro's contribution has been."[74]

Rose had mentored many women at the center by the time she retired in 1942, and they in time took over the maintenance, cataloging, and acquisition of its materials.[75] Perhaps the most integral woman at the center after Rose was Catherine Latimer, the meticulous head cataloger and reference librarian until 1947. She came to the Harlem branch in 1920 at age twenty-five and was the first professionally trained black librarian in the New York Public Library system. Like Porter, she, too, attended Howard and Columbia and worked as a university archivist (Tuskegee Institute) before coming to New York to serve the African American community directly. After Schomburg died, Latimer continued his charge to make materials accessible for "digging up the Negro past," often by reorganizing the items already on the shelves. Adjustments and expansions of the Dewey Decimal System were necessary for much of the center's holdings in race history, she explained, especially when it inadequately highlighted the variety of texts available on Negro culture. Latimer frequently removed books about Africa from their traditional spots in the travel section and placed them in ethnology and history. Likewise she reshelved many of the books formerly indexed under slavery "in numbers more appropriate to the subject"; several she regrouped under ethnohistory, race relations, and social and economic history. Latimer hoped that these simple changes would make it easier for patrons to happen upon materials and perhaps be inspired to research the everyday lives of African Americans themselves.[76]

Her efforts paid off. The Schomburg Center, like the Moorland Foundation, was increasingly recognized as a repository of rare and original race works, so much so that soon Latimer required her staff to be expertly trained in handling a range of research requests, including ones for materials in languages other than English. One woman just starting on the job recalled how busy the reference department was in 1942:

We conducted individual and group tours explaining the background and growth of the collection. . . . Others who came have been research workers, authors, writers of magazine articles, artists, students (college, high school and university), study clubs, newspaper men, housewives, and men and women who came to read magazines, newspapers, books on a particular subject relating to the Negro. . . .

In addition to preparing new books and bindery books for the shelves, filing shelf cards, making numerous changes in recataloguing . . . my work has been the answering of reference questions.

Some of these have been telephone requests from Government agencies, newspapers and from worthwhile organizations for the material of the Negro in the present and the previous wars. An important agency concerned with race relations wanted the names and address[es] of outstanding Negro Sociologists and Economists. Others wanted examples of the integration of Negroes in Defense industries, and practically all the questions one could think of concerning the use and treatment of Negroes in the war effort.

Many of these requests that came required much probing and searching of Documents, newspaper clippings, magazine articles, pamphlets, of old, rare and new books.[77]

Porter's and Latimer's efforts were unmatched in the collection of Negro history, and yet they understood that the headway they achieved was only a beginning. The need for information had not been completely met for the increasing number of researchers who approached them about race materials. As early as 1934 Latimer published a general reference article in the *Crisis*, "Where Can I Get Material on the Negro?" hoping to stem the tide of inquiries to the center. Equally concerned with accessibility, Porter compiled *A Selected List of Books by and about the Negro* through the U.S. Government Printing Office and "Library Sources for the Study of Negro Life and History" in 1936.[78] In the 1940s Porter and Latimer reaped the benefits of a national HRS program "to bring under scholarly control all 'records created by or relating to the American Negro.'" African American colleges, the Frederick Douglass Memorial, and the Schomburg Center and the Moorland Foundation received government money with which to compile the most complete listings of race materials to date. HRS worker Edith Dodson classified manuscripts into subcollections with Arthur Schomburg until just two weeks before his death, and Latimer employed the help of WPA librarians to put together her most comprehensive research tool yet, the "clippings file," along with the *Calendar of the Manuscripts in the Schomburg Collection of Negro Literature* (1942).[79] Porter also took advantage of federal funds to publish *A Catalogue of Books in the Moorland Foundation* and to compile *The Union Catalog of Works Relating to the Negro* (1938). This bibliographic reference guide drew from the titles in the Moorland and Schomburg collections, the Library of Congress, the Henry Slaughter Collection, and archives at Duke, North Carolina, Fisk, Hampton Institute, and public libraries, making it the most comprehensive index of Negro history in the country.[80]

Porter continued to submit bibliographic pieces to the *American Scholar*, the Bibliographical Society of America, and the *JNH* about the obscure, unused, and missing sources of Negro history. But soon a new generation of black women librarians joined her in making sources accessible. Virginia Lacey and Miriam Matthews added to the finding aids with "United States Government Publications on the American Negro, 1916–37" (1938) and "The Negro in California, 1781–1910: An Annotated Bibliography," respectively. Jessie Parkhurst Guzman (Tuskegee Institute), Ellene Bentley (Atlanta University), Mollie Dunlap (Wilberforce University), and dozens of custodians of race collections became compilers and bibliographers, and several even became collectors themselves.[81] Dunlap's "Special Collections of Negro Literature in the United States" (1935) cited the existence of collections kept by Fannie Barrier Williams in New Orleans and the librarians at the George Cleveland Hall branch of the Chicago Public Library. In many ways these women were not different from the thousands of others who, as Woodson had already discovered, had been collecting privately for generations.[82] By the 1930s the impact of women archivists and bibliographers was especially apparent in the prefaces of the books written by up-and-coming race scholars. James Weldon Johnson expressed his appreciation for the efforts of Latimer and her Schomburg staff in *Black Manhattan* (1930), as did Nancy Cunard in *Negro: An Anthology* (1934). Vernon Loggins acknowledged Ernestine Rose and Catherine Latimer in *The Negro Author, His Development in America* (1931), and to Porter he gave special thanks for checking the accuracy of his bibliographies.[83]

Indeed, women were committed to making the raw materials of race history accessible to researchers, and yet they continued to collect items and encourage research in areas that revealed more about the experiences of men than themselves. In 1934 Georgia Fraser Goines, for example, one of Porter's most generous individual donors, deposited about 60 books and 100 periodicals—items overwhelmingly by and about African American men—in honor of her mother.[84] This tendency of women collectors like Goines deserves attention, since it is once again so unique. As white women and black men became more involved in historical work, stories of their collective pasts came forth as a natural result of their heightened historical awareness. Why was this less the case for African American women? Certainly it was not due to a lack of interest. Archivists and collectors such as Porter, Latimer, and Elbert were more than happy to acquire written works by women if they could find them, but African American women left little documentation of their past. Much of this is explained by a general lack of literacy or access to modes of publication before the twentieth century, but there is also a deeper explanation for why their thoughts rarely made it to paper.

Only with hindsight have scholars suggested that the African American woman's silence on the past reflects a self-imposed invisibility, or practice of "dissemblance." The building of facades frequently served as her modus operandi in the nineteenth century, as she tried to shield herself from white and male oppressors. Moira Ferguson concurs, noting that an author's ability to "mask the distance, rearrange chronologies, and alter characteristics" empowered her to feel a degree of personal security—and of course, there was the strategy of fictionalizing one's life or refusing to write about it altogether. Although dissemblance was a defensive measure, on one hand, its practice continues to hinder the African American woman seeking to recover an empowered past. Privileged women like Terrell may have whitewashed memories of victimization in their writings, but other women offered no memories of the past at all.[85]

Porter and Latimer did not diagnose the problem as dissemblance, but they certainly knew firsthand the frustration of finding few materials by or about women. Latimer confirmed this dearth of sources when she compiled the *Bibliography on the Contribution of Negro Women to American Civilization* in 1940. Another general listing of Schomburg materials produced by the WPA in 1942 revealed that women were only peripherally represented in the center's collections. Of the 239 entries in its biographical index, only 17 pertained to women, and many of them were white antislavery advocates. Two original volumes of Phillis Wheatley's poetry were practically the center's only rare items written by a woman, with the exception of books by Harriet Beecher Stowe. The Bruce, Crummell, West Indies, and Haiti Collections, some of the center's most exhaustive, contained little pertaining to women, despite the fact that women librarians, archivists, and catalogers were responsible for their maintenance.[86]

As professional librarians, Porter and Latimer had been trained to value *written* sources as the most functional pieces of historical evidence. Yet perhaps revering the written document to that extent caused historical women to elude them. It was not until the late 1930s that they gradually expanded their definition of historical materials to include nonwritten forms that revealed women in the past. Zora Neale Hurston and Ophelia Egypt had just explored women's oral culture, and the WPA had just distributed personal testimonies as part of its slave narrative project. Oral history collections at the Schomburg Center and the Moorland Foundation were in desperate need of additions, as both Porter and Latimer discovered when a writer named Pearl Graham sent them on a hunt for a slave named Sally Hemmings.

Graham's primary objective was to substantiate a historical rumor that had gone uninvestigated for 150 years: that Thomas Jefferson had fathered Negro children. Graham's intention was to get to the bottom of the muffled allegations and, if they were accurate, to restore the memory of Jefferson's mixed offspring with a slave she believed to be named Sally Hemmings. Latimer was excited about the project, for documents she unearthed independently suggested inconclusively that Graham's suspicions had merit. Moreover, she understood the influence that this finding could have on the popular interpretation of African American women in the Revolution and the early republic. Whereas former slaves such as Nat Turner and Frederick Douglass had become race icons in the post-Reconstruction years, black women had barely scratched the surface of national memory. If a woman slave were proven part of the narrative of the nation's Founding Fathers, the discovery could give the African American woman the historical attention and validation that had been denied her for so long.[87]

Graham realized that such a revisionist interpretation of an American idol like Jefferson could incite the ire of white Americans if not rendered without "a mountain of incontrovertible evidence." "Most white observers, at any rate, are going to take a cynical, 'Oh, yeah?' attitude," she predicted. "The whole story of Sally Hemings, etc., is so completely foreign to most Americans' conception of Jefferson. . . . But if he's going to be canonized, I think it should be for the virtues which he possessed, and not for those in which he was conspicuously lacking." Graham had already investigated a fair amount on her own, pursuing all leads that professional archivists had given her, but these experts, including Jefferson's biographers, rejected outright the possibility of black descendants. She lamented that "so many Jefferson students either ignore the subject completely, or mention it merely to dismiss it as political slander." The editor in chief of the Jefferson materials at Princeton was willing to make rare documents available to her, but oddly, none of the researchers who had already seen them had ever alluded to the controversy.[88]

Latimer regrettably could find few items that shed light on Hemmings's identity. She referred Graham to Porter and to Daniel Murray's widow, a woman who was little known to scholars but who owned some of the most obscure slave documents in existence, including the unpublished letters of two of Jefferson's alleged daughters. Murray confirmed the existence of Jefferson's mulatto children, but then Graham inquired further of Porter about this woman whom she knew as "Sally Heming, Hemings, or Hemmings." Of course, Porter suggested that Graham look in the traditional places: archives known to keep Jefferson memorabilia, such as Princeton and the Library of Congress. But she also advised a visit to her colleague Luther Jackson at Virginia Union University; he likely knew where to find ownership and genealogical records for slaves who lived in the state.[89]

Porter hoped that this paper trail would provide some initial leads, yet her previous searches had taught her that written documentation would turn up little where African American women were concerned. Independently she began her own inquiries through a word-of-mouth network of older black women, only to find that her own mother was acquainted with Lucy Williams, a Boston woman who claimed to be a descendant of Jefferson and Sally Hemmings. Porter's mother visited with the aging woman and corroborated some of the information that Graham had gathered about Hemmings's descendants. *"Please write to her because Princeton wants what she has,"* Porter's mother urged. "She has a few other relics which she will tell you about." Thus, unlike the Jefferson scholars who had preceded them, Graham turned to Williams's oral testimony and family keepsakes for historical leads.[90]

Initially, Graham was reluctant to rely on Williams for factual information about her genealogy. "I think her family tradition is a shade confused —as all family traditions become when they have to rely solely upon oral transmission," she confided. Nonetheless, the testimony from Williams and two other women claiming to descend from Jefferson provided evidence of family affairs that no amount of official paperwork would even subtly suggest. Williams explained that she had a great-grandmother named Sallie who took care of Jefferson's wife. "Sallie Hemmings was in Mrs. Jefferson[']s room when she died," she explained. "I have the bell given Sallie that she rang for the servants while ill." She contended that Sallie received the bell as the favored female servant, and she also confirmed that because of her status in Jefferson's home, her great-grandmother was the slave he took to France as a nurse for his daughter.[91] Further interviews with Williams's sisters revealed slight discrepancies between their oral family history and the genealogical information Graham and Jackson were able to find in legal files. However, the women were still able to provide information that Graham needed to put the pieces of the larger puzzle in place. Ownership records Graham obtained through Jackson were limiting in that they revealed more about male than female descendants. Williams, on the other hand, furnished family mementos that appeared to be passed down matrilineally. Graham obtained enough information about the mementos to draw up a chart of their transmission: from Jefferson to Sally Hemmings, to her daughter Harriet Hemmings, to her daughter Mary Frances Captain Coles, to Lucy Williams.[92]

Although not entirely conclusive, too many of the factors had come together for Graham to doubt the allegations. Other testimony corroborated Williams's claims that Hemmings joined Jefferson and his children on an extended trip to France and nursed his daughter for the duration of their stay abroad. Legal records showed, too, that Jefferson suspiciously freed all the Hemmings men from slavery. Graham was convinced that they were likely his son and grandsons, especially after she recovered Jefferson's "Farm Book," in which the statesman himself wrote about Hemmings's children. Pictures that Lucy Williams showed Graham even revealed several of her relatives as likenesses of Jefferson, with his same stature and "sandy red hair." "Jefferson probably was the father of Sally Hemings' four children," Graham concluded in 1949. "The Mendelian Law, and the physical characteristics of Sally's descendants, support those descendants' family tradition."[93]

In search of evidence about the life of a single African American woman, Graham proceeded down avenues that professional historians refused to take, but she took her lead from the research traditions established by archivists Catherine Latimer and Dorothy Porter. Already committed to finding evidence of the unrecovered African American past, they finally applied their knowledge to the retrieval of nonwritten sources that better revealed an African American woman named Sally Hemmings. Like Zora Neale Hurston, Porter understood that such personal histories were often embedded in the stories that women passed down to one another through word of mouth, not through written forms. DNA testing has since proven conclusively what Graham's legwork led her to believe in the 1940s. Nevertheless, her investigation of oral evidence was the most effective means at the time to illuminate otherwise irretrievable truths about the private life of an African American woman. Porter, Latimer, and Graham performed this work of recovery with little fanfare, in effect upholding Bethune's supposition about the African American woman and history: Just as her historical role occurred behind the "front ranks," so did her contributions to race historiography and memory. As educators and custodians of culture at the grassroots level, African American women proved as important in the end as front-rank scholars who have since been remembered as the fathers of New Negro history.

For the time being, the women of the New Negro History Movement seemed content to operate behind the front ranks, and yet there were subtle indications that a distinctive brand of African American women's history lay waiting to be discovered and produced. Sadie Daniel and Hallie Brown had begun to fashion it in the 1930s, but in the 1940s more African American women would recover the past to use it to their advantage. Club movement leaders in particular created their very own commemorative events, institutional histories, and even a repository in Washington dedicated to their legacy in public service and named fittingly after Bethune. They understood that by erecting institutions and rewriting the past, they infused their accomplishments with valued meaning and historical status that validated them in their current time and place.

In stark contrast to African American race workers, the white leaders of the woman's rights movement had always been conscious of their historical legacy, so much so that they achieved and shaped the memory of their political goals almost simultaneously. The histories, commemorations, and collections that came out of organized feminism in the early twentieth century provide poignant examples of literal "history in the making." African American race reformers left few histories, let alone reflections about them. However, white feminists left plenty of published and unpublished historical works and personal papers that reveal their intentions for and disagreements about their collective history over several generations. Suffrage pioneers purposefully stored the written sources from which future chronicles were written and, in fact, recollected and documented these accounts themselves so that the movement would not lack for eyewitnesses to the past. Unfortunately this abundance of firsthand accounts did not culminate in greater clarity about movement events; rather, it created a vacuum of consensus about how the past should shape the future. Like the women of the New Negro History Movement, woman's rights activists recognized the social and political influence their histories could wield, but they could never agree on what message they wanted to convey about their movement, its leaders, or woman's identity in the public sphere. They make an excellent case study of historical consciousness-raising nonetheless, and for turning the process of remembering into a subject of history itself.

Chapter 6
Remembering Organized Feminism

The historical projects of Dorothy Porter seem worlds apart from the exposé writing of Angie Debo or the patriotic history of Alice Earle, and yet taken together they speak to the varied social agendas of American women in the twentieth century and the need to construct new versions of the past to carry them out. The growing authority of the academic establishment quieted the voices of these women in one sense, but it certainly never silenced them or diminished their influence in their local communities. Women educators, preservationists, regionalists, and race workers continued to find ways to explore the pasts of marginal groups, using social and cultural perspectives much the same way women historians had before the professional turn. When the production of history and the shaping of memory are viewed from the margins, women suddenly emerge front and center as innovators of social change. History became their instrument for achieving justice for laborers, Native Americans, and members of the African American community—but what about for themselves as political beings? Indeed, just as women invoked the past for race and class reform, they also made history a conscious instrument of woman's rights in the twentieth century. In the decades before and after the passing of woman suffrage in 1920, organized feminists turned the writing of history into a programmatic act, a political gesture for woman's rights in the public sphere.

The agenda made explicit in the histories of the woman's rights movement had been implicit in the historical writings of domestic women since the nineteenth century. Alice Earle might have seemed more nostalgic than visionary in her rejection of cultural pluralism, yet at the same time she subtly sought recognition for women's public activities that made her modern in appeal. Her colonial writings discreetly endorsed professional pursuits for women (including her own as a writer) by harking back to the days when mothers and wives participated in the labor economy outside the home. Women in the generation after Earle's continued to seek careers in the public sphere and wrote histories of women's work to confirm that a precedent had long been set for them. Elisabeth Dexter's *Colonial Women of Affairs* (1924), like Abbott's *Women in Industry*, proved that women in the preindustrial age had been effective contributors to the family wage outside the domestic sphere. Women in various professional fields also picked up the historian's pen to advance their current standing in their respective occupations. In 1907 nurses Adelaide Nutting and Lavinia Dock produced the first of four volumes of *A History of Nursing*, and several decades later Dr. Kate Hurd-Mead chronicled female accomplishment in the masculine world of medicine (*A History of Women in Medicine* [1938]). These histories lent credence to the more brazen claims to rights of entry into public and political life made at the same time by historians of the woman's rights movement.[1]

Whether implicitly or explicitly, women in the early twentieth century were successfully making a case for an expansion of their public roles and professional identities by invoking the past. Yet their rationales for their presence in the workforce did not remain static over time. Mead's history of medical women, for example, reflected the growing preference of her younger generation to seek equality with men in public and professional pursuits. The first college-educated nurses of Nutting and Dock's generation, on the other hand, sought equitable value for their public work based on their distinctive feminine attributes, not a presumption of gender equality. Although both histories chronicled the accomplishments of medical women of the past, they inadvertently revealed the sensibilities of the medical women writing them in the present. Mary Beard tried to explain in *On Understanding Women* that this was always the case with written history; embedded in interpretations of the past were clues to the author's current time, place, and state of mind. Thus by extension, she believed, a historical text, its subtext (the hidden meanings behind the text), and even its *para*text (the conditions surrounding the production of the text) became enlightening of one another.

Beard's premise holds true for the histories women constructed about their professional work but also about their activism for political rights. Indeed these narratives divulged a range of shifting views about gender equality and difference, which more than likely reflected the opinions of other professional and activist women forging careers at the time they were written. In the decades before and after the passing of the Nineteenth Amendment, feminists wrote dozens of historical accounts that recollected aspects of the American woman's rights movement. Some were biographies of suffrage pioneers; others were institutional accounts that charted developments in the suffrage cause or advancements of American women in public life. Regardless of their focus, each was derived from a set of historical conditions that can be mined for the hidden meanings undergirding the text itself. In nearly all the histories to come out of the woman's rights movement, shifting subtextual disputes over political strategy and gender ideology were waged again and again as historians revisited the people and events of the movement and recast them in a modern mold. Yet whether they believed the feminist legacy was about equal or equitable standing, radical action or conservative contemplation, sexual autonomy or maternal responsibility in the political sphere, historians of the woman's rights movement sought to revise the past to fashion a legacy for women in the future.

The historians and histories that follow shed new light on women's heightened historical consciousness in the twentieth century, but also on one another. Feminist historians were a relatively homogeneous group. Most belonged to the first two generations of middle-class, college-educated women in America and with this common experience likely received similar cultural messages about history and activism. It should not be surprising that shared tropes, metaphors, and belief systems informed their stories. Nearly all movement historians expected American history to advance along a trajectory of democratic progress and thus told the story of the suffrage movement as an inevitable event along the nation's upward climb toward democratic perfection. Despite having this master narrative in common, however, suffrage historians made individualized choices that caused them to render remarkably different interpretations of the same people and events. These distinctive facets of their histories reveal much in turn about the women of this small activist community—as individuals and as ideological and generational cohorts. The calculated nature of their published accounts reveals the activist agendas of feminist leaders but also confirms that American feminists acquired an awareness of the power dynamics tied to the act of remembering.

Constructing a Usable Past for Woman Suffrage

The centennial commemorations held throughout the nation in 1876 inspired Susan B. Anthony and Elizabeth Cady Stanton to reflect more deeply than ever on their place in national memory, and they decided to write an elaborate history of the suffrage movement. Already their organized efforts had a rich thirty-year past worth chronicling in an official record. Six years earlier, Paulina Wright Davis had collected transcripts of the movement's key meetings, conferences, and speeches and published them as *A History of the National Woman's Rights Movement* (1871), but Anthony was intent on compiling something more grandiose for posterity. Having saved more than $4,500 of lecture fees to go toward production costs, she began work on her ambitious history of the suffrage movement in 1880 with Stanton and suffragist Matilda Joslyn Gage by her side.[2]

The actual compiling and writing of a suffrage movement history would be no easy task. Documents containing accurate names, dates, and places remained scattered among dozens of suffrage leaders; no one had kept files of newspaper clippings, schedules, or official correspondence, partly because no headquarters existed to house them. Moreover, leaders wrote about movement business and strategy in personal correspondence, not in official memorandums that had been dated and systematically stored. Still, as central figures in the organized movement, Anthony, Stanton, and Gage had an idea of who may have held onto certain papers and that few of these items had left the confines of New England or New York. Anthony herself had kept trunks and boxes of unorganized material in her attic in Rochester. When the three suffragists sat down to compile the history in Stanton's New Jersey home, Anthony and other movement leaders sent their papers and biographical information there. From November 1880 until late 1886, Anthony and company were consumed by the work that culminated in three massive volumes of the history of woman suffrage.[3]

Anthony was undoubtedly the most heavily invested of the three in the project. Her thankless clipping of papers and raising of funds reveal that in her mind the completed history could become the suffrage movement's greatest tool for advancement. She and her sister Mary lived for months at a time in cramped quarters overrun by boxes of pages, bindings, and books at all stages of completion. Over the next seventeen years she patiently waited for more lecture fees to come in to pay for binding, distribution, and storage costs for the 1,000 unbound books and lithographs in her possession. With the generous gifts of friends and supporters, she eventually bought out the rights of the publisher of the third volume and mailed copies to libraries and politicians at her own expense.[4] In Anthony's mind no price was too high for disseminating a movement history set in the words of its own leaders. She hoped that *The History of Woman Suffrage* would become the standard text to which future researchers referred when writing their own works on woman's rights in America. "Into whatever library the student may go seeking information upon this question," she insisted, "it is to these volumes he must look to find it in collected and connected form."[5]

The authors of the *History* boasted that they had "furnished the bricks and the mortar for some future architect to rear a beautiful edifice." Yet in claiming to lay the foundations of the history of woman suffrage, they would soon discover that they were not without critics within the movement itself. Lucy Stone, first and foremost, was an integral figure in the antebellum and abolitionist work highlighted in volume 1 of the *History*. She distrusted the authors' claims to compile an official and impartial account of the whole suffrage movement or to use her materials to good effect. Refusing to lend any biographical information or personal correspondence to the project, her important role was drastically reduced in the finished manuscripts sent to press.[6]

The *History*'s authors claimed to write for the entire organized movement, but suffragists other than Stone soon contested their account. Fundamental disagreements between the suffrage leadership had already led to a formal break into rival factions in 1869, and the *History* only exacerbated the schism. Led by Anthony and Stanton, the National Woman Suffrage Association (NWSA) formed shortly after breaking with abolitionist allies. Its members perceived that radical Republicans and male backers had no intention of enfranchising women along with African Americans under the Fifteenth Amendment. Moreover, their brand of egalitarian feminism was driven by natural rights ideology that ran counter to prevailing attitudes about women's distinct realm of influence in Victorian society. Stone, along with her husband Henry Blackwell, Mary Livermore, and Julia Ward Howe, formed the leadership of the opposing American Woman Suffrage Association (AWSA), a faction that understood the battle for the vote to be one of tactical alliances and incremental change. Its leaders supported the Fifteenth Amendment and the enfranchisement of African American men as a step in the right direction. More important, their suffrage work was not fueled by the assumption that women were naturally equal to men but, rather, that women were men's moral superiors, making them a necessary influence in the corrupted realm of politics.[7]

Given the different ideologies and personal antagonisms involved in the movement's split, AWSA leaders saw the *History* as undervaluing not only Stone's individual efforts but the collective work of their faction and its primary figures. Volume 1 paid some attention to these leaders, who in the early stages of the movement were not yet in disagreement about its direction. However in volume 2, which recorded the years of greatest conflict between the factions (1860s and 1870s), the authors stopped telling a unified story. The actions of the NWSA drove the narrative and became the foreground of the account, and had Stanton's daughter Harriot Stanton Blatch not intervened, the AWSA likely would have been omitted completely from the second volume. "If the *History of Woman Suffrage* had appeared with no mention of the American Association, a deluge of adverse comment would have fallen on the book," Blatch justified, inserting a 106-page final section that included steel engravings of Lucy Stone and Julia Ward Howe. Unfortunately, much of the damage had already been done; her additions seemed little more than token gestures compared with the book's first fifteen chapters of coverage.[8]

The *History*'s authors decorated volume 1 with a frontispiece of Frances Wright, a symbol of the egalitarian ideology they claimed for all American suffragists. Yet in reality this focus did not match the sentiment prevalent in American suffragism at the time of publication in 1881. The movement was gaining its momentum in the club and temperance ranks, where arguments of domestic protection and maternal moralism were winning pro-suffrage converts more successfully than the egalitarianism presented by Stanton, Anthony, and Gage. The story told in the *History* was primarily an account of a heroic, single-headed nucleus of equal rights activists who sought the vote through federal government action—not the multifaceted mix of parties, ideologies, and gradual change in sentiment that the suffrage battle had really become.[9]

Soon enough the biased recounting of events in the *History* caused suffrage leaders to come forward one by one to revise the movement's past and their roles in it. Friends had warned Mary Livermore, for one, that her "decease would inevitably be the signal for the appearance of unauthorized, unreliable, and shabby biographies" and that she should write about her participation in suffrage activities before it was too late. She quickly rose to the occasion, as did close associates of AWSA leaders Julia Ward Howe, Caroline Severance, Anna Shaw, and Frances Willard in the 1890s and 1900s, shoring up versions of suffrage events that they believed NWSA women distorted for personal ends.[10] Stanton and Anthony, in turn, were moved to reassess their individual places in popular memory, for while their version of the movement's history was known more widely than any other, their personal legacies were threatened by the life stories of other suffragists. Anthony asked loyal protégé Ida Harper to write an endearing account of her life and legacy, ultimately approving every word before it went to press. Harper explained in later years that Anthony's precautions were warranted; between Stone's bitter allegations and Stanton's "indiscretions," it was "no wonder she wanted her Life written while she was yet alive!" Indeed Stanton had become increasingly estranged from the movement for her unorthodox ideas about organized religion and sexual autonomy. In 1898 her friends and family urged her to gather papers to write her life story, *Eighty Years and More*, hoping that this version of movement events would resituate her front and center in the popular mind.[11]

Today it is commonplace for biographies to defame some individuals and bolster the reputation of others, yet remarkably few early movement biographers resorted to slander of suffrage pioneers. In 1890 the AWSA and the NWSA formally reunited as the NAWSA, and while tensions lingered in the ranks, in suffrage biographies they were detectable in silences rather than in overt insults. It remained an unwritten code to preserve a unified front to the outside world for the purpose of maintaining an enduring legacy for future activism; dishonoring the memory of any pioneer would have undermined the advancements this generation collectively achieved in woman's rights. Victoria Woodhull, however, would prove the exception to this rule; her legacy was one with which no one wanted to be associated after 1872.[12] She came on the suffrage scene like a whirlwind in late 1870, and for a time she had allured Gage and Stanton with her radical program for social change and Anthony with her congressional strategies for woman suffrage. The more conservative AWSA membership was generally repelled by her eccentric lifestyle and her ideas on free love, but soon her unsavory connection with the Beecher-Tilton sex scandal solidified her unequivocal banishment from all the biographies of suffrage pioneers. Future historians would also discover that Woodhull's contributions to the movement could not be broached without opening old factional wounds or stigmatizing individuals by association.[13]

Perhaps the more conspicuous void in these years was any biographical work on Lucy Stone, who died in 1893 before writing her personal memoirs. It is likely that a life story written immediately after her death would have matched the influence of Harper's *The Life and Work of Susan B. Anthony* (1899). Stone was an attractive figure among suffrage converts in women's clubs and moral reform groups, where sentiments resembled hers rather than Anthony's or Stanton's. Nonetheless, her silence allowed the pioneer generation to maintain an appearance of unified leadership in the historical literature passed on to twentieth-century feminists. This code of silence against dissension in the ranks remained unbroken—at least in the pioneers' lifetimes. As historians of later generations rewrote movement history to support their changing views on gender and modern women, they would revisit these old ideological feuds, even taking sides.

Anthony had already anticipated some of these twentieth-century contests at the end of the nineteenth century, when she started to think about compiling another volume of woman's rights history. No one understood her plan better than Ida Harper, who as Anthony's official biographer and traveling companion, not only chronicled the hardships of producing volumes 1 through 3 of the *History* but was urged by the dying pioneer to write volume 4, carrying the story to 1900. Harper believed that Anthony's plan made sense; by this time Stanton and Gage had passed away, and the materials necessary to write volume 4 had been collected and stored in Anthony's home, where she was already spending much of her time writing the volumes of Anthony's *Life and Work*.[14] Volume 4 became a two-and-a-half-year ordeal, over the course of which Harper claimed to have written 2,000 inquiries for documentation. Anthony proofread the manuscript and financed the project with donations and gifts received on her eightieth birthday. "This volume, after much labor on your part," she wrote Harper in 1903, "came in . . . clothed for the battle to be placed by the side of its three predecessors—the four huge volumes completing the records of the Nineteenth Century."[15]

With the publication of volume 4 in 1902, Harper brought the nineteenth-century movement into the twentieth century. Her timing was fitting because as both a suffragist and a historian, she, like the woman's movement itself, embodied transition. In a literal sense she stood directly between the old and new guards of the suffrage movement. The pioneers about whom she wrote in the 1890s were either dead or in their seventies and eighties; she was in her forties, and the youngest of the suffrage ranks were generally still in college. In the seven years Harper spent writing volume 4 of the *History* and *Life and Work*, Anthony had given her much insight into the older mentalities that allowed rifts like the ones between the AWSA and NWSA to exist. She also came to understand the Victorian culture that often made marriage and spinsterhood, motherhood and activism, such definitive and mutually exclusive paths for Anthony's generation. On the other hand, like a growing number of younger activists, Harper proved less torn between her private life and public activism, since she had married, had a child, and even divorced in the course of her activist life. And like many of the younger professionals who would join the suffrage ranks in the twentieth century, she received a university education and became a self-sufficient professional writer, contributing to publications such as the *New York Sun* and *Harper's Bazaar*.[16]

In many ways the tone of volume 4 of the *History* reflected Harper's dual consciousness as an old-guard suffrage pioneer and a feminist activist with modern sensibilities. Like her predecessors, she largely concealed any factionalism within the suffrage movement, cloaking rifts between the NWSA and AWSA and the factional fallout after they reunited in 1890. On the other hand, the tone of volume 4 acquired a heightened element of distance, as Harper seemed less intimately connected to the expanding network of local and state suffrage players that peopled yet never humanized her account. The personalities that colored volumes 1 through 3 were increasingly muted in volume 4 and were overtaken by the names, dates, and venues of state campaigns.[17] Harper's decidedly different narrative voice echoed the changes in professional history writing as well as suffrage activism by 1900; just as history had become a field of scientific experts, an expansive and disciplined suffrage bureaucracy gradually replaced the charismatic leadership of individual suffrage pioneers. Harper discarded the idealistic rhetoric that saturated the pages of volumes 1 through 3 for descriptions of the politically oriented, expedient strategies of twentieth-century suffrage tacticians.[18]

Carrie Chapman Catt, Anthony's successor to the NAWSA presidency, had much to do with this modern face of organized suffragism. Eventually she oversaw the production of the fifth and sixth volumes of the *History* to make them reflect her modern sensibility and focus. Nonetheless, in the nearly twenty-year span between the printing of volume 4 and volumes 5 and 6, other movement histories had already begun to reflect the shifting attitudes of organized feminists. In 1908, for example, Harper published her third and final posthumous volume of Anthony's *Life and Work* to re-create a model of suffrage heroism inspiring to younger women. It made a timely appearance; the progress of NAWSA campaigns, then under the direction of Anna Howard Shaw, slowed to a near standstill on state and local levels. Harper's latest installment of Anthony's life story rekindled memories, accurate or otherwise, of a more effectual age in woman's rights activism.[19] Anthony's durability as a feminist icon came to depend on more than Harper's nostalgic recollection of her accomplishments, however; in this twentieth-century biography, Anthony was recast into a distinctly modern mold, released from the Victorian trappings of her pioneer generation. Harper's Anthony was lovable but hardly sentimental, wise but not worldly, and impassioned but never emotive or overly dramatic. She was disciplined to the point of rigidity and dependent on rigorous routine, wearing the same plain clothes and eating the same bland meals even on special occasions. Harper hoped that Anthony's Spartan simplicity as depicted in *Life and Work* would not seem puritanical or old-fashioned but, rather, efficient and pragmatic, given her objectives. When compared with ideologues like Stanton or Stone, Anthony would seem a suffragist all the more modern.[20]

Women had indeed formed new ideas about the traits the suffrage heroine embodied. No longer the maternal martyr or the radical ideologue, she was a deft tactician, a self-sufficient doer, and a pragmatic feminist—not only in thought but in constant action, particularly in the political ring. Catt's brand of leadership, as portrayed by younger movement historians, had a certain appeal that would not have endeared her to older suffragists. She made a clean break from both the maternalist and the egalitarian ideologues of the pioneer generation, claiming not to know whether the vote was woman's right, duty, or privilege, and in the end not much caring. She was a professional organizer undistracted by stray emotions and personal loyalties. According to twentieth-century suffrage historians, in her two terms as the NAWSA president, Catt embodied more qualities of the modern leader than did Anna Howard Shaw, a moving orator but an inept political tactician and organizer.[21] In *Susan B. Anthony: The Woman Who Changed the Mind of a Nation* (1928), Rheta Childe Dorr described Shaw as a "roly-poly little Methodist preacher, rather narrowly educated, rather inexperienced in life, brimming with harmless egotism." Although she disagreed with Catt's gradualist suffrage strategies, she preferred in Catt what she claimed to see in the timeless and "unemotional" Susan B. Anthony: a modern intellectual sense, "a handsome face and figure," "a genius for organization," "knowledge of parliamentary law," and "an executive ability and power to raise money." Catt was the model presiding officer of a modern activist bureaucracy, as was the younger NWP leader Alice Paul, whom suffrage historian Doris Stevens likened in *Jailed for Freedom* (1920) to V. I. Lenin: "a master strategist . . . cool, practical, rational, sitting quietly at a desk and counting the consequences, planning the next move before the first one is finished."[22]

This modern shift in suffrage focus and leadership style was no more evident than in the contrasting writings of suffrage leaders who attempted to become historians themselves. Shaw's *Story of a Pioneer* (1915) resembled the works of earlier Victorian writers with its personal, anecdotal style. Shaw recounted the organizational activities in which she took part, but she shifted focus from the finer details of suffrage business to offer insights into the bond she shared with Anthony, her spiritual mentor, speaking of her "humor," "sympathy," and "selflessness," not her meticulous tactical sense as younger historians would. Shaw's life story was tinged with a yearning for the same close-knit intimacy shared among movement leaders of an earlier time—so much so that her thoughts seemed more connected to the nineteenth century than the present.[23]

In contrast to Shaw's historical writing, all nostalgia was removed from Catt's *Woman Suffrage and Politics: The Inner Story of the Suffrage Movement* (1923), written with the aid of NAWSA secretary Nettie Shuler. In the style of Ida Tarbell's popular histories of big business at the time, Catt's work served as exposé, the "inner story," as the subtitle suggests. Unlike the self-congratulatory histories of the pioneer generation, Catt's version was devoid of personal anecdotes about individuals. The primary protagonists in her analysis were "interests" and "forces"—namely, woman suffrage versus government, big business, and the liquor lobby. Like many of the accounts now written by "scientific" historians, Catt's was unabashedly argumentative, chock full of statistics and expert testimony, and driven by the assumption that bureaucracies, systems, and material interests—not individuals—ultimately acted as agents of change. "Circumstantial and direct evidence supported by affidavits carefully preserved by the National Woman Suffrage Association during a period of fifty years, shows the liquor interests in active opposition to woman suffrage on the following counts," she argued. After listing the counts, she provided footnotes that cited government reports and other investigative studies as evidence.[24]

Catt's penchant for empirical data and scientific argumentation contrasted starkly with the historical writing of the preceding generation of suffragists, whose historical accounts were peopled and personal, rhetorical rather than analytical. Her summary of the movement's legislative battles is a perfect example: "To get the word male in effect out of the constitution cost the women of the country fifty-two years of pauseless campaign thereafter," she wrote. "During that time they were forced to conduct fifty-six campaigns of referenda to male voters; 480 campaigns to urge Legislatures to submit suffrage into State constitutions; 277 campaigns to persuade State party conventions to include woman suffrage planks; 30 campaigns to urge presidential party conventions to adopt woman suffrage planks in party platforms, and 19 campaigns with 19 successive Congresses."[25] Catt assured readers that her facts and figures could be substantiated through the documentation she organized into an official NAWSA archive. As she wrote *Woman Suffrage and Politics*, she paid Ida Harper to use this material to construct an official, updated movement history—what ultimately became *The History of Woman Suffrage* volumes 5 and 6.[26]

Although Catt did not play the active part that Anthony did in writing the first four volumes of the *History*, her influence over volumes 5 and 6 was unmistakable; for just as she made suffrage activism professional and bureaucratic, she did the same for the movement historian and her history. Harper did not write the individual chapters but, rather, compiled state-by-state synopses written by research specialists hired by Catt. This systematized process proved both a relief and a frustration; although Harper was no longer solely responsible for gathering data that had expanded manyfold since she wrote volume 4, dozens of women now documented in minute detail developments in each U.S. state, Canada, Great Britain, and Europe that often seemed unrelated. Harper enjoyed complete control over the entire contents of volume 4 but grew impatient with efforts to impose continuity on the individually written chapters for volumes 5 and 6. Many of her writers turned in drafts of chapters that lacked names, dates, and general coherence. Dissatisfied with Grace Hebard's revisions of the Wyoming chapter, Harper finally rewrote it herself. In the end, volumes 5 and 6 were a product of an assembly line of historical production. Harper lamented that they read more like a disjointed patchwork of people and places than a unified story of a single movement.[27]

Catt, however, was pleased with the outcome, managing with Harper's assistance to take over the reins of both the NAWSA leadership and its official history. Unfortunately she did not grasp that forces outside her control were already fragmenting the unified movement and the memory she was trying to protect. By 1912 a distinct faction had formed within the NAWSA's congressional committee that eventually broke from the organization altogether. This group, led by Alice Paul and Lucy Burns, formed into the NWP in 1916 and led a campaign for the vote based on civil disobedience for a federal suffrage amendment. Highlighting the work of the NAWSA, Catt's "official" history barely mentioned the NWP or other suffrage groups active in the passing of the Nineteenth Amendment or differences within the ranks of the NAWSA itself. The generally younger members of the NWP rejected Catt's state-by-state strategy and what they perceived as the passive complacency of the matronly NAWSA membership. Dissatisfied with the organizational consensus that the vote should be won based on women's inherent differences from men, they insisted instead that the fundamental equality of the sexes legitimated women's claims to the vote. In their public demonstrations, and soon in their movement histories, they presented themselves as the rebellious young spirits of the organized woman's movement who no longer cared to wait for incomplete suffrage goals.[28]

In the years immediately before and after the passage of the Nineteenth Amendment, radical sympathizers with Alice Paul wrote movement histories that revised the suffrage memory ensconced by Harper and Catt. Inez Irwin, Doris Stevens, Rheta Childe Dorr, Katharine Anthony, and Harriot Stanton Blatch were all women associated with the NWP who wrote full-length suffrage histories or historical biographies in these years. Their works, some of which have been mentioned already, gave the legacy of woman's rights a much-needed broadening after 1920, providing models of feminist heroism that extended beyond the outmoded role of the moralizing suffragette to appeal to younger women. The historians of the NWP were professionals, generally in their late twenties and early thirties when they joined the movement. They were college educated and cosmopolitan, and several participated in pacifist and militant suffrage movements in Europe after college. They bore relatively few children and identified themselves by their professional work rather than their domestic duties. Both Dorr and Irwin, for example, were journalists who earned a living primarily through their craft. Dorr raised a son single-handedly while she wrote for publications like the *New York Evening Post, Everybody's Magazine*, and *Hampton's*, and she served as editor of the *Suffragist*. Irwin belonged to several professional writers' organizations and had by all accounts a happy, egalitarian marriage.[29] Irwin, Dorr, Stevens, and Anthony belonged to the radical feminist group Heterodoxy in New York's Greenwich Village; at meetings they fleshed out the ideas that eventually found expression in their histories of the suffrage movement.[30]

In every sense, these NWP women were already living the independent lifestyles heroines fought to achieve for all women in their movement histories. They scripted the fight for political rights not as a moral imperative but as the right of autonomous beings to the political status they deserved. In some ways their spiritual mother (and biological mother in the case of Blatch) was Elizabeth Cady Stanton; like them, she understood women's subjection as rooted not solely in the inability to vote but also in American society's need for a deeper cultural reorientation. NWP radicals also shed the assumption that women fundamentally differed from men, but their broader feminist vision for political, sexual, and economic equality and independence more closely resembled the feminism of Charlotte Perkins Gilman, who also appealed to their twentieth-century predilections as professional women. To varying degrees the feminism of NWP historians also fell under the rubric of a larger socialist philosophy of egalitarianism tinged with sympathy for the working class. This may be why socialist biographer Rheta Childe Dorr found Susan B. Anthony, an advocate for labor later in her career, more attractive to write about in 1928 than Stanton, despite Stanton's modern resonance as a sex activist. In radical suffrage histories the working-class militant became a symbol of grassroots fortitude, in contrast to the middle-class matron of NAWSA accounts.[31]

History had taught radical NWP women that the demure tactics of the NAWSA had not worked in America or elsewhere. Accordingly, their intent when revising movement history was to relocate the American suffrage legacy away from the maternalist politics of their conservative counterparts and closer to a tradition of radical agitation. They soon discovered that the most effective way to revise movement memory to this end was to reappropriate the most widely recognized suffrage icon, Susan B. Anthony, as the matron saint of feminist militancy. NWP historians linked Anthony explicitly to their expedient suffrage program, referring to the national suffrage amendment as the Susan B. Anthony Amendment or "Susan's child." Doris Stevens asserted in *Jailed for Freedom* that Anthony "was the first woman to defy the law for the political liberty of her sex. . . . In the national election of 1872 she voted in Rochester, New York, her home city, was arrested, tried and convicted," thus making her "the first militant suffragist." In *Susan B. Anthony* Dorr similarly clarified the raison d'être of the NWP as a campaign to retain "Susan's own militant spirit . . . to carry out the instructions of the great leader."[32]

The NWP's recasting of Anthony as a champion of the national amendment completely contradicted Shaw's and Catt's personal memories of Anthony's activism. The former linked Anthony to the work they did together in the states, and the latter insisted that to link Anthony's name to the federal amendment would be to distort the memory of Lucretia Mott championing it before her. Nevertheless, Anthony's radical remaking by NWP historians was nearly complete. Once it was firmly established that Anthony was their spiritual mother, NWP historians portrayed Alice Paul, not Carrie Chapman Catt or Anna Shaw, as Anthony's spiritual daughter. In *Jailed for Freedom* Stevens even described Paul and Anthony as physical and spiritual likenesses of each other. Both women retained an egalitarian ethic and a strong moral compass from their Quaker upbringings; they dressed plainly, worked avidly, never married, were shrewd political tacticians, and devoted their lives to woman's rights.[33]

This reworking of movement history was inevitable. Just as older historians reconstructed the past to ingratiate themselves in the public sphere, younger women fashioned a history that suited their needs as professionals and modern activists looking to the future. NWP historians remade suffrage heroism to match their militant brand of activism, sometimes blurring the line between historical representation and fictional characterization in the process. Irwin, for example, touted *The Story of the Woman's Party* (1921) not as history but as "feministic literature" designed to promote the NWP.[34] Although she maintained that her characters were transparent representations of real militant feminists, often she reduced these individuals to a single stylized type: the youthful martyr. Indeed, most militant feminists were younger and more willing than the average NAWSA suffragist to act out defiantly for woman's rights. Nevertheless, the heroines featured in radical histories maintained a youth and beauty that may have been more than slightly embellished. Stevens and Irwin described militant feminists indiscriminately as vigorous "youths at heart," regardless of their age or rank. They referred to both Alice Paul and Lucy Burns as "girls" and implied the youth of the militant movement metaphorically by referring to the NAWSA as the "mother" group and NWP suffragists as rebellious, idealistic daughters. "The attitude of the Woman's Party," Irwin explained, ". . . was like that of a girl who wants a college education. She teases her father for it without cessation, but she goes on loving him just the same."[35]

These embellished depictions of youth may have been due in part to Irwin's and Stevens's own romantic notions about what militancy represented and entailed. Stevens described it as more than just a label for NWP tactics but as "a state of mind, an approach to a task," and its adherents as "those who in their fiery idealism do not lose sight of the real springs of human action." Irwin associated the militant mentality to her coming of age at Radcliffe, when she first was drawn to the tactics of the Pankhurst women in England: "When they threw the first brick my heart was tied to it," she fondly recalled. Gone were the days when the matronly suffragette waxed rhetorical in sewing circles and reform clubs; the militant feminist, as depicted by NWP historians, was a young, idealistic renegade and athlete, with a constitution to sustain beatings, starvation, and constant rigorous activity. "It is one of the chief glories of the Woman's Party that these organizers came to them younger and younger," Irwin remarked, "until at the end they were fresh, beautiful girls in their teens and early twenties." In *Jailed for Freedom* Stevens introduced the "young, small, slender" militant Hazel Hunkins, who "had climbed up onto the pedestal and was throwing logs into the pool of oil when two huge policemen descended upon her." Mildred Morris, on the other hand, was quick enough to run away from the police after "fasten[ing] some asbestos coils among the White House trees." In *The Story of the Woman's Party*, Irwin claimed that such physical vigor was necessary in the daily campaigns of suffrage militants, compared with the more passive deliberations of NAWSA members.[36]

Radical historians wrote about dozens of women who symbolized the youth and vigor of militant heroism, but none more than Inez Milholland, the radical martyr who died at age thirty, only four years before suffrage was won. "She loved work and she loved battle," Stevens eulogized, ". . . with a loveliness beyond most, a kindliness, a beauty of mind and soul . . . the symbol of light and freedom." Irwin dedicated a whole chapter of *The Story of the Woman's Party* to Milholland's memory; other NWP historians enhanced their memorials with photographs of Milholland posed in sweeping gowns, wearing white, and atop a horse, all of which displayed her natural beauty and vigor. Like biographers of Anthony, Milholland's historians blurred the distinctions between the myth and the woman. No NWP history listed her actual accomplishments for suffrage with any detail or revealed whether the cause of her death was even linked to the militant acts for which she achieved martyrdom. Regardless, as one of the young, courageous, physical, beautiful, "human sacrifices offered on the altar of woman's liberty," Milholland served her purpose as an effective icon for militant feminism.[37]

Suffrage Is Won but Our Work Is Not Done:
Adapting and Contesting the Memory of Suffrage Pioneers

The leaders of the suffrage movement documented their past so that future generations would never forget the pains they took to advance American women and democracy. Forward-looking Stevens, Irwin, Harper, and Catt wrote their histories immediately after women won the vote, not only to distinguish their suffrage faction as the most efficacious but also to win public acceptance to attack gender inequalities beyond suffrage. The NWP continued under the same name after 1920, but the NAWSA spawned the postsuffrage organization the League of Women Voters (LWV). The league only enjoyed about 5 percent of the nearly 2 million members the NAWSA had at its peak, not because women stopped organizing after 1920 but, rather, because former suffragists now scattered their energies in multiple directions. The strong, unified front presented in movement histories had never been the reality among feminists before suffrage was won, but the pretense was easier to uphold when the primary focus of so many women's organizations was to achieve formal equality in the political sphere through the vote. In the postsuffrage years the differences among women—racial, religious, ideological, and otherwise—became more prominent and their club activity more specialized. Nancy Cott suggests that women's diversified activities after 1920 revealed their "dual sense of themselves as members of a sex and as individuals possessing singular characteristics and designs." As more American women entered the professions and combined careers with marriage and motherhood in the 1920s and 1930s, their organizations increasingly operated outside the model of separate spheres idealized by suffrage pioneers, intersecting, as Cott explains, "with government bureaucracy, universities, research institutes, trade unions, hospitals, and so on."[38]

Younger generations of American feminists set their sights on goals different from those aspired to by the preceding generation of collective and separatist agitators; no longer united with other women in the singular battle for suffrage, they became introspective, seeking to understand themselves as autonomous, self-fulfilled individuals equal to any man—not as members of a separate feminine sphere or female collective. These independent "new women," so to speak, had been fashioning themselves in various guises since the 1890s. In the postsuffrage years they were professional, sexual, and as Rheta Childe Dorr described them, wanting to "belong to the human race, not to the ladies' aid society." As many of the professionals who remained active in woman's rights diverted their energies to the Equal Rights Amendment, professional advancement, and party politics after 1920, movement historians recognized the need to revise the past in ways that appealed to women as careerists, sexual beings, and individuals on a par with professional and political men.[39] The sanitized accounts of spinsters uniting for political equality no longer inspired married and career women with individualist sensibilities. The postsuffrage historian thus began to focus anew on psychological and sexual identity, in effect undergirding the tale of woman's rights with a wholly different but resonant metanarrative: the triumph of the eccentric individual over social restrictions and gender conventions.

Unveiling subconscious identities and hidden sexuality, biographers recast historical figures with a heightened sense of realism and complexity lacking in earlier accounts of women's collective agitation. The burgeoning fields of Freudian psychology and sexology validated these new explorations of the subconscious and sexual in the twentieth century. Formerly, Victorian biographers had typecast women reformers and activists as two-dimensional caricatures: religious saints, as in the case of Frances Willard, or licentious troublemakers, as in the case of Victoria Woodhull. In the postsuffrage years, however, these figures were recast and fleshed out as sexual, troubled beings whose complexity made them attractive and incredibly functional as biographical subjects. By revealing the personal inner conflicts deeply embedded within their subconscious, feminist biographers could explore broader feminist concerns that suffrage activism had not previously addressed—namely, the social and sexual norms that denied women deeper self-realization in American society.[40]

This shift to modern ways of remembering was no more apparent than in the range of works written on Margaret Fuller in the late nineteenth and early twentieth centuries. As a forerunner of the modern feminist movement, Fuller had defied facile categorization and frustrated Victorian biographers, who included her in volumes of "Extraordinary Women" and "Eccentric Personages" at the same time. "Her character alternately repels and charms, but her story is always sad," one concluded in 1883. Friends Thomas Wentworth Higginson and Julia Ward Howe wrote of her trials in more sympathetic life stories at the end of the nineteenth century, but at the expense of rendering impersonal accounts of Fuller the writer and social critic, not the deeply tormented woman.[41] Finally in 1920 radical feminist Katharine Anthony exposed Fuller, sexuality and all, in *Margaret Fuller: A Psychological Biography*. "Margaret was, after all, more interesting as a personality than as a writer," Anthony told readers. Her goal was to apply "a new method to old matter": "by means of modern psychoanalysis . . . to analyze the emotional values of an individual existence, the motivation of a career, the social transformation of a woman's energies." In Anthony's mind, such an approach would reveal the flesh-and-blood person Fuller's previous biographers had failed to expose. Anthony distinguished between Fuller's "inner" and "outer" struggles yet drew connections between them; Fuller's miserable relationships in adulthood, for instance, Anthony linked to her sublimated incestual feelings as a child for her father. She described Fuller in girlhood as a clinical picture of Freud's future hysteric and accused previous biographers of misdiagnosing her hysteria or simply ignoring it altogether. These intensely personal, psychosexual conflicts explained the phenomenon of Margaret Fuller, Anthony believed, as well as her modern, individualistic brand of feminism.[42]

It was no mystery why Katharine Anthony was drawn to Fuller's ideas and life story. As a lesbian socialist she had long searched for a vehicle through which to explore broader feminist issues, and the suffrage movement had not been it. Heterodoxy was one forum in which she expressed unconventional ideas about gender and sexuality, but another outlet was the writing of feminist biography. Her psychological Fuller resembled the complex modern woman who sought to reconcile romantic love with individual autonomy. Anthony assured readers that while Fuller's multifaceted feminism had lost resonance in the years when " 'woman's rights' narrowed down to a strictly suffrage basis," it would be redeemed now that suffrage was won and women longed for more. She confessed that she much identified with Fuller, "a modern woman who died in 1850"; then again, she seemed to relate easily to all her biographical subjects, from Mercy Otis Warren to Louisa May Alcott and, eventually, Susan B. Anthony. To varying degrees, each subject allowed her to explore the historical construction of feminine norms as individuals who lived despite them; they defied convention, validating Anthony's own eccentric life choices and feminist views.[43]

Like Fuller, the formerly shunned Victoria Woodhull became an acceptable if not titillating subject of a biography by Emanie Sachs called *"The Terrible Siren"* (1928). As the title suggests, Woodhull was depicted as an alluring and sexual figure—"a witch," "a storm centre," "a firebrand," and "a fearless muckraker" all rolled into one. Sachs revisited Woodhull's childhood as a psychiatrist would a patient's, uncovering the "scar tissue on the psychic wounds" that unlocked the mysteries of Woodhull the woman. She guaranteed readers that "her story [wa]s as strange as her personality," and that she was a woman of endless contradiction: "a dual personality, half saint, half sinner, but altogether fascinating." In Sachs's mind this complexity made Woodhull the quintessentially modern woman who was merely misunderstood by an earlier generation. Sachs recast the former misfit as a feminist counterheroine, "a pioneer suffragist . . . a social reformer who suffered for views now generally accepted."[44]

In June 1929 Inez Irwin finished reading *"The Terrible Siren"* and wrote former NAWSA leader Maud Wood Park with her thoughts: "Never, *literarily*, was I so torn between triumph and disgust as when I read that book," she confessed. Woodhull and her sister Tennessee Claflin "made me blush not only for my sex but for the whole human race. At the same time, I could not help taking a rich and wicked joy in the way they walked roughshod, spike-heeled and copper-toed over the entire male sex. As I love to see women beat the masculine game, I suppose the triumph triumphed over disgust."[45] Irwin's reaction to the Woodhull biography indicated the change in sentiment among organized feminists in the immediate postsuffrage years; although initially offensive to her ingrained sense of propriety, ultimately the sexual and assertive woman was her feminine model of choice.

Ida Harper could sense this new face of feminism taking shape as early as 1908 when she introduced her third volume of *Life and Work* to younger generations of American women. It was difficult to recall Anthony as an attractive feminine figure when women increasingly viewed spinsterhood and homosociability as unattractive life choices. Fiction authors already were depicting single activists as "fanatically driven" and "incomplete," and Freudian disciples had diagnosed women like Anthony as sexually repressed individuals who sublimated sex into overwork.[46] Propelling Anthony's memory to the forefront of the American consciousness was even more difficult in the postsuffrage years. Feminists who lived through the suffrage battle detected that their own daughters and granddaughters had little desire to perpetuate the memory of pioneer suffragists as role models. "The average young woman today has no notion of the ordeal through which that woman went," grumbled one aging feminist to another as she reflected on Anthony's accomplishments. Instead, younger women seemed to take for granted the politically and economically independent status they had inherited, without questioning the desirability of their professed equality with men in the public sphere or what women before them had sacrificed to obtain it for them. Lucy Anthony's concern over what to do with Susan's keepsakes was indicative of the generational divides among feminists in the postsuffrage years. She deposited some of Susan's key letters at the Library of Congress, fearing that her great niece, Susan B. Anthony II, would use them to write a biography "from the standpoint of the young radical generation"—as if Stevens, Irwin, and other NWP women had not already.[47]

Indeed, second- and third-generation feminists had rewritten Anthony's legacy since Harper had first done it in 1908, and several even dressed her in modern, sexually liberated attire. To them the separatist reform culture in which Anthony once operated seemed outmoded and cranky, and Anthony herself, as depicted in the earliest histories, seemed a schoolmarm rather than a radical woman's activist. She never married or had children, nor did she seem to interact much with men, making a modern makeover awkward. In *Susan B. Anthony* Dorr attempted one anyway, effectually reducing the former AWSA/NWSA split to different takes on women's sexuality. As the leaders of the renegade wing, Stanton and Anthony looked like rebellious sex radicals compared with Lucy Stone and Julia Ward Howe, matrons "as puritanically conservative as Plymouth Rock." Because radicals such as Dorr remade Anthony this way, feminists continued to place Anthony, a single-minded suffragette, in a position of perpetual primacy in the woman's movement even when the vote no longer remained the focus. Both the NWP and the LWV touted her as a "Great American Emancipator" like the male icons Abraham Lincoln and George Washington, whose accomplishments should be equally weighted in the national record.[48]

Dozens of feminists, young and old, worked on projects to preserve Anthony's memory in the years following the passing of the Nineteenth Amendment. Yet why was this the case when Anthony seemed so unbefitting of a modern makeover? Certainly Dorr's depiction of her as a sex radical was a stretch, if not wholly inaccurate. In more ways than Anthony did, Stanton provided the intellectual inspiration for the sexual, secular, individualistic strain of feminism that prevailed among the movement's younger generations of professional women, and yet she was not the subject of a biography until her daughter Harriot Stanton Blatch intervened in 1940. Ellen DuBois suggests that Stanton may not have been appropriated as a radical icon of the NWP because of Alice Paul's ideological differences with Blatch. Nonetheless, this does not explain why Matilda Joslyn Gage also fell into relative obscurity; she, one can argue, embodied feminist militancy more definitively than either Stanton or Anthony before Paul even entered the organized suffrage scene. She had been so far to the left, in fact, that she refused to join Anthony in the reunification of the NWSA and AWSA in 1890, establishing the more radical Women's National Liberal Union instead. Nonetheless, younger feminists preferred to recall Anthony's strategies, not Gage's, as the foil to the "polite propagandizing" of AWSA rivals.[49]

Anthony's resilience as a feminist icon can be attributed to many things, not the least of which was Ida Harper's ability to portray her early in highly adaptable terms. In *Life and Work* Anthony appeared as a single renegade yet a universal mother, an ally of reform but also of the working class, and deeply committed to women's escape from dependence, as broadly as later generations chose to construe this. In her ability to lead, Anthony was likened to great men such as Lincoln and Napoleon Bonaparte. At the same time, Harper's recounting of the suffragist's quieter moments made her never appear too mannish. In making Anthony too complex to classify yet likable at any extreme, Harper created a malleable feminist symbol for both conservative and radical feminists over several generations. Anthony's historical litheness may also be attributable to the fact that she never left her own rendition of her life to posterity. The fact that Harper consulted Anthony at all junctures of the drafting of *Life and Work* was irrelevant to younger generations of biographers, who could later claim to compose a more authentic life story. Throughout the twentieth century, writers looked for the elusive personal documents that were thought to contain the inside truth about Anthony's relationships and feminist views, all the while reinvoking her memory as her contemporaries fell deeper into anonymity. When all was said and done, Anthony had, in essence, never aged. Her silence on her own life and legacy allowed others to remake her over and over to conform to changing preferences in the twentieth century.[50]

By the 1930s the NWP had gone so far as to form a memorial committee to publicize, broadcast, and propagate Anthony's memory among the American populace. "We are endeavoring to make her name known throughout the world as the great reformer and leader which she was, whose contribution to the civilization of two centuries has been unequalled by that of any man," committee members declared. "She should have her place in history equal to that of Washington or Lincoln. Her name and place should become as well known to every man, woman and child in the nation, and her beautiful and noble features as quickly recognized as are the portraits of Washington and Lincoln and her birthday February 15th should eventually receive equal honor with theirs in years to come."[51] The committee mailed press releases to more than 2,500 publications in the 1930s, urging editors to print publicity about Anthony's accomplishments. To give "the younger generation of men and women some comprehension of what [Anthony] accomplished," Rheta Childe Dorr wrote a fifteen-minute radio address that circulated to 400 local stations. "Every woman who holds a good job, who goes to college, who is a lawyer, doctor, scientist, teacher, as well as every mother who has power to protect her children, and above all, every woman who votes or holds office owes a debt of gratitude [to Anthony] that can never be repaid," she claimed. Meanwhile her *Susan B. Anthony* was reprinted and made available to the public for a fifth of its original price, and the NWP donated copies to local schools and libraries. The memorial committee campaigned in local legislatures to rename public parks, schools, playgrounds, bridges, and highways and eventually lobbied the postmaster general to issue a commemorative Anthony stamp in a popular three-cent denomination printed in the white and purple colors of the NWP.[52]

The memorial committee proved highly successful in getting communities across the country to remember Anthony. They saw Susan B. Anthony Day passed in local legislatures, her life story taught in public schools, and her biographies exhibited in the windows of libraries and bookstores. Women in New York turned her Rochester home into a national memorial and museum, while the California memorial committee helped to create a Susan B. Anthony Collection in the Los Angeles Public Library and made their state the first to observe her birthday in public schools. A tree was planted for the suffrage pioneer in Sequoia National Park next to those for other famous patriots and statesmen. Not for lack of effort, the NWP stopped just short of having her likeness sculpted into the side of Mount Rushmore alongside the heads of the other Great American Emancipators.[53]

Anthony's place in the history of woman's rights and American democracy remained secure thanks to the commemorators of the NWP, and yet as organized feminists collectively cast Anthony as their spiritual figurehead, children of other suffragists reevaluated Anthony's legacy in an attempt to rekindle the memory of their own mothers as feminist pioneers. In 1922 Theodore Stanton and Harriot Stanton Blatch revived their mother with an edited version of her letters, diaries, and personal reflections. They did little to recast her ideas in a modern light, for Stanton herself predicted in *Eighty Years and More* that they would be better received by women in later generations. "The trouble was not in what I said, but that I said it too soon, and before the people were ready to hear it," she reflected. "It may be, however, that I helped them to get ready; who knows?" True enough, by the 1920s Stanton's ideas on woman's right to self-sovereignty had become mantras among a growing feminist following. More women took up her views on the right to divorce and practiced what they preached. Younger women increasingly understood her reason for interrogating not only their lack of political rights but also the religious and legal dogma that defined their inferior social status. Her children promised that her reprinted writings would prove that as far back as 1889, she, not Anthony, first anticipated the militant suffrage movement.[54]

Lifting "the veil hiding the personality" of their mother, Stanton's children hoped to reveal a multifaceted private life that Anthony seemed to lack—one that was resonantly modern. Whereas Anthony the single-minded spinster remained consumed with the work of suffrage, Stanton was the three-dimensional wife, mother, and activist occupied with multiple pursuits. In her version of the months writing the *History*, it emerged only occasionally as a peripheral distraction from her immediate domestic tasks of making "pumpkin pies for Thanksgiving" and "plum pudding for Christmas." As the true intellect of the pioneer movement, the updated Stanton was said to have miraculously written Anthony's speeches while keeping a spotless home and rearing seven children.[55] Unfortunately, though her children depicted her as modern in some senses, younger feminists did not perceive Stanton's matronly persona and domestic lifestyle as matching her radical vision. She epitomized the reform ideologue of the abolitionist years, writing of the ideal world but rarely leaving the comforts of her cozy domestic existence. She never suffered the stigma of spinsterhood or the desexing Anthony endured at the hands of her Victorian peers; rather, she seemed to fall in line with the middle-class status quo as the most ideal of mothers and housekeepers. Ida Harper's depiction of Stanton in *Life and Work* as domestic and sedentary endured in the postsuffrage years, much to the chagrin of Stanton's children.[56]

Blatch and Stanton were not the only offspring with personal stakes in rewriting Anthony's legacy. Alice Stone Blackwell, the daughter of Lucy Stone, sought to fill her mother's thirty-year silence in *Lucy Stone: Pioneer of Woman's Rights* (1930). Blackwell conceded that she worried about the repercussions of revisiting the past to rectify points of contention, especially given the fact that she and Blatch had been instrumental in reuniting their mothers in 1890. In the end, however, her family loyalties outweighed her desire to depict a unified movement. Whenever possible, she uprooted Stanton and Anthony from their positions as originators to pronounce her mother "the morning star of woman's rights." She dismissed *Life and Work* and *The History of Woman Suffrage* as intentional distortions of movement memory, disclosing their inaccuracies and then vindicating her mother for her selfless decision not to expose them sooner. Stanton and Anthony's national association was wrongly titled, she contended; it consisted of an insular clique of New York radicals, while Stone's brand of activism won more widespread approval.[57] Blackwell recounted the story of women's progress as the history of women's entrance into higher education and the professions, the public spheres in which her family's pioneering role was most apparent. She boasted of her mother becoming "the first Massachusetts woman to take a college degree" and of her aunts Elizabeth Blackwell and Antoinette Brown Blackwell becoming the first American woman physician and ordained minister, respectively, professional role models for modern women with careers.[58]

Much the same way Stanton's children depicted their mother as a woman with modern sensibilities, Blackwell portrayed Stone as the ultimate feminist visionary. A large section of her biography was devoted to the courtship of her parents, which seemed to mirror the companionate, egalitarian partnership idealized by younger feminists. Touting her mother's decision to retain her maiden name at a time when it was nearly unthinkable, Blackwell portrayed Stone as a model of modern independence. Meanwhile, she cast Anthony as Stone's unpleasant antithesis—the cold Victorian separatist who "did not like to have the suffrage lecturers fall in love and marry." Blackwell hoped that younger activists would identify with her mother's struggle to reconcile romantic love with woman's rights. Her ability to occupy roles as mother and editor, wife and activist, appealed to feminists who by 1930 were seeking the same balance as private and professional women.[59]

Indeed, Blackwell's well-rounded portrayal of her mother struck a chord, for eight years after the publication of *Lucy Stone*, Maud Wood Park adapted it for the stage. Shortly thereafter, feminist Mary Peck wondered why the same appealing storyline could not just as easily be applied to a play about her dear friend Carrie Chapman Catt, also an independent woman who found love and autonomy in a modern egalitarian marriage. Peck began working through the rough details of such a production, scripting childhood and courtship scenes similar to those Park had adapted from Blackwell.[60] Catt's life never made it to the stage, but Peck eventually exploited Blackwell's formula and in 1944 published a full-length biography of the suffrage leader. *Carrie Chapman Catt: A Biography* was a labor of love for Peck but also the generator of undue stress. She was fully aware of the historical wrongs Catt hoped she would correct through her reinterpretation of suffrage events. A close confidante recalled the pressure Peck was under: "The writing of any biography is difficult, the writing about a friend is twice as difficult; to write about a friend of Mrs. Catt's caliber while she lived, and do it in constant consultation if not collaboration with her seems to me a superhuman achievement." Catt wanted to be redeemed after being upstaged by Anthony, whom the general public recognized as the more dynamic leader of the NAWSA, and by Paul, whom younger women viewed as the mastermind of the federal amendment strategy. In the end Peck loyally placed Catt atop the movement pedestal as a noble leader above the fray of factional infighting. Peck's Catt was, in essence, the modern savior of the declining woman's movement under the outmoded leadership of Anthony.[61]

Like Blackwell and Peck, Blatch hoped to trim Anthony down to human size through revisionist history, but her mother left her with little material to use. In *Eighty Years and More* Stanton only praised her younger companion as a "most upright, courageous, self-sacrificing, magnanimous human being."[62] Not until 1940 with the publication of Blatch's own autobiography, *Challenging Years*, did a rendition of a nearly dislikable Anthony appear in print. Blatch described her as a humorless woman who tied her hair back too tight and invoked fear in all the Stanton children. Meanwhile her mother appeared as the definitive "scribe as well as the legal mind" of the pioneering suffrage duo. Writing her memoirs as a woman on the verge of infirmity herself, Blatch arranged her account with the assistance of NWP historian Alma Lutz, who also wrote the first full-length biography of Elizabeth Cady Stanton, *Created Equal*, that same year. Both the Blatch and Stanton biographies celebrated Stanton's formerly extremist views on sex and marriage and placed her firmly in position as the spiritual mother of radical feminism.[63] Characterizing Anthony as "the secondary attraction" and Stanton as "the drawing card," Lutz attempted to revise the suffrage history of the preceding fifty years. Yet even at this, Blatch took issue with Lutz's designation of the Nineteenth Amendment as the "Anthony Amendment" and insisted that such a label belied historical fact: "It should have been called the Elizabeth Cady Stanton Amendment to honor my mother who made the first demand for woman suffrage in 1848."[64]

Blatch's protests did little to preempt future snubs of her mother by LWV and NWP women, who seemed to forget that Stanton had organized the first Woman's Rights Convention with Lucretia Mott or that she was the first president of the NAWSA. Adding insult to injury, the NWP launched a twenty-year campaign to induct Anthony as the sole suffragist representative in the National Hall of Fame in New York City. Despite successful campaigns to venerate her, Anthony was never a shoe-in; only seven of seventy-seven inductees between 1900 and 1930 were women, and suffragists fared especially poorly. Of the four nominated, Anthony was consistently the favorite, receiving nominations between 1930 and 1945 yet never enough votes for induction. The hall's election process was based on the subjective opinions of a few individuals who voted in a new class of honorees every five years, yet feminists understood that induction was a telltale sign of historical greatness to the average American.[65] Feminists gave one last push to induct Anthony in 1950, a year in which the field of 186 nominees was particularly strong. Only 10 of 117 Hall of Fame board members were women, none of whom had formal connections to the suffrage movement.[66]

On the other hand, feminists had reason to be optimistic. Electors were not immune to the fact that thirty-three states had since passed Susan B. Anthony Day as an official holiday and that her birthday was commonly acknowledged in printed calendars and date books. Collections of her papers existed in New York, Washington, and California, and the Susan B. Anthony Memorial in Rochester was now a nationally recognized historic site. Her nomination was backed by the DAR, the Woman's Christian Temperance Union, and other groups whose history books taught them that they had her to thank in some small way for their successes as organizations of modern women.[67] Thus it was not much of a surprise when after her fifth appearance on the ballot, Anthony finally became one of six new inductees into the Hall of Fame in 1950, ahead of Theodore Roosevelt and Alexander Graham Bell in the voting. The twenty-year battle for Anthony was a small victory for organized feminists, but it did not inspire duplicate efforts for any other suffrage pioneer. After receiving three votes for induction in 1935 and 1940, Stanton, to the disappointment of her children, was never nominated again.[68]

Even after the memorial committee won Hall of Fame status for Anthony, NWP women continued to reinvent the suffrage pioneer in biographies for modern audiences. In 1954 Katharine Anthony performed the most complete sexual makeover of Susan B. Anthony yet in *Susan B. Anthony: Her Personal History and Her Era*. She characterized "Susan" as a woman motivated yet also terrorized by her underlying sexuality. Suffering from an "ugly duckling" syndrome, she was said to have eventually diverted her energies away from wooing men, where she thought failure was imminent, and toward antislavery and woman's rights activism instead. By attempting to understand Susan B. Anthony as a personality, not a figurehead, Katharine Anthony hoped to appeal to readers too young to identify with the collective action of the pioneer generation. This same strategy that she employed in her biography of Fuller in 1920 unfortunately was less successful in endearing Susan B. Anthony, the single, childless feminist, to women in the conservative aftermath of World War II. Her attempt to reinvent the suffragist nevertheless suggests that Katharine Anthony understood the perpetual need to revise history for the cause of woman's rights.[69] Failing to inspire women with Stanton's biography in 1940, Alma Lutz also reinvented Susan B. Anthony in 1959 with "something readable and swift-moving, not ponderous with too much detail"—the "baby" paperback as she called it—"to rouse [women] from the doldrums of apathy and IGNORANCE with which they seemed satisfied."[70] Forty years after suffrage was won and sixty years after Susan B. Anthony had stepped down as a suffrage leader, she remained feminists' icon of choice.

In the 1940s NWP efforts to shore up suffrage history revolved largely around Susan B. Anthony's commemoration, but they also expanded into other directions and institutions of national stature, including the Library of Congress. Mary Beard had long insisted that a congressional collection was appropriate, given the NWP's focus on suffrage through congressional means. Such a collection would attract widespread attention to the organization's accomplishments, Beard predicted, provided parts of it were displayed in library cases and accommodations made for its immediate use. "A really competent history of the NWP should be written on the basis of this material," she recommended, in addition to definitive biographies of Alice Paul and Doris Stevens and a study on suffrage supporters in Congress based on NWP files. In May 1941 the Library of Congress began receiving the first installments of organization records dated from the group's inception to the passing of the Nineteenth Amendment. Later that year NWP leaders held a ceremonial opening of the Alma Belmont Library in the coach house of the party's Washington headquarters. Again, its installation in the U.S. capital was an intentional effort to solidify the militant movement's place front and center in national memory.[71]

Feminists independent of the NWP also established collections in the 1940s to shore up their versions of the movement's contested past. For a half-century Maud Wood Park had played an integral role within the ranks of organized feminism, serving as head of the congressional committee of the NAWSA and as the first president of the LWV. Over the years she had amassed an impressive assortment of suffrage and woman's rights documents, including organizational records and classic works dating back to the eighteenth century, and she sought to deposit them where they could serve as the nucleus of a woman's rights collection. Her decision to place them at Radcliffe College was natural; she was an alumnus and with Inez Irwin had started the College Equal Suffrage League there in 1900. For her forty-fifth-year college reunion in 1943, she transferred her documents and took part in a special ceremony marking the occasion. Younger feminist Edna Stantial maintained the collection and acquired other NAWSA-related materials to add to Park's original items. Inez Irwin, Park's lifelong friend, spearheaded the publicity for the 1943 opening, much to the disapproval of Carrie Chapman Catt. More than any other former suffragist, she had been obsessed with shaping woman's rights history, associating much of it with her own personal legacy. Having spent nearly forty years preserving materials to ensure that the NAWSA would be remembered as the organization responsible for woman suffrage, Catt feared that Irwin's participation in the Woman's Rights Collection would divert too much attention to the NWP's version of suffrage events.[72]

Sure enough, Irwin was responsible for most of the NWP materials Park allowed into the collection, causing Catt to look for other repositories for her organizational papers.[73] Despite pleas at Radcliffe for her to reconsider, Catt even tried to defuse rumors that the Woman's Rights Collection was the definitive source on suffrage history, telling former colleagues that the materials needed to write this history remained scattered, uncataloged, and unknown to the general public. What researchers needed, she insisted, was a massive inventory of feminist materials in the nation's repositories and a master index of them in the Library of Congress, the Huntington Library, and New York City, where more researchers could access the information.[74] To aid in fulfilling her prophecy, Catt placed much of her NAWSA collection in the Library of Congress, where she hoped it could be made readily available yet carefully guarded from theft. Her paranoia about movement papers likely stemmed from fear for her own historical legacy as much as for the movement itself; despite calls to consolidate movement papers, she quietly burned select personal items that she did not want relinquished for public consumption.[75]

Catt's decision to destroy records was ironic to say the least. In the nick of time she had convinced Lucy Anthony to spare Susan's diaries and deposit them at the Library of Congress, where they were sealed for a period of years until she was ready to have them seen by the public. Catt nevertheless disclosed only so much about her relationships with others in the movement to future historians. She stipulated to her executors that her letters at the New York Public Library remain sealed until 1965, when parties mentioned in them would likely be deceased. She also persuaded Alice Stone Blackwell to burn several letters she had written during her NAWSA presidency, since they revealed bitter fallout with Susan B. Anthony. Woman's Rights Collection archivist Edna Stantial hoped that the few that remained would ultimately reveal Catt, not Anthony, as the wronged party in the dispute. With biographers so anxious to write new life stories of Anthony, Catt's letters could shed critical light on the mythologized pioneer.[76] In 1941 Stantial urged Catt yet again to reconsider depositing the last of her letters, if not at Radcliffe, then somewhere: "Please, please do not have a bonfire of your speeches," she implored.

> They are a part of the history you talked with me about during my visit with you. If you don't want to have them shipped here to Mrs. Park to be added to her collection, won't you mark them so that some day they

may be added to the Library of Congress collection of suffrage material? Dear Mrs. Catt, you must not be modest about this. They belong with the papers that are already there and those that are now being organized for later deposit. . . . Mary Gray Peck agrees with me and I hope she will keep after you and blow out the matches as quickly as you light them![77]

Stantial assured Catt that her intention was not to defame others through her papers but, rather, to accomplish what Catt had always envisaged: a centralized collection of feminist history. In time the aging suffragist was sufficiently impressed by Stantial's ability to organize mass quantities of material with indexes and comprehensive cross-referencing systems, and she took greater comfort in her exhaustive collecting philosophy, which seemed to resemble her own. As the younger feminist compiled files on individual women, she scrounged for supplementary materials to fill in missing information about their personal lives. She added newspaper clippings to the letters, journals, and official documents women donated to the collection. "These help no end in understanding a person," Stantial explained, but of course Catt needed no justification. These individual files proved to her that Stantial wanted to present a complete historical view of the larger movement, which like its members, had a birth, an awkward adolescence, and a pulse of its own. Stantial incorporated the writings of Mary Wollstonecraft, Lucretia Mott, Paulina Wright Davis, and other women who were early influences on the modern movement. Their writings revealed ideological debts to equal rights philosophers, Quakers, and abolitionists, giving the woman's rights movement the broader historical scope Catt wanted for it. Stantial organized the collection to make Anthony no longer appear the center of the movement but, rather, a single participant in a longer, multifaceted women's revolution.[78]

The Woman's Rights Collection never received Catt's total blessing, but she had faith that Stantial was committed to historical truth and would not let Irwin overextend her influence. "I charge you to fulfill this job for us old girls," Catt wrote when she finally handed over her papers to Stantial. In a sense the gesture symbolized a passing of the guard. Throughout Catt's feminist career she stood in the shadows of Anthony's bright historical legacy, but now she hoped that the revisions to come out of Stantial's collection would right the historical wrongs where she was concerned. In her old age Catt remained determined to rectify the damage done by both NWP historians and Anthony loyalists such as Ida Harper. "The final story must include the knowledge of the federal amendment's origin," she insisted. Like Blatch, she resented that Anthony's name had become attached to it when others were more deserving of the honor.[79]

After Catt died in 1947, Mary Peck sorted and distributed some of her items unrelated to the NAWSA. She claimed to know Catt well enough to assume that she would want nothing put in the Woman's Rights Collection that appeared trivial, unfinished, or "in grab-bag chaos," selecting what she considered important items to pass on to Stantial and destroying files that were hard to read. It was "inhuman to expect people to plow thru it!" she justified. "[Catt] herself would certainly draw the line at having odds and ends handed down to posterity."[80] Peck did not reflect on her decisions again until several years later, when she disclosed to Stantial that she still possessed some of Catt's controversial papers. She and Catt "almost came to blows" when discussing their placement, but in the end Catt decided to keep them with Peck. "It took quite a little communion with my own soul before I concluded to preserve it as is," Peck wrote before sending Stantial the material that Catt "never intended for posterity." Stantial eased Peck's conscience by agreeing to cut select excerpts and letters from the final collection index. By the time Catt's papers passed inspection, certain items had been omitted, carefully edited, rearranged, and incorporated seamlessly into the larger Woman's Rights Collection, unbeknownst to almost everyone.[81]

In this way Stantial made important decisions about how personal and public personas of the suffrage movement would be presented to researchers in the public domain. She was no different in this regard from any archivist who imposed organization on deposited papers, privileging certain interpretations of people and events through her edits, cross-references, and removals. Ultimately she had little control over how researchers would interpret the papers, and yet she wielded a deceptive power over suffrage history by choosing how and which papers would be grouped. In the end her decision of greatest consequence was to consolidate Catt's and Blackwell's personal papers into a single NAWSA collection, an idea that first originated in 1940. By this time Alice Stone Blackwell was too infirm to catalog her considerable collection and asked Stantial to be its executor. Peck described the jumble of papers, books, pamphlets, and clippings piled up in Blackwell's den as "one *HOLY MESS*" but a priceless source of woman's rights history once someone organized it. Stantial straightened and incorporated the items into the collection of Catt's personal and NAWSA papers she later compiled.[82] "Wherever we put them, let's put them all together," she wrote Peck. "I'm convinced that is the important thing to do. I can put all the duplicates together for the New York Library or for any other place you think important. . . . Miss Blackwell has a wonderful lot of letters from Mrs. Catt. That is why I think it's got to be done all together—the Blackwell papers and the National and Mrs. Catt's."

With that, Stantial inextricably fused the activist careers of all the people represented in the three collections with the legacy of the NAWSA.[83]

Catt's vision for a completely consolidated collection of American woman's rights history was still not yet achieved. Anthony, Stanton, and other key feminist leaders had already deposited their personal papers in separate installments at the Library of Congress, where Catt had always wanted a centralized woman's collection.[84] Knowing full well what Catt's intentions had been, Peck carefully approached Park with the idea of moving the Woman's Rights Collection from Radcliffe to Washington: "In view of the fact that Susan B. Anthony and Mrs. Catt placed their feminist libraries in the Congressional Library, and now the League [of Women Voters] is adding to the collection, does it not seem to you that the material which we sent to you and Edna Stantial after going over Mrs. Catt's papers . . . ought to be placed in the N.A.W.S.A. Collection in the Congressional Library? Especially since the Blackwell papers are going there?"[85] Park understood the logic of placing the NAWSA materials in Washington, especially since the NWP had recently done the same. She relinquished control over the papers of her close associates but left her own personal items at Radcliffe.[86] In the meantime Stantial continued to cross-reference Catt's materials with Blackwell's and then with those she salvaged from former NAWSA women to create a larger NAWSA file. To these papers she added the items turned over from Park's Woman's Rights Collection, with an eye toward housing them together in the Library of Congress.[87]

As Stantial and Peck gathered materials for Washington, they kept Catt's credo of accessibility in mind. Their priority was to complete sets of material for the library of Congress and from there to disperse duplicates to Radcliffe and Smith Colleges and microfilm original papers. Stantial transferred duplicate NAWSA bulletins from Radcliffe to Washington and redistributed volumes of the *Woman Citizen* and Stanton and Anthony's *Revolution* to university collections. By 1947 the *Woman's Journal* had already been microfilmed to supplement the complete set of volumes in Cambridge and Washington. Copies of Catt's papers found homes in the rare books collection of the New York Public Library, as did extra copies of the *Woodhull and Claflin Weekly*, since as Peck reasoned, New York was where Woodhull had become "a thorn in the respectable side of the suffrage movement."[88] Whereas Catt had once refused to keep the controversial publications of Victoria Woodhull in the organizational archive, Peck was now trying to find proper air-conditioned facilities for a complete set in Washington. Stantial also welcomed materials pertaining to antisuffragists and their campaigns, for the story of these adversaries was intertwined with the history of feminism and woman's rights. This open-mindedness aside, she and Peck continued to omit items of the NWP, perhaps because the organization was still alive and well. "The Woman's Party can show nothing comparable supporting their claim to fame," Peck boasted as the NAWSA collection neared completion.[89]

After nearly two decades of hands-on work preparing these materials, however, Stantial would not be so self-congratulatory. Perhaps better than anyone, she could confirm that suffrage papers were being made accessible to the public but also hoarded and protected by families of suffrage pioneers.[90] Along with personal and factional politics, financial troubles also began to weigh heavily on the integrity of the NAWSA collection. Stantial had been determined to process it quickly, but her lack of financial and human resources made this impossible. The cost of materials and travel from Boston to Washington had made it difficult for her to shoulder the burden alone. Friends of Blackwell and Catt started funds to expedite the cumbersome operation, but they were insufficient to cover all of Stantial's costs. As Stantial rummaged through thousands of documents without the benefit of paid assistants, the processing of the collection dragged on through the end of 1960. Stantial conceded that over time the organizational scheme for the collection might have lost it original continuity. As she became more desperate to finish the work, it is conceivable that she also became more lax in deciding which materials entered (or never entered) the collection. Of course one can only surmise how Stantial's views about the materials changed over this time; the collection in 1961 might have looked very different had it been completed while older feminists were still alive.[91]

It is likely that the final collection contained omissions of which even Stantial was not aware. Minutes from many NAWSA meetings were never found, and Ida Harper admitted in earlier days that lack of funds prevented several sets from being printed in the first place. This is not to say that all memory of these meetings was lost, for personal anecdotes were passed down by word of mouth through generations of movement insiders. Peck, for instance, knew things about NAWSA committee meetings in 1900 that documents would not reveal, having heard directly from attendees that personal resentments almost tore the organization apart from the inside. The documents of the NAWSA collection revealed the NWP as the organization's greatest adversary within the movement, while the unofficial oral history of insiders often revealed its greatest enemy as itself. Documents in the collection allude to the existence of this insider history, but sadly none of the movement's oral tradition was recorded for posterity.[92]

By 1961 a collection that included even the most minor state suffragists was nonetheless tucked away in a prestigious Washington archive, just as

Catt had envisioned. A new generation of researchers with no personal memory of suffrage events could now use the written and printed materials that Stantial put together to retell the history of woman's rights. Alma Lutz commented when writing her biography of Susan B. Anthony that the collection's exhaustive index allowed her to record more information in an hour than she had been able to gather all day from Anthony's personal collection at the Library of Congress. Of course, Lutz would never know that in the end Stantial and Peck withheld valuable papers from her, preferring not to divulge them to a woman with NWP affiliations.[93]

Ironically the papers of Carrie Chapman Catt, the suffrage leader most adamant about accessibility, remained the most scattered and elusive for suffrage scholars. In her overzealous attempt to deposit papers in the most conspicuous places, Catt donated bits and pieces of her personal collection to too many repositories for Stantial to regather them all. Eleanor Flexner inquired of Peck about some of Catt's absent materials as she researched her manuscript for *Century of Struggle* (1959), but she came away empty-handed. "I feel that I face a great responsibility in trying to do an objective and authoritative piece of work," she professed to Peck. "I want to write the best possible book in gratitude and honor to the wonderful women who did so much for me and my generation." Her intentions to pay homage were noble, but Flexner was forced to negotiate the many gaps, deliberate or otherwise, in the collections feminists left behind. In the end she found plenty of material on the early suffrage movement before Anthony's death, yet the twentieth-century movement, which she described as the "far more complicated period," remained a partial mystery to her. Many living suffragists were only a generation removed from Flexner, but the factional politics that plagued the advancement of organized feminism and its efforts to collect its own history ultimately debilitated later historians seeking to advance the movement's memory.[94]

Catt died in 1947 still believing that embedded in the documents was a single truthful account of movement history—"the final story"—waiting to be revealed and that Stantial would ultimately reveal it. Yet even Stantial admitted that she had become too involved in choosing, arranging, and editing the collection to think of movement history the same way again. After nearly two decades of work on the Woman's Rights and NAWSA materials, she doubted more than ever that her labors advanced a greater degree of historical accuracy. "I'm sure that in a few years it won't matter what we wrote to one another," she conceded, "—for the generation working on the papers then won't believe most of it could possibly have been true." As younger women reshaped the legacies of suffrage pioneers in the twentieth century, they learned some valuable lessons about the function and nature of historical memory. Interpretations of the past would always be contested, they recognized, so long as those connected directly or indirectly to the past had different reasons for remembering it. They also learned that feminist history would not inspire women in the present if it did not continue to evolve. Blackwell, Peck, Blatch, Harper, Stantial, and other second- and third-generation feminists understood these truths, making their own modest revisions to the historical record after 1920.[95]

Postscript

Despite Stantial's protectiveness of Catt's legacy, in the end she left correspondences in the NAWSA collection that revealed some of the heated words and personal jealousies Catt never intended for the historical record. One set of letters exposed better than any other the personal insecurities and self-conscious machinations behind Catt's shaping of feminist memory. The letters told of her participation on a subcommittee to commission a history of women's activism for the Chicago World's Fair in 1933. She had hoped that a broadly conceived account of women's "progress" as public organizers would motivate new generations of women back into the LWV and other women's groups, but she grew leery when Inez Irwin was asked to oversee the project. Several letters (perhaps items Park permitted Irwin to donate to Radcliffe in 1943) further reveal how Irwin agreed to take on this mammoth history, though not without reservation. She admitted to friends that she was overwhelmed by its scope; how was she going to appeal to all American women with a singular account of women's progress? She only had several months to complete what in her mind was really six histories in one: a history of women's education, trade unions, temperance, antislavery, and club work, as well as suffrage. Even at that, she wondered what realms of women's activity she might be leaving out.[96]

It was not long before Irwin found herself in the same position as Ida Harper a decade earlier as she compiled volumes 5 and 6 of the *History*; somehow her task became to impose cohesion on the patchwork of loose data on piles of disorganized note cards turned in by untrained researchers. Her husband Bill Irwin trekked to the New York Library "innumerable times" to confirm much of the data she received, and together they attempted to smooth out the discrepancies, fill in the gaps, and balance out the inordinate amount of attention researchers paid to some topics at the expense of others. The result was a history of women's public work that included all white clubwomen, reformers, and professionals. It was devoid of any trace of ideological divisions between women organizers, such as those between AWSA and NWSA suffragists and radical and conservative feminists; these rifts were addressed in a cursory way and written off as distinctions without real difference. All white women who organized, regardless of their class or ideological orientation, belonged to an American tradition of woman's rights—at least as it was happily related by Irwin.[97]

She titled the completed work *Angels and Amazons*, betraying her hope that this history might reunite old guard and new, radical and conservative, in more than just a title but a reinvigorated feminist movement. Unfortunately, as encompassing as Irwin tried to make her account of women's progress, her manuscript received fifty-six pages of criticism, a considerable portion of which was launched by Catt.[98] Not surprisingly, the former NAWSA president was not concerned with the first half of the 100 years Irwin covered in the history but, rather, with Irwin's bias toward the NWP in the final years of the suffrage campaign. Surprisingly, however, she reserved her greatest disapproval for how Irwin depicted some of the movement pioneers, including Susan B. Anthony, whom Irwin ambiguously linked to the breach of confidence that started the Beecher-Tilton scandal in the 1870s. "Tainting the memory of persons who are dead and gone is not the best way to record History," she warned Irwin. In a return letter Irwin expressed her exasperation over Catt's misreading of her account of the controversy. It had always been her intention to avoid assigning blame for it, for Stanton still had a living daughter in the movement whom Irwin did not want to offend by implicating her mother outright. She bitterly replied to Catt, "I have never received such a stab as your words. . . . I respect, revere, venerate the memory of Susan Anthony beyond my poor powers of expression." She then went on the counteroffensive, attacking Catt for the lack of conventional respect she paid her suffrage foremothers in *Woman Suffrage and Politics*, which said almost nothing about individual pioneers, let alone Susan B. Anthony.[99]

True enough, Irwin's manuscript minimized the role of the NAWSA in the final years before suffrage was won, telling nothing of Catt's "Winning Plan" or the congressional work of the NAWSA more generally. She conceded to Maud Wood Park that the lack of attention she gave to the NAWSA might in some way have resulted from her former affiliations with the NWP. "It is perhaps beyond my poor powers to be cool and impartial on what was after all the most precious civic experience of my life," she confessed. But her admission of bias extended beyond her ideological leanings; indeed she admitted that her personal relationships with individual suffragists impaired her ability to judge the major players in the movement fairly, especially Catt: "Naturally I wrote a great deal more about you. I became a little frightened that I had made you more prominent than Mrs. Catt," she wrote

Park. "I would have liked to do that of course; for I have always thought you the abler of the two."[100] Irwin eventually conceded to Catt that her handling of the twentieth-century suffrage battle was "horribly shaky," especially since she occasionally relied on her own heavily weighted recollections to recount the chain of events leading up to the passing of the Nineteenth Amendment. Before sending the manuscript to press, Irwin tried to make amends, inserting a separate chapter on the NAWSA written from documents supplied by Park. However, by then it was clear that Irwin had reopened old wounds that had never fully healed.[101]

Irwin lamented that rifts between old factions survived in the postsuffrage years. Alice Paul had always insisted that no suffragist should criticize another, regardless of the organization to which she belonged. Irwin heeded her advice and sought never to defame NAWSA members in print, but she informed Catt that this courtesy had not been extended in return: "After a careful examination of your book and Ida Husted Harper's book, I feel, that the day for that chivalry is past. And of course in my reminiscences, I shall have to tell the truth as I see it." Irwin's sentiments confirmed that the code of respectable silence upheld by suffrage pioneers had been broken once and for all. Catt's harsh criticisms and Irwin's defense of *Angels and Amazons* suggest that much was at stake in how past events were interpreted for contemporary audiences. The details of the nineteenth-century scandal that sparked the heated exchange between Catt and Irwin may seem insignificant, given the time that had passed since the affair occurred. Perhaps they even seemed insignificant to Stantial, since she included the private letters that unveiled the controversy in the NAWSA collection without worry of factional fallout. However, Catt's and Irwin's letters reveal to later generations of historians the charged and contested nature of feminist history, an important fact that helps us to read critically between the lines of suffrage texts.[102]

In the end the most lamentable consequence of the lingering disputes between organized feminists was not that they still existed, but that the leaders who engaged in them had not considered their lack of relevancy to a diversified population of younger American women. The life of the organized woman's rights movement no longer depended on a unified story of its past suffrage battles; rather, it relied on multiple narratives of activism that resonated with women of varying social backgrounds—the kind of history that Flexner was trying to write with little help from organized feminists themselves. Irwin understood this as time wore on and tried to convince Catt that their arguments over finer points would be rendered insignificant over time: "It is only the beginning—better books on the same subject will be written again and I hope, again and again. And of course naturally as time goes on and historians can look down a long perspective of this period, they will see it quite differently from you or me." Unfortunately, by the time Irwin died in the early 1970s, historians who chronicled the second-wave feminist movement did not see things all that differently. They, too, failed to take the diversity of American womanhood into account when scripting their stories of white women of privilege. Still, the lessons women learned from writing movement history in the twentieth century were important. Like women of the New Negro History Movement, American feminists recognized that to take ownership of the past was to own the present and determine the future. They constructed usable history that feminists continue to draw from and refine for themselves— just as Irwin had predicted they would.[103]

IV

Establishing
Women's
History as a
Field

Chapter 7
Creating a Usable Past for Women

For women in the work of history, 1940 was a momentous year. Caroline Ware published her compendium of cultural history papers as Zora Neale Hurston's WPA colleagues completed hundreds of interviews of former African American slaves and printed them for public and university libraries. Alma Lutz finished her biographies of Elizabeth Cady Stanton and Harriot Stanton Blatch, and Angie Debo found a willing publisher for *And Still the Waters Run*. It was also the year that Dorothy Porter gathered items for a women's exhibit at the American Negro Exposition in Chicago and Sue Bailey Thurman began printing regular features on Negro women's history as editor of the *Aframerican Woman's Journal*. Women were gaining legitimacy as historians of the formerly inarticulate, which increasingly also meant as historians of women themselves. Certainly the Woman's Rights Collection at Radcliffe helped bring attention and institutional clout to women's history, but other ventures brought validation to nonwhite and working women as historical subjects and even historical experts. In essence the 1930s and 1940s marked the beginnings of the institutionalization of American women's history, a process that once again did not occur from the core of the academic establishment but, rather, from the social and professional peripheries where women historians mustered their greatest force.

As early as 1931, women in history departments of northeastern women's colleges correlated their secondary status as professional scholars to the misinterpretation (or underinterpretation) of women's work and expertise in the past. Several formed the Berkshire Conference of Women Historians for the dual purposes of bolstering their status as academic practitioners and promoting women as worthy historical subjects. Berkshire members were all too aware that the intellectual and social climate of the academy was hostile to research on women; like the youngest historians of the woman's movement, they believed that they could never advance a program for women's history until they established a respected position of authority in the same professional arenas in which men had always excelled. Thus while the writing of women's history was ultimately the conference's raison d'être, in its initial years the priority was to make men acknowledge women's history as a scholarly pursuit—and that first required establishing the woman historian as a scholar in her own right.

Mary Beard was promoting women's history at the same time as the Berkshire women, but her deeply seated philosophies about its practice and function differed in fundamental ways. History was a creative endeavor for all women, she insisted, not the scientifically trained few. Thus there was no reason to seek the support of academic institutions for history that needed no scholarly affirmation; all women had a past regardless of the methods they employed to retrieve it. The real dilemma to her was how such wide-ranging accounts of women would ever be assembled. Like Lucy Salmon, she argued that the only way to capture a broad range of human experience was to expand on the scientific scholar's methodologies and assumptions about where history took place. It became necessary to collect sources that were written and nonwritten, official and private, extraordinary and routine, and historical as well as sociological, anthropological, and literary. Such an immensely ambitious project, she believed, could not be approached in the individualistic academy but, rather, in a collective of women established solely for this purpose. Such was her vision when she founded the World Center for Women's Archives (WCWA) in 1935.

Beard would insist that the enterprise of women's history be removed not only from the academic milieu but from the men who defined professional history in masculine terms. The Berkshire women, on the other hand, were less interested initially in women's history as a field than in women historians as respected experts alongside men. In this sense they resembled a labor union within the university itself, a class of employees mobilizing for equity in the workplace. When all was said and done, they fundamentally disagreed with Beard over whether to use history to call for an integration of the sexes or to render them distinct in the twentieth century. They did agree, however, that politics infused the production of history. The past never changed, but representations of the past always would so long as the social, cultural, personal, and institutional context of the historian shaped the form and function her renditions of the past assumed. Having already focused on historical methodologies, here we examine the activities of women as members of a professional interest group and an independent institution that politicized history and women's roles as historians. Together, Beard and the Berkshire Conference refined the notion of a usable past in institutions created by and dedicated to American women and introduced a larger cross section of women to historical practice as interpreters, creators, researchers, and subjects worthy of the historical record.

The Berkshire Conference of Women Historians

The collective consciousness of Berkshire women did not emerge suddenly; rather, it evolved as they made opportunities to convene away from men to discuss their discontents. Over time they realized that their professional conditions were shared, and even attributable to their common experience of gender. The personal correspondence of Mary Williams, Lucy Salmon, and others reveals that women historians in the academy had long been clamoring (amongst themselves, at least) for better recognition as scholars—whether in the form of academic jobs with upward mobility, better pay, more research funds, or just fewer teaching responsibilities. Some resented the exclusionary practices of male colleagues at professional conferences and AHA meetings. Viola Barnes, for one, would have much preferred to attend "smokers" with other male scholars who practiced in her field of Revolutionary history and smoked along with her. Lucy Salmon complained as early as 1905 that segregated conditions were insulting, and DAR executive Mary Lockwood had threatened to resign from the AHA altogether if women did not start to achieve some parity. These isolated grumblings did nothing to integrate the socializing at AHA proceedings until 1917, however, and the AHA leadership did not relinquish sex segregation completely until decades after that.[1]

A male historian confessed to Vassar's Louise Fargo Brown that the exclusion of female colleagues from professional activities was often intentional, particularly at J. Franklin Jameson's annual retreat, the Convivium Historicum. "The informality, one of the most valued features of the meetings, would inevitably disappear if women were asked to attend," he explained. Brown would feel even worse as she sat with Louise Ropes Loomis of Wells College on the train ride home from yet another disappointing AHA annual meeting in 1929. So many of their colleagues felt isolated as the only female faculty members in university history departments, and they attended annual meetings only to find that they felt no better connected afterward. In those instances when women did enjoy the company of female colleagues (which almost always only occurred at women's colleges), they rarely found themselves in close proximity to women who worked in similar fields to provide constructive criticism of their research. Ever conscious of the intellectual isolation of their colleagues, Brown and Loomis proposed planning their own annual retreat where women could benefit from camaraderie and professional collaboration. In the early spring of 1930 they invited female historians from women's colleges in New England and New York to attend the first meeting of what came to be called the Lakeville Conference. Women from Barnard, Wellesley, Smith, Wells, Vassar, Wheaton, Mount Holyoke, Elmira, Connecticut College, New Jersey College for Women, and Hunter Teachers College met at a rustic inn in rural Connecticut for a social gathering like the one they imagined Jameson organized for men.[2]

Initially the Lakeville Conference was a social gathering and nothing more. The attendees took walks in the woods and chatted on topics other than the slights they felt as women in the historical profession. "We organized to get acquainted and also to enjoy the beauty of the landscape," Viola Barnes recalled of the conference in early years. "I think our group accomplished its purpose, which was to bring individuals from various centers together, for there seemed to be no place for us at the American historical association meetings, where the older, well-established members paid us no attention and neither did anybody else." By all accounts the first few annual meetings had been pleasant, even escapist. Margaret Judson reminisced fondly about the carefree mood of the attendees in the 1930s: "Although each was already a friend as a result of other contacts, it was good to renew both personal and professional talk with them, as we walked, climbed mountains, or enjoyed leisurely meals." Word of the conference spread quickly; Judson invited Caroline Robbins of Bryn Mawr and Mary Albertson of Swarthmore College to the annual gatherings after Emily Hickman had invited her. Albertson later confided "how much it meant to her to meet and talk into the small hours with women young and old, from other colleges about history." Soon after the first meeting Barnes moved the annual event to the more comfortable Stockbridge Inn in the Berkshires; hence the name by which the conference is still known today.[3]

The organizers received positive feedback from the women who participated in the first weekend retreats, but they questioned why more had not accepted invitations to attend. Sixty-seven women from fifteen colleges were invited to the conference before the second meeting, yet fewer than half of them showed. In 1932 twenty-three delegates from thirteen colleges attended, and only seventeen delegates from nine colleges came the following year. When Barnes became president of the group in the mid-1930s, she discovered that the social interaction men enjoyed at the Convivium Historicum was not sufficient enticement for all women historians to finance the weekend retreat. One colleague told her that the group was "too light hearted" and did not engage in enough serious discussion of the woman historian's professional interests. In some ways she merely confirmed what

Barnes had already sensed herself: that the Berkshire Conference needed to be a formal entity, one that actively pursued its members' special interests and addressed their professional concerns. Barnes drafted a new agenda for the next meeting, which essentially transformed the Berkshire Conference from a lazy weekend retreat to an interest group for professional women historians.[4]

Conference members spent the next few years discussing issues of prime interest to women historians in the academy. Several collected data on comparative pay scales for male and female historians and designed plans to promote equal pay for equitable work. The Berkshire women believed that their academic research should be the primary determinant of their professional status, but they understood that the stigma placed on teaching continued to have detrimental effects on their promotion and earning potential. In the minds of male colleagues, teaching had always been tangential to scientific research. The greater attention it received at the Berkshire Conference, however, was no indication of women's proclivities as educators but of their understanding that pedagogy and femininity continued to be conflated in the field. The esteem attributed to teaching had everything to do with the valuation of women as historical professionals. Moreover, many of their female students had become secondary school teachers who also felt the devaluation of classroom work. In 1936 the conference called for heightened standards of pedagogical training in the hopes of bringing clout and greater compensation to educators. Members also urged state authorities to adopt minimum standards for the preparation of teachers and a system of certification, jump-starting the process with an investigation of standards set by the New England History Teachers Association at the secondary and collegiate levels.[5]

The Berkshire women grew increasingly concerned that the devaluation of teaching, but also women's professional isolation, was to blame for their low rate of promotion, as many of their colleagues were the only female and nontenured faculty in college history departments. One conference member expressed the problem this way: "The limited number of positions open to women means that women are likely to remain in the same institutions throughout their teaching careers. They thus miss the refreshment and stimulus coming from variety and experience that men are very likely to get, through accepting posts in different places."[6] The conference superficially addressed these concerns as early as 1931 when it surveyed interest in ·a "faculty exchange." The idea was that women historians would spend a year at another college or university while other conference members filled their posts. The response of Berkshire women was overwhelmingly positive, particularly among those at small colleges. "Such a system if ideally carried out, would broaden and stimulate the exchange of individuals, and would bring about an interchange of ideas and methods," wrote a respondent from Hunter Teachers College. "It would also give instructors all opportunity to improve their positions, or to make a change in college positions should their work be unusually good."[7]

Unfortunately the replies of male department heads, especially outside the Northeast, were mildly favorable at best. Many said they would be unwilling to back the exchange with adequate salaries or housing for visiting historians. At coeducational universities—Michigan, Wisconsin, Iowa, Berkeley, Stanford, and Washington—administrators maintained that there would be financial difficulties with the exchange since women in the Northeast were often paid salaries comparable to those of their male colleagues. They alleged that few women in their departments were interested in leaving anyway, for there was no evidence of collective discontent. Of course no respondent elaborated on whether or not he had asked women historians themselves how they felt.[8]

This rejection by western administrators reinforced a fact already abundantly clear to Berkshire leaders: The conference retained a regional identity that proved difficult to shed. Nevertheless, this would start to change in the late 1930s with a new set of tactics centered on the business of the AHA. Conference members believed that the association had become women's greatest source of professional marginalization, but as a prominent national organization it could also become their best means for consolidation. Its annual meeting provided the ideal venue for men to gather and discuss collective action with a wider representation of practitioners, so why could not the same be true for women? The Berkshire Conference thus sponsored an annual breakfast meeting, where women convened, collaborated, and demonstrated their growing numbers to AHA men. Isabel Abbott was relieved to find so many women at these early breakfasts, having no sense from her isolated post at Rockford Seminary that the national community of women practitioners was as large as it was. She took comfort in the company of women colleagues and became part of a growing network of historians with raised awareness of the collective obstacles women faced in the field. Exasperated by a hectic teaching schedule and continually postponed tenure, Abbott could at least take comfort in knowing that she was hardly alone.[9]

At the same time Berkshire women built up a conspicuous female presence at annual meetings, they tried to galvanize their growing ranks to elect individual women to AHA leadership positions. Since 1920 historians, primarily from women's colleges in the Northeast, had made some headway on key committees. It was no longer unusual, for instance, to see a woman on the nominations, program, or prize committees, which were particularly powerful positions from which to arbitrate professional standards. Nellie Neilson, Julia Orvis, and Louise Fargo Brown, faculty at Seven Sister colleges, found their way onto the Herbert Baxter Adams Prize Committee and other influential seats, and in the 1930s Kathleen Bruce and Viola Barnes earned spots on the Dunning Prize Committee. By 1933 five women boasted previous posts on the AHA's Executive Council, and three years later Bessie Pierce, Caroline Robbins, and a dozen other women appeared on the annual meeting program as elected council members and presenters of original research. Despite this clear increase in female representation, however, the Berkshire historians still insisted that their influence was not commensurate with their increasing numbers in the profession. The only way to win more power, they thought, was through a targeted campaign to place women in the most prestigious AHA seats.[10]

This shift in tactics reflected the conference's expanding agenda in several ways. Without a doubt, infiltrating the AHA bureaucracy from its higher rungs would help the Berkshire group shed its regional identity and bolster the status of individual members. The final objective was not prestige in and of itself, however. From positions on AHA panels and committees, Berkshire women hoped to promote not only women as researchers but also research in women's history, for they increasingly saw the two goals as intertwined. In 1937 the Conference voiced disapproval when the editors of the AHA *Papers* refused to publish the work of Louise Fargo Brown, the one female participant in a series of panels on historiography at the preceding annual meeting. Executive Secretary Conyers Read tried to make amends and requested a list of women to be considered for future panels. Berkshire members saw this as an opportunity for themselves as professionals but also as a chance to advance women's history. They lobbied men on the program committee to approve panels centering on women's experience as they launched campaigns to fill program committee seats with Berkshire members who would eventually force these changes themselves.[11]

In 1939 the Berkshire Conference urged women to unite to nominate Violet Barbour of Vassar College to a seat on the AHA Executive Council. Although women's votes were likely insufficient in themselves to win Barbour the seat, the hope was that this voting bloc would leave an impression on the nominating committee for the following year. Again a Berkshire subcommittee geared up for the next annual meeting, selecting a slate of representatives to be endorsed as candidates for key committees. Louise Fargo Brown, Caroline Ware, and Emily Hickman were chosen as candidates for seats on the council, nominating, and program committees.[12] It was hardly a coincidence, given the groundwork women had already laid in the preceding years, that the AHA also approved a panel on women's activism for its annual meeting. Mildred Thompson served as the panel chair, and Alma Lutz and Vera Brown sat in as commentators. Jeanette Nichols spoke on American feminism, and Lillian Fisher addressed the status of women after the Mexican Revolution. Two years later the program committee responded again to pressure for another panel, this time on women's influence in ancient civilizations. Women by no means were becoming commonplace subjects of AHA panels, but the virtual moratorium had been lifted.[13]

In 1941 and 1942 the nominations blitz continued, and by 1943 the Berkshire women felt the time was right to lobby vigorously for the AHA presidency.[14] Whomever they presented as a candidate had to be a respected scholar in the eyes of male AHA members but also dedicated to furthering the position of women in the profession. This was not the first time women pressed for a female president of the AHA. In 1932 Mary Williams had orchestrated a campaign to have Mount Holyoke's Nellie Neilson elected, and she urged women to inundate the one woman on the nominating committee, Louise Phelps Kellogg, with letters supporting Neilson's presidency. In 1934 the AHA leadership appointed Neilson to the editorial board of the *AHR*, and this was as far as Williams pushed her candidacy. Perhaps the most honored woman historian in the American academy to date, Neilson seemed a natural choice again in 1938, when Violet Barbour was made chair of the nominations committee. More than fifty women supported her candidacy with petitions, but again she lost to a male historian—this time to James Westfall Thompson. Another opportunity to elect Neilson presented itself in 1940, when Judith Blow Williams, a Berkshire member from Wellesley, was elected to the nominations committee. With the aid of several sympathetic male committee members she succeeded in getting Neilson elected second vice-president. The following year the Berkshire women campaigned for Neilson's presidency again; her success was a foregone conclusion the year after that.[15]

In 1943 the Berkshire women finally put one of their own in the highest position of the most elite organization in the history profession. Neilson was nearing the end of her life and was hardly able to lead with the same tenacity she had displayed at earlier junctures of her impressive career. Nevertheless, her tenure represented an important stepping-stone for women in the field of professional history. After 1943 the number of women on AHA committees or in well-paying university jobs would not start exceeding or even meeting the number of men in similar positions. However, in a symbolic sense the dam had been broken, and women, while still a minority in the profession, no longer felt that their natural lot was as its proletariat class of lecturers, instructors, and nonentities. No one disputed that Neilson embodied the scholarly traits and accomplished the goals that professional men had come to seek for themselves. She proved that when given the opportunity, a woman could succeed in the world of academic history.

Yet perhaps the more significant result of Neilson's presidency was the lesson it taught women historians about collective action. After 1943 the Berkshire Conference grew larger and extended its regional boundaries to include historians from around the country. With its new demographic came a gradual focus on new goals, as members ultimately concluded that the promotion of women's history as a field could achieve more for women in and out of the historical profession than packing AHA committees. This lesson was one that Mary Beard had been trying to teach professional women for some time, arguing that their efforts in the academy and its organizations were misplaced. Nevertheless, the Berkshire women believed that the legitimization of women as both historical practitioners and subjects went hand in hand; acknowledged for their ability to analyze history, they hoped to create interpretations of the past that supported a case for women's heightened social status in the present. In time their most lasting influence would not be as promoters of women's career advancement but as scholars placing women into historical consciousness and national memory—a goal Mary Beard tried to achieve with the WCWA.

Mary Beard and the WCWA, 1935–1940

The Berkshire Conference raised awareness of women in the academy as Mary Beard eschewed academia to pursue women's history through the WCWA. She had long rejected the masculine culture of the university as an appropriate setting for the nascent field, turning instead to pockets of women nearly anywhere else for support. The WCWA served as a manifestation of all that she envisioned for an institution of women's history. It was run exclusively by women and collected relics of the social and cultural past regardless of ethnic, racial, religious, and regional origins. Without the rigid disciplinary structure of the university impeding her, Beard promoted the application of a broader range of social science methodologies to bring women's contributions to "civilization" to the fore and, she hoped, to elevate women's status in American society.

Beard never believed in historical omniscience; she was sure that the historical influences weighing on the historian would always color the history she rendered on the page. Indeed her own historical works were undoubtedly both a reflection of and a window into her own personal history as a Progressive who operated within a feminine reform culture. Although she shared with the women of the Berkshire Conference the understanding that gender biases had bearing on the production of history, she would certainly come up with different, if not conflicting, methods for advancing women's history despite them. She was never interested in promoting the professional identity of the woman historian. As far as she was concerned, the historian of women could be a scholar, a mother, a laborer, an immigrant—anyone who contributed to a diversified narrative of the past. The more varied women's history became, the more she believed it could discredit the fiction of feminine and masculine spheres and promote an array of roles for women in the present-day world. If anyone questioned a woman's place as a politician, a world leader, or a laborer who worked outside the home, she hoped one day to be able to refer to a more complete historical record to verify that what women were doing was not new but consistent with the past.

Beard's logic concerning women and history might on the surface seem contradictory. On one hand, she denounced women with professional career aspirations, including academic historians, insisting that terms of professional culture were set by men who devalued women's historical contributions to civilization and modern society. On the other hand, as the eventual director of the WCWA, one of her greatest imperatives was the collection of papers from women who worked in fields perceived as staunchly masculine, such as politics, medicine, and academia. She proposed studies on "Women Politicos," for example, to debunk assumptions that women historically took little interest in all things political, and she assigned WCWA members to projects such as "Women in Diplomacy" and "Women in Science." One researcher, a statistician, collected materials on women in mathematics, while Beard urged others to examine "woman as leader" and women "in public service," "in industry as owners," "in social movements," "in scholarship," "in exploration," "as managers and employees," and "as landlords and tillers of the soil."[16] She explained that her interest in these topics was by no means hypocritical; in fact, a view of women's pursuits over the course of long history would prove that seemingly masculine endeavors only found that designation in the modern age.

It was thus her unremitting belief in historical and cultural relativism, and specifically in the fluidity of gender roles through space and time, that explained the contradiction in her call for a separate women's history that simultaneously celebrated women's roles in an integrated professional culture. Just as she broke down historical myths about masculine work, she ascribed feminized sectors of endeavor with a heightened sense of social value. She believed that as mothers and nurturers, women had wielded a humane influence in the world and on the development of its professions. Thus as WCWA director she coveted the papers of women in philanthropy, education, and caregiving fields. One of her specific recommendations to researchers was to trace the history of the woman social worker, whose influence on the modern field had been largely obscured: "The humanitarian primordial urge of women has found expression in this line of public work to an important degree, but every founder and promoter of every kind of social work can go off the record and only men associated with social work in its well-organized stage may get on the record." Through the "hidden" history of social workers, Beard hoped to undo the damage historians inflicted on modern-day professional women. Her historical corrective worked at dual purposes: It set the record straight about women's work as it distorted the picture drawn by men to reveal women as complex and complete human beings.[17]

The origins of the WCWA can be traced back to Europe near the turn of the twentieth century, when Hungarian activist Rosika Schwimmer started to compile one of the largest collections of international feminist and pacifist materials in the world. Having fled to the United States as a political refugee in 1921, Schwimmer feared for the preservation of her collection, which by this time included letters, pamphlets, leaflets, and books on the controversial Neo-Malthusian League and birth control movement.[18] She found herself in dire financial and political straits eight years later when the U.S. government refused to grant her citizenship and she was forced to flee again. In hopes of keeping her collection intact, she wrote American feminists in 1935 with proposals to establish a woman's archive. Harriot Stanton Blatch and Dorothy Bromley suggested that she talk to Mary Beard, a feminist whom Schwimmer knew through the International Woman Suffrage Alliance. She agreed that Beard was the best person to head such a project as one of the few American women who maintained collegial connections with feminists not only in the former NAWSA and NWP camps but also in the current equal rights amendment lobby and the LWV. Moreover, her books *On Understanding Women* and *America through Women's Eyes* showed, if nothing else, her sincere interest in reclaiming the history of women as seen through their own perspectives.[19]

The two former pacifists agreed that the misrepresentation of women in history was largely attributable to the dearth of collected source materials by women themselves. Schwimmer regretted that in the current war-ridden age enormous quantities of documents revealing women's "life and labor, their public interests, and their social leadership," had been destroyed.

"From private homes where the care of documents is burdensome . . . priceless data pertaining to women of affairs regularly moves into the fire," she lamented. Women's personal papers had become casualties of "lack of protective foresight," in part because of the assumption that documents of women were of little historical consequence. She and Beard were optimistic, however, that this could change with the opening of a renowned archive of women's history. The primary function of the WCWA, as Schwimmer and Beard envisioned it, was to recover source materials relating to the past experiences of women and then to make them available to researchers throughout the country and eventually throughout the world.[20]

The WCWA was initially twenty women strong but grew to several hundred dues-paying members within a year of its founding. This membership was a mix of society and professional women that included notable figures Eleanor Roosevelt, Frances Perkins, Inez Irwin, Doris Stevens, and others active in organized feminism and government agencies. Beard also recruited professional librarians in anticipation of a massive collection of donated papers, but the WCWA remained an archive only in theory until revenues could be raised to rent storage space to accommodate documents. Beard estimated that an annual income of $30,000 would be necessary to maintain the proper fireproof vaults and study facilities for students and scholars. For now, the center was merely a vacant room and reception area with adequate space and lighting for three or four student desks.[21]

As Schwimmer's political situation grew increasingly precarious, she removed herself from the official business of the WCWA, finally relinquishing complete control to Beard. It was at this embryonic stage that Beard was thus able to mold the center's work as she saw fit, immediately expanding Schwimmer's original focus on the collection of white, middle-class pacifist and feminist materials.[22] Over the next five years the agenda she brought to the directorship of the WCWA mirrored the objective accomplished in her women's histories: to unearth historical evidence of women's persistent adeptness and contributions to civilized culture broadly construed. Given her mission, there was not a single item that she intended to refuse once the center was ready to accept donations; all materials collected by and about women, she believed, would serve as valuable evidence of their social worth and accomplishment. "Budgets of housewives and housekeeping records are proper for the Center," she assured members, as were diary entries that seemed to contain little more than gossip. By revealing the common, private, and routine, such treasures disclosed women's experience in its totality.[23]

For Beard the more plaguing dilemma was not deciding which materials would be appropriate for the archive but, rather, figuring out how to gather a range of materials this eclectic. Ultimately she believed that the success of the WCWA relied on its ability to appeal to women of all socioeconomic, racial, and ethnic persuasions—if not as financial sponsors then more crucially as donors of personal items. Together their materials would prove conclusively that the restrictive gender norms in modern America were not fixed but culturally relative. The items of minority women in small towns, factories, farms, and working families would sustain the WCWA as the repository of social and cultural knowledge she envisioned. Unfortunately, while well-to-do white women proved willing to make donations of personal and family keepsakes, a diverse cross section of American women remained unaware of her call for materials. Her plan in the end would thus require her to practice what she preached in her histories of women, to approach collecting from the bottom up. This meant restructuring the WCWA bureaucracy to level the hierarchy that separated her from potential members at large and to expand her appeal to American women from all walks of life. The driving force for her grassroots campaigns would not be the wealthy sponsor but the untrained volunteer in state and local WCWA branches. In a figurative sense, Beard would disperse her message alongside these rank-and-file members in the trenches, as she threw herself into the work of researching, publicizing, and speaking at remote venues where elite members refused to go.[24] However naive, she believed that if women were better informed about the past struggles of other women, they would come to appreciate the culture they shared rather than let differences divide them.

To entice a larger mix of supporters, Beard's publicity described the WCWA not as an institution but as a "majestic cultural movement" of revolutionary proportions, which "enlist[ed] the interest of widely representative women" to undistort the historical record. The tyranny of the traditional male historian had taken its toll, she insisted, and the future of women's history, truthfully told, was in jeopardy. "Pledges cannot be postponed," her promotional literature warned, "owing to risks of annual destruction, diffusion in scattered depositories multiplying year by year, and the urgent need of teacher and general education in women's social role." The WCWA *Bulletin* described the plight of Helen Lewis, for example, whose records fell prey to the hurricanes of 1938. Warnings about the "hazards connected with the private holding of documents" were sounded in nearly every issue, and Beard was likely responsible for their dire tone.[25] Assuming the persona of a grassroots insurrectionist of the people, she disseminated strict instructions to her insurgents in state branches through memorandums that read like manifestos: "And so, strength to your courage and your eyes, your telephones and your [e]ars: With full appreciation of your consent to serve this grand new women movement headed toward a finer human movement, I am, Mary R. Beard." WCWA publicity smacked of her agenda for social history down to the very rhetoric invoked in its handbills and pamphlets: "The past is peopled for us by gigantic figures of men and shadows of women," one read. "Hearing historians lecture, one might surmise that no great woman ever lived, except, perhaps, Cleopatra, Elizabeth of England and another queen or two." The motto most frequently printed by the WCWA was a favorite of Beard's taken from Fustel de Coulanges: "No documents, no history."[26]

Always in search of a broad, diversified audience of women, Beard worked with fellow WCWA members to write a series of history programs for radio called *Gallant American Women*. In 1939 the Federal Radio Project assisted in airing broadcasts such as "Women on the Land," "Women Explorers," "Mothers of Great Americans," "Women and the Law," "Women as Providers," and "Seafaring Women." The National Broadcasting Company aired the programs on more than ninety radio stations, and the U.S. Department of Education printed synopses of the shows for distribution to thousands of high schools across the country. In a moment of self-congratulation, Beard attributed the popularity of the programs to groups such as the Not Listening Club, whose members were tired of the "romances that crowd the airwaves," preferring "history instead of blubber." Unlike the textbooks written by phlegmatic academics, these radio presentations, Beard hoped, would inspire women en masse to make history for themselves.[27]

The broadcasts were an example of the less pretentious means through which Beard hoped to stir women to action. Sure enough, they drew women outside the Northeast into WCWA state and local branches. By 1939 auxiliaries in Michigan, South Carolina, and New Mexico established collecting niches that revealed American women as culturally and regionally distinct. The Washington, D.C., branch took advantage of its proximity to materials on women in political office and civil service. From its headquarters in the new annex of the Library of Congress, its members searched for items pertaining to first ladies, wives of high officials, national headquarters of women's associations, women lobbyists and party workers, and other categories devised to reveal the feminine influence in the masculine world of Washington politics and the public and political spheres generally.[28]

In addition to new legions of women in state branches, members of organizations and academic institutions joined Beard's brigade of grassroots promoters and collectors. Gladwys Jones, an executive member of the National Deans of Women, agreed to pass out WCWA press releases at the National Convention of Educators in 1936, while local units of the AAUW pledged to support historical studies of college women. Indiana University faculty and students researched prominent women graduates and then collected and cataloged their personal papers for the center. Beard also encouraged the collecting of oral and local history through the national Camp Fire Girls organization in 1938, designing activity plans that allowed young girls to get acquainted with the history of women in their local communities. "Why not begin with your grandmothers?" Beard proposed. "You might inquire whether there are any legends in your community about women who once lived there. . . . Are there memorials in your community to any women?" Like the researchers in Indiana, the Camp Fire Girls promised to donate their findings to the WCWA once the repository was open for business.[29]

The letters Beard received from across the country suggest that her publicity blitz filtered down to local communities successfully. A state supervisor for the HRS in Arizona agreed to prepare a summary of findings on women, and a member of the Indiana Council of Black Women sent the WCWA a history of her small organization, assuring Beard that a new version would be drafted for the council's golden anniversary in 1942. White and African American teachers and sorority administrators wrote letters requesting materials for their educational programs, yet Beard was most gratified that women unaffiliated with organizations were also inspired to locate family papers in their attics and basements. One New York woman offered to donate the diary of her mother, "the first married woman to teach school in this part of the country." Another woman offered the Civil War diaries of her husband's father's second wife, a sister of President William McKinley.[30]

American women were willing to share the materials that told their history, much to Beard's satisfaction, since there were many holes in the historical record that she hoped to fill with them. Nonetheless, some realized through the course of their searching that finding women in the past was not always easy. One California librarian reported that her state's "greatest historian," Hubert Howe Bancroft, "did not include women in his pioneer register," let alone mention women of Spanish or Native American descent. Beard was hardly surprised. "To think that Hubert Howe Bancroft included no women in his pioneer register is to remember the neglects all along the line," she responded. Yet she proposed that a shrewd rereading of these sources might still bring some hidden truths about women to light; that same year Julia Cherry Spruill had proven it possible as she recovered the lives of southern women.[31]

Frustrating as such projects could be, Beard was pleased that this researcher was eager to focus on colonial women somewhere other than New England. Whatever material she discovered would assist in recounting the national past from what Beard deemed its "real" beginnings: "From the aborigines our plan calls for exploring Spanish and French families in the Pacific region and the Southwest in a search for papers revealing the women of the original conquests and settlements," she explained. "From there we propose to work up through the story of pioneering, through social history-making to the present day."[32] Beard hoped that, in time, the collection of information on women of cultures and regions other than Protestant New England would flesh out the heterogeneous, precolonial, preformally political history of the Americas broadly. As a consequence, popular memory of American history would inevitably extend beyond historians' traditional nineteenth-century Anglo focus.

Beard believed this a necessary outcome for two reasons: First, the solidification of Anglo-Protestant gender roles that took place in the nineteenth century ultimately obscured the historian's view then and afterward of empowered women's cultures that developed before, during, and after the Victorian period. Second, it was during the nineteenth century that white, middle-class American feminists began to define the woman's movement narrowly as a battle for legal and political "rights," not, as Beard would have it, as a fundamental critique of social relations between the sexes. If historians were less entrenched in Victorian ideologies about history and gender, Beard figured they would render a more balanced view of women as contributors to civilization over the course of long history, not merely as legal and political nonentities over the preceding 100 years. Her reperiodization of history stretched out the otherwise brief record of the United States to allow longer-standing patterns of parity between the sexes to come into view. Once America's past was reconceived as a relatively recent consolidation of a nation-state, a modern chapter in a longer history of cultural change, Beard predicted that several historically based assumptions would be overthrown—the most important being the cultural primacy of Western man.

The anthropological studies of Native Americans by Mary Austin, Alice Fletcher, and Angie Debo had already brought such assumptions of primacy into question, but Beard hoped that this was only the beginning. She had always found Native American history appealing for its potential to provide alternative models of gender to white historians, and she made it a special mission to bring materials of Indian women to the WCWA. She wrote tribal folklorists requesting printed versions of matriarchal legends and then appealed to the Indian Arts and Crafts Board for "documents of all possible sorts which will reveal [women's] role in Indian societies." Alas, in making such requests she showed a naïveté about Indian history. Like African American women prior to the twentieth century, Native American women did not leave written documents so much as oral and artistic expressions of their past. The more daunting task for Western historians like Beard, however, was accounting for what Native Americans defined as history in the first place. The oral traditions of Indian groups conveyed a mix of stories and legends that were simultaneously spiritual and corporeal, mental and physical, recurring and singular. Many cultures, as Beard discovered, had no concept of linear time, let alone empirical methods for retrieving the past. In the end, Beard had trouble discerning whether native accounts were history or myth, a difference that to her scientific sensibility seemed nonnegotiable.[33]

Until the WCWA sought materials on Native American women, Beard had not realized just how indoctrinated she had become with scientific methods of historical research. Indeed, her husband helped to codify the brand of empirical objectivity achieved through written documents alone. The limitations of the Beards as scientifically trained historians were evident in the conspicuous absence of detailed discussion of Native American cultures in the texts they coauthored through the 1920s. Initially Mary's methodological biases led her to insist that the WCWA limit its collecting to written documents only; the acceptance of art in any form, she decided, would make the center a museum, not an archive. Only later did her reverence for anthropological models come to bear on her collecting philosophy and did she come to accept both emic and etic perspectives of the Native American past coexisting at the center to contribute to her plan for a wide-ranging women's history. Recanting her former position, she expanded her search for relics to provide an inside and outside perspective of the Indian past, including photos, specimens of art, and "symbols of feminine leadership." "We cannot compete with a museum," she conceded, "and yet it may be that only in visual objects can the Indian woman be revealed."[34]

The center's research of Native Americans brought Beard just that much closer to a diversified women's history. It successfully revealed roles for women other than those documented in Anglo New England, as did projects on Catholic and Jewish women's history. Beard employed the help of nuns from the International Missionary Council to start a Catholic women's collection, while the National Council of Jewish Women offered to donate the papers of its founder as the beginnings of a Jewish women's collection.[35] Florence Frank, director of the center's research on Jewish women, warned against collecting materials merely on the "Edna Ferbers, the Dorothy Parkers, et. al.—or even the prominent Jewish clubwomen or civic lights." "What seems to me valuable for the Archives—is the material that evidently interests you," she wrote Beard, "the social conditions in the various Jewish settlements in America." Through her collected documents

Frank hoped to enlighten future scholars on how the cultural conditioning of Jewish women impinged on their American experience in distinctive ways. She was especially interested in the unexamined perspective of Jewish women in agricultural and western settings. "Their experience was different in kind from that of Jews in the large Eastern cities," she discerned, "but almost all of our records are those of urban groups. . . . Every novel about American Jews, except two, had New York as a background." As a corrective, Frank collected the personal papers of her grandmother in Atchinson, Kansas.[36]

Beard appreciated Frank's project for a host of reasons. It deflated the stereotypical view of the urban American Jew, but it also helped an individual woman get in touch with her historical roots, a goal Beard hoped all women could someday achieve. The project also supported Beard's personal pet undertaking to expose the historical roles of agricultural women to modify presumptions that men were natural producers and women were natural consumers. They easily defied such rigid distinctions, acting as physical, indelicate laborers and producers of raw materials, at the same time assuming feminine roles as domestic nurturers and consumers. Beard had already collected papers of rural women on the frontier to draw out this history, as well as to prove that male historians, Frederick Jackson Turner in particular, depicted masculine ruggedness in the West at the expense of more accurate portrayals of heroic women in daily frontier life. "Indian and early day white women were probably exciters of adventure, creative leaders of economic activity, and certainly the bearers of social culture to every succeeding frontier," she maintained. The morsels of evidence she had gathered from diaries of women in coal mining communities also indicated a feminine influence on frontier life just waiting to be discovered.[37]

Women's labor—whether in the California coal mines or the New York factories—had been Beard's long-term interest as a woman with an extensive record of participation in labor activism. Ever since she had written *Woman's Work in Municipalities* (1915) and *A Short History of the American Labor Movement* (1920), she had been compelled to find more sources that revealed women's integral role in labor activities and acquired the personal papers of unionists and labor activists. Grace Hutchins, Fanina Cohn, and Rose Schneidermann donated their papers to the WCWA twenty years after working with Beard in the WTUL, and Mary Dreier offered the papers of Leonora O'Reilly's work in both the Knights of Labor and the American Federation of Labor. Her activism so intertwined with a critique of twentieth-century capitalist enterprise, Beard considered these items some of the center's most prized possessions. She hoped that the documentation of women's collective labor agitation could be used to enlighten future research on women's participation in the manly realm of union and industrial activity and perhaps even provide alternative ideologies for big business in the future.[38]

Beard's belief in the activist potential of history grew ever apparent in her labor collection. Working and ethnic women certainly piqued her interest, yet of all the center's projects, she was most adamant about building an African American collection as a weapon against race oppression. Well before the WCWA was under way, she had complained that black women remained conspicuously absent in the historical record. Over the years she had spoken about historical projects with Lucy Slowe and Mary McLeod Bethune and served as a consultant for promoting history in black colleges and race organizations. Beard strongly encouraged the membership of the WCWA's only two African American women sponsors but had not made race history a priority until 1938, when the WCWA finally pitched a Negro collection at the annual convention of the NCNW. By this time Bethune was president of the NCNW and the ASNLH. She agreed to appoint a chairperson to head an archives committee for the WCWA, which immediately began its collection and programming in Negro women's history from NCNW headquarters in Washington.[39]

Even with the launching of the Negro Women's Committee, Beard worried that an all-encompassing multicultural history would not be achieved. Collections of American women's items alone would not render the larger picture of long history she thought necessary for bringing out women's diversified experience. As Schwimmer had initially, Beard began to search beyond national borders to find a collective pan-women's history broader in temporal, regional, and cultural scope. She assigned researchers to projects on women in Asia, Australia, Latin America, Canada, Central Europe, India, and the Arab nations and sent board members to the International Conference of Women and the International Federation of Business and Professional Women in the hopes of generating donations abroad. One WCWA member, a scholar of the German Republic, returned to Europe for three months to research the role of women in the 1848 revolts. In 1937 another member traveled to the Far East with a list of research objectives and desired materials, while another translated the center's prospectus into Spanish and created a card index of prominent women educators, historians, and diplomats in Latin American history. By August 1940 the WCWA had acquired papers from the wives of ex-presidents and women political officials, with files of the feminist movement in the Dominican Republic forthcoming. In the meantime, Beard collaborated with women in Japan and Austria to compile an international encyclopedia of women's history.

Her scattered efforts seemed to create more confusion than clarity about women's past, but to some degree this was her design—to use the pasts of the broadest range of women to defy reductive typecasting of them in the future.[40]

By all indications the WCWA was progressing toward its goal of promoting an eclectic history of women. Publicity and exhibits sparked interest on the grassroots level, and diverse groups of women from home and abroad offered keepsakes to the center: Hebrew memoirs of a seventeenth-century diarist, sketches of Japanese women, testimonies of farm women, speeches of public officials, and diaries of anonymous workers, to name just a few.[41] Still, these promises were little more than good intentions until Beard could bankroll an archive, and this was not happening quickly enough. One board member admitted that "within the group there were no women with money-raising qualities."[42] The WCWA hosted formal publicity events in efforts to attract wealthier sponsors. Amelia Earhart's husband ceremoniously donated his wife's aeronautical charts and personal letters at a fund-raising dinner at the New York City Biltmore in 1937. Meanwhile Eleanor Roosevelt spoke to society women at a Washington luncheon about the need to support such an important movement, but all to little avail. It proved even more difficult to generate interest among male corporate sponsors, who hardly viewed a woman's archive as an imperative, given the depressed economy and impending world war. Although Abby Rockefeller expressed personal interest, the Rockefeller Foundation was not enthused, nor was the William C. Whitney or the Carnegie Foundation. Beard was forced to transfer more than $3,000 of her personal savings to keep the WCWA afloat, but before long she could barely cover costs for day-to-day operations.[43]

Taking extra measures to attract wealthy sponsors, Beard had surely succumbed to the financial pressures she was so desperate to avoid. She had long believed that the economic inequalities prevalent in industrial America had halted true democracy among its citizenry, and now these inequalities threatened her egalitarian vision for the WCWA. Soon enough, the class-based contradictions inherent in her conception of the archive began to surface. As she encouraged the preservation of the materials of the common laborer, she sought more prominent women's papers in order to bring in money, publicity, and prestige. While she urged members to collect materials from women who lived in the most remote areas, she insisted that the center remain in a high-rent district in New York City, where recognition by the elite was assured.[44] By 1939 it became difficult to determine which was more crippling, financial hardships or the heated disputes among the WCWA leadership. Beard criticized middle-class members for not being "liberal enough to care about drawing the documents of bona fide working women and their leaders into the collection." On the flipside, however, she conceded that "even the labor women ha[d] egotistic leaders," who rigidly opposed collecting documents not pertaining to labor or providing anticapitalist critiques. The range of class interests among WCWA women reflected the heterogeneous character Beard sought for the archive, on one hand. On the other hand, it created a conflict of identity that could not be concealed from potential supporters.[45]

Ironically some disputes between board members, many of whom belonged to feminist organizations, reflected the ideological schisms that Schwimmer thought Beard, an unaffiliated woman's activist, would easily defuse. Fundamental debates about sexual equality or difference fragmented the collective view of the materials the center should acquire. Beard, too, grappled with these issues and carried strong opinions. Why demand equality in a modern masculine world, she wondered, when the history of women from primitive times had proven that a distinctive feminine culture needed to be nurtured for the "civil" aspect of civilization to be preserved? She faulted equal rights feminists for their lack of strategic foresight in their postsuffrage battles; they demanded equal access to politics and education without questioning the masculine individualism of either institution.[46]

Beard strongly encouraged WCWA women to keep this interpretation of women's history in mind when seeking materials for the collection. Yet in her cautious moments she tried to defuse arguments over the merits of equal rights ideology, encouraging activists of all persuasions to contribute to the archive. She implored women to consider feminism of all kinds as only a single, relatively modern development in a larger history of women that still needed to be told in its entirety. To appease feminist board members she stressed that "an attempt had been made to make all groups and interests among women identified with the [WCWA] leadership." Regardless, Carrie Chapman Catt and other former NAWSA leaders were concerned that too many members were NWP sympathizers, and they advised colleagues to deposit their papers elsewhere. Alice Stone Blackwell first pledged her support to the WCWA only to relinquish connections to it shortly afterward. The likely cause for her change of heart was news of former NWP member Inez Irwin stepping in as the board chairman. "It has grieved me very much that the proposed World Center for Women's Archives seemed spoiled for you by the personnel," Beard wrote Blackwell in 1938. "It would be a very specialized set of archives if only one or a few feminine attitudes toward life and labor were assembled, you will agree I am sure." Despite the loss of key endorsements, Beard continued to solicit the documents of suffrage militants such as Alva Belmont, insisting that they could "not be left neglected if the true and comprehensive story of the winning of the vote [wa]s to be on record."[47]

Despite her attempts to maintain the middle ground, Beard, too, grew frustrated with board members who supported the Equal Rights Amendment she adamantly opposed. These feminists did not see the value in her broad view of history or the importance of collecting documents that did not pertain directly to women's struggles for legal and political rights. Yet in reality Beard's historical theories did not appeal to nearly any ideological or even generational cohort of organized feminists at the center. Her ambitions to collect materials about women's unique social experience did not match the agendas of younger members who by the late 1930s had come to embrace modern professional and political culture as their own. Her desire for a separate institution of women's learning was more consistent with the separatist feminism of their mothers and grandmothers and was hardly an attractive goal for them. Attempting to identify the problem, one younger WCWA sponsor explained that the difference between men and women was "more and more disappearing in modern life" and that Beard's "chip-on-the-shoulder attitude" no longer appealed to her generation.[48]

Even more intense than the ideological conflicts between board feminists became the racial discord within the WCWA's local Washington unit. White members of the branch refused to integrate collecting efforts with the Negro Women's Committee, and thus, to Beard's great lament, the two groups continued to work as separate entities. Beard tried to paper over any signs of animus among the white Washington membership by redefining the Negro Women's Committee as a direct auxiliary of the WCWA national. The white branch chairwoman resigned amidst the controversy, but Beard refused to be forthcoming to the Negro Women's Committee about the growing tensions. "Though the Washington Unit lags about choosing a successor," she wrote committee chair Dorothy Porter in 1940, "it is certainly important that the quest for important documents on Negro women should not be held back. . . . Proceed without further confusion . . . [and] work under my direction." Nonetheless, Beard did not fool everyone into thinking that racial animosities did not exist. Board member Miriam Holden resented her seeming inaction, construing it as affirmation of the racist attitudes of the white women in Washington. Only in hindsight did Beard finally admit that racial issues were real and paralyzing, both to archival efforts in Washington and to the larger goal of a diversified women's history.[49]

Beard envisaged an archive that celebrated differences among women past and present. But perhaps she was too idealistic in believing that a single, centralized institute could unite individuals of disparate backgrounds and ideologies through its all-inclusive women's history. In practice highlighting differences among women also brought out underlying resentments and conflicts of interest. The feuding feminist groups, labor activists, and women of color who participated in the WCWA were plagued and ultimately defeated by these tensions before they attracted widespread support for women's history. In her attempts to make the WCWA an appropriate repository for all women, Beard created for it a beleaguering crisis of identity. It is not altogether clear whether she wanted to gain recognition for individual women as historical greats or whether she preferred to rid the world of the notion of great history altogether. Her advice to researchers suggests the latter, for she advised them to remove the word "great" from the titles of their projects, as it affirmed the individualist ethic she despised in the modern industrial order. Nevertheless, she undoubtedly wanted greatness for the WCWA and found it necessary to resort to an individualistic mindset to secure it. Whether or not her strategies justified her desired end, the crisis of identity persisted.[50]

In some ways this crisis paralleled Beard's own as a woman wanting to be recognized as a historical authority yet also as an organizer unattached to elite institutions and uninhibited by professional culture. In this regard she suffered a crisis similar to Carter Woodson's in the 1920s, for he, too, sought professional affirmation for a historical movement that was non-professional and grassroots at its core. She had hoped that the success of the WCWA would bring her distinction as her name became synonymous with its directorship, and yet there were moments when she privately repelled public scrutiny. Ironically, Beard urged women to hold on to their papers for the sake of accurate historical recollection, but she destroyed many of her own before depositing the remainder anywhere. Later in the 1940s she requested that the copies of her speeches at Smith College be burned, fearing that they would be poorly received without a chance for her to respond to the criticism. After refusing to donate materials to the Swarthmore Peace Collection, she resolved that she had never really been "archive-minded to that extent." "It has not been concern for my own archives which has thrust me into the big archives business," she justified. "I am a typical woman, I suppose, in my indifference in this matter." Those close to her, however, knew that what she maintained as indifference was more than likely just the opposite.[51]

Restricting membership of the WCWA to women only, Beard hoped to eliminate masculine influences on the history collected, researched, and written in the ranks. Yet she quickly learned that men were not the WCWA's most devastating enemy; the seeds of demise grew from within the organization. Sex separatism proved an impossible stance to maintain, given the differences that led women themselves to promote history for cross-purposes. Moreover, by the time Beard rallied women together, it was already the preference of WCWA professionals to be integrated with other professional men. Thus while it became a common goal to claim the present by reclaiming the past, there was never a singular past for American women to reclaim or a singular reason for reclaiming it. The different strategies women employed to reconstruct history in the twentieth century reveal how distinct they perceived their circumstances to be as academicians, advocates, professionals, and race reformers and how varied their paths would be in the future.

Chapter 8
Legacies for Women's History in the Twenty-First Century

The WCWA was short lived, formally dissolving in 1940, and yet it was noteworthy as an example of Beard's intent to make the pursuit of women's history an interactive endeavor with social implications. As envisioned, it promoted a creative and participatory exchange between the woman-at-large and the history that shaped her current social condition. It rejected the elitist assumption that credentialed men were the only people with access to documentary evidence and its proper interpretation, and it encouraged women of all backgrounds to collect, produce, and interpret history for themselves. Better than Beard's written histories, the archive articulated her plan for combining historical learning with women's activism, idealist thought with grassroots action, and feminist theory with social practice—if only for a brief time.

All that Beard had achieved in historical archiving was not lost when the WCWA disbanded. Rosika Schwimmer finally regrouped her papers with those of pacifist Lola Maverick Lloyd in the New York Public Library, which also became home to Carrie Chapman Catt's first installment of NAWSA papers. Catt deposited other items in the manuscripts division of the Library of Congress, where Director Archibald MacLeish was making good on his promise to Beard to neglect women no longer. Already he had acquired papers from prominent suffragists and one of the first American woman historians, Mercy Otis Warren. The spirit of the WCWA also lingered in the ongoing efforts of former local branches. The Michigan auxiliary, for example, quietly established a state women's archive, another indication that Beard generated interest in women's history in ways we may never fully know.[1]

Beard never stopped criticizing institutions of higher education for their neglect of women in course curricula and archival collections. Nevertheless, after 1940 she began to see greater appreciation for women's history than ever before in the academic sector. The presidents of Bryn Mawr, Haverford, and Swarthmore Colleges met to discuss plans for a "communal Women's Library and Archive" in the Philadelphia area. Meanwhile, librarians continued to acquire women's materials at Duke, Scripps, Vassar, Goucher, and other small women's colleges. Collections at Northwestern University, the Medical Women's Archive in Louisiana, and the William Clements Library at the University of Michigan had been in existence already, but after 1940 they were augmented with materials that had been promised to the WCWA. Purdue University received the maps and charts of Amelia Earhart, and the Teachers College of New York requested the center's collection on women educators. The Institute of Women's Professional Relations at Connecticut College received the items from the WCWA's former Women in Science project, and Barnard College agreed to house its WPA records.[2]

Signs indicated that the African American clubwomen Beard collaborated with in the WCWA were also ready to advance their history on a grander scale in 1940. At the World's Fair in New York City, Phillis Wheatley, Dorothy Maynor, Jane Bolin, and Marian Anderson appeared on the Wall of Fame, and curators cited several women as distinguished race achievers on the Schomburg Collection Historical Honor Roll. Bethune took these events and the WCWA's collapse as a signal to create an autonomous identity for the Negro Archive Committee, and the NCNW approved her recommendation to acquire a building that would serve as national headquarters to an archive of black women's history.[3] The "Report of the Archives Committee" laid out its primary objective in 1941: "to locate and collect materials and documents of importance which record the history and achievements of American Negro women." Proof of achievement would come from many realms of human endeavor and include "manuscripts (including musical compositions), citations for special services and various accomplishments, scrapbooks of clippings, certificates, diplomas, letters, diaries, . . . [from] teachers, artists, musicians, business women, physicians, authors, housewives, lawyers or domestic employees."[4]

When boiled down, the list betrayed a preference for professional accomplishment—and *written* sources—that overwhelmingly favored the urban, middle-class experience. Unlike Beard or Hurston, the clubwomen on the archives committee largely celebrated the exceptionally articulate and respectable examples of Negro womanhood. Nevertheless, their effort to institutionalize black women's history was a beginning. Dorothy Porter remained the head of the new committee until 1942, when her obligations at the Moorland Foundation forced her to relinquish the position. Sue Bailey Thurman took over as chair in 1944, and the following year her mother, a retired Arkansas schoolteacher, donated $1,000 toward the development of the Archives and Museum Department. Rallied by Bethune and Thurman, Washington women renewed their commitment "to collect material significant, unusual and rare which is documentary evidence of accomplishments of Negro women in the development of the social, economic, political or cultural patterns of American life."[5]

Many members of the new archive committee were clubwomen who had participated in the history campaigns of the New Negro History Movement and the WCWA, and they borrowed strategies from both experiences to promote the collection of African American women's history. Much like the WCWA *Bulletin*, the NCNW *Aframerican* urged women not to "underestimate the value of that bit of history in your possession. Pictures, books, mementos link the story of the past to the action of the present. Send them to the Archives, registered or insured for safety."[6] On June 30, 1946, the NCNW organized a National Archives Day that resembled the first Negro History Week twenty years earlier. Harking back to methods that worked so well for them then, women publicized events to ministers, librarians, and heads of organizations in Washington and sponsored local pageants, essay contests, and presentations celebrating "Negro Women in the Vanguard" in local schools. Bethune served as a grand pageant master of sorts, taking from Beard a lesson that Woodson sorely overlooked: The support of a wide body of social, ethnic, and labor organizations—the Young Women's Christian Association, the National Council of Jewish Women, the National Council of Catholic Women, the General Federation of Women's Clubs, the Congress of Industrial Organizations, and the American Federation of Labor, in addition to race organizations like the National Association for the Advancement of Colored People—was essential to the propagation of African American women's history. Who better to rally than groups who had suffered similarly at the hands of a distorted, incomplete historical record?[7]

As part of the June festivities the NCNW played a radio address over station WWDC called "On This We Stand" and urged local groups to form listening parties for the broadcast. Melodies of "America the Beautiful" and "Yankee Doodle" played in the background as the narrator praised the twentieth-century Negro clubwoman as patriot and mother: "In 1935, Negro women in the United States made a pledge to their country. They spoke through twenty of their National Women's Organizations affiliated together to form the National Council of Negro Women. They lent the dignity of formal statement to the whispered dreams and hopes, to the prayers sung to a sleepy baby cradled in the warm arms of his Negro mother."[8] "On This We Stand" invoked some of the traditional tropes of white commemorators to appeal to the radio audience's comfort with the familiar. Now, however, the protagonists of this well-rehearsed historical tale were African American women. Sojourner Truth and Harriet Tubman served as the leads. As they told of their travails under slavery, "Go Down Moses," "When the Old Chariot Comes," and "Nobody Knows the Troubles I've Seen" gradually drowned out the cheerful patriotic tunes playing in the background.[9] After years of commemorating the accomplishments of other African American men and white women, the members of the NCNW archive committee had finally celebrated their legacy and incorporated it into a narrative of the national past. Their local efforts in Washington were small in scale, but they culminated into something larger: the National Archive of Black Women's History, which still exists today. Indeed, Beard's persistent prodding of Bethune for an organized campaign in Negro women's history did not end in vain.

Building Institutions of Women's History: Debates over a Usable Past

The NCNW was not the only party Beard inspired to build institutions of women's history. By 1943 Radcliffe President Wilbur Jordan had announced plans to open a women's archive on campus and asked Beard to be a consultant to the advisory board. He assured her that the project was well supported and would be undertaken in cooperation with Harvard librarians, who agreed to "surrender to Radcliffe the major responsibility for the accumulation of research materials in this general field."[10] In earlier years Beard might have viewed such overtures of Harvard men as an attempt to co-opt women's efforts, but now she admitted that the "Radcliffe-Harvard combination" could be a good thing, possibly bringing to women's history the prestige she had failed to generate for the WCWA. She demanded that Radcliffe seek sources in and outside the United States that revealed women of all walks of life. Regardless of how many volumes were on the shelves, she advised that they be complemented by a women's studies curriculum that brought faculty and students into active participation with archival holdings. The interactive environment she encouraged at Radcliffe defied the prevailing mindset of academic librarians, many of whom, to her frustration, preferred to collect on esoteric topics for specialized research. "I have been warned that the library air is positively charged with hostility to professors and thus to students and that librarians with that animus are hoping to specialize more and more in tight little neat museum collections," she remarked to Jordan. Nevertheless she implored him to resist this trend; women's history remained too much of a mystery to fall prey to narrow treatment.[11]

Beard gave $1,000 to the Radcliffe fund drive and offered some of her prized materials to the collection. She had already donated Alice Stone

Blackwell's volumes of the *Woman's Journal* in 1940, and to those she added some eighteenth- and nineteenth-century women's diaries, autobiographies, travel journals, and novels, many taken from her personal library. Hopeful that Radcliffe would become the "revival of the Woman Center for Woman's Archives," she also donated center records, including lists of supporters who could likely be persuaded to deposit their personal materials. Inez Irwin, a proud Radcliffe alumnus, proved ready and willing, promising all her books by and about women and eventually her personal papers. Beard persuaded the founders of the National Consumer's League and Barnard College to amend their wills to leave their papers at Radcliffe. Meanwhile sculptor Nancy Cushman, a former WCWA supporter, turned over personal materials and offered to work in a research capacity.[12]

Jordan succeeded in carrying out many of Beard's initial recommendations. Blueprints for fireproof facilities in Byerly Hall already indicated that he had thought beyond the mere theoretical archive the WCWA had been, and the board budgeted for yearly appropriations toward maintenance and archival expansion and applied for grants to purchase rare materials. By 1945 Jordan was reporting plans for a library annex with intimate spaces for fireside discussions, and the breakdown of the annual budget generally met Beard's specifications. Sizable portions were set aside for the hiring of trained research librarians, bibliographical research, and publications.[13] Jordan's "Plan for Advanced Research for Women" proposed to attract researchers with generous stipends and housing in the college's graduate facilities, arrangements both Beard and the Berkshire historians could enthusiastically endorse:

> Relatively few opportunities are available for mature women scholars to gain occasional periods of leisure in which scholarly interests may be pursued. It may be said that women, by and large, finish their graduate training quite as well equipped as men. . . . [But] all too frequently the woman scholar's sole contribution is her doctoral dissertation which often remains unpublished. . . .
>
> Most women scholars, because of the rigid structure of the academic hierarchy, find teaching positions in colleges for women which have not as yet undertaken to contribute to the advancement of learning. . . . These institutions are teaching colleges, too often their facilities lie under the pall of an academic inferiority complex, and they do not possess the library facilities, the intellectual stimulation, or the traditions that must undergird research at its highest levels.
>
> Moreover, those women who receive appointments to the faculties of co-educational colleges and universities, though better situated in many

respects, are not normally encouraged by their colleagues to carry on with research and scholarly writing of the best type. Though there are a few brilliant exceptions, these women tend to remain teachers rather than scholars and all too often their academic career is limited by the restraints and handicaps that follow from continued tenure in the junior ranks of the academic hierarchy.

Radcliffe College, with unique facilities and with an interest in the problem . . . believes it can assist in setting up and administering an experiment designed to remedy the difficulties.[14]

Beard and Jordan were of like mind regarding the archive's layout and the content and scope of its collections. Unfortunately it was not long before Beard realized that Jordan was nearly alone in wanting a women's archive in the first place. A report drafted by Harvard administrators provided a more accurate gauge of consensus; it essentially reasserted the university's primary objective to train "Christian gentlemen" rather than squander resources on a women's collection. Beard felt somewhat duped into thinking that the archive had full administrational support: "Just where Radcliffe students . . . come into the educational program of training Christian gentlemen, I can't even imagine," she huffed. Jordan remained sympathetic, as did advisory board member Arthur Schlesinger, who had shown a sincere appreciation of women's historical role in his research and donated etiquette books to the archive at his own expense. Nevertheless, Beard described the reaction of Harvard deans as "positive hostility" when she proposed her outline for the study of women's history; one man even walked out of the meeting before she finished. Later he explained that his hasty exit was motivated by the conviction that anything women learned beyond domestic pursuits was simply unnecessary.[15]

Male administrators were not the only opponents Beard faced at Radcliffe. At a meeting of the Graduate Women's Club, one female administrator remarked that educators needed "to begin with the little boys," not worry about the collected materials of women. Beard suffered this response in front of academic women again. At Vassar teachers insisted, "We are people now," and hence a separate women's history was unnecessary; another professor of women exclaimed that she wanted engraved on her tombstone, "Born a woman; died a person."[16] To Beard these sentiments only underscored the need for her separatist brand of women's history, even if women themselves did not see it that way. "The proposal to elevate the history of women to a position of equal importance in the schools with that of men—the only honest basis of 'equal education'—has no warrant in the popular mind," she complained.

Women professors in fact, are sometimes the most hostile to the suggestion. Having risen to posts of prominence and importance by special adaptability to the existing curriculum and taking for granted that they demonstrate by such adaptability the very equality prized by feminists, members of the gild [*sic*] have been heard to declare with heat that "the time had come to forget women" and eliminate sex from thinking. Nevertheless, the "sexless" education upon which they insist is not, after all, abstract to any degree. It is basically a sex education—masculine in design and spirit.[17]

Little did Beard realize that the assault university women launched against her history was soon to be outdone by some of her former suffragist colleagues who had designs of their own for the Radcliffe archive. As Beard urged Jordan to collect materials with an open mind, Maud Wood Park was pressing him to do just the opposite, wanting nothing to overshadow her Woman's Rights Collection. Jordan never mentioned to Beard that Park's donation of suffrage materials had been contingent upon it serving as the nucleus of a memorial to the NAWSA. Her items were designated for the Alice Mary Longfellow Hall until a permanent space could be built in expanded facilities, and Park was determined to give even this temporary space her distinctive mark, conceiving of a room set in Victorian ambience with framed photographs of state and national suffrage workers. Edna Stantial had already started to raise the estimated $3,000 to pay for Park's adornments, much to the approval of the archive advisory board. The collection room was titled "Remember the Ladies," a saying taken from a letter Abigail Adams wrote to her husband when he was drafting the Declaration of Independence. To Beard the choice was telling; it indicated that Park's collection would focus narrowly on American women's quest for legal and political rights.[18]

Beard's fears for the "Remember the Ladies" room materialized quickly. The organization of materials in it rendered a discrete narrative divided into three parts: The first revealed a feminist tradition that, according to Park, began with Seneca Falls and moved on to the legal battles for education, property rights, and eventually, suffrage. The papers of the Grimké sisters, Lucretia Mott, Elizabeth Cady Stanton, and Carrie Chapman Catt were found here, as were those of other white women who made up the ranks of the organized suffrage movement. The second section paid homage to the work of suffragists at the state level and included complete volumes of the *Woman's Journal*, the *Woman Citizen*, and publications of city and college suffrage organizations. The final section celebrated the legal and political accomplishments of feminists since 1920, with papers documenting the passing of the Cable and Reclassification Acts, the lives of women in political positions and parties, and the activities of the LWV. Against Beard's better judgment, this display played out perfectly what she critically referred to as the "1848 narrative"; it emphasized the accomplishments of a few elite women who measured progress by their increasing ability to imitate men in the political sphere.[19]

Beard insisted that focusing solely on the woman's rights movement was a mistake. Researchers using the collections would assume that the papers in front of them told the whole story, or at least all that was important about women in the past. They would never detect the silences embedded in the tactical selection of the documents before them, nor would they have the knowledge with which to speculate about where evidence of women's broader experience could be found. Beard guaranteed Jordan that such a limited view of women's past, both topically and chronologically, "would help to freeze like the icyness [sic] of a glacial age the interpretation of history of masculine tyranny and feminine subjection." To accept this rendition of history was to fall prey to a destructive "feministic jingoism," which in the end would do nothing to advance the social position of women.[20]

Despite Beard's desperate pleas, archivists continued to focus almost exclusively on the historical materials of American women, and white feminists in particular, insisting that in-depth attention to any topic in women's history was better than none at all. Beard disagreed: "The [Radcliffe archivists] knew nothing about realistic history," she charged. "They clung naively to the absurd Seneca Falls 1848 interpretation of women which made women the subjects of men through all history since a romantic golden age." In one last meeting with Harvard administrators, she urged them to conceive of women's history since the age of "pre-historic women who launched civilization by inventing the industrial arts and tilling the soil." "We must start with the first women in order to start thinking straight about women," she reiterated. But in the end she could only conclude that she "had been too optimistic about Radcliffe's intentions," and she started to look elsewhere to carry out her plan for women's history.[21]

Dozens of Beard's associates sympathized with her attack on the "1848 narrative," but no one more than Smith College librarian Margaret Grierson. Smith had long housed an impressive collection of alumnae materials; but not until 1940 did President Elizabeth Cutter Morrow seek to revitalize general collections, and she hired Grierson as head librarian in charge of the college's archives. Grierson also believed that a focus on American feminism was limiting and that an archive with an eclectic blend of materials would better reveal women's varied social roles in the past. Thus as Beard's hopes dissolved in Cambridge, she turned her attention to Smith.[22]

Herbert Davis, the new president of the college, had a limited notion of what Beard and Grierson's vision entailed, but he proved more supportive than Radcliffe administrators and organized the Friends of Smith College Library to raise funds for materials. Beard removed from storage former WCWA items, including her own unpublished articles, that did not fit into specialized collections elsewhere and gave them to Grierson. Convinced that Smith would be the more nurturing environment for international materials, she also donated her texts on Japanese and Arab women before tracking down the primary sources she had used to write *America through Women's Eyes*, including a history of a female academy founded in 1787, etiquette books by Frances Trollope, and an 1838 edition of Harriet Martineau's *Retrospect of Western Travel*. Grierson's staff graciously accepted the items other archivists considered too eccentric, including a German woman's account of her botanical exploration of Surinam in 1699. Before long, the library had acquired enough material to inaugurate what came to be known as the Sophia Smith Collection.[23]

Beard continually warned Grierson not to cater to the whims of feminist donors by allowing the Sophia Smith Collection to be transformed into a memorial for woman's rights. She monitored inventories and acquisition reports for the disproportionate abundance of partisan donations, in one instance even urging staff members to remove a mural given to the library, on the grounds that it was "a strictly 19th century feminist presentation of the case for women" and thus "too unhistorical." Yet in the same breath she also insisted that the Smith collection not preclude documents on women's fights for political and legal autonomy altogether. These items did, after all, shed light on one recent episode in a larger history of women that Beard wanted to present to patrons, and therefore she encouraged Grierson to find materials that represented woman's rights in proportion to the whole of women's past. Specifically, the acquisition of NWP materials should be of highest priority, she argued, to balance the representation of NAWSA women at Radcliffe. Beard conceded that recently acquired papers from the LWV were "*musts* of course," but she offset these with copies of the speeches she had delivered to Congress as an NWP activist in 1917. Her rationale for such precise recommendations may have seemed arbitrary to any bystander, yet her sense of balance and historical scope seemed to coincide with Grierson's own.[24]

Beard's opinions about the limited views of equal rights feminists and professional women never changed, and yet in her attempt to be true to an all-inclusive women's history, she sought to make both part of the Sophia Smith Collection. Anyone who influenced the thoughts or actions of women deserved a place in the inventory, she told staffers. Remarkably, the collection thus eventually included Sigmund Freud, one of the originators of the "women's submission" ideology to which Beard believed modern feminists had fallen prey. She worried that women accepted Freud's "so-called wisdom" so willingly "that it seem[ed] impossible to get them up on their feet to use their heads for knowing and judging themselves." Nevertheless, as artifacts "indicating the depths to which that sex interpretation has gone and still goes," his writings served as valuable cultural resources.[25] Women professionals, some of Freud's most gullible converts, according to Beard, were important contributors to the archive even if their desire to integrate into masculine institutions seemed hopelessly misplaced; their papers became useful to defy historical generalizations about women's work and natural proclivities. Nutting and Dock's *History of Nursing* revealed what Beard considered an essential chapter in the history of women's work in America, as did Mead's *History of Women in Medicine*, which she admired despite its careerist undertones. The published histories of Nellie Neilson and the books of social scientists Mary Follett and Margaret Mead were just some of the professional works that made her list of recommendations for the Sophia Smith Collection.[26]

In 1951 Elizabeth Borden, the new director of the Radcliffe archive, wrote Mary Beard asking her to serve yet again as a consultant. Apparently she knew little about the animus between Beard and administrators several years earlier, but Beard felt obliged to set the record straight:

> I not only turned over to Radcliffe data on persons who had helped disseminate the idea of a World Center for Women's Archives . . . but I also contributed $1,000 for the promotion of an important Archive at Radcliffe. . . . Having lured many women to believe that Radcliffe was the best place in the U.S. for a great collection of books and documents respecting women's roles in American and other history, I have regretted that Radcliffe, as far as I knew, was in no great sense apparently warranting that belief.[27]

As harsh as her words were, they barely expressed her frustration with the path the Radcliffe project had taken. Borden seemed amenable to her suggestions for women's education, yet Beard expressed doubt to Grierson: "She has to operate within the confines of the Harvard-Radcliffe circumference. . . . At present she is not mentally prepared to burst that boundary."[28] To her surprise, however, Borden did embrace the plans Beard once articulated for a seminar in women's history. Her seminar on women included Elizabeth Schlesinger, Alma Lutz, Elisabeth Dexter, and scholars who presented papers on the history of women in religion, the professions, labor, and suffrage.[29] Having convened continuously for eight years, in 1955 members even invited Grierson to speak about the Sophia Smith Collection. In turn Grierson made a compact with Borden to exchange bibliographies, books, catalogs, and materials that dealt with families or alumnae connected to the other's respective institution. With this collegial cooperation, Radcliffe and Smith were on their way to becoming the academic forerunners of women's collecting.[30]

Mary Beard the Anachronism

Thanks to Beard's Herculean efforts, by 1950 thousands of items were available for the writing of women's history. Yet Beard could only stand back and bemoan women's relative lack of interest in the collections. Individuals sought out these materials only occasionally, not to the extent of forging inroads into unexplored areas of women's past as Beard had hoped. The initial interest in women's history at Smith and Radcliffe was increasingly difficult to maintain or replicate anywhere, for that matter.[31] Faculty at women's colleges remained most apathetic of all; when Beard tried to convince one college president of the importance of women's source materials, she responded that she did not think students really wanted to know about women's past. Likewise, Mildred McAfee, president of Wellesley, confessed that the reason she did not accept membership in the WCWA or support Beard's efforts afterward was because she did not think it "vitally important . . . to recreate the story of 'woman as compared to man.' "[32] Women faculty continued to embrace the masculine pedagogy to which they were subjected as graduate students without questioning its underlying value for women. The opposing opinions of one professor at Vassar caused Beard to conclude that her efforts had done almost nothing to alleviate ignorance of woman's "historic force." "She is sunk by the blithe feminist cult," Beard sadly concluded. "She has nothing at all to give college girls, in my opinion. She is up against the pressure in college circles to drive woman *exclusively* to the nursery."[33]

Despite this academic's response to Beard, several Vassar colleagues expressed interest in women's history courses and a repository, an indication that perhaps a glimmer of Lucy Salmon's legacy was alive and well on the campus. Ultimately, however, administrators were repelled by the cost of building fireproof facilities. As for the earlier proposal of Swarthmore, Bryn Mawr, and Haverford administrators to build a communal women's library, it, too, seemed to fade without contention.[34] The years following the dissolution of the WCWA witnessed a brief piquing of interest in women's collections, but by the 1950s those that had materialized were, to

Beard's continued disappointment, too specialized and poorly promoted on university campuses. Many of them sat untouched in what she described as a "museum-like state," virtually inaccessible to the undergraduate student of average curiosity. "It's a war on all campuses," Beard declared. "The little museum idea for colleges is not only ridiculous. It would reduce education to child's play. . . . It must not get a death grip on our new social content." But in the end even Beard conceded that she was waging a losing battle. She promoted the knowledge of women's long history to an extent, but never to the revolutionary proportions she envisioned.[35]

Looking back over her own long history, Mary Beard saw a mixed legacy of great successes and irrefutable failures. Much of her acclaim came as a collaborator with husband Charles Beard; between 1915 and 1942 they wrote some of the most influential historical textbooks the country had ever seen, including their most celebrated three-volume work, *The Rise of American Civilization*. Like all their textbooks, the first of this series proclaimed the Progressive hope that the history of civilization, "if intelligently conceived," could be an instrument of civilization itself. It was a bold statement to make at the time, but Mary Beard took comfort in conspiring with her husband to create their reform-minded interpretations of the American past. In fact, she relied so much on Charles's reputation to lend weight to their histories that she often eschewed recognition for their collaborations altogether. Humbly she told Merle Curti in 1938, "I try to help CAB [Charles] escape the burden of carrying me. . . . It is commonly assumed that I injected women into the thought of history and just that." When Grierson asked if she could use Beard's name to promote the Sophia Smith Collection, she responded with humility once again: "Of course you are welcome to use it, though I doubt whether it has the pull which you think it has."[36]

Mary Beard's rejection of academic careerism certainly lent to her preference for anonymity, but her personal insecurities also played a part in her decision to let Charles shoulder most of the criticism and praise for their joint productions. By 1940 she had good reason for concern; the books for which she claimed sole responsibility almost always received harsh feedback from all directions, and her name alone proved insufficient to carry the WCWA into the more prosperous years after World War II. Aware of her husband's more commanding reputation, Mary even joked that when it came to printing her solo works, publishers "cr[ied] out paper shortage." After publishing *Laughing Their Way: Women's Humor in America* (1934) with Martha Bruere, she concluded that "very few laughed with us, judging from the fact that the book was not reprinted." One critic for the *New York Times* remarked that the work had "an under-tow of resentment," but of course Beard's only resentment was that so few understood her simple goal: to prove that women laughed throughout the course of American history and made men laugh with them.[37]

On Understanding Women and *America through Women's Eyes* did not resonate with all audiences either. Reviewers suggested that part of the problem was Beard's writing style. It could be cumbersome, unlike her husband's straightforward prose, and at times her data became unwieldy: "She beguiles you with detail until you feel you may as well cry 'uncle' or 'aunt,'" wrote one otherwise sympathetic woman critic. While some admired her marshalling of massive amounts of evidence, it was often the scholarly appraisal that her interpretation of women's accomplishments to civilization was peculiar and ridden with inconsistency. Because she wrote about women since the days of antiquity, she treaded against the academic current of specialization; scholars described her historical coverage as dauntingly broad, as she worked her way through cultures across the globe from primitive to present times. While feminists were less critical of her lack of disciplinary convention, most were uneasy with her underlying interpretation of women's past. It, too, defied prevailing sentiments by showing a historical precedent for the separatist ideologies of older suffragists, not the integration of men and women that professionals increasingly preferred.[38]

Here we see the interrelated nature of Beard's historiographical and feminist worldviews as well as her own personal transformation after women won the vote in 1920. An active NWP suffragist in the late 1910s, she eventually questioned Alice Paul's battle for women's social and political equality with men. The organized movement's "obsession with natural rights and the idea of equality in self-interestedness" had caused feminism, in her eyes, to grow "vigorously individualistic," "humanistically anemic."[39] She looked to the past for evidence of women's contributions to the progress of a gentler civilization, only to discover that equal rights feminism had relied on a historical falsehood for its ideological basis: "the myth of women's subjection." She urged women not to determine their current status using legal identity as the sole measure, for a longer view of history proved that their lack of power on paper did not reflect the quality of women's experience in or outside Western culture until modern times. A broader view proved that women's nineteenth-century fight for legal rights was a misguided battle at the expense of life-giving culture. Once they placed the modern feminist movement in this proper perspective, women would recognize that their "imitativeness of men [wa]s a brief, recent phase," and that "feminine energy and initiative have marked history" in the longer term. For decades Beard armed herself with this interpretation of women's past, hoping not only to convince younger feminists that they were trying to knock down a fictitious wall of subjection but that her long history would alleviate what were, in fact, real inequalities in modern life.[40]

To this diehard Progressive, the parasitic capitalism of the modern age had robbed America of its humanistic and civilizing elements. The individualist ethic of industrialists was a threat to American democracy and required a reassertion of the historically feminine—collectivism, humanism, and maternalism—to rebalance society and foster democratic progress. Beard's *Woman as Force in History* attacked capitalists, politicians, and professionals in the presentist mode, and eventually she turned a critical eye on the feminist movement of which she was once a part. It came as no surprise that reactions to her book were mixed to negative overall. One female reviewer wondered why Beard sounded "so cross"; had not she herself proven that modern women could marry, enjoy equitable relationships with husbands, and have children while engaging their own intellectual pursuits? A feminist editor for the *Independent Woman* thought the book a "hellish thing," while another reviewer wondered how Beard could list twenty-six pages of bibliographic references and yet still complain that scholars had ignored women in history.[41] Others found her claims of "woman as historical force" wholly unconvincing. In "Fools Gold for Women," a male critic concluded that "Mrs. Beard misse[d] the heart of the historical problem, which is that equality for women is a chimera where the material foundations for it are lacking." "She cannot fool us," insisted a writer for the *New York Book Review*. "We know who was mainly behind those trends and developments and movements. For better or for worse, it was the men."[42]

Beard never claimed to account for the tastes of male critics, but by 1947 she was disconcerted that women were not reading *Woman as Force in History* to the extent that she had hoped. The book did go into a third printing that year, but she called its 7,500 copies sold "a washout" compared with the tens of thousands already sold of the first printing of Ferdinand Lundberg and Marynia Farnham's *Modern Woman: The Lost Sex*. It bothered her to no end that women willingly became "the major consumers of books which ever damn their sex," especially when hers offered an empowered view of women's role for the future. Lundberg and Farnham's biological determinism lacked historical perspective, she complained; with the popular writings of Philip Wylie it, in her eyes, was the by-product of an uncritical "Freudian cultism" that women seemed to accept wholeheartedly. Nonetheless, by 1949 her greater lament as she traveled from campus to campus was that Simone de Beauvoir had cast a virtual spell on university women. How could they accept her depiction of them as victims of history lock, stock, and barrel, as well as her prescription to seek equality with men in the modern work world? Beard called *The Second Sex* (1949) "perfectly ridiculous" and its author "a most pretentious person" for pretending to have "knowledge of [the] primitive, to give long history as background," and then to wrongly assert that "man made woman till the fields." If only younger women listened to her like they listened to this French theorist of counterhistory, she thought, then they would develop their own institutions of learning and measure accomplishment on their own terms.[43]

Beard concluded that *The Second Sex* was "utter nonsense in view of actual long history," but de Beauvoir was hardly the only woman she grumbled about in her later years. The social scientists on whom she once relied for a more complete perspective of women in the past were now failing to support her outmoded agenda. Margaret Mead, for instance, once provided anthropological backbone for Beard's claims about women's roles in primitive culture, but now, according to Beard, Mead was close to rejecting the notion of ancient matriarchy altogether. Karen Horney was another social scientist whom Beard had once praised, only to conclude by 1944 that "she needs to study the history of 'cultures' " before drawing any essential conclusions about the genders. By the late 1940s the women from whom Beard borrowed relative models seemed to essentialize gender like the dreaded Freudians and had won converts. "Naturally I am drawn into the contest for the capture of youthful thinking about boys and girls," she wrote. "BUT I HAVE LITTLE DOUBT THAT THE PSYCHIATRISTS AND SEXOLOGISTS WILL BE THE VICTORS and girls [will] become more 'confused' than ever."[44]

By the early 1950s Beard's assaults against feminists, academics, sexologists, and other "experts" even extended to professional writers of women's history. Two of the unsuspecting victims, Alma Lutz and Elisabeth Dexter, felt Beard's wrath as participants in Radcliffe's first women's history seminar. Both had used the archive's new collections, but Beard felt that their research left much to be desired. Lutz's works on the suffrage pioneers were two-dimensional, particularly *Created Equal*, which "lack[ed] any concern with Mrs. Stanton's mind—with her sharp analysis of Woman, Church, and State." Indeed, Lutz's Stanton appeared more obsessed with equal rights than with the analysis of cultural attitudes that made her, in Beard's mind, the more sophisticated thinker. In the end Beard concluded that Lutz herself was "far from a thinker . . . on account of her lack of knowledge or fear of woman in long history."[45] As for Dexter, Beard chided her for her undying "careerism," much like she did the "Dumb clucks" of the AAUW, whose " 'packaged thinking' seem[ed] never to burst a package." In 1950 she refused to endorse Dexter's most recent work, *Career Women of America*, on the grounds that it did not place women's "careers" in proper context.

Still, Dexter's imposition of twentieth-century notions of careering was not unlike most historians', informed by what Beard disparagingly referred to as "feministic historiography," or the 1848 frame of reference. Dexter had "fall[en] into feminist formulas," Beard lamented. "I abhor the word 'career' for women. It trivializes their operations."[46]

Dexter defended her lack of knowledge of women's long history; sources were limited, she explained, especially since women researchers continued to be "deprived of access to book collections" and "were not welcome in libraries." Of course, this claim only incited Beard's ire by perpetuating the myth of female victimization she was trying to demystify. Dexter's excuse implied that male institutions continued to reign supreme and that without access to them, women remained defenseless and ignorant. "I wanted to ask how Lydia Maria Child got at sources for her book on women in history which she published years before 1848," Beard sniped.[47] She resented women's reliance on male institutions, especially since history proved that this had not always been the case; before they had access to the university, women had commonly educated other women about the past. Now, however, collegians were indoctrinated to believe that the only authorities on the past were male professors who considered women inconsequential. She complained in the *Independent Woman*: "Women at large do not know that their sex has a lively history, because they too have been instructed merely in the history of the male."[48] Dexter's comments made Beard more adamant than ever to establish an institution where both feminist and masculine narratives of history could be taken to task and the myth of victimization banished once and for all. Until one existed, women would never be more than "mental children," Beard concluded, "just parrots learning to speak what men teach them to say."[49]

In the early 1950s Beard drew up the plans for such an institution, what she and Grierson termed "The Woman's Institute." Her experience at Radcliffe convinced her that it could not exist at a school where male figureheads controlled the curriculum, but she sensed that Smith was "freer than Barnard and Radcliffe from the pull-back of university men." The institute would be a segregated environment at first, "until women catch up with themselves as knowers of their background and philosophers of their foreground," but gradually the learning community would be open to men.[50] Admittedly, few women had sufficient training to teach an entire women's history course from beginning to end, but within a year or two Beard believed that Smith could be ready to offer courses in particular specializations. She already had former backers of the WCWA in mind for the experiment; their fields ranged from women in music to women in religion since prehistoric times.[51]

Her call for what was essentially a women's studies program piqued the interest of several educators, who developed experimental programs in women's history. Dean Eunice Hilton at Syracuse University, a former WCWA supporter, structured a course on the history of women's "responsibilities" in America, which Beard was happy to report had gone "beyond the customary mere sentimentality connected with the word 'responsibilities.'" Sixty women took the course in its first year, inspiring school librarians to collect more source materials for student research. Another dean at the University of Wisconsin consulted Beard about structuring a course called Representative Women, and faculty at Purdue sought input on a syllabus for a seminar starting with women's "social origins" as inventors of the arts. Unfortunately, the institute at Smith was never to be. Its downfall was to some extent one of the shortcomings of the WCWA; although her close associates knew better, to outsiders Beard seemed to focus on the minutest details of long history at the expense of a tangible plan for women's learning in the university. Potential sponsors deemed her ideas about women's education too theoretical to be practically applied to course curricula and classroom exercises.[52]

Despite another failed project, Beard continued to write about women's role in long history. In 1951 she peddled a manuscript on Japanese women, only to confirm that publishers, like most academics, wanted little to do with her conception of women's history. "My favorite publisher agrees with all the others who rejected my Ms," she wrote Grierson. "There is no reading public for it. . . . Books must be simple and appeal to emotions rather than to such history as I have tried to tell." An editor at Macmillan told her that he could not "gamble on unsalable books," and to her surprise editors at the University of Minnesota Press (which according to Beard was entirely "run by women") "were harshly emphatic that they didn't want this book." She wrote Grierson in sheer dismay, announcing her resignation from book writing altogether. The letter proved disingenuous, for her final book was still four years away: a posthumous biography of Charles Beard that an editor had no reservations about printing. But indeed it would be the end of her writing on the history of women, aside from her disgruntled scribblings to Grierson and other confidantes who cared to listen.[53]

Final Thoughts: Linking Historical Pioneers to the Present

In the 1950s Mary Beard's ideas about history and its activist potential lost resonance with scholars and the public at large. The relativism she espoused for the writing of history was never a moral relativism, yet after World War II relativism of any stripe was unnerving, given the depths of human depravity the Holocaust had proven possible. Americans seemed less critical of disparities of wealth and social status at home, for they had witnessed so much more instability abroad and looked forward to consuming their way to a standard of living higher than ever before. Introspection about one's cultural biases or responsibilities to America's less fortunate citizens was not demanded of the historian, a fact reflected in the scholarship produced in the postwar years. John Higham observed that "the progressive synthesis of American history broke down [as] . . . historians called for recognition of the continuities in American history and belittled the magnitude of the many crises, upheavals, and 'watersheds' Progressive historians had reveled in." Peter Novick describes the moment as one in which academic historians "identif[ied] with those who exercise[d] power." "Orthodoxy, not heterodoxy, was à la mode. 'Radical' interpretations were abandoned; dissidents were increasingly marginalized." "If one had to choose a single term to characterize the dominant tendency in postwar American historical writing," he concludes, " 'counterprogressive' would seem the best choice."[54]

As the Red Scare intensified after World War II, hundreds of left-leaning scholars fell prey to censorship and removal, and historians in particular were careful to relinquish ties with the Communist Party.[55] Aside from a few renegades, most remained content to write American history within the Free-World-versus-Totalitarianism framework, casting national enemies not as exploitative insiders but, rather, as alien outsiders who sought to infiltrate American culture at its weakest link. Politicians and scholars insisted that a fortified, patriotic history was the nation's best instrument of defense. As Adlai Stevenson encouraged Smith graduates to fight the good fight as patriotic mothers and wives in the home, Thomas Bailey used his latest diplomatic history to chastise Americans who amidst the "Communist menace" did not "[bear] their new burdens cheerfully and responsibly."[56]

The academy turned hostile to criticism of institutions of power, giving Beard more reason than ever to point an accusatory finger at the university historian and his phlegmatic history. Unfortunately it appeared that students and women themselves were taking comfort in postwar narratives of American heroism and consensus. Once the dauntless reformer, Beard now lived in an age in which historians no longer wrote history to confront injustice or heighten social consciousness but, rather, to celebrate the dawning of a new age of peace, prosperity, and domestic bliss. Popular and academic historical discourse blotted out the socioeconomic differences that continued to exist between men and women of various ethnic, racial, and religious backgrounds, casting them uniformly in "an overwhelmingly affirmative stance toward the American experience"—or so it would super-ficially appear.[57]

One would think that in the domestic quietude of the 1950s, Beard's historical scrutiny of corporatism, consumerism, and all relations of social power would be construed as harmless, but in fact it was a dangerous act of dissension, perhaps because she was not alone. The postwar years became host to a discourse of consensus, but if we look hard enough we can also trace less prominent discourses of discontent. Voices of opposition sounded occasionally in many sectors of American society, including history depart-ments and publishing houses, though they were often quickly suppressed. Higham and Novick concede that the consensus school's program to under-play the dialectic of progressive history "was vulnerable to internal frac-tures."[58] Nonetheless, neither seriously considers women, Beard included, as disrupters of consensus or as significant voices of dissent. Certainly in this study we have tried to disprove any essentialist claims about the gender of historical practices or historiographical traditions. But we have seen that women's relationship to structures of power made them advance progres-sive projects in ways many male historians did not, and this tendency quietly continued in the 1950s.

In fact, some women who appeared the avatars of domesticity were Beard's disgruntled coconspirators; Betty Friedan is one of the better-known examples. She claimed to play the role of housewife to perfection in the 1950s before identifying the "feminine mystique," but Daniel Horowitz now insists that this is only half her story. He can trace her awakening to social inequality (not only in terms of gender but also of class and eth-nicity) back to her radical activities in the 1940s. She was not alone in her early commitments to the laboring class. As we learn about the little-publicized activities of Friedan and other left-leaning women, we are dis-covering that the social critiques of progressive feminists did not altogether dissipate in the 1950s but went underground, only to inform threads of second-wave feminism a decade later. Left feminists looked the image of contented domesticity, but their campaigns for "the masses" indicate that they were hardly content in the McCarthy years. Some protested covertly through Communist activities; others worked through labor unions. And there were those, like Progressive historians before them, who turned his-tory itself into a tool of labor and social reform.[59]

Two of these women, Gerda Lerner and Eleanor Flexner, deserve special attention, not only because they understood that racial, class, and gender inequalities continued to exist in American life, but also for bravely pi-oneering new avenues of women's history that acknowledged such differ-ence. Ironically, as fewer and fewer women entered history departments or championed Beardian history in the conservative 1950s, Lerner and Flexner wrote women's history that was undoubtedly shaped by their activities in leftist organizations, the most influential of which was the Congress of American Women (CAW), the U.S. branch of the Women's International Democratic Federation. Amy Swerdlow recalls that the very preamble of this pacifist group revealed an identification with women's democratic struggles in the past, invoking Anne Hutchinson, Harriet Tubman, Sojourner Truth, Susan B. Anthony, Lucretia Mott, the Lowell Mill girls, and "the women garment workers of the early twentieth century who struck for economic justice."[60] Lerner taught women's history at the CAW's Los Angeles chapter as early as 1949 and published "The Lady and Mill Girl" under its auspices. Flexner, Lerner's CAW compatriot, agreed that her participation in radical circles heightened her awareness of the diversity of American experience but also of the sad truth that "leftist organizations—parties, unions—were also riddled with male supremacist prejudice and discrimination."[61]

As Flexner became involved in unionization campaigns of the Congress of Industrial Organizations, the Foreign Policy Organization, and the Association of Colored Graduate Nurses in the 1940s, she grew to appreciate how racial, ethnic, and gender biases intersected in the special burdens of laboring women of color whose histories had been left unrecorded. Inez Irwin's *Angels and Amazons* made no mention of black women's organizing, she noted, nor did the biographies that came out of the suffragist camps. She offered women's history courses at the Jefferson School of Social Science, a Communist Party academy, hoping to empower part-time working students with this history. She also turned to writing what became *Century of Struggle*, one of the first scholarly treatments of American women's history and assuredly the first rendition of woman's rights that included black and working women.[62]

Beard would have taken solace in knowing that during her research Flexner used the Radcliffe and Smith collections that had sat untouched in Beard's lifetime. Flexner's insistence on including black women in her account also led her to Dorothy Porter at the Moorland-Spingarn Research Center and Jean Blackwell Hutson, the new director at the Schomburg Center. Like W. E. B. Du Bois, these women had shown enthusiasm for the projects of African American researchers of New Negro history. Unlike Du Bois, however, they embraced Flexner's vision for women's history and directed her to sources. Her interest in women of color and the working class was not altogether new, but her consideration of them in a connected story was an idea to which no one other than Beard had given much thought before and immediately after *Century of Struggle* came out in 1959.

"Struggle" was what united her historical women she decided, even if they did not share a common experience.[63]

For the re-release of *Century of Struggle* in 1996, Ellen Fitzpatrick attached a foreword that described Flexner's activist state of mind leading up to the writing of the final manuscript, now acknowledging that these details were vitally important to the text itself. Flexner agreed that her early social convictions and radical activities inescapably determined her later work as a historian: "In all honesty I have to say that my real concern and interest in women came out of my connection with the radical movement in the thirties," she remembered.

> The Communist Party, and Marxist publications like *New Masses* and others, did have enormous impact on the nearly non-existent (among whites) interest in black history and black thought and writing, and much later, the area of women's rights and ideology. . . . I can definitely trace the origins of my book . . . to some of my contacts with Communists like Elizabeth Gurley Flynn and Claudia Jones (who was quite unknown to the larger white community). . . . It was from [Flynn] . . . that I first heard about people like the Lowell mill girls and other early activists of American working women.[64]

It may seem surprising that today's historians know so little about Flexner's radical origins and how they factored into her pioneering of women's history. On the other hand, Horowitz and Swerdlow insist that such silence was the lasting legacy of McCarthyism, a phenomenon that obscured the Old Left's ties to the New Left, civil rights, women's liberation, and even women's and minority history writing in the 1950s and 1960s. The CAW only lasted four years before it was forced to disband due to government intolerance of political dissent of any kind. The accomplishments of its members seemed swept under the rug, much like Friedan's dismissal of her own radical activities before McCarthyism.[65] Indeed, the censorship of the 1950s has limited our understanding of the work of women activists, scholars, and historians much like the masculine process of professionalization had at the turn of the twentieth century. While Flexner, Lerner, and Beard helped to raise historical consciousness in ways that resonate with multicultural historians today, most of us credit men with similar agendas for creating this bottom-up history later—once the fear of reprisal had receded.

Joyce Antler's work on the Emma Lazarus Federation (ELF) attempts to fill in some of these voids in women's historiography, for she shows that the Emmas succeeded in Beard's goal of combining diverse women's history with social action through the McCarthy years. The ELF grew out of the Jewish People's Fraternal Order after World War II and became an independent organization of Jewish women in 1951. Its originators included Clara Lemlich (Shavelson) and other workingwomen with ties to labor radicalism in the 1900s and 1910s, and from this unique perspective they came to understand that they and women of color suffered injustices that were no better clarified in history texts that defined Americanness as male, white, and middle class. The Emmas recognized that their fights for wartime victims, labor, Israeli independence, and racial and ethnic tolerance relied on a reworking of the historical record. Thus amidst the trepidation of the 1950s they did not remain silent but promoted historical education that celebrated cultural pluralism and Jewish identity. Nearly 5,000 strong in the 1950s, the Emmas set out to educate Americans with a history that recognized diversity as well as "linked identity," that accounted for the combinations of gender, culture, politics, race, and ethnicity and revealed experiences in the American past as both shared and fundamentally unique.[66]

Many of the women in this study likely inspired the historical projects of the ELF. The Emmas initially combated anti-Semitism (which they perceived as analogous to racism) with a history of women of accomplishment, much like the women of the New Negro History Movement. Their narratives instilled ethnic pride in Jews as they informed non-Jews of a past that defied ethnic stereotypes, but like Beard and the first womanist writers, the ELF soon advanced this history further. Antler describes histories, for example, set within a tradition of "dissident women" (i.e., courageous martyrs such as Ethel Rosenberg alongside rebellious Protestant Anne Hutchinson). But the Emmas also offered alternative models of accomplishment that were culturally unique to Jewish women (i.e., the distinctive radicalism of turn-of-the-century garment workers). That is not to say that these heroines fought for women or Jews alone. The ELF sponsored a biography of Ernestine Rose, a nineteenth-century woman whose experience as an eccentric immigrant Jew provided her with insight into social inequalities across the board. The Emmas praised her as a radical feminist, abolitionist, peace activist, and overall cultural dissenter who believed in "human rights without distinction of sect, party, sex or color." Through Rose, the ELF showed that Jews and Gentiles, whites and nonwhites, and men and women were interrelated in the American past, a claim Beard had hoped to prove through her all-encompassing women's history.[67]

Indeed the ELF succeeded where Beard's WCWA had not, mobilizing a wide range of American minorities, including African Americans, to promote women's history as a means of social reform. In this sense the Emmas better resembled Mary McLeod Bethune as she galvanized racial, ethnic, and religious groups for her black women's history campaigns in the late 1940s—although unlike hers, ELF histories functioned both ways: Just as they promoted Jewish history in race organizations, the Emmas authored some of the most innovative African American history of the 1950s and 1960s, including study guides on Harriet Tubman, Sarah Douglass, and Ida Wells Barnett. Moreover, they backed their historical teachings with like-minded social action, recognizing the achievements of civil rights activist Rosa Parks, for instance, and participating in Negro History Week, Freedom Rides, and Freedom Summer by 1965. In some small way they had finally achieved Beard's unrealized vision, despite the closed-mindedness of academic historians and much of American society in the postwar years.[68]

Radical women quietly carried out Beard's plan through the 1940s and 1950s while privileged university women seemed uninterested in women's history. Little did Beard know that as she was being heckled by Radcliffe collegians in the 1940s, one of them was being groomed to produce the scholarship she envisioned. Anne Firor Scott simultaneously embarked on her dissertation in the American civilization department while starting a family and writing for LWV publications. When she left the LWV to complete her research in 1953, she received two going-away presents: Simone de Beauvoir's *Second Sex*, but also Beard's *Woman as Force in History*. Like so many before her, Scott was overwhelmed by too many distractions to complete her graduate work swiftly, but she secured an AAUW fellowship that allowed her "at last—seven years and three children beyond the preliminary examination"—to complete the dissertation. Much the same way Arthur Schlesinger encouraged Julia Cherry Spruill to recover the lives of southern women in the 1930s, in the 1940s and 1950s another Harvard historian, Oscar Handlin, pushed Scott to pursue the southern Progressives. "As I searched the record . . . I kept stumbling over women: well dressed, well-spoken southern ladies taking a strong hand in social and political issues," she noted with surprise. Jane Addams had been the only woman north or south whose life Scott had researched to that point, yet by 1961 she was ready to present "The 'New Woman' in the New South" to the Southern Historical Association, and soon Spruill was appealing to her to write a full manuscript on the subject. "[Spruill] was like a retired athlete urging a younger runner on around the track," Scott recalled before finally completing *The Southern Lady* in 1970. Had Beard been alive, she likely would have been next to Spruill cheering Scott along.[69]

Indeed, had Beard lived longer, she would have witnessed the stemming of the conservative tide of the 1950s, a renewed questioning of power in academic circles, and a reinvigorated political culture. With the rise of the New Left, the civil rights movement, antiwar protests, and women's liberation, she would have also witnessed the prolific rewriting of social and cultural history by university scholars who aligned themselves with these causes and, like her, drew an ethical connection between social conviction and historical research. Just as Beard had rejected the role of scholar as it had come to be defined in the twentieth century, by the late 1960s young academics increasingly scrutinized the elitism of the university, as well as its stance on social issues. They looked at anonymous individuals in local settings, seeking to understand limitations to the American Dream of social mobility from the bottom up. They no longer construed Beard's former condemnation of academicians, experts, and capitalists as an uppity assault on omniscient men, nor did they deem progressive "self-criticism" the "national neurosis" diagnosed by an AHA president only years earlier. This was the brand of reflectivity expected of a public intellectual, whose view of power was unobstructed by the fray of institutional politics. A woman with connections to university men and politicians, Beard had enjoyed exceptional privilege that in some respects made her a social and political insider. Yet to younger generations it was her position as an outsider—which she assumed automatically as a woman but imposed on herself as a nonestablishmentarian—that ultimately gave her the greatest historical insight.[70]

In 1967 the *AHR* confirmed that this repudiation of consensus history was not merely the sounded angst of a radical few but a pervasive requestioning of power in a progressive vein. John Higham recalls,

> Four groups that had earlier appeared only on the margins of American history and had received little notice from professional historians sprang into prominence at the annual meetings and in the lists of doctoral dissertations: blacks, Indians, women, and the white working class. . . . The stifled, empathic feelings that could not attach themselves to America as a whole or to its dominant sectors poured forth in a flood of books on the outgroups that seemed from a progressive or radical point of view the victims of American history.

Historiographers rightfully insist that men had written on such people before, but not with matched prolificacy or a desire to show how struggle brought Americans depth and dignity. Higham claims that as a professional collective, academic historians suddenly exclaimed, "Here, incontestably, were histories worth telling." We have seen, however, that women, as a collective of sorts, had deemed these stories worth telling all along.[71]

Until her death Beard excoriated scholars for defining national history as the story of the great man—whether embodied by the rugged pioneer or the capitalist entrepreneur. She failed in her lifetime to convince women that this rendition of the national past robbed them of the broader self-knowledge they had once achieved before reifying the authority of male experts. Had she lived to see the rise of cultural feminism by the early 1970s, she would have witnessed communities of women newly invested in invoking long history to find the primitive origins of woman's life-giving force. As some even renounced their place in the social order to live communally with other women, they celebrated their special maternal knowledge and asserted that sisterhood was powerful because it indeed had historical precedent. By the late 1970s it was clear that this feminist ideology would never sustain a mass political movement, yet academics such as Estelle Freedman still urged women to reconsider "Separatism as Strategy," the battle cry Beard shouted to deaf ears for decades after the Nineteenth Amendment was passed. Her call for autonomous institutions like the WCWA and the Woman's Institute no longer appealed after first-wave feminism, yet second-wave feminists such as Freedman could look down the road of long history far enough to see that the idea had once changed the gender order in ways that should never be forgotten. These second-wavers, now professional scholars of women's history, even revived Beard's eclectic collecting efforts at the Radcliffe archive, which in 1965 was renamed the Schlesinger Library on the History of Women in America.[72]

Of course, academic women historians would still have things to gripe about. Despite trends toward democratization in American universities in the 1960s, the influx of minorities into history departments yielded a female contingent of only 12 percent, compared with 20 percent between 1910 and 1940.[73] In 1976 several historians of women gathered their thoughts in a volume of essays called *Liberating Women's History*, in which they continued to note the gender biases Beard had pointed out among scientific scholars in the 1930s. In "The Invisible Woman: The Historian as Professional Magician," Dolores Barracano Schmidt and Earl Robert Schmidt lamented, "There is a one hundred percent likelihood that an American woman college student majoring in education will take an American history course," and yet "the chances that the course will be designed so that she will better understand the society in which she lives and/or that the materials selected are relevant to her experience as a member of the largest minority in American culture are considerably lower." Her probability of having a woman history professor at a women's college was 33 percent; at a coeducational university, 5.5 percent. "Assuming, even, that a woman college student taking an American history survey course breaks the odds and draws a woman professor," they concluded, "there is no possibility whatever at this writing that the textbook she will use will be written by a woman, [for] . . . Beard's *Basic History of the United States* is now out of print." Looking through the twenty-seven leading history texts at the time, they noted that authors devoted as little as .05 percent of their material to women and that when percentages were higher, it was generally to depict women in pictures, not written text or through personal testimonies of women themselves. Even in the 1970s it appeared that professional historians preferred women to be seen rather than heard.[74]

Nonetheless, while the problems of women in history persisted, women historians found a voice of authority as scholars who had every right to seek solutions. The essayists of *Liberating Women's History* wrote as professionals whose opinions merited the backing of a university press and likely the support of the history departments through which they were employed. While they expressed their explanation for women's absence from American history in terms slightly different from Beard's, in the end their diagnoses were virtually the same. In "The Problem of Women's History," Ann Gordon, Mari Jo Buhle, and Nancy Schrom Dye noted that "historians' neglect of women" continued to be "a function of their ideas about historical significance." "Their categories and periodization have been masculine by definition," they added, "for they have defined significance primarily by power, influence, and visible activity in the world of political and economic affairs." Mary Beard would have undoubtedly agreed.[75]

A woman who shied away from the scrutiny of others, Beard would have also been discomfited to discover that by this time she had become the subject of many books, articles, and women's studies courses by professional women historians. Since the 1970s, Berenice Carroll, Carl Degler, Ann Lane, Barbara Turoff, Loretta Zimmerman, Bonnie Smith, Suzanne Lebsock, Nancy Cott, and a substantial number of graduate students writing dissertations in women's history have acknowledged Mary Beard on her own merits, not merely as Charles Beard's collaborator. When it was unpopular to study women's past, to shift the historical focus from political men, to employ history as a tool for social change, and to question the unitary perspective of the scientific historian, Beard went against the grain, unknowingly anticipating the paradigms that would prevail in today's university. Despite her critics, it is likely that she helped to sway intellectual currents toward that direction. "By opening the historical narrative to multiple voices, multiple points of view," Bonnie Smith concludes, "Mary Beard significantly advanced the history of women, and even history itself."[76]

Recently historians have been intrigued by Beard as a representative thinker of the Progressive Age, yet they have found her nearly postmodern sensibility most fascinating of all. She, too, seemed to take for granted that history was an interpretive act, despite the positivist consensus of her generation. Although she believed like most historians of her time that historical truth was ultimately knowable, she qualified that it was only achievable through a multiplicity of perspectives, including those of non-whites, non-Protestants, the laboring class, and of course, women. She never used the term "gender" to describe her belief in the relative nature of social relationships between the sexes, or "multicultural" to describe her history of American women. Nonetheless, like social and cultural historians today, she undoubtedly sought to reveal the malleability of men's and women's social roles and cultural pluralism in the American past. The questions she posed in her 1934 syllabus on women's history leave little doubt that her mission was nearly the same:

What part did women play in the American and French Revolutions?
Were they "sex conscious?"
What is meant by social history?
Is race a factor in American sex discriminations?
With what kinds of classes of women have historians been mainly concerned, if with any?
Study the inequities which prevail as between women and women.

This eclectic line of questioning seemed to lack focus or significance in 1934, but Beard's inquiries indicate an intuition about the interrelatedness of race, class, and gender and the corresponding dynamics of power that we have only begun to unravel in the postmodern age.[77]

Nonetheless, this study has shown that a sophisticated understanding of power was not Beard's alone. Lucy Salmon, Zora Neale Hurston, Angie Debo, Caroline Ware, Mari Sandoz, Susan B. Anthony, Edith Abbott, Dorothy Porter, Gerda Lerner, and Eleanor Flexner also recovered the hidden lives of the poor, the oppressed, and the disenfranchised, even though at the time these women were not recognized as historians of note. In hindsight we can see that they were all savvy innovators of historical method and interpretation, and their recovery of the historically inarticulate provided a precedent for the projects of multicultural historians in the twenty-first century. Marginalized by gender, race, and institutional politics, they came to understand the intricacies of power that men of the university simply took for granted and achieved power for themselves by taking over the interpretive reins of the past.

The fact that so many of these women have become recent subjects of historical analysis is proof alone of their current resonance as multicultural scholars. Robert Hemenway was one of the first biographers to properly acknowledge Hurston, for example, "as the most important collector of Afro-American folklore in the country." "A black social scientist trying to destroy racial stereotypes held by the majority culture," he remembers, "she simultaneously urged black people to be proud of the folk heritage." Nonetheless Hurston, while popularizing folk culture in ways no academic could claim, never earned more than $943.75 in royalties for any of her books.[78] Despite her successful depathologizing of African Americans, she died in obscurity, and her legacy was not reevaluated until the early 1970s. Alice Walker, one of the first to retrieve her, recalls the moment she became acquainted with her work:

> In late 1970 I was writing a story that required accurate material on voodoo practices among rural southern blacks of the thirties; there seemed none available I could trust. A number of white, racist anthropologists and folklorists of the period had, not surprisingly, disappointed and insulted me. They thought blacks inferior, peculiar, and comic, and for me this undermined—no, *destroyed*—the relevance of their books. Fortunately, it was then that I discovered *Mules and Men*. . . . Because [Hurston] immersed herself in her own culture even as she recorded its 'big old lies,' i.e., folktales, it was possible to see how she and it . . . fit together. The authenticity of her material was verified by her familiarity with its context, and I was soothed by her assurance that she was exposing not simply an adequate culture, but a superior one.[79]

Hurston continues to receive more attention from literary critics than from historians, and as limited as this coverage has been, it is undoubtedly more generous than that afforded many of the African American women in this study. Mary McLeod Bethune, Dorothy Porter, Gertrude Mossell, Mary Church Terrell, Delilah Beasley, Catherine Latimer, Elizabeth Ross Haynes, and Jessie Parkhurst have been revisited by historians in the past two decades, but as clubwomen, librarians, and educators—not also as shapers of memory in their own right. Within the past ten to fifteen years scholars have made opening gestures toward establishing a field of African American women's historiography. Hopefully as more studies come out on womanist reform, their contributions to race history will continue to surface and find their proper place in narratives about national memory.[80]

Though scholars have not sufficiently acknowledged African American women historians, several writers have finally paid their intellectual debts to other women highlighted here. Robert Dorman has been one of the first to appreciate Mari Sandoz's contributions to regionalist memory, even crediting her with foresight never achieved by male historians of her day. "She had gone very far conceptually toward apprehending the frontier myth as myth rather than . . . conceiving it as objective reality," he concluded in 1993. "She was well on her way to a modernist conceptualization of history . . . in which culture—rather than fate, or Providence, or geography, or blind force—was the determinative factor in history." In 2001 Bonnie Smith and Nicholas Adams reassessed Lucy Salmon's legacy and concluded that she, too, was a pioneer of American modernism. Despite constraints of gender, she expanded traditional methodologies and historical focus in the academic establishment. Her commitment to education and social reform made her appear antiquated to her "scientific" colleagues, and yet scholars today appreciate the balance she struck as a university teacher, a prolific scholar, and an early multicultural feminist intellectual.[81]

Perhaps more successfully than any other Salmon student, Caroline Ware integrated scholarship and social action as a professor at Sarah Lawrence College and then for nearly twenty years at Howard University. Ware's student Pauli Murray, later a prominent figure in the civil rights and women's liberation movements, recalled her mentor's commitment to social justice as a participant in sit-ins and protests toward the end of her teaching career. Ware understood that her African American students' feelings of defensiveness and inferiority in the classroom reflected how they felt in white society. Murray credited Ware for providing a "broader perspective on [her] minority status," and for helping her to see "the parallels between racism and sexism" that ultimately shaped her feminist convictions. Ware's mentoring in this sense was not unlike that she received from Salmon in the 1920s; lessons she instilled in the classroom could indeed be carried over into civic life and internalized to shape the individual woman and the way she viewed the world.[82]

Few have fully acknowledged the impact of Salmon's beliefs on historical methods or social activism in the twentieth century, yet Ware's successful integration of them extended her influence into New Deal agencies, the civil rights movement, and even second-wave feminism. Ware herself was fittingly featured in Susan Ware's collection, *Forgotten Heroes*, in 1998. Professional historians chose a mix of men and women for this volume, ironically about 100 years after Sarah Bolton compiled her collective biographies, *Famous Womanhood* and *Leaders among Women*. Indeed, the later volume of heroes provides different prescriptions for gender than Bolton's, which sought more recognition for women's influence on history's great men than for Bolton's own influence as a woman historian. Nonetheless Bolton, Alice Earle, and other late Victorians paved the way for American women to be validated as historical interpreters and empowered through their ability to remember the past.

Perhaps most fitting of all, Angie Debo, the woman once shunned by almost all practicing historians of the West, finally won the praise of academic historians she desperately sought in her younger years. Better yet, she won over the public at large as the Oklahoma Board of Education finally lifted the ban on her books and permitted legislators to use them for the consciousness-raising she intended. A 1988 PBS documentary acknowledged her as an authority on Native American history, a visionary, and a historical heroine in her own right. Reviewing the film for the *Journal of American History*, Richard White credited Debo with having practically "invented the 'new' Indian history long before there was a name for it." Her sincere engagement of the native perspective, the defining feature of ethnohistory, is also one of the cornerstones of the New Indian History project of the twenty-first century. Today her contributions to her field are virtually uncontested. In 1993 an AHA survey listed Debo's *And Still the Waters Run* as the one book written before 1945 that scholars continue to cite as most influential in the field.[83]

In 2000 Shirley Leckie posthumously turned Debo into the subject of a full biography appropriately titled *Angie Debo: Pioneering Historian*. Her rendition of Debo's life, like the one presented here, is a tale of irony: a talented and compassionate truth-seeker fallen prey to institutional politics of race and gender. She endures and, despite the rejection of male academics, carves out a space where she can recover hidden truths with social purpose. Now in the twenty-first century as her portrait sits in the rotunda of the Oklahoma statehouse, Debo is no longer a historical victim but a heroine, much like the Native American women she had once revealed with such conviction in her histories. Throughout time most historians, women especially, have come to see themselves as anonymous by definition; as Mercy Otis Warren believed, historians do not make history, they just relate it. Debo and the women in these pages prove, however, that the converse may be just as true. Historians have indeed made history in more ways than one, and perhaps their anonymity should itself become a thing of the past.

Notes

ABBREVIATIONS

In addition to the abbreviations found in the text, the following
are used in the notes:

BUL   Brown University Library, Brown University, Providence, R.I.
GCA   Goucher College Archives, Goucher College, Baltimore, Md.
JAAUW   *Journal of the American Association of University Women*
JHL   John Hay Library, Brown University, Providence, R.I.
LC   Library of Congress, Washington, D.C.
MHASC   Mount Holyoke College Archives and Special Collections,
       Mount Holyoke College, South Hadley, Mass.
MSRC   Moorland-Spingarn Research Center, Howard University,
       Washington, D.C.
NABWH   National Archive of Black Women's History, Bethune Council House,
       Washington, D.C.
OHS   Oregon Historical Society, Portland
SC   Schomburg Center for Research in Black Culture, New York, N.Y.
SL   Schlesinger Library, Radcliffe College, Cambridge, Mass.
SSC   Sophia Smith Collection, Smith College, Northampton, Mass.
TJGC   Thomas Jefferson Genealogical Collection
WCA   Wellesley College Archive, Wellesley College, Wellesley, Mass.

INTRODUCTION

1. Nina Baym, *American Women Writers and the Work of History, 1790–1860* (New Brunswick: Rutgers University Press, 1995), 93; Mercy Otis Warren, *The History of the Rise, Progress, and Termination of the American Revolution* (Boston: Manning and Loring, 1805).

2. Thomas Woody, *A History of Women's Education in the United States* (New York: Science Press, 1929), 64, 178, 182, 318, 418; "Terms of Admission," college catalog, Mount Holyoke Female Seminary, 1884–85, MHASC, 20; "Requisites for Admission," Smith College circular, Smith College, 1885, SSC, 2.

3. Lucille A. Pollard, *Women on College and University Faculties: A Historical Survey and a Study of Their Present Academic Status* (New York: Arno Press, 1977), 61–62; Woody, *History of Women's Education,* 460, 483, 499–500.

4. Bessie L. Pierce, *Public Opinion and the Teaching of History in the United States* (New York: Knopf, 1926), 6–16.

5. Baym, *American Women Writers,* 35.

6. These and other preservationists are discussed in Charles B. Hosmer Jr., *Presence of the Past: A History of the Preservation Movement in the United States before Williamsburg* (New York: Putnam, 1965), 113, 118–19.

7. Mrs. Joseph Rucker Lamar, *The National Society of Colonial Dames of America:*

Its Beginnings, Its Purpose, and a Record of Its Work, 1891–1913 (Washington, D.C.: The Society, 1913), 12. See also *National Society of Colonial Dames of America Constitutional Acts in Council, 1921* (Washington, D.C.: Gibson Brothers, 1921), 6; David Glassberg, *American Historical Pageantry: The Uses of Tradition in the Early Twentieth Century* (Chapel Hill: University of North Carolina Press, 1990), 18, 39, 135–37.

8. Jacqueline Goggin, "Bessie L. Pierce and the Creation of *Public Opinion and the Teaching of History*," series 8, box 21, Berkshire Conference of Women Historians Papers, SL, 5–7; James Lindgren, " 'A New Departure in Historic, Patriotic Work': Personalism, Professionalism, and Conflicting Concepts of Material Culture in the Late Nineteenth and Early Twentieth Centuries," *Public Historian* 18 (Spring 1996): 42; Hosmer, *Presence of the Past*.

9. Baym, *American Women Writers*; Bonnie Smith, *The Gender of History: Men, Women, and Historical Practice* (Cambridge: Harvard University Press, 1998); Bonnie Smith, "The Contribution of Women to Modern Historiography in Great Britain, France, and the United States, 1750–1940," *AHR* 89 (June 1984): 711.

10. Joyce Appleby, Lynn Hunt, and Margaret Jacob, *Telling the Truth about History* (New York: Norton, 1994), chap. 2, 52–53; Peter Novick, *That Noble Dream: The "Objectivity Question" and the American Historical Profession* (New York: Cambridge University Press, 1988), 21.

11. David A. Hollinger, "Inquiry and Uplift: Late Nineteenth-Century American Academics and the Moral Efficacy of Scientific Practice," in *The Authority of Experts: Studies in History and Theory*, ed. Thomas L. Haskell (Bloomington: Indiana University Press, 1984), 150–51; Margaret W. Rossiter, *Women Scientists in America: Struggles and Strategies to 1940* (Baltimore: Johns Hopkins University Press, 1982); Bonnie Smith, *Gender of History*, 1.

12. Alice Walker, "In Search of Our Mothers' Gardens," in *In Search of Our Mothers' Gardens* (San Diego: Harcourt, Brace, Jovanovich, 1983), 231–43.

CHAPTER 1

1. Mary Louise Booth, *History of the City of New York, From Its Earliest Settlement to the Present Time* (New York: W. R. C. Clark and Meeker, 1859); Alice Morse Earle, *Colonial Days in Old New York* (New York: Charles Scribner's Sons, 1896); Esther Singleton, *Dutch New York* (New York: Dodd, Mead, 1909); Mrs. Schuyler van Rensselaer, *History of the City of New York in the Seventeenth Century* (New York: Macmillan, 1909).

2. Will B. Johnstone, "Why Was It Left for Women to Write the Most Authentic Histories of New York?," *New York Evening World*, 1921, series 1, box 1, folder 5, Martha J. Lamb Papers, SSC.

3. Piece read before the New Jersey Historical Society, 28 September 1888, and "A Notable Work by a Notable Worker," *Baltimore American*, 28 May 1882, series 1, box 1, folder 5, Lamb Papers, SSC.

4. Martha J. Lamb, *The Homes of America* (New York: Appleton, 1879); *Wall Street History* (New York: Funk and Wagnalls, 1883).

5. Transcripts of miscellaneous writings; "Famed Historian Native of Hilltown," 7 August 1963, series 1, box 1, folder 5, Lamb Papers, SSC.

6. Contract between Lamb and Funk and Wagnalls for *Wall Street History*, 12 September 1883, series 2, box 6, folder 35; Susan E. Lyman, *Lady Historian Martha J. Lamb* (Northampton, Mass.: Smith College Library, 1969), 27–28, Lamb Papers, SSC.

7. Transcripts of miscellaneous writings; "Famed Historian Native of Hilltown"; "Mrs. Lamb's Quuer [sic] Ways: She Was the Only Woman Historian in America," *The Press*[?], n.d., series 1, box 1, folder 5, Lamb Papers, SSC.

8. Sarah K. Bolton, *Pages from an Intimate Autobiography*, ed. Charles Bolton (Boston: Thomas Todd, 1923), 94–95. The original manuscript of Bolton's autobiography is in the Sarah Bolton Collection, SL. The bibliography lists Bolton's historical biographies.

9. Bolton, *Pages from an Intimate Autobiography*, 102–3.

10. Sarah K. Bolton, *Famous Types of Womanhood* (New York: Crowell, 1892), 104, 125, 149.

11. Bolton, *Pages from an Intimate Autobiography*, 96–97, 101.

12. Frances Willard and Mary Livermore, eds., *A Woman of the Century: Fourteen Hundred-Seventy Biographical Sketches Accompanied by Portraits of Leading American Women in All Walks of Life* (Buffalo: Charles Wells Moulton, 1893); Phoebe A. Hanaford, *Daughters of America; or, Women of the Century* (Boston: B. B. Russell, 1883); Louisa C. Moulton, *Our Famous Women. (An authorized and complete record of the lives and deeds of distinguished American women of our times)* (Hartford: A. D. Worthington, 1883); Frances Willard, *Women in the Pulpit* (Washington, D.C.: Zenger, 1889). More of these collective biographies are listed in the bibliography.

13. Some of Ellet's collective biographies include *Women Artists in all Ages and Countries* (London: Richard Bentley, 1859); *The Women of the American Revolution*, 4th ed. (1850; reprint, New York: Haskell House, 1969); *The Queens of American Society* (New York: Charles Scribner, 1870); *Pioneer Women of the West* (New York: Charles Scribner, 1852); *The Court Circles of the Republic; or, The Beauties and Celebrities of the Nation: Illustrating life and society under eighteen presidents; describing the social features of the successive administrations from Washington to Grant* (Philadelphia: Philadelphia Pub. Co., 1872).

14. Nina Baym, *American Women Writers and the Work of History, 1790–1860* (New Brunswick: Rutgers University Press, 1995), 222.

15. Anne H. Wharton, *Through Colonial Doorways* (Philadelphia: Lippincott, 1893), 3–4.

16. Anne H. Wharton, *Colonial Days and Dames* (1894; Philadelphia: Lippincott, 1898), 130–31.

17. Anne H. Wharton, *Martha Washington* (New York: Charles Scribner's Sons, 1897), vii. The other four books in the series are Catherine Schuyler, *Mary Gay Humphreys*; Eliza Pinckney, *Harriet Horry Ravenel*; Maud Wilder Goodwin, *Dolly Madison*; Alice Brown, *Mercy Warren*.

18. Wharton, *Through Colonial Doorways*, 65.

19. Alice Morse Earle, *Colonial Dames and Good Wives* (Boston: Houghton Mifflin, 1895), 106.

20. Advertisements in back matter of Wharton, *Martha Washington*.

21. "New woman" is a term used loosely to delineate between Victorian ideals of femininity and the "new" sensibilities of women in the twentieth century, in terms of fashion, social and economic independence, and heightened sexual liberation. "New woman" described the modern woman of the stage and magazines as early as the 1890s, as well as the "flapper" of the 1920s. See "The Steel Engraving Lady and the Gibson Girl," *Atlantic Monthly*, July 1901, 105–8; Rosalind Rosenberg, *Beyond Sepa-*

rate *Spheres: Intellectual Roots of Modern Feminism* (New Haven: Yale University Press, 1982), 54–83; Earle, *Colonial Dames and Good Wives*, 159, 240–41, 45.

22. "Notable Work by a Notable Worker," Lamb Papers, SSC; *Springfield Republican* quoted in Lyman, *Lady Historian Martha J. Lamb*, 18.

23. Joyce Appleby, Lynn Hunt, and Margaret Jacob, *Telling the Truth about History* (New York: Norton, 1994), 52–53.

24. Bonnie Smith, *The Gender of History: Men, Women, and Historical Practice* (Cambridge: Harvard University Press, 1998), 85–86; Peter Novick, *That Noble Dream: The "Objectivity Question" and the American Historical Profession* (New York: Cambridge University Press, 1988).

25. David D. Van Tassell, "From Learned Society to Professional Organization: The American Historical Association, 1884–1900," *AHR* 89 (October 1984): 943; "Graduate Studies in History at Brown University, 1887–1897," J. Franklin Jameson Papers, BUL.

26. "Paleography file" in Isabel Abbott's graduate course notes, Isabel Abbott Papers, BUL.

27. John Martin Vincent, *Aids to Historical Research* (New York: Appleton-Century, 1934), 27, 104; Herbert B. Adams, *The Study and Teaching of History* (Richmond: Whittet and Shepperson, 1898).

28. Bonnie Smith, *Gender of History*, 138; Joan W. Scott, "American Women Historians, 1884–1984," in *Gender and the Politics of History* (New York: Columbia University Press, 1988), 182–83.

29. Lamb was the first woman to speak in front of the New Haven Historical Society. She frequently lectured before the New-York Historical Society. See diary entry, 4 July 1854, series 2, box 6, folder 30; "Gardiner's Island," n.p., series 1, box 1, folder 5, Lamb Papers, SSC.

30. Bonnie Smith, *Gender of History*, 104–28; Franklin Jameson, "The American Historical Association, 1884–1909," *AHR* 15 (October 1909): 3.

31. Susan R. Williams, "In the Garden of New England: Alice Morse Earle and the History of Domestic Life" (Ph.D. diss., University of Delaware, 1992), 98, 122, 123–24.

32. Piece read before the New Jersey Historical Society, 28 September 1888, Lamb Papers, SSC.

33. Susan R. Williams, "In the Garden of New England," 154–57; Alice Morse Earle, "The Pleasures of Historiography," in *Chap-Book Essays* (Chicago: Herbert S. Stone, 1896), 47–53.

34. Bonnie Smith, "The Contribution of Women to Modern Historiography in Great Britain, France, and the United States, 1750–1940," *AHR* 89 (June 1984): 720; Alice Morse Earle, *Child Life in Colonial Days* (New York: Macmillan, 1899), viii–ix.

35. Susan R. Williams, "In the Garden of New England," 144; Earle, "The Pleasures of Historiography," 47.

36. For a discussion of the construction of amateur history of the late nineteenth century and professional history in the twentieth century, see Harold E. Mahan, *Benson J. Lossing and Historical Writing in the United States: 1830–1890* (Westport, Conn.: Greenwood Press, 1996), chaps. 1, 10.

37. Bonnie Smith, *Gender of History*, 67.

38. For a description of historical amateurism, see ibid., chap. 2, "The Birth of the Amateur."

39. J. Franklin Jameson charted the progress of historical method since the seven-

teenth century, describing this gradual evolution as a series of stages leading from the conception of "historical literature" to "historical science." See Jameson, *The History of Historical Writing in America* (Boston: Houghton Mifflin, 1891), chap. 1, "The Historian in the Seventeenth Century"; Mahan, *Benson J. Lossing*, 130–32; Bonnie Smith, *Gender of History*, 7. Earle's fallout with Scribner's caused her to go to Macmillan in 1897. See Susan R. Williams, "In the Garden of New England," 145–50; Frances Victor to Judge Matthew Deady, 24 December 1888, Frances Victor Letters, OHS (microfilm).

40. Frances F. Victor, "She Discourseth upon Popular Literature," *San Francisco Daily Morning Call*, 22 August 1875, quoted in Jim Martin, *A Bit of Blue: The Life and Work of Frances Fuller Victor* (Salem, Ore.: Deep Well, 1992), 141–43.

41. Frances Victor to Professor Frederic Young, 20 September 1897; to Matthew Deady, 24 December 1888, 1 December 1872, Victor Letters, OHS.

42. Frances Victor to Professor Frederic Young, 5 December 1898, Victor Letters, OHS.

43. Hazel Emery Mills, "The Emergence of Frances Fuller Victor, Historian," *Oregon Historical Quarterly* 62 (December 1961): 310, 333; Victor, "She Discourseth upon Popular Literature," 1; June J. Bube, " 'No True Woman': Conflicted Female Subjectivities in Women's Popular Nineteenth-Century Western Adventure Tales" (Ph.D. diss., University of Washington, 1995), 228–32.

44. Frances Victor to Professor Frederic Young, 5 December 1898; to Matthew Deady, 3 November 1886, 24 December 1888, Victor Letters, OHS; Martin, *Bit of Blue*, 165. The four books she displayed at the exhibition were *History of Oregon I and II*, *History of Washington, Idaho, and Montana*, and *History of Nevada, Colorado, and Wyoming*. The authorship controversy is covered in Hazel Emery Mills, "Emergence of Frances Fuller Victor," 324–30. See also William A. Morris, "The Origin and Authorship of the Bancroft Pacific States Publications: A History of a History," *Quarterly of the Oregon Historical Society* 4 (December 1903): 287–364.

45. Lorraine J. Crouchett, *Delilah Leontium Beasley: Oakland's Crusading Journalist* (El Cerrito, Calif.: Downey Place, 1990), 40–41; Delilah Beasley, *The Negro Trail Blazers of California: A compilation of records from the California Archives at Bancroft Library, University of California at Berkeley; also from diaries, old papers, conversations of old pioneers in California* (Los Angeles: Times Mirror, 1919).

46. Earle, "Pleasures of Historiography," 47; Susan R. Williams, "In the Garden of New England," 155, 165, 184–85, 207–9.

47. Bonnie Smith, *Gender of History*, 132.

48. *Boston Transcript* quoted in Lyman, *Lady Historian Martha J. Lamb*, 18.

49. *New York Graphic*, 20 November 1886, series 1, box 1, folder 5, Lamb Papers, SSC.

50. Transcripts of miscellaneous writings; Johnstone, "Why Was It Left for Women to Write the Most Authentic Histories of New York?"; "Mrs. Lamb's Quuer [*sic*] Ways," Lamb Papers, SSC.

51. "Notable Work by a Notable Worker," Lamb Papers, SSC.

52. Piece read before the New Jersey Historical Society, 2; "Informative Influences," *Forum*, March 1891, series 1, box 1, folder 5, Lamb Papers, SSC.

53. Coman had been on the faculty at Wellesley since 1880 and a full professor since the 1890s, but she never earned a Ph.D. degree. See Joan McCrea, "Katharine Coman, a Neglected Economist" (paper presented at the meeting of the History of

Economics Society, University of Illinois, Champaign-Urbana, 25 May 1979, Katharine Coman biographical file, WCA); William B. Hesseltine and Louis Kaplan, "Women Doctors of Philosophy in History," *Journal of Higher Education* 14 (May 1943): 254.

54. "Special Requirements of the Department of History and Economics and Politics"; preliminary exams and seminary exams of Isabel Abbott at Bryn Mawr College, 1927–30 (English History from 1450 to 1600, International Law, Europe since 1815, American History from 1776–1815, Historical Bibliography and Criticism, European History Seminary, Comparative Government Seminary), Preliminary Exams File, Abbott Papers, BUL.

55. Jessie Tatlock and Nellie Neilson, "The Teaching of History at Mount Holyoke, 1837–1937," unpublished paper in General File, Mount Holyoke History Department Files, 4–5; Nellie Neilson, "The Department of History and Political Science," *Mount Holyoke Alumnae Quarterly* 4 (April 1920): 1, General Material, box 1, folder 1, MHASC.

56. "Subjects of Honour Papers," 1924–37, General File, box 1, folder 1; Nellie Neilson to President Woolley, 25 June 1934, series B, box 1, folder 1; "Report from the Department of History and Political Science, 1928–29," Reports File, box 1, folder 1; "List of Women with graduate degrees in History from Mount Holyoke" and "Suggestions for the Restatement of Courses for 1938–39," Subject File, box 4, folder 10; Tatlock and Neilson, "Teaching of History at Mount Holyoke," 12; "Report of the Department of History and Political Science," 9 June 1937, series B, box 1, folder 1, History Department Records, MHASC. The percentage given here has been estimated using the figures in Hesseltine and Kaplan, "Women Doctors of Philosophy in History," 255–56.

57. To a lesser degree, Woolley's research philosophy existed in the history departments at other women's colleges, including Wellesley. See Patricia Palmieri, *In Adamless Eden: The Community of Women Faculty at Wellesley* (New Haven: Yale University Press, 1995), 48, 68 (tables); Oral History of Viola Barnes, 1972, *Mount Holyoke in the Twentieth Century*, MHASC, 5.

58. Neilson earned her Ph.D. at Bryn Mawr, and Putnam did her undergraduate study there only. See Margaret Hastings and Elisabeth G. Kimball, "Two Distinguished Medievalists: Nellie Neilson and Bertha Haven Putnam," *Journal of British Studies* 18 (Summer 1979): 142–43.

59. Ibid., 153–58.

60. Tatlock and Neilson, "Teaching of History at Mount Holyoke," 9–10.

61. Hastings and Kimball, "Two Distinguished Medievalists," 142–51.

62. Neilson quoted in Joan W. Scott, "American Women Historians," 180–81; Barnes quoted in "Comments of Questionnaire," series 3, box 12, folder 1, Viola Barnes Papers, MHASC.

63. Margaret A. Judson, *Breaking the Barrier: A Professional Autobiography by a Woman Educator and Historian before the Women's Movement* (New Brunswick: Rutgers University Press, 1984), 109.

64. Rosalind Rosenberg, "The Limits of Access: The History of Coeducation in America," in *Women in Higher Education in American History*, ed. John Mack Faragher and Florence Howe (New York: Norton, 1988), 113–14; Rosenberg, *Beyond Separate Spheres*, xv, 1–27; Ely Van de Warker, *Woman's Unfitness for Higher Coeducation* (New York: Grafton Press, 1903).

65. Patricia Albjerg Graham, "Expansion and Exclusion: A History of Women in American Higher Education," *Signs* 3 (Summer 1978): 764; Rosenberg, *Beyond Separate Spheres*, 44; Committee of the Association of Collegiate Alumnae, *Contributions towards a Bibliography of the Higher Education of Women* (Boston: Trustees of the Public Library, 1897); Emilie J. Hutchinson, *Women and the Ph.D.: Facts from the Experiences of 1,025 Women Who Have Taken the Degree of Doctor of Philosophy since 1877* (Greensboro: Institutes of Women's Professional Relations at North Carolina College for Women, 1930), 15; Emilie J. Hutchinson, "Data Concerning the Degree of Masters of Arts," *JACA* 11 (March 1918): 428; Geraldine J. Clifford, ed., *Lone Voyagers: Academic Women in Coeducational Universities, 1870–1937* (New York: Feminist Press, 1989), 15–16.

66. Van Tassel, "From Learned Society to Professional Organization," 946. Confirming Van Tassell's estimates, Peter Novick also contends that academic history had grown geometrically from the 1890s to the 1970s. He bases his conclusions on data on history jobs, but also on data on the size of history departments and growth of professional journals, university presses, and fellowship programs. See Novick, *That Noble Dream*, 204; Hesseltine and Kaplan, "Women Doctors of Philosophy in History," 254.

67. "List of Doctoral Dissertations in History Now in Progress at the Chief American Universities, December, 1913," *AHR* 19 (January 1914): 450–66.

68. Graham, "Expansion and Exclusion," 775–76; Lucille A. Pollard, *Women on College and University Faculties: A Historical Survey and a Study of Their Present Academic Status* (New York: Arno Press, 1977), 29; Ellis Caswell, "Preliminary Report of Committee W, on the Status of Women in College and University Faculty," *American Association of University Professors Bulletin* 7 (October 1921): 21–32; Rosenberg, "Limits of Access," 124; Rosenberg, *Beyond Separate Spheres*, 45; Penina Glazer and Miriam Slater, *Unequal Colleagues: The Entrance of Women into the Professions, 1890–1940* (New Brunswick: Rutgers University Press, 1987), 67; Clifford, *Lone Voyagers*, 5.

69. Glenda Riley, "Frederick Jackson Turner Overlooked the Ladies," *Journal of the Early Republic* 13 (Summer 1993): 218–19; Louise Fargo Brown, *Apostle of Democracy: The Life of Lucy Maynard Salmon* (New York: Harper and Brothers, 1943), 68–69; Palmieri, *In Adamless Eden*, 167. Adams is quoted in Bonnie Smith, *Gender of History*, 113.

70. Future academics Gertrude S. Kimball and Mary E. Woolley attended Jameson's seminars; however, the majority of other women participants were teachers seeking terminal master's degrees in education. Of the seminar students between 1887 and 1897 for which postgraduate records exist, six of twenty-five were women. See "Graduate Studies in History at Brown University"; "Minutes of the Sessions of the Historical Seminary at Brown University, 1891–1901," vol. 2, Jameson Papers, BUL.

71. "Minutes of the Sessions of the Historical Seminary at Brown University," 19 May 1898, Jameson Papers, BUL.

72. In 1896 Jameson published Kimball's *The East-India Trade of Providence from 1787–1807* (Providence: Preston and Rounds, 1896) as part of the printed series Papers from the Historical Seminary of Brown University. He also assisted in publishing Mary Woolley's *The Early History of the Colonial Post-Office* (Providence: n.p.) in 1894.

73. The Convivium Historicum is discussed in Louise Fargo Brown, "Brief History of the Berkshire Conference," 1951, box 1, folder 1, Berkshire Conference of

Women Historians Papers, SL; Jacqueline Goggin, "Challenging Sexual Discrimination in the Historical Profession: Women Historians and the American Historical Association, 1890–1940," series 6, box 16, Berkshire Conference on the History of Women Collection, SL, 8–9.

74. Judson, *Breaking the Barrier*, 35.

75. Ibid., 34, 109.

76. Ibid., 112.

77. Herbert B. Adams, "Report of the Organization and Proceedings, Saratoga, 9–10 September 1884," in *Papers of the American Historical Association* (New York: Putnam, 1885), 1:6; Jameson, "American Historical Association," 1–19.

78. Herbert B. Adams, "Report of the Organization and Proceedings," list of members; Herbert B. Adams, "Report of the Proceedings of the Second Annual Meeting of the American Historical Association, Saratoga, 8–10 September, 1885," in *Papers of the American Historical Association* (New York: Putnam, 1886), 2:5, 67; Lyman, *Lady Historian Martha J. Lamb*, 34–35.

79. Lucy M. Salmon, "History of the Appointing Power of the President," in *Papers of the American Historical Association*, 1:291–419; Nicholas Adams and Bonnie Smith, eds., *History and the Texture of Modern Life: Selected Essays* (Philadelphia: University of Pennsylvania Press, 2001), 3.

80. The majority of women attending AHA annual meetings were high school history teachers and history enthusiasts in patriotic societies such as the DAR and the SCD. Adams quoted in Van Tassell, "From Learned Society to Professional Organization," 952–53. See also Jacqueline Goggin, "Challenging Sexual Discrimination in the Historical Profession: Women Historians and the American Historical Association, 1890–1940," *AHR* 97 (June 1992): 786–87.

81. Those other women speakers were Lilian Johnson, Ellen Churchill Semple, Annie Abel, and Sophonisba Breckinridge. No women were listed as speakers on the program for the annual meeting in 1910, for example. See "The Meeting of the American Historical Association at Indianapolis," *AHR* 16 (April 1911): 456–57, 467; Edna Moffett to Professor Pendleton, 2 June 1924, History and Political Science Department, Annual Reports, WCA.

82. Donnan joined the executive council in 1930, yet she managed to rise to an assistant editorship at the *AHR* as early as 1911 and remained there for seven years. See "Historical Association Elects New President," *Springfield Republican*, 31 December 1930, Elizabeth Donnan biographical file, WCA. Percentages in the text are estimates of Arthur Link in Joan W. Scott, "American Women Historians," 184.

83. Herbert B. Adams, "Report of the Organization and Proceedings," ii, 5, 67; Salmon, "History of the Appointing Power of the President"; Van Tassell, "From Learned Society to Professional Organization," 937.

84. Jameson, "American Historical Association," 10, 12, 16.

85. "Program of the 21st Annual Meeting of the American Historical Association," Baltimore, Maryland, 26–29 December 1905; "Programs of Meetings," Madison, Wisconsin, 27–31 December 1907, of the AHA, AEA, APSA, ASS, AALL, and MVHS, JHL; Goggin, "Challenging Sexual Discrimination," *AHR*, 787.

86. Goggin, "Challenging Sexual Discrimination," *AHR*, 780; Nellie Neilson, "Boon Services on the Estates of Ramsey Abbey," *AHR* 2 (January 1897): 213–24; Mary Woolley, "The Development of the Love of Romantic Scenery in America," *AHR* 2 (October 1897): 56–66.

87. Louise Phelps Kellogg, Annie Abel, Ella Lonn, and Gertrude Kimball generally wrote on western, southern and northeastern topics, respectively, and all were university trained. For examples of reviews of their works and works they reviewed in the *AHR*, see 5:309, 6:348, 9:158, 14:184, and 20:672. Abel contributed an article to the *AHR* in 1910 titled "The Indians and the Civil War" (15:281–96). For *AHR* reviews of Putnam's *William the Silent*, "Calendar of State Papers, Colonial," *Historic New York*, and *Medieval Princes*, see 1:329, 7:764, 4:547, and 10:917, respectively. For reviews of Earle's *Margaret Winthrop, Home Life in Colonial Days, Child Life in Colonial Days, Stage-Coach and Tavern Days*, and *Costumes in America*, see 1:374, 4:544, 5:765, 6:580, and 10:170, respectively.

88. Lucy Salmon, "Book Review of *William the Silent, Prince of Orange: The Moderate Man of the Sixteenth Century. The Story of his Life as told from his own Letters, from those of his Friends and Enemies, and from Official Documents*," *AHR* 1 (January 1896): 329.

89. Williams is quoted in Jacqueline Goggin, "Mary Wilhelmine Williams: Feminist, Activist, and Historian" (paper presented at the Eighth Berkshire Conference on the History of Women, Douglas College, 9 June 1990, series 8, box 19, 1990, Berkshire Conference on the History of Women Collection, SL), 1. See also Goggin, "Challenging Sexual Discrimination," Berkshire Conference on the History of Women Collection, SL, 10, 15.

90. Louise Fargo Brown, *Apostle of Democracy*, 143; "Dr. Gallagher Tells about Her Dogs," *Goucher College Weekly*, 2 February 1945, Katharine Gallagher Faculty File, GCA; "Tribute to Miss Kendall and Miss Chandler," 1920, Elizabeth Kendall biographical file, WCA; Clifford, *Lone Voyagers*, 29.

91. Transcript of Susan Ware's interview with Caroline Ware, 27–29 January 1982, Women in the Federal Government Project, OH-40, SL, 36; "Biographical notes," box 16, folder 8, Elisabeth Dexter Papers, JHL; Elisabeth Dexter, *Colonial Women of Affairs* (Boston: Houghton Mifflin, 1924).

92. Graham, "Expansion and Exclusion," 771; Clifford, *Lone Voyagers*, 24; Rosenberg, *Beyond Separate Spheres*, xxii; Nellie Neilson to President Allyn, 16 June 1932; to Mary Woolley, 14 June 1933, series B, box 1, folder 1, History Department Records, MHASC.

93. Oral History of Viola Barnes, 1; Louise Fargo Brown, *Apostle of Democracy*, 194; Responses to Questionnaire, 1931, box 1, folder 2, Berkshire Conference Papers, SL; Palmieri, *Adamless Eden*, 52, 68, 98–99, 136.

94. Caswell, "Preliminary Report of Committee W," 21–32; Ella Lonn, "Academic Status of Women on University Faculties," *JAAUW* 17 (January 1924): 5–8.

95. Lonn, "Academic Status of Women on University Faculties," 5–8; Hutchinson, *Women and the Ph.D.*, 17, 86–87. Hutchinson surveyed 1,575 women who received Ph.D. degrees in American institutions between 1877 and 1930; 1,025 women replied, an unknown number of which were historians. See Hutchinson, "Data Concerning the Degree of Masters of Arts," 428.

96. Of the 1,025 female doctorates who responded to Hutchinson's study, 597 became teachers, while only 81 became professional researchers. See Hutchinson, *Women and the Ph.D.*, 15, 57, 182; Mary Williams to President Hans Froelicher, 17 May 1929, Mary Williams folder, President's File, GCA.

97. Responses to Questionnaire, Berkshire Conference Papers, SL; Lois Kimball Mathews, *The Dean of Women* (Boston: Houghton Mifflin, 1915); George Herbert

Palmer, *The Life of Alice Freeman Palmer* (Boston: Houghton Mifflin, 1908), 96–101. Pierce's and Gillespie's extracurricular duties in the University of Chicago history department are discussed in Michael Kammen, *In the Past Lane: Historical Perspectives on American Culture* (New York: Oxford University Press, 1997), 42–43; Edna Moffett to Professor Pendleton, 11 June 1928, History and Political Science Department, Annual Reports, WCA.

98. Hutchinson, *Women and the Ph.D.*, 87; Hesseltine and Kaplan, "Women Doctors of Philosophy in History," 257–58.

99. Louise Fargo Brown, *Apostle of Democracy*, 107, 110, 216; Responses to Questionnaire, Berkshire Conference Papers, SL; interview of Dorothy Stimson, 18 March 1971, Goucher College, 9–10; R. I. Grassfield to Dorothy Stimson, 23 June 1917, Incoming Letters file; Helen Myers, "Educator Returns for Second Time to Vassar to Head New Course," series 1, box 1, clippings file, Dorothy Stimson Collection, GCA.

100. Judson, *Breaking the Barrier*, 36; Goggin, "Challenging Sexual Discrimination," Berkshire Conference on the History of Women Collection, SL, 12.

101. [E.Do?] to President W. W. Guth, 30 April 1915, Mary Williams folder, President's File; *New York Graphic*, 20 November 1886; Frederic Paxson to Eleanor Lord, 29 May 1915; D. C. Munro to Lord, 29 May 1915, Katharine Gallagher folder, President's File, GCA.

102. Novick, *That Noble Dream*, 169.

103. Jo Freeman, "Women on the Social Science Faculties since 1892, University of Chicago" (transcript of speech delivered at the minority workshop of the Political Science Association Conference, the University Panel on the status of women at Chicago, Winter 1969), statistical appendix; Clifford, *Lone Voyagers*, 1–37; Kammen, *In the Past Lane*, 31.

104. Hutchinson, *Women and the Ph.D.*, 182–83.

105. Isabel Abbott to Margaret Morriss, 7 November 1933, Correspondence: Graduate Study and Job Search, Abbott Papers, BUL.

106. Isabel Abbott to Howard Gray, 29 November 1932, "Correspondence with and related to Howard L. Gray" file, Abbott Papers, BUL.

107. Guy Stanton Ford to Isabel Abbott, 24 March 1928; Howard Gray to Abbott, 27 October 1924, 17, 22 April, 15 June 1929; Abbott to Gray, 30 April 1932, "Correspondence with and related to Howard L. Gray" file, Abbott Papers, BUL; Isabel Ross Abbott, "Taxation of Personal Property and of Clerical Incomes, 1399 to 1402," *Speculum* 17 (October 1942): 471–98; Abbott to Gray, 20 July 1940, "Gray Correspondence"; "Book Reviews Folder"; Abbott to Ford, 14 January 1949, "Correspondence relating to book reviews"; Abbott to Professor Collier, 7 May 1947; Abbott to Charles W. David, 7 May 1947, Correspondence: Graduate Study and Job Search, Abbott Papers, BUL.

108. Hesseltine and Kaplan, "Women Doctors of Philosophy in History," 255–56.

109. Ibid., 259.

110. Harry Kelsey, "A Dedication to the Memory of Annie Heloise Abel-Henderson, 1873–1947," in *Arizona and the West* (Tucson: University of Arizona Press, 1973), 1–2, Annie H. Abel Henderson Faculty File, GCA.

111. Mary Williams to President Hans Froelicher, 17 May 1929, Mary Williams folder, President's File; Henry Allen Moe to Dorothy Stimson, 8 March 1929, series 1, box 1, "Incoming Letters" folder, Stimson Collection, GCA.

112. The thirty-eight women who responded to the questionnaire came from

Smith, Vassar, Wellesley, Wells, Mount Holyoke, Hunter, Skidmore, Elmira, Barnard, and Wheaton Colleges and New Jersey College for Women. See Responses to Questionnaire, Berkshire Conference Papers, SL.

113. "Lakeville Historical Conference Report on Discussion of the Agenda Submitted by the Planning Committee," 1934, box 1, folder 3, Berkshire Conference Papers, SL. The two works Coman produced after her sabbatical in 1902 were "The Negro as Peasant Farmer," *American Statistical Association Publication* 9 (1904–5): 35–54, and "History of Contract Labor in the Hawaiian Islands," *American Economic Association Publications* 4 (1903): 68. See Olga S. Halsey, "Katharine Coman," *Survey*, 23 January 1915, Katharine Coman biographical file, WCA.

114. "Lakeville History Conference Full Report of the Discussion of the Agenda Submitted by the Planning Committee of the AHA," 1933, Berkshire Conference Papers, SL; Julia Orvis to President, 7 July 1921, History and Political Science Department, Annual Reports; History 302, Wellesley College; *Bargaining in Benefices: An Episode in Renaissance Diplomacy* (Cambridge: Harvard University Press, 1934), in General File, Department of History, WCA; Committee of the Planning of Research, American Historical Association, *Historical Scholarship in America: Need and Opportunities* (New York: Ray Long and Richard R. Smith, 1932), 105.

115. In 1932 Nellie Neilson, the acting departmental chair, wrote to President Allyn, "The fundamental question seems to me to be whether the college values and requires some productive scholarship of a high character from some at least of its staff, and is willing to make allowance of time for it. I myself firmly believe that a college without such requirements of its faculty necessarily falls into a low place, both because productive scholars,—even women, who have practically no research positions open to them,—hesitate to come to an institution where they are too burdened, and also because the students suffer if they get no perspective from instructors on higher forms of learning" (Nellie Neilson to President Allyn, 16 June 1932, series B, box 1, folder 1, History Department Records, MHASC). See also Neilson to Mary Woolley, 25 June 1934, 9 June 1931, series B, box 1, folder 1; Viola Barnes, "Field Majors in other Colleges," 1937, General File, box 1, folder 1; "Report from the Department of History and Political Science, 1927–28," Reports folder 1, History Department Records, MHASC; Oral History of Viola Barnes, 7; Glazer and Slater, *Unequal Colleagues*, 33; Hastings and Kimball, "Two Distinguished Medievalists," 146.

116. Mary Albertson, Dorothy Louise Mackay, and Judith Blow Williams are just a few of the historians who also won AAUW prizes between 1913 and 1940. See "Report of the Committee on Fellowships," *JACA* 6 (March 1913): 44, and 7 (May 1914): 80; Kelsey, "Dedication to the Memory of Annie Heloise Abel-Henderson"; Oral History of Viola Barnes, 7; "Report of the Fellowship Committee," *JAAUW* 15 (July 1922): 119–20.

117. Elizabeth Kendall and Katharine Coman biographical files; Elizabeth Hodder to Ellen Pendleton, 3 June 1932, History and Political Science Department, Annual Reports, WCA; "Lakeville Historical Conference Report on Discussion of the Agenda Submitted by the Planning Committee," Berkshire Conference Papers, SL; Louise Fargo Brown, *Apostle of Democracy*, 262; Goggin, "Challenging Sexual Discrimination," *AHR*, 780; Joan W. Scott, "American Women Historians," 189–90.

CHAPTER 2

1. Biographical notes, series 1, box 1, folder 1, Mary Sheldon Barnes Papers, SSC.

2. In 1911, for example, Sarah Riggs of the Iowa State Teachers College discussed

the preparation of grade school history teachers, and the following year women from the Michigan State Normal College and the Normal School in Trenton proposed alternative pedagogical methods to those advocated by the AHA Committee of Eight. See "The Meeting of the American Historical Association at Indianapolis," *AHR* 16 (April 1911): 456–57, 467; "The Meeting of the American Historical Association at Buffalo and Ithaca," *AHR* 17 (April 1912): 469, 474–75.

3. *HTM* 1 (September 1909), cover; "Correspondence," *HTM* 1 (December 1909): 76; "Preliminary Report of the Committee of Five," *HTM* 1 (February 1910): 128–29; "Eleven Hundred History Teachers," *HTM* 3 (September 1911): 14. See Williams's monthly feature "Periodical Literature"; "The Meeting of the American Historical Association at Buffalo and Ithaca," *AHR* 17 (April 1912): 474–75.

4. Mary S. Barnes, ed., *Studies in Historical Method* (Boston: Heath, 1896), 57–63. Student contributions in the same volume include Anna Kohler, "Special Study on the Historic Memory of Children," 81–92; Alma Patterson, "Special Study on Children's Sense of Historical Time," 94–104.

5. Rosalind Rosenberg, *Beyond Separate Spheres: Intellectual Roots of Modern Feminism* (New Haven: Yale University Press, 1982), 110; Mary O. Furner, *Advocacy and Objectivity: A Crisis in the Professionalization of American Social Science, 1865–1905* (Lexington: University Press of Kentucky, 1975), xii–xiii; Peter Novick, *That Noble Dream: The "Objectivity Question" and the American Historical Profession* (New York: Cambridge University Press, 1988), 69. Several of the dissertations in progress in 1913 included Maud Huttmann, "Persecution and Toleration in the Early Fourth Century," Columbia University; Anne Burlingame, "The Antislavery Movement in England and France in the Eighteenth Century," Columbia University; Carrie Lewis, "A History of the Literature of Abolition," Cornell University; Hazel Kyrk, "Development of State Policies of Control in the United States," University of Chicago; Florence Robinson, "Social Movements [in America], 1825–1860," University of Wisconsin; Elsie Rushmore, "Indian Policies during the Grant Administration," Columbia University. See "List of Doctoral Dissertations in History Now in Progress at the Chief American Universities, December, 1913," *AHR* 19 (January 1914): 450–66.

6. Sanford worked to preserve Minnesota's forests, provide health care for the native tribes of Montana, and raise funds for African American schools and churches in the South. Hebard participated in regional organizations, such as the Wyoming Teachers' Association, the Wyoming Pioneer Association, the Wyoming Federation of Women's Clubs, and national women's groups like the AAUW and the WTUL. See Geraldine Clifford, "'Best Loved' . . . and Besieged: Maria Louise Sanford, 1836–1920," in *Lone Voyagers: Academic Women in Coeducational Universities 1870–1937* (New York: Feminist Press, 1989), 60–61; Janell M. Wenzel, "Dr. Grace Raymond Hebard as Western Historian" (master's thesis, University of Wyoming, 1960), 21–22; Patricia Palmieri, *In Adamless Eden: The Community of Women Faculty at Wellesley* (New Haven: Yale University Press, 1995), 48, 130; Rosenberg, *Beyond Separate Spheres*; Helene Silverberg, ed., *Gender and American Social Science: The Formative Years* (Princeton: Princeton University Press, 1998); Bonnie Smith, *The Gender of History: Men, Women, and Historical Practice* (Cambridge: Harvard University Press, 1998), 199.

7. Silverberg, *Gender and American Social Science*, 7, 11, 3–27; Rosenberg, *Beyond Separate Spheres*, xviii, 35, 49–51, 83.

8. Ware quoted in Bonnie Smith, *Gender of History*, 199. Some of Coman's pub-

lications on women's labor are "A Sweated Industry," *Life and Labor,* January 1911, 13–15; "The Supreme Court Decision on the Oregon Ten Hour Law," *Publication of the Association of Collegiate Alumnae* 18 (December 1908): 31.

9. Jacqueline Goggin, "Challenging Sexual Discrimination in the Historical Profession: Women Historians and the American Historical Association, 1890–1940," series 6, box 16, Berkshire Conference on the History of Women Collection, SL, 19–20; "Dr. Gallagher Speaks about First Feminist," *Goucher College Weekly,* 23 November 1934, Katharine Gallagher Faculty Record, 1930, Faculty Files; Katharine Gallagher folder, President's File; "Report for Ella Lonn—Record of Writings, Lectures, Service on Committees, 1937–1941," Lonn folder, President's File, GCA.

10. Mary Williams won the Winsor Prize for *Anglo-American Isthmian Diplomacy* (Washington, D.C.: AHA, 1916) in 1914. Louise Fargo Brown's *Political Activities of the Baptists and Fifth Monarchy Men in England during the Interregnum* (Washington, D.C.: AHA, 1912) won the Herbert Baxter Prize in 1911. Louise Phelps Kellogg won the Winsor Prize in 1903 for *The American Colonial Charter: A Study of Its Relation to English Administration* (Washington, D.C.: Government Printing Office, 1904). Annie Abel won the Winsor Prize in 1906 for her Yale University doctoral dissertation, "The History of Events Resulting in Indian Consolidation West of the Mississippi," which was published in *Annual Report of the American Historical Association* (Washington, D.C.: Government Printing Office, 1908), 233–450.

11. Harry E. Barnes, *The New History and the Social Studies* (New York: Century, 1925), vii; Arthur M. Schlesinger, *New Viewpoints in American History* (New York: Macmillan, 1922).

12. Ernst A. Breisach, *American Progressive History: An Experiment in Modernization* (Chicago: University of Chicago Press, 1993), 43, 42–45; Novick, *That Noble Dream,* 69.

13. Charles A. Beard, *An Economic Interpretation of the Constitution of the United States* (New York: Macmillan, 1913).

14. Breisach, *American Progressive History,* 44; Joyce Appleby, Lynn Hunt, and Margaret Jacob, *Telling the Truth about History* (New York: Norton, 1994), 137–42; Novick, *That Noble Dream,* 92–99.

15. Catherine B. Shaw, "Katharine Coman," *Margin,* Fall 1991, 79; Olga S. Halsey, "Katharine Coman," *Survey,* January 1915, Katharine Coman biographical file, WCA; Palmieri, *In Adamless Eden,* 29, 169.

16. Jo Freeman, "Women on the Social Science Faculties since 1892, University of Chicago" (transcript of speech delivered at the minority workshop of the Political Science Association Conference, the University Panel on the status of women at Chicago, Winter 1969), 2–3; Nancy Folbre, "The Sphere of Women in Early-Twentieth-Century Economics," in Silverberg, *Gender and American Social Science,* 44.

17. Lela B. Costin, *Two Sisters for Social Justice: A Biography of Grace and Edith Abbott* (Urbana: University of Illinois Press, 1983), 19–27, 28.

18. Ibid., 28–35.

19. Ibid., 38; Edith Abbott, "A Sister's Memories," *Social Science Review* 3 (September 1939): 355.

20. Edith Abbott, *Women in Industry: A Study in American Economic History* (New York: Appleton, 1910), 8–9, xiii–xiv. Abbott's tables and charts were prepared primarily by her former students at Wellesley College and her students in the School of Civics and Philanthropy at the University of Chicago. See *Women in Industry,* 365

n. 1. Abbott's struggle to balance "objective social science" and "applied research" is discussed in Ellen Fitzpatrick, *Endless Crusade: Women Social Scientists and Progressive Reform* (New York: Oxford University Press, 1990), xii, 66–69, 171–94.

21. According to Nancy Folbre, the conventions, paradigms, and traditional subject matter of academic economists in the early twentieth century were distinctly masculine, making the labor studies of Abbott and Breckinridge completely unprecedented in the American academy. See Folbre, "Sphere of Women in Early-Twentieth-Century Economics," 35–54; Abbott, *Women in Industry*, vii–xii.

22. Mary Roberts [Smith] Coolidge, *Chinese Immigration* (New York: Holt, 1909); Mary Beard, *Woman's Work in Municipalities* (New York: Appleton, 1915). See also Edith Abbott, *Historical Aspects of the Immigrant Problem* (Chicago: University of Chicago Press, 1926). More immigration histories are listed in the bibliography.

23. Katharine Coman, "The Negro as Peasant Farmer," *American Statistical Association Publication* 9 (1904–5): 35–54; Helen Sumner Woodbury, "History of Women in Industry in the United States," in *Report on Conditions of Women and Child Wage Earners* (Washington, D.C.: U.S. Bureau of Labor, 1910), vol. 9. Appleton published *Women's Work in Municipalities*, but it was part of the National Municipal League Series. See Mary Beard, *A Short History of the American Labor Movement* (New York: Worker's Education Bureau of America, 1920). For more examples, see the bibliography.

24. Woodbury's shift to government work is discussed in Kathryn Kish Sklar, "American Female Historians in Context, 1770–1930," *Feminist Studies* 3 (Fall 1975): 184, 180–81; Folbre, "Sphere of Women in Early-Twentieth-Century Economics," 42–43. Some of Woodbury's collaborations include Helen L. Sumner Woodbury, John R. Commons, David J. Saposs, E. B. Mittelman, H. E. Hoagland, and John B. Andrews, eds., *History of Labor in the United States* (New York: Macmillan, 1921–35); Helen L. Sumner Woodbury and J. R. Commons, *The Causes of the Union-Shop Policy* (n.p.: American Economics Association Publications, 1905).

25. Costin, *Two Sisters for Social Justice*, 29.

26. See Helen T. Catterall, *Judicial Cases Concerning American Slavery and the Negro* (Washington, D.C.: Carnegie Institution of Washington, 1929); Elizabeth Donnan, *Documents Illustrative of the History of the Slave Trade to America*, 4 vols. (Washington, D.C.: Carnegie Institution of Washington, 1926–35).

27. August Meier and Elliott M. Rudwick, *Black History and the Historical Profession, 1915–1980* (Urbana: University of Illinois Press, 1986), 3–4; Earl E. Thorpe, *Black Historians: A Critique* (New York: William Morrow, 1971), 27, 47.

28. Jim Martin, *A Bit of Blue: The Life and Work of Frances Fuller Victor* (Salem, Ore.: Deep Well, 1992), 183–84.

29. Harry Kelsey, "A Dedication to the Memory of Annie Heloise Abel-Henderson, 1873–1947," in *Arizona and the West* (Tucson: University of Arizona Press, 1973), Annie H. Abel Henderson Faculty File, GCA, 1–2. Abel's published Native American histories are listed in the bibliography.

30. College of Arts and Sciences, Department of History, *Angie Debo: An Autobiographical Sketch, Eulogy, and Biography* (Stillwater: Oklahoma State University, 1988), 1–2; Shirley A. Leckie, *Angie Debo: Pioneering Historian* (Norman: University of Oklahoma Press, 2000), 26–34.

31. Leckie, *Angie Debo*, 60, 82–83.

32. Mrs. Joseph Rucker Lamar, *A History of the National Society of the Colonial Dames of America, from 1891 to 1933* (Atlanta: Walter W. Brown, 1934), 28; Martha

Strayer, *The D.A.R.: An Informal History* (Westport, Conn.: Greenwood Press, 1958), 28, 31, 56, 93.

33. *National Society of Colonial Dames of America Constitution Acts in Council, 1921* (Washington: Gibson Brothers, 1921), 6; Strayer, *D.A.R.*, 43; Mrs. Joseph Rucker Lamar, *The National Society of Colonial Dames of America: Its Beginnings, Its Purpose, and a Record of its Work, 1891–1913* (Washington, D.C.: The Society, 1913), 12.

34. Michael Kammen, *Mystic Chords of Memory: The Transformation of Tradition in American Culture* (New York: Knopf, 1991); Susan R. Williams, "In the Garden of New England: Alice Morse Earle and the History of Domestic Life" (Ph.D. diss., University of Delaware, 1992), 1, 9, 16, 164–65; T. J. Jackson Lears, *No Place of Grace: Antimodernism and the Transformation of American Culture, 1880–1920* (New York: Pantheon, 1981), xiii. See also Esther Singleton, *Furniture of Our Forefathers* (Garden City, N.Y.: Doubleday Page, 1900); Anne H. Wharton, *Heirlooms in Miniatures* (Philadelphia: Lippincott, 1898).

35. Anne H. Wharton, *Through Colonial Doorways* (Philadelphia: Lippincott, 1893), 7–8.

36. Alice Morse Earle, *Colonial Dames and Good Wives* (Boston: Houghton Mifflin, 1895), 69.

37. James Lindgren, " 'A New Departure in Historic, Patriotic Work': Personalism, Professionalism, and Conflicting Concepts of Material Culture in the Late Nineteenth and Early Twentieth Centuries," *Public Historian* 18 (Spring 1996): 44–45.

38. Lears, *No Place of Grace*, xiii, xiv, 60–61.

39. The 1894 regulations regarding the membership of Negro women are listed in Strayer, *D.A.R.*, 46–47; see also 27, 57–58, 82–83, 93, 124, 132–34; Charles B. Hosmer Jr., *Presence of the Past: A History of the Preservation Movement in the United States before Williamsburg* (New York: Putnam, 1965), 86–87.

40. Novick, *That Noble Dream*, 80–82. The questions posed to history teachers are taken from a 1919 questionnaire of the Rhode Island commissioner of public schools; they are similar to the questions asked in most U.S. states at this time. See Bessie L. Pierce, *Public Opinion and the Teaching of History in the United States* (New York: Knopf, 1926), vii–viii, 72, 113, 115, 124–25, 199, 206, 245, 275–96.

41. Strayer, *D.A.R.*, 63.

42. Lamar, *History of the National Society of the Colonial Dames*, 74; Anne H. Wharton, *Second Address of Miss Anne Hollingsworth Wharton, National Historian, before the Council of the National Society of the Colonial Dames of America* (Manchester, N.H.: John B. Clarke, 1902), 15; *Minutes of the National Society of Colonial Dames of America*, May 25–27, 1921 (Washington, D.C.: Gibson Brothers, 1921), 27.

43. Pierce, *Public Opinion and the Teaching of History*, vii–viii. See also Lamar, *National Society of Colonial Dames of America*, 62–66. Pierce assisted Schlesinger in planning a conference titled "The History of American Patriotism." See Arthur Schlesinger to Bessie Pierce, 8 December 1931, Schlesinger Papers, in Jacqueline Goggin, "Bessie L. Pierce and the Creation of *Public Opinion and the Teaching of History*," series 8, box 21, Berkshire Conference of Women Historians Papers, SL, 2.

44. Robert L. Dorman, *Revolt of the Provinces: The Regionalist Movement in America, 1920–1945* (Chapel Hill: University of North Carolina Press, 1993), 107–8.

45. *The Study of History in Schools: Report to the American Historical Association* (New York: Macmillan, 1899), 160; Howard R. Boozer, "The American Historical Association and the Schools" (Ph.D. diss., Washington University, 1960), 75; Lucy

Salmon, *What Is Modern History* (Poughkeepsie: Vassar College, 1917), 34; Salmon quoted in Nicholas Adams and Bonnie Smith, eds., *History and the Texture of Modern Life: Selected Essays* (Philadelphia: University of Pennsylvania Press, 2001), 12. For an example of similar commentaries by a professional woman historian, see Ella Lonn, *Problems in Americanization: A Course of Suggested Readings for Native Born Americans* (Baltimore: Women's Civic League, 1920).

46. Louise Fargo Brown, *Apostle of Democracy: The Life of Lucy Maynard Salmon* (New York: Harper and Brothers, 1943), "Appendix 3: Examination Papers, 1907–1926," 279.

47. Ibid., 117–19.

48. Helen Campbell, *Household Economics* (New York: Putnam, 1897); Katharine Gallagher, "Domestic Service during the Italian Renaissance" (paper presented at the Historical Society of Colleges and Preparatory Schools in Middle States and Maryland, n.d.); Woodbury, "History of Women in Industry in the United States"; Helen L. Sumner Woodbury, "The Historical Development of Women's Work in the United States," *Proceedings of the Academy of Political Science in the City of New York* (New York, 1929).

49. Adams and Smith, *History and the Texture of Modern Life*, 6; Lucy M. Salmon, *Domestic Service* (New York: Macmillan, 1897); Lucy M. Salmon, *Progress in the Household* (Boston: Houghton Mifflin, 1906), vii–viii.

50. Salmon's letter to Underhill quoted in Adams and Smith, *History and the Texture of Modern Life*, 8–9.

51. Lucy M. Salmon, "Some Principles in the Teaching of History," in *First Yearbook of the National Society for the Scientific Study of Education* (Chicago: University of Chicago Press, 1902), 13; Salmon quoted in Adams and Smith, *History and the Texture of Modern Life*, 14.

52. Louise Fargo Brown, *Apostle of Democracy*, 279, appendix 3, 244–46; Lucy M. Salmon, *The Newspaper and the Historian* (New York: Oxford University Press, 1923), xli, xlii; Lucy M. Salmon, *The Newspaper and Authority* (New York: Oxford University Press, 1923).

53. Salmon, "Some Principles in the Teaching of History," 21; Lucy M. Salmon, "The Curriculum," *JAAUW* 15 (April 1922): 91.

54. Talbot quoted in Adams and Smith, *History and the Texture of Modern Life*, 7.

55. Lucy M. Salmon, *Main Street* (Poughkeepsie: Lansing and Broas, 1915). Salmon's essay about unearthing historical evidence in the backyard is in her *Historical Material* (New York: Oxford University Press, 1933); see also Bonnie Smith, *Gender of History*, 208, 228–32. For a discussion of Salmon's modernist thought and writing style, see Adams and Smith, *History and the Texture of Modern Life*, introduction.

56. For a discussion of Salmon's battle to keep her job at Vassar, see Bonnie Smith, *Gender of History*, 207–9.

57. Lucy M. Salmon, *Why Is History Rewritten?* (New York: Oxford University Press, 1929); Salmon, *Historical Material*.

58. Transcript of Susan Ware's interview with Caroline Ware, 27–29 January 1982, Women in the Federal Government Project, SL, 18–19.

59. See Susan Ware's introductory notes to interview with Caroline Ware, SL; Thomas Dublin, "Caroline F. Ware: Crusader for Social Justice," in *Forgotten Heroes: Inspiring American Portraits from Our Leading Historians*, ed. Susan Ware (New York: Free Press, 1998), 251–52; Adams and Smith, *History and the Texture of Modern Life*, 6.

60. Oral History of Viola Barnes, 1972, *Mount Holyoke in the Twentieth Century*, MHASC, 36–37, 86.

61. For discussions of the masculine biases in turn-of-the-century social science disciplines, see the essays in Silverberg, *Gender and American Social Science*.

62. Kamala Visweswaran, " 'Wild West' Anthropology and the Disciplining of Gender," in Silverberg, *Gender and American Social Science*, 87–113; Silverberg, *Gender and American Social Science*, introduction; Rosenberg, *Beyond Separate Spheres*, 162–64.

63. Fletcher quoted in Joan Mark, *Four Anthropologists: An American Science in Its Early Years* (New York: Science History Publications, 1980), 67; Visweswaran, " 'Wild West,' " 108.

64. Elsie Clews Parsons, *The Old-Fashioned Woman: Primitive Fancies about Sex* (New York: Putnam, 1913); Rosenberg, *Beyond Separate Spheres*, 147, 163; Elizabeth Fee, "The Sexual Politics of Victorian Anthropology," in *Clio's Consciousness Raised*, ed. Mary Hartman and Lois Banner (New York: Harper and Row, 1974), 86–102; Robert Hemenway, *Zora Neale Hurston: A Literary Biography* (Urbana: University of Illinois Press, 1977), 89, 103; Zora Neale Hurston, *Mules and Men* (Philadelphia: Lippincott, 1935); Margaret Mead, *Sex and Temperament in Three Primitive Societies* (New York: Morrow, 1935).

65. Carl Becker, *Everyman His Own Historian* (Chicago: Quadrangle Books, 1963); Charles A. Beard, "Written History as an Act of Faith," *AHR* 39 (1934): 219–31; Novick, *That Noble Dream*, 89, 104, 143–44, 161.

66. Caroline Ware, ed., *The Cultural Approach to History* (New York: Columbia University Press, 1940), 12.

67. Adams and Smith, *History and the Texture of Modern Life*, 21.

68. Ann Lane, ed., *Mary Ritter Beard: A Sourcebook* (Boston: Northeastern University Press, 1988), 1–8.

69. Bonnie Smith and Nancy Cott argue for Mary Beard's influence in her husband's shift to relativism. See Bonnie Smith, "Seeing Mary Beard," *Feminist Studies* 10 (Fall 1984): 403; Nancy Cott, ed., *A Woman Making History: Mary Ritter Beard* (New Haven: Yale University Press, 1991), 44–46; Nancy Cott, "Two Beards: Coauthorship and the Concept of Civilization," *American Quarterly* 42 (1990): 287–88; Mary Beard, *On Understanding Women* (New York: Grosset and Dunlap, 1931), 13; Mary Beard, *America through Women's Eyes* (New York: Macmillan, 1933), 1–2. Beard's anthropological influences are discussed in Cott, *Woman Making History*, 25–26; Mary Beard, "Memory and Human Relations," *Key of Kappa Kappa Gamma*, December 1936, 309–10.

70. Mary Beard, *On Understanding Women*, 32, 33.

71. Mary Beard, *America through Women's Eyes*, 1–2.

72. For a discussion of Mary Beard's Progressive activism, see Loretta Zimmerman, "Mary Beard: An Activist of the Progressive Era," *University of Portland Review* 26 (Spring 1974): 15–36; Lane, *Mary Ritter Beard*, chap. 1; Cott, *Woman Making History*, 8–13.

73. Mary Beard to Florence Cross Kitchelt, 18 May 1928, folder 113, Florence Kitchelt Papers, SL; Zimmerman, "Mary Beard," 15–36. Full citations for the books the Beards cowrote appear in the bibliography.

74. Mary Beard referred to these and other "amateur" women historians throughout *America through Women's Eyes*; see esp. 11, 27, 56, 187, 268, 300, 358.

75. Ibid., 126, 265, 304.

76. Gilman's adoption of Ward's ideas is discussed in Rosenberg, *Beyond Separate Spheres*, 37–40.

77. Mary Beard to Margaret Grierson, 28 December 1950, box 1, Mary R. Beard Papers, SSC; Charlotte P. Gilman, *The Home: Its Work and Influence* (New York: Charlton, 1910), 6. See also Charlotte P. Gilman, *The Man-Made World; or, Our Androcentric Culture* (New York: Charlton, 1911).

78. Anna G. Spencer, *Woman's Share in Social Culture* (New York: Mitchell Kennerley, 1913), ii–x, "analysis of contents."

79. Jane Addams, *The Long Road of Woman's Memory* (New York: Macmillan, 1916), xiii; Review of *The Long Road of Woman's Memory*, *Book Review Digest*, December 1916, in *Jane Addams Papers*, ed. Mary McCree Bryan (Chicago: University of Illinois, 1985, microfilm).

80. Both Mary Beard and Jane Addams were active in the WILPF. See Spencer, *Woman's Share in Social Culture*; Mary Beard, *On Understanding Women*; Rosenberg, *Beyond Separate Spheres*, 34–40; Rosalind Rosenberg, "The Limits of Access: The History of Coeducation in America," in *Women in Higher Education in American History*, ed. John Mack Faragher and Florence Howe (New York: Norton, 1988), introduction, xvi–xvii.

81. Mary Beard, *A Changing Political Economy as It Affects Women* (Washington, D.C.: AAUW, 1934), 5–6, 8–9.

82. Exam in Women in the Middle Ages folder, Teaching Medieval Europe box, Isabel Abbott Papers, BUL.

83. See, for example, Mary Williams, "Outline for the Incidental Teaching of Hispanic-American History in the Secondary School," *Historical Outlook* 9 (June 1918): 335–37; Ella Lonn, "A Course in Methods of Teaching the Social Studies in High Schools," *Historical Outlook* 15 (December 1924): 387–91; Helen Myers, "Educator Returns for Second Time to Vassar to Head New Course" and "Goucher Ex-Dean to Join Faculty as Science Teacher," Articles folder, series 1, box 1, Dorothy Stimson Collection, GCA.

84. Mary Williams to President David A. Robertson, 27 January 1932, Mary Williams folder, President's File, GCA; Jacqueline Goggin, "Mary Wilhelmine Williams: Feminist, Activist, and Historian" (paper presented at the Eighth Berkshire Conference on the History of Women, Douglas College, 9 June 1990, series 8, box 19, 1990, Berkshire Conference on the History of Women Collection, SL), 8.

85. "Larger Place for Women in Histories of Future Seen by Prominent Writers," *Washington Post*, 31 December 1934, in Elizabeth Donnan biographical file, WCA.

CHAPTER 3

1. Julia Cherry Spruill, *Women's Life and Work in the Southern Colonies* (Chapel Hill: University of North Carolina Press, 1938), 172. Spruill classified her source materials as "Manuscripts," "Newspapers," "Official Documents," and "Letters and Journals" in the bibliography at the end of the book.

2. Caroline Ware, ed., *The Cultural Approach to History* (New York: Columbia University Press, 1940), 8.

3. Ibid., 4–5.

4. Anne Firor Scott provided the introduction for a reprint of Spruill's 1938 manuscript. See Julia Cherry Spruill, *Women's Life and Work in the Southern Colonies* (New York: Norton, 1972).

5. Debo's biographer Shirley Leckie uses "intercultural broker" to describe Debo, but she borrows the term from Western historian Peggy Pascoe, who used it to describe women writers of Western genres generally. I will use the term to refer to women who wrote history from the geographic as well as the social and professional margins. See Shirley A. Leckie, *Angie Debo: Pioneering Historian* (Norman: University of Oklahoma Press, 2000), 7.

6. See Anne Firor Scott, *Unheard Voices: The First Historians of Southern Women* (Charlottesville: University Press of Virginia, 1993).

7. Genevieve McMillan, "History of Higher Education of Women in the South" (master's thesis, University of North Carolina, 1923). Odum's intellectual project is discussed in Robert L. Dorman, *Revolt of the Provinces: The Regionalist Movement in America, 1920–1945* (Chapel Hill: University of North Carolina Press, 1993), 51–52.

8. Spruill, *Women's Life and Work in the Southern Colonies* (1938), preface.

9. Guion Griffis Johnson, *Ante-Bellum North Carolina: A Social History* (Chapel Hill: University of North Carolina Press, 1937).

10. Anne Firor Scott, *Unheard Voices*, 1–4, 54; Guion Griffis Johnson, *Ante-Bellum North Carolina*, bibliography.

11. Anne Firor Scott, *Unheard Voices*, 13–15, 65, 67; Virginia Gearhart, "The Southern Woman, 1840–1860" (Ph.D. diss., University of Wisconsin, 1927).

12. One male historian denounced Hebard's degree as "a pure fake" from "a school notoriously loose in the granting of degrees." Furthermore, Hebard's doctoral training was in political science, not history. See Janell M. Wenzel, "Dr. Grace Raymond Hebard as Western Historian" (master's thesis, University of Wyoming, 1960), 7; Geraldine Clifford, " 'Best Loved' . . . and Besieged: Maria Louise Sanford, 1836–1920," in *Lone Voyagers: Academic Women in Coeducational Universities 1870–1937* (New York: Feminist Press, 1989), 60–61.

13. Catharine C. Cleveland, *The Great Revival in the West, 1797–1805* (Chicago: University of Chicago Press, 1916), xi–xii. Rachel Eaton's life and work are discussed in Jennifer Scanlon and Sharon Cosner, eds., *American Women Historians, 1700s–1900s: A Biographical Dictionary* (Westport, Conn.: Greenwood Press, 1996), 65–66.

14. For insight into the regional resentments that led to the establishment of societies such as the Mississippi Valley Historical Association and the Southern Historical Association, see Peter Novick, *That Noble Dream: The "Objectivity Question" and the American Historical Profession* (New York: Cambridge University Press, 1988), 180–82.

15. "A Statistical Report on the Participation of Women in the Southern Historical Association, 1935–1985," *Journal of Southern History* 52 (May 1986): 285.

16. Buck quoted in Dorman, *Revolt of the Provinces*, 117.

17. Abel's contributions to the *MVHR* include "Trudeau's Description of the Upper Missouri" (edited), 8 (June 1921): 149–79; "Mackay's Table of Distances," 10 (March 1924): 428–46. Examples of Lonn's submissions to the *MVHR* include "The Journal of John Sutherland," 4 (December 1917): 362–70, and "The French Council of Commerce Relative to American Trade," 6 (September 1919): 192–219. See "Review of *Reconstruction in Louisiana*," 5 (December 1918): 366–68. Lonn wrote or was written about in the following volumes of the *Journal of Southern History*: 1:410; 3:234; 6:135; 7:68, 73; 8:294; 11:81, 89, 90; 12:85, 450; 13:83, 88; 14:104; 16:49, 52. For synopses of her papers, see 2:70–71; 6:73. For reviews, see 5:268–69; 8:134–35; 9:420–21; 10:360–62; 14:554–56; 16:338–41. See also "Reconciliation between North and South," 13 (Febru-

ary 1947): 3–26; presidential address appraised, 16 (February 1950): 36; "Salt as a Factor in the Confederacy" (review), 1 (May 1935): 241–43; "Desertion during the Civil War" (noted), 2 (May 1936): 141; "Foreigners in the Confederacy" (review), 6 (November 1940): 561–63; "Colonial Agents of the Southern Colonies" (review), 11 (August 1945): 426–27. See "Statistical Report on the Participation of Women in the Southern Historical Society," 282.

18. Jane Berry, "Indian Policy of Spain in the Southwest," *MVHR* 3 (March 1917): 462–77; Hallie Farmer, "The Economic Background of Frontier Populism," *MVHR* 10 (March 1924): 406–27; Helen Broshar, "First Push Westward of Albany Traders," *MVHR* 7 (December 1920): 228–41; Dorothy Dondore, "Points of Contact between History and Literature in the Mississippi Valley," *MVHR* 11 (September 1924): 227–36.

19. Barbara Howe, "Women and Architecture," in *Reclaiming the Past: Landmarks in Women's History*, ed. Page Putnam Miller (Bloomington: Indiana University Press, 1992), 31–35, 57n, 59n; Michael Wallace, "Reflections on the History of Historic Preservation," in *Presenting the Past: Essays on History and the Public*, ed. Susan Porter Benson, Steven Brier, and Roy Rosenzweig (Philadelphia: Temple University Press, 1986), 169–72; Charles B. Hosmer Jr., *Presence of the Past: A History of the Preservation Movement in the United States before Williamsburg* (New York: Putnam, 1965), 68.

20. Luther H. Evans, *The Historical Records Survey: A Statement on Its Program and Accomplishments Presented to the Sub-Committee of the Senate Committee on Education and Labor, in Connection with the Bill to Create a Permanent Bureau of Fine Arts* (Washington, D.C.: HRS Division of Women's and Professional Projects, WPA, 1938); Luther H. Evans, *Preservation of the Nation's Records*, address delivered before the 48th Continental Congress, National Society of the Daughters of the American Revolution, Washington, D.C., 19 April 1939 (New York: HRS, 1939), 3–10; John C. L. Andreassen, *The National Survey County Archives* (Washington, D.C.: Historical Records Survey, 1938), 1–6; Nancy Bruns, "The Federal Writers' Project and the Historical Records Survey" (master's thesis, University of Cincinnati, 1961), 29–39.

21. There were more than 8,000 men and women working for the HRS in the late 1930s. The evidence on women workers is largely anecdotal; I have found no statistical data indicating how HRS employment broke down by sex. See Bruns, "Federal Writers' Project and Historical Records Survey," 32.

22. College of Arts and Sciences, Department of History, *Angie Debo: An Autobiographical Sketch, Eulogy, and Biography* (Stillwater: Oklahoma State University, 1988), 1–2; Levi S. Peterson, *Juanita Brooks: Mormon Woman Historian* (Salt Lake City: University of Utah Press, 1988), 102–3; *The Historical Records Survey: What Is It?* (n.p.: California HRS, n.d.); Bruns, "Federal Writers' Project and Historical Records Survey," 46, 76; Robert Hemenway, *Zora Neale Hurston: A Literary Biography* (Urbana: University of Illinois Press, 1977), 161, 330.

23. Constance McLaughlin Green, "The Value of Local History," in Ware, *Cultural Approach to History*, 275, 285–86.

24. Juanita Brooks, "Let's Preserve Our Records," *Utah Humanities Review* 2 (July 1948): 259–63; Levi S. Peterson, *Juanita Brooks*, 2, 45, 108.

25. Christopher D. Felker, " 'Adaptation of the Source': Ethnocentricity and 'The Florida Negro,' " in *Zora in Florida*, ed. Steve Glassman and Kathryn L. Seidel (Orlando: University of Central Florida Press, 1991), 146–57; Zora Neale Hurston, *Dust*

Tracks on a Road: An Autobiography, 2nd ed. (Urbana: University of Illinois Press, 1970), xvi; Hemenway, *Zora Neale Hurston*, 61, 85–86.

26. Mary S. Barnes, ed., *Studies in Historical Method* (Boston: Heath, 1896), 20.

27. Mary H. Eastman, *The American Aboriginal Portfolios* (Philadelphia: Lippincott, Grambo, 1853); Mary H. Eastman, *Chicora and Other Regions of the Conquerors and the Conquered* (Philadelphia: Lippincott, Grambo, 1854); Susan Wallace, *Land of the Pueblos* (New York: J. B. Alden, 1888).

28. Many of these accounts of the West are listed in the bibliography.

29. Brigitte Georgi-Findlay, *The Frontiers of Women's Writing: Women's Narratives and the Rhetoric of Westward Expansion* (Tucson: University of Arizona Press, 1996), 106. For more on the literary genres of western women, see June J. Bube, " 'No True Woman': Conflicted Female Subjectivities in Women's Popular Nineteenth-Century Western Adventure Tales" (Ph.D. diss., University of Washington, 1995); L. L. Lee and Merill Lewis, eds., *Women, Women Writers, and the West* (Troy, N.Y.: Whitson, 1979).

30. Emma Helen Blair dedicated her *Indian Tribes of the Upper Mississippi Valley and Region of the Great Lakes* "to Frederick Jackson Turner who long has led the van of research in the history of the great Middle West, and has done most to make known its importance in the development of the American nation." See dedication to Blair, *The Indian Tribes of the Upper Mississippi Valley and Region of the Great Lakes as Described by Nicholas Perrot, French Commandant in the Northwest; Bacqueville de la Potherie, French Royal Commissioner to Canada; Morrell Marston, American Army Officer; and Thomas Forsyth, United States Agent at Fort Armstrong* (Cleveland: Arthur H. Clark, 1911); Glenda Riley, "Frederick Jackson Turner Overlooked the Ladies," *Journal of the Early Republic* 13 (Summer 1993): 218–19, 221; Susan H. Armitage, "Women's Literature and the American Frontier: A New Perspective on the Frontier Myth," in Lee and Lewis, *Women, Women Writers, and the West*, 5–6.

31. Pascoe cited from Leckie, *Angie Debo*, 7.

32. Abigail Scott Duniway, *Path Breaking: An Autobiographical History of the Equal Suffrage Movement in Pacific Coast States* (Portland, Ore.: James, Kerns and Abbott, 1914).

33. Elizabeth Ellet, *Pioneer Women of the West* (Philadelphia: Porter and Coates, 1852, 1873); William W. Fowler, *Woman on the American Frontier: A valuable and authentic history of the heroism, adventures, privations, captivities, trials, and noble lives and deaths of "Pioneer mothers of the Republic"* (Hartford: S. S. Scranton, 1876).

34. Georgi-Findlay, *Frontiers of Women's Writing*, 242–43, 239–40; Valerie S. Mathes, *Helen Hunt Jackson and Her Indian Reform Legacy* (Austin: University of Texas Press, 1990), 10–11.

35. Wenzel, "Dr. Grace Raymond Hebard," 29–33.

36. Grace R. Hebard, *The Pathbreakers from River to Ocean: The Story of the Great West from the Time of Coronado to the Present* (Chicago: Lakeside Press, 1911), preface; Grace R. Hebard, *The History and Government of Wyoming: The History, Constitution, and Administration of Affairs* (San Francisco: C. F. Weber, 1906, 1923), 47.

37. Georgi-Findlay, *Frontiers of Women's Writing*, 12–13, 291.

38. Agnes C. Laut, *Pathfinders of the West* (New York: Macmillan, 1904); Dorman, *Revolt of the Provinces*, 174.

39. Dorman, *Revolt of the Provinces*, 170.

40. Ibid., xiv, 172, 181; Leckie, *Angie Debo*, 54, 84; Dorothee Kocks, *Dream a Little: Land and Social Justice in Modern America* (Berkeley: University of California Press, 2000), 63–99.

41. Dorman, *Revolt of the Provinces*, 69, 172, 174.

42. Lydia M. Child, *The First Settlers of New England; or, Conquest of the Pequots, Narragansetts and Pokanokets. As related by a mother to her children* (Boston: Munroe and Francis, 1829).

43. Mathes, *Helen Hunt Jackson*, 23.

44. Helen Hunt Jackson to Caroline Dall, 8 February 1881, reprinted in Valerie S. Mathes, *The Indian Reform Letters of Helen Hunt Jackson* (Norman: University of Oklahoma Press, 1998), 176.

45. Jackson is quoted in Mathes, *Helen Hunt Jackson*, introduction, 36.

46. Joan Mark, *Four Anthropologists: An American Science in Its Early Years* (New York: Science History Publications, 1980), 62–69; Kamala Visweswaran, " 'Wild West' Anthropology and the Disciplining of Gender," in *Gender and American Social Science: The Formative Years*, ed. Helene Silverberg (Princeton: Princeton University Press, 1998), 87–113.

47. Mathes, *Helen Hunt Jackson*, xiv.

48. Frances F. Victor, *The Early Indian Wars of Oregon* (Salem, Ore.: Frank Baker, 1894), v–vi; Jim Martin, *A Bit of Blue: The Life and Work of Frances Fuller Victor* (Salem, Ore.: Deep Well, 1992), 183; Harry Kelsey, "A Dedication to the Memory of Annie Heloise Abel-Henderson, 1873–1947," in *Arizona and the West* (Tucson: University of Arizona Press, 1973), Annie H. Abel Henderson Faculty File, GCA, 2.

49. Mary Austin, *The Land of Little Rain* (Boston: Houghton Mifflin, 1903); Mary Austin, *The American Rhythm* (New York: Houghton Mifflin, 1913). Austin is quoted in Dorman, *Revolt of the Provinces*, 35–36.

50. Annie H. Abel, ed., *The Official Correspondence of James S. Calhoun while Indian Agent at Santa Fe and Superintendent of Indian Affairs in New Mexico* (Washington, D.C.: Government Printing Office, 1915); Annie H. Abel, *The American Indian as Slaveholder and Secessionist: An Omitted Chapter in the Diplomatic History* (Cleveland: Arthur H. Clark, 1915); Annie H. Abel, *The American Indian as Participant in the Civil War* (Cleveland: Arthur H. Clark, 1919); Annie H. Abel, *The American Indian under Reconstruction* (Cleveland: Arthur H. Clark, 1925).

51. Blair, *Indian Tribes of the Upper Mississippi Valley and Region of the Great Lakes*.

52. Ibid., 18–19.

53. Flora W. Seymour, *The Story of the Red Man* (New York: Longmans, Green, 1929), 2, 18.

54. Ibid., 6, 214–15, 223–25.

55. Grace R. Hebard, *How Woman Suffrage Came to Wyoming* (New York: W. D. Embree, 1940) (posthumous publication); Grace R. Hebard, "The First White Women in Wyoming," *Washington Historical Quarterly* 8 (January 1917): 29–31; Grace R. Hebard, *Sacajawea: A Guide and interpreter of the Lewis and Clark Expedition, with an account of the travels of Toussaint Charbonneau, and of Jean Baptiste, the expedition papoose* (Glendale: Arthur H. Clark, 1933).

56. Hebard, *Sacajawea*, 216–17.

57. Ibid., 20–21.

58. Wenzel, "Dr. Grace Raymond Hebard," 87, 47–49, 77, 92.

59. Hebard, *Sacajawea*, 17–18, 50, 290, 215–16.

60. Angie Debo, *The Rise and Fall of the Choctaw Republic* (Norman: University of Oklahoma Press, 1934), 18.

61. Leckie, *Angie Debo*, 54.

62. Debo quoted in an oral interview videotaped for *The American Experience: Indians, Outlaws, and Angie Debo*, American Experience Series (Boston: WGBH, 1988).

63. Robin K. Berson, *Marching to a Different Drummer: Unrecognized Heroes of American History* (Westport, Conn.: Greenwood Press, 1994), 86–92.

64. Mari Sandoz, *Crazy Horse* (New York: Knopf, 1942); Kocks, *Dream a Little*, 91–92, 218–19n.

65. Kocks, *Dream a Little*, 66, 72, 77; Helen Winter Stauffer, *Mari Sandoz: Story Catcher of the Plains* (Lincoln: University of Nebraska Press, 1982).

66. Sandoz quoted in Dorman, *Revolt of the Provinces*, 72, 244. See also Kocks, *Dream a Little*, 93–94, 98; Helen Stauffer, "Mari Sandoz and Western Biography," in Lee and Lewis, *Women, Women Writers, and the West*, 55–67.

67. Dorman, *Revolt of the Provinces*, 233; Kocks, *Dream a Little*, 69–70, 71.

68. Kocks, *Dream a Little*, 69. Debo is quoted in Dorman, *Revolt of the Provinces*, 171, 172.

69. College of Arts and Sciences, Department of History, *Angie Debo*, 1–2; Kocks, *Dream a Little*, 90.

70. Juanita Brooks, *Quicksand and Cactus: A Memoir of the Southern Mormon Frontier* (Salt Lake City: Howe Brothers, 1982), xxviii–xxix; Levi S. Peterson, *Juanita Brooks*, 4, 122; Fawn M. Brodie, *No Man Knows My History: The Life of Joseph Smith, the Mormon Prophet* (New York: Knopf, 1945); Juanita Brooks, *The Mountain Meadows Massacre* (Stanford: Stanford University Press, 1950).

71. Kocks, *Dream a Little*, 66, 73–74, 89–90; Leckie, *Angie Debo*, 5, 6, 193.

CHAPTER 4

1. Robert Hemenway, *Zora Neale Hurston: A Literary Biography* (Urbana: University of Illinois Press, 1977), 21, 82, 87–89, 92–93, 99–100.

2. Carla L. Peterson, *"Doers of the Word": African-American Women Speakers and Writers in the North, 1830–1880* (New York: Oxford University Press, 1995), 5, 8.

3. In *"Doers of the Word"* Carla L. Peterson discusses black women's historical uniqueness as articulated by Truth, Jacobs, Harper, and other nineteenth-century women.

4. The slow rise of the black press is discussed in Donald Joyce, *Gatekeepers of Black Culture: Black-Owned Book Publishing in the United States, 1817–1981* (Westport, Conn.: Greenwood Press, 1983).

5. Dorothy (Porter) Wesley [Dorothy B. Porter], "Black Antiquarians and Bibliophiles Revisited, with a Glance at Today's Lovers of Books and Memorabilia," in *Black Bibliophiles and Collectors: Preservers of Black History*, ed. Elinor Sinnette, Paul Coates, and Thomas C. Battle (Washington, D.C.: Howard University Press, 1990), 5; Dorothy B. Porter, "The Organized Educational Activities of Negro Literary Societies, 1828–1846," *Journal of Negro Education* 5 (October 1936): 555–75; Jeffrey Stewart and Fath Davis Ruffins, "A Faithful Witness: Afro-American Public History in Historical Perspective, 1828–1984," in *Presenting the Past: Essays on History and the Public*, ed. Susan Porter Benson, Steven Brier, and Roy Rosenzweig (Philadelphia: Temple University Press, 1986), 311.

6. Wayman Harrison, "The American Negro Historical Society of Philadelphia and Its Officers," *Colored American Magazine*, February 1903, 288.

7. John W. Cromwell, *History of the Bethel Literary and Historical Association*

(Washington, D.C.: R. L. Pendleton, 1896), box 5-1, folder 4, Bethel Literary and Historical Association Collection, MSRC, 4–27.

8. Carla L. Peterson, *"Doers of the Word,"* 13–14.

9. William C. Nell, *The Colored Patriots of the American Revolution, with Sketches of Several Distinguished Colored Persons: To Which, is Added a Brief Survey of the Conditions and Prospects of Colored Americans* (Boston: R. F. Wallcut, 1855); James M. Guthrie, *Campfires of the Afro-American; or, the colored man as a patriot, soldier, sailor, and hero, in the cause of free America* (Philadelphia: Afro-American Pub. Co., 1899).

10. Mary Curtis, *The Black Soldier: The Colored Boys of the United States Army* (Washington, D.C.: A. D. Morris, 1915); Laura Wilkes, *Missing Pages in American History, Revealing the Services of Negroes in the Early Wars in the United States of America, 1641–1815* (Washington, D.C.: R. I. Pendleton, 1919).

11. Robert M. Adger, *A Portion of a Catalog of Rare Books and Pamphlets Collected by R. M. Adger, Philadelphia—upon Subjects Relating to the Past Condition of the Colored Race and the Slavery Agitation in this Country* (n.p., 1894); Robert M. Adger, *Catalog of Rare Books on Slavery and Negro Authors on Science, History, Poetry, Religion, Biography, etc. from the Private Collections of Robert M. Adger* (n.p., 1906); Wendy Ball and Tony Martin, *Rare Afro-Americana: A Reconstruction of the Adger Library* (Boston: G. K. Hall, 1981), 28.

12. Ball and Martin, *Rare Afro-Americana*, 19, 24–25. Male collectors of "Negroana" considered themselves "bibliophiles"—that is, race workers using history books to create social change for African Americans. As Wendy Ball and Tony Martin explain, "the connection between race activism and book collecting was an obvious one and necessary for nineteenth-century Afro-Americans. Books were not only a means of educational advancement for a race still largely denied adequate educational opportunities. The writing and preservation of books on the past and present achievements of the race also provided evidence to refute the pervasive pseudoscientific theories of Black inferiority" (*Rare Afro-Americana*, 18). See Sinnette, Coates, and Battle, *Black Bibliophiles and Collectors*, preface; Porter, "Black Antiquarians and Bibliophiles Revisited," 5–10. White's records are now part of the Leon Gardiner Collection at the Historical Society of Pennsylvania, Philadelphia.

13. G. K. Cook, Supt. of D.C. Schools, 23 February 1895; George Gorham to J. W. Cromwell, 27 May 1895; Frank Edward Kittredge, "A Brief History of the Douglass Monument," in *The Man with the Branded Hand* (Rochester, N.Y.: H. L. Wilson, 1899); "Program of the Commemoration of the Birth of Frederick Douglass under the Auspices of the Pen and Pencil Club," 14 February 1903, box 24-2, folder 43; "Invitation to the Anniversary Dinner of the Birthdate of Frederick Douglass tendered by the Liberal Culture Society of Chicago," 19 February 1914; "Program for the Republican League Banquet in Honor of the Anniversary of the Birth of Lincoln and Douglass," Westchester County Negro League, Yonkers, N.Y., 1909; "Address of Gov. Whitman before Douglass Commemorative Society," Rochester, N.Y., 15 February 1917, box 24-2, folder 45, Cromwell Family Papers, MSRC.

14. Dorothy Salem, *To Better Our World: Black Women in Organized Reform, 1890–1920* (Brooklyn: Carlson, 1990), 75.

15. William Huff to Charles Ferguson, 28 February 1912, box 39-8, folder 60, Archibald H. Grimké Collection; "Library of Congress, Division of Bibliography, list

of References on Frederick Douglass," n.d.; Arthur Schomburg, comp., "Bibliography of Writings of Frederick Douglass" (ANA, n.d.), box 24-2, folder 44, Cromwell Family Papers, MSRC.

16. Mary C. Terrell, *A Colored Woman in a White World* (Washington, D.C.: Ransdell, 1940; reprint, New York: Oxford University Press, 1996), xxxviii; Emma F. G. Merritt, "Douglass Day: Why Not Make It National," *Voice of the Negro*, April 1906, 279–81; Thomas J. Calloway to A. H. Grimké, 26 December 1911, box 39-8, folder 60, Archibald H. Grimké Collection, MSRC; Laura Wilkes, *The Story of Frederick Douglass* (Washington, D.C.: R. I. Pendleton, 1909), preface. (The first edition of *The Story of Frederick Douglass* was published in 1899 by Howard University.)

17. Rev. F. J. Grimké to Dear Sir, 16 December 1911, box 39-8, folder 160, Archibald H. Grimké Collection, MSRC; "Souvenir Program, Dedicatory Exercises of the Frederick Douglass Memorial Home, Cedar Hill, Anacostia, D.C.," 12 August 1922, box 28-2, folder 44, Frederick Douglass Collection, MSRC, 11; Salem, *To Better Our World*, 115–17.

18. Mary Talbert, "Concerning the Frederick Douglass Memorial," *Crisis*, August 1917, 167; "The Frederick Douglass Home," *Crisis*, February 1917, 174; "Souvenir Program, Dedicatory Exercises of the Frederick Douglass Memorial Home," 9–10.

19. Mary Talbert to Archibald Grimké, 31 May 1922, box 38-9, folder 160, Archibald H. Grimké Collection, MSRC; "Records of the National Association of Colored Women Concerning the Frederick Douglass Memorial Home," box 28-2, folder 44, Douglass Collection, MSRC.

20. "Souvenir Program, Dedicatory Exercises of the Frederick Douglass Memorial Home."

21. "To All Descendants of Early New England Negroes," n.d.; Florida Ruffin Ridley to Carter Woodson, 22 August 1930, April [?]; "Society of the Descendants of Early New England Negroes Registration Blank," n.d., container 6, reel 3, Carter G. Woodson Papers, LC.

22. Mary C. Terrell, "Susan B. Anthony, the Abolitionist," *Voice of the Negro*, June 1906, 411; Terrell, *Colored Woman in a White World* (1940), 279–80; Mary C. Terrell, "Announcement of the Centenary of the Birth of Harriet Beecher Stowe," n.d., box 102-3, folder 56, Mary Church Terrell Papers, MSRC.

23. Carla L. Peterson addresses this question of authorship in *"Doers of the Word,"* 13.

24. Ibid., 50–51. For a discussion of African American women writers' negotiation of white ideals of femininity, see Hazel Carby, *Reconstructing Womanhood: The Emergence of the Afro-American Woman Novelist* (New York: Oxford University Press, 1987); Joanne Braxton, introduction to Mrs. N. F. Mossell, *The Work of the Afro-American Woman*, 2nd ed. (Philadelphia: George S. Ferguson, 1908; reprint, New York: Oxford University Press, 1988), 10.

25. Annie Wittenmyer, *History of the Woman's Temperance Crusade. A Complete Official History of the Wonderful Uprising of the Christian Woman of the United States Against the Liquor Traffic, Which Culminated in the Gospel Temperance Movement* (Philadelphia: Office of the Christian Woman, 1878); Mary A. Livermore, *The Story of My Life* (Hartford: A. D. Worthington, 1897).

26. Susan King Taylor, *Reminiscences of My Life in Camp with the 33rd United States Colored Troops, Late 1st S.C. Volunteers* (Boston: The author, 1902; reprint, New

York: Arno Press, 1968); Addie W. Hunton and Kathryn M. Johnson, *Two Colored Women with the American Expeditionary Forces* (Brooklyn: Eagle Press, 1920).

27. Jennie C. Croly, *Sorosis: Its Origins and History* (New York: J. J. Little, 1886); Jennie C. Croly, *The History of the Woman's Club Movement in America* (New York: Henry G. Allen, 1898).

28. *A History of the Club Movement among the Colored Women of the United States of America* (Washington, D.C.: National Federation of Afro-American Women, 1902); Elizabeth L. Davis, *Lifting as They Climb* (Washington, D.C.: NACW, 1933; reprint, New York: G. K. Hall, 1996). Between the publication dates of these two histories, Davis also wrote *The Story of the Illinois Federation of Colored Women's Clubs* (1921; reprint, New York: G. K. Hall, 1997).

29. Susan L. Shorter, *Heroines of African Methodism* (Xenia, Ohio: The author, 1891).

30. Lawson A. Scruggs, *Women of Distinction* (Raleigh: L. A. Scruggs, 1893); M. A. Majors, M.D., *Noted Negro Women: Their Triumphs and Activities* (Chicago: Donohue and Henneberry, 1893); Benjamin Griffith Brawley, *Women of Achievement* (Chicago: Woman's American Baptist Home Mission Society, 1919).

31. Majors, *Noted Negro Women*, ix–x, 44, 154, 93.

32. Mossell, *Work of the Afro-American Woman*, 10; Carla L. Peterson, *"Doers of the Word,"* 5.

33. Anna J. Cooper, "The Higher Education of Woman," *Southland* 2 (April 1891): 189–90, box 23-5, folder 63, Anna J. Cooper Papers, MSRC.

34. Anna J. Cooper, *A Voice from the South* (Xenia, Ohio: Aldine, 1892; reprint, New York: Negro University Press, 1969), iii, 28.

35. Some of the historical articles in *Voice of the Negro* in 1904 and 1905 include Mary C. Terrell, "The Progress of Colored Women," July 1904, 292–94; Josephine B. Bruce, "What Has Education Done for Colored Women," July 1904, 292–98; Anna H. Jones, "A Century's Progress for the American Colored Woman," August 1905, 632–33.

36. Nannie H. Burroughs, "Not Color But Character," *Voice of the Negro*, July 1904, 278; Addie W. Hunton, "Negro Womanhood Defended," *Voice of the Negro*, July 1904, 281–82.

37. The institutionalized racism of the early twentieth-century historical profession is discussed in August Meier and Elliott M. Rudwick, *Black History and the Historical Profession, 1915–1980* (Urbana: University of Illinois Press, 1986), 3–4; Jacqueline Goggin, "Countering White Racist Scholarship: Carter G. Woodson and the *Journal of Negro History*," *JNH* 68 (Fall 1983): 355–56, 358; Jacqueline Goggin, "Carter G. Woodson and the Collection of Source Materials for Afro-American History," *American Archivist* 48 (Summer 1985): 263.

38. In 1931–32 African American men comprised 43.2 percent of the African American college student population, and black women comprised 56.8 percent. At public, four-year colleges, 501 men received degrees, compared with 778 women. Nearly 61 percent of all African Americans in junior colleges and normal schools in these years were women. See Florence Murray, ed., *The Negro Handbook* (New York: Wendell Malliet, 1942), education section.

39. Lucy D. Slowe, "The Education of Negro Women and Girls," delivered at Teachers College, Columbia University, 11 March 1931, and reprinted in *Journal of the College Alumnae Club of Washington*, January 1939, 14–15; Lucy D. Slowe, "The

Colored Girl Enters College—What Will She Expect?," *Opportunity*, September 1937, 276–78, box 90-6, Lucy D. Slowe Papers, MSRC.

40. Herman V. Ames to Carter Woodson, 14 March 1922, box 5, reel 3, Woodson Papers, LC.

41. Darlene Clark Hine, *Hine Sight: Black Women and the Reconstruction of American History* (Brooklyn: Carlson, 1994), 244; Stewart and Ruffins, "Faithful Witness," 314; Drusilla D. Houston, *Wonderful Ethiopians of the Ancient Cushite Empire* (Oklahoma City: Universal Publishing, 1926; reprint, New York: African Missions Publications, 1988).

42. Ball and Martin, *Rare Afro-Americana*, 30.

43. Arthur A. Schomburg, "The Negro Digs up His Past," in *The New Negro: An Interpretation*, ed. Alain Locke (New York: Albert and Charles Boni, 1925), reprinted in Nathan Irvin Huggins, ed., *Voices from the Harlem Renaissance* (New York: Oxford University Press, 1976), 220, 217; Robert Hill, "On Collectors, Their Contributions to the Documentation of the Black Past," in Sinnette, Coates, and Battle, *Black Bibliophiles and Collectors*, 47–55.

44. Schomburg, "Negro Digs up His Past," 217.

45. Robert Adger, William Carl Bolivar, John Bruce, William Dabney, and Daniel Murray were just a few of the men involved in these organizations. See "Agenda for the Twenty-Ninth Annual Meeting of the American Negro Academy," 28–29 December 1925, box 24-2, folder 40, Cromwell Family Papers, MSRC; Hugh M. Browne to Archibald Grimké, 15 June 1905, 25 March 1904, 24 July 1908, box 39-8, folder 155, Archibald Grimké Collection, MSRC.

46. Wellesley College Alumnae Association 1942 biographical record, 1 October 1941; Ella L. Smith minibiography, n.d., Ella Smith Elbert biographical file, WCA; "Ella Elbert," biography in Elbert Gifts File, Wellesley College Special Collections, Wellesley, Mass.

47. Meier and Rudwick, *Black History and the Historical Profession*, 3–4; Earl E. Thorpe, *Black Historians: A Critique* (New York: William Morrow, 1971), 9–10; Earl E. Thorpe, *Negro Historians in the United States* (Baton Rouge: Fraternal Press, 1958), 52–53.

48. Not all academics in race organizations favored an emphasis on slave history. Alain Locke, for example, agreed with Arthur Schomburg that the African roots of the Negro should be emphasized over the more recent phenomenon of American slave culture. See Elinor Sinnette, "Arthur Alfonso Schomburg (1874–1938), Black Bibliophile and Collector," in Sinnette, Coates, and Battle, *Black Bibliophiles and Collectors*, 36.

49. Arthur Schomburg to John Cromwell, 24 December 1912, box 24-1, folder 14; Jack Thorne, "A Plea for Social Justice for the Negro Woman," NSHR, Occasional Paper, no. 2, 1912, box 24-16, folder 192, Cromwell Family Papers, MSRC.

50. Carla L. Peterson, *"Doers of the Word,"* 16–17.

51. Hallie Q. Brown, ed., *Homespun Heroines and Other Women of Distinction* (Xenia, Ohio: Aldine, 1926; reprint, New York: Oxford University Press, 1988), 220.

52. Sadie I. Daniel, *Women Builders* (Washington, D.C.: AP, 1931), xiii, xv–xvi.

53. Alice Walker, *In Search of Our Mothers' Gardens: Womanist Prose by Alice Walker* (San Diego: Harcourt, 1983), xi; Janet J. Montelaro, *Producing a Womanist Text: The Maternal as Signifier in Alice Walker's "The Color Purple"* (Victoria: University of Victoria, 1996), 12–14; Elsa B. Brown, "Womanist Consciousness: Maggie Lena

Walker and the Independent Order of Saint Luke," in *Unequal Sisters: A Multicultural Reader in U.S. Women's History*, 2nd ed., ed. Ellen C. DuBois and Vicki Ruiz (New York: Routledge, 1994), 268–69.

54. For a discussion of the sexual stigmatization African American women endured after slavery, see Bell Hooks, *A'int I A Woman* (Boston: South End Press, 1982), 51–86; Carla L. Peterson, "*Doers of the Word*," 20.

55. Deborah Gray White, "Private Lives, Public Personae: A Look at Early Twentieth-Century African American Clubwomen," in *Talking Gender: Public Images, Personal Journeys, and Political Critiques*, ed. Nancy Hewitt, Jean O'Barr, and Nancy Rosebaugh (Chapel Hill: University of North Carolina Press, 1996), 107.

56. For discussions of the suppression of the personal and sexual in African American women's writing, see Carby, *Reconstructing Womanhood*; Darlene Clark Hine, "Rape and the Inner Lives of Black Women in the Middle West: Preliminary Thoughts on the Culture of Dissemblance," in DuBois and Ruiz, *Unequal Sisters*, 342–45.

57. Matilde Weil, the Writer's Workshop, to Mary Church Terrell, 19 November 1932, box 102-2, folder 40, Terrell Papers, MSRC; Beverly W. Jones, *Quest for Equality: The Life and Writings of Mary Eliza Church Terrell, 1863–1954* (Brooklyn: Carlson, 1990), 62.

58. Deborah Gray White, "Private Lives, Public Personae," 110–11.

59. Terrell, *Colored Woman in a White World*. In the reprinted version Nellie McKay describes Terrell's intentions when writing her autobiography (1996, pp. xvi–xxxvi); see also Deborah Gray White, "Private Lives, Public Personae," 117–20.

60. Several woman-authored Howard theses include "The Negro and the Supreme Court to 1900" (1936), "The Anti-Slavery Activities of Negroes in New York" (1936), "The Attitude of the Negro toward Slavery" (1936), and "The Anti-Slavery Activities of Negroes in Pennsylvania" (1937). At Boston University, Edythe Mae Gordon researched "The Status of the Negro Woman in the U.S. from 1619–1865," but her interest in African American women was not the norm. See Marie Elizabeth Ruffin Carpenter, *The Treatment of the Negro in American History School Textbooks: A Comparison of Changing Textbook Content, 1826 to 1939, with Developing Scholarship in the History of the Negro in the United States* (Manasha, Wis.: George Banta, 1941), bibliographic references and footnotes.

61. Zora Neale Hurston, *Dust Tracks on a Road: An Autobiography*, 2nd ed. (Urbana: University of Illinois Press, 1970), xvii.

62. Hurston's *Mules and Men* (Philadelphia: Lippincott, 1935) is quoted in Hemenway, *Zora Neale Hurston*, 62.

63. Hemenway, *Zora Neale Hurston*, 63, 91.

64. Hurston, *Dust Tracks on a Road*, 170–71; Hurston, *Mules and Men*; Mary Katherine Wainwright, "Subversive Female Folk Tellers in 'Mules and Men,'" in *Zora in Florida*, ed. Steve Glassman and Kathryn L. Seidel (Orlando: University of Central Florida, 1991), 62–75. Other examples of Hurston's anthropological studies include Zora Neale Hurston, "Characteristics of Negro Expression" and "Shouting," in *Negro: An Anthology*, comp. Nancy Cunard (London: Wishart, 1934, reprinted in Huggins, *Voices from the Harlem Renaissance*); Alice Walker, *In Search of Our Mothers' Gardens*, 237.

65. Ophelia Egypt, "Unwritten History of Slavery," Social Science Documents, no.

1 (1945), Social Science Institute, Fisk University, Nashville, Tenn., 11–12. The typed manuscript is in Ophelia Egypt Papers, MSRC.

66. Although Egypt conducted the interviews for this monograph between 1929 and 1930, they were not published in book form until 1968. See ibid., 11–12.

67. Jacqueline Goggin, "Challenging Sexual Discrimination in the Historical Profession: Women Historians and the American Historical Association, 1890–1940," *AHR* 97 (June 1992): 769; Meier and Rudwick, *Black History and the Historical Profession*, 98–99, 113, 130–31.

CHAPTER 5

1. Lucy D. Slowe, "The Education of Negro Women and Girls," delivered at Teacher's College, Columbia University, 11 March 1931, and reprinted in *Journal of the College Alumnae Club of Washington*, January 1939, 14–15.

2. August Meier and Elliott M. Rudwick, *Black History and the Historical Profession, 1915–1980* (Urbana: University of Illinois Press, 1986), 104–5; Marion Cuthbert, *Education and Marginality: A Study of the Negro Woman College Graduate* (New York: Columbia University Press, 1942); Edna Colson, "An Analysis of the Specific References to Negroes in Selected Curricula for Teachers" (Ph.D. diss., New York Teachers College, Columbia University, 1940).

3. Marie Elizabeth Ruffin Carpenter, *The Treatment of the Negro in American History School Textbooks: A Comparison of Changing Textbook Content, 1826 to 1939, with Developing Scholarship in the History of the Negro in the United States* (Manasha, Wis.: George Banta, 1941), 16, 59–60.

4. Bethune is quoted in Dorothy Salem, *To Better Our World: Black Women in Organized Reform, 1890–1920* (Brooklyn: Carlson, 1990), 253.

5. Carter G. Woodson, "Ten Years Collecting and Publishing the Records of the Negro," *JNH* 10 (October 1925): 600; Meier and Rudwick, *Black History and the Historical Profession*, 3–4; Jacqueline Goggin, "Countering White Racist Scholarship: Carter G. Woodson and the *Journal of Negro History*," *JNH* 68 (Fall 1983): 355–56, 358.

6. Carter G. Woodson, "Negro Historians of Our Times," *NHB*, April 1945, 155.

7. The three Rockefeller trusts that helped to fund ASNLH research were the Rockefeller Foundation, the Laura Spelman Rockefeller Memorial, and the General Education Board. For information about the white philanthropic organizations that backed the ASNLH, see Darlene Clark Hine, *Hine Sight: Black Women and the Reconstruction of American History* (Brooklyn: Carlson, 1994), 203–17; "Proceedings of the Second Biennial Meeting of the Association for the Study of Negro Life and History," *JNH* 4 (October 1919): 475–82; Meier and Rudwick, *Black History and the Historical Profession*, 45.

8. Herbert Wright interview with Charles H. Wesley, 5 March 1970, Oral History file I19, MSRC, 7.

9. James Hugo Johnston, Rayford Logan, Lorenzo Greene, and Charles Wesley were a few men who worked under Woodson and eventually earned distinguished reputations in the field of academic history. See Woodson, "Negro Historians of Our Times," 156; Meier and Rudwick, *Black History and the Historical Profession*, 94.

10. Woodson, "Ten Years Collecting and Publishing the Records of the Negro," 604; Zora Neale Hurston to Carter Woodson, n.d., container 5, reel 3, Carter G. Woodson Papers, LC; Meier and Rudwick, *Black History and the Historical Profession*,

47; Irene Wright, comp., "Dispatches of Spanish Officials Bearing on the Free Negroes and Indians," *JNH* 9 (April 1924): 144–95.

11. Carter G. Woodson, "Review of *The Negro Trail Blazers of California*, by Delilah Beasley, Los Angeles, CA, 1919," *JNH* 5 (January 1920): 129.

12. Laura Wilkes to Carter Woodson, 22 July 1921, container 6, reel 3, Woodson Papers, LC.

13. Carter G. Woodson, "Review of *Reconstruction in Louisiana*, by Ella Lonn, Assistant Professor in Grinnell College, G. P. Putnam's Sons, NY, 1919," *JNH* 5 (January 1920): 131; "Review of *Documents Illustrative of the History of the Slave Trade to America*," vols. 2 and 3, *JNH* 18 (April 1933): 215–16; Carter G. Woodson, "Review of *Tell My Horse*, by Zora Neale Hurston, Philadelphia: J. B. Lippincott Company, 1938," *JNH* 24 (January 1939): 116–18.

14. Robert Hemenway, *Zora Neale Hurston: A Literary Biography* (Urbana: University of Illinois Press, 1977), 84, 87–89, 95–96. Hemenway does not indicate conclusively that Parsons donated the necessary funds but suspects this was the case.

15. Zora N. Hurston, "Cudjo's Own Story of the Last African Slaver," *JNH* 12 (October 1927): 648–63; Zora Neale Hurston, *Dust Tracks on a Road: An Autobiography*, 2nd ed. (Urbana: University of Illinois Press, 1970), 198–204. Robert Hemenway has noted that controversy surrounded the publication of the Cudjo Lewis interview. He claims that only 25 percent of Hurston's research was original, and the rest came from a book written by Emma Langdon Roche titled *Historic Sketches of the Old South*. Hurston did not acknowledge Roche in the article, and her plagiarism remained undetected until linguist William Stewart discovered it in 1972. See Hemenway, *Zora Neale Hurston*, 96–97.

16. Jessie (Parkhurst) Guzman [Jessie Parkhurst], "The Role of the Black Mammy in the Plantation Household," *JNH* 23 (July 1938): 349.

17. Dorothy B. Porter, "Sarah Parker Remond, Abolitionist and Physician," *JNH* 20 (January 1935): 287.

18. Elizabeth R. Haynes, "Negroes in Domestic Service in the United States," *JNH* 8 (October 1923): 384–442.

19. Carter G. Woodson, "The Negro Washer Woman: A Vanishing Figure," *JNH* 15 (April 1930): 269–77.

20. Robert Hemenway maintains that between 1919 and 1930 black writers, women included, published in greater numbers than they would again until the 1960s. See his *Zora Neale Hurston*, 36.

21. E. C. Williams, "Review of *Unsung Heroes*, by Elizabeth Ross Haynes, NY: DuBois and Dill, 1921," *JNH* 7 (April 1922): 224–25; Carter G. Woodson, "Review of *Two Colored Women with the American Expeditionary Forces*, by Addie W. Hunton and Katherine M. Johnson," *JNH* 6 (July 1921): 224–25.

22. Anna Bustill Smith to Carter Woodson, 11 June 1925, container 6, reel 3, Woodson Papers, LC; Anna B. Smith, "The Bustill Family," *JNH* 10 (October 1925): 638–44. See also Leila Pendleton, "Our New Possessions: The Danish West Indies," *JNH* 19 (July 1934): 324–29; Alice Dunbar-Nelson, "The People of Color in Louisiana," *JNH* 1 (July 1916): 359–74; Mary M. Bethune, "Clarifying Our Vision with Facts," *JNH* 23 (January 1938): 10–15; Mary M. Bethune, "The Association for the Study of Negro Life and History: Its Contribution to Our Modern Life," *JNH* 20 (July 1935): 406–11.

23. Often the women who received attention in the journal as historical subjects

were deemed exceptional for their roles as teachers. Some of the earliest articles, for example, were about educator Prudence Crandall and the Virginia mother and daughter Maria Louise Moore and Fannie M. Richards, who were praised as trainers of the race. See Mary C. Terrell, "History of the High School for Negroes in Washington," *JNH* 2 (July 1917): 259; Loretta Funke, "The Negro in Education," *JNH* 5 (January 1920): 1–21; G. Smith Wormley, "Prudence Crandall," *JNH* 8 (January 1923): 72–80; W. B. Hartgrove, "The Story of Maria Louise Moore and Fannie M. Richards," *JNH* 1 (January 1916): 23–32; Grace Hays Johnson, "Phases of Cultural History of Significance for Negro Students," *JNH* 12 (January 1937): 29–37; Mary M. Bethune, "The Adaptation of the History of the Negro to the Capacity of a Child," *JNH* 24 (January 1939): 9.

24. Goggin, "Countering White Racist Scholarship," 365, 374.

25. By 1933 the ASNLH had been completely cut off from the General Education Board and Rosenwald Fund grants. See Meier and Rudwick, *Black History and the Historical Profession*, 59–61; Darlene Clark Hine, "Black Women's History, White Women's History: The Juncture of Race and Class," in Hine, *Hine Sight*, 203–21.

26. Woodson, "Ten Years Collecting and Publishing the Records of the Negro," 603; Hine, *Hine Sight*, 219–21.

27. Pledge Sheet for the Association of Negro Life and History, 1928?, box 398, folder 145, Archibald H. Grimké Collection, MSRC. Statistics gathered between 1915 and 1925 indicate that more than $48,500 in general contributions were collected during these years compared with $11,400 collected through subscription fees and $2,950 collected in membership fees. Philanthropists maintained a research fund of just over $20,000 during these ten years, less than half that gathered through contributions in the community. See Woodson, "Ten Years Collecting and Publishing the Records of the Negro," 603; Hine, *Hine Sight*, 219–21.

28. Maria Baldwin to Carter Woodson, 4 March 1917; Janie Porter Barret to Woodson, 4 September 1925, container 5, reel 3, Woodson Papers, LC.

29. For details on the items that could be found in Woodson's Library of Congress collection, see Jacqueline Goggin, "Carter G. Woodson and the Collection of Source Materials for Afro-American History," *American Archivist* 48 (Summer 1985): 261–70; Abigail Richardson to Carter Woodson, 2 June 1924, container 6, reel 3, Woodson Papers, LC.

30. Mary T. Higginson to Carter Woodson, 12 October 1925, container 5, reel 3; Annie Rogers Knowlton to Woodson, 6 October 1926, container 3, reel 3, Woodson Papers, LC.

31. Laura Deitz Howard to Carter Woodson, 24 October 1928, container 5, reel 3; Leota Clair to Woodson, 7 November 1921, container 5, reel 5; M. Viola Johnson to Woodson, 29 January 1928, container 3, reel 3, Woodson Papers, LC.

32. "Proceeding of the Spring Conference of the ASNLH held in Philadelphia, 3–4 April 1924," *JNH* 8 (July 1924): 375.

33. Margaret Washington to Carter Woodson, 4 September 1922, container 6, reel 4, Woodson Papers, LC.

34. Nettie Ashbury to Carter Woodson, 31 December 1929, container 5, reel 3; Mary Talbert to Woodson, 9 July 1917; Florida Ruffin Ridley to Woodson, April 19??, 22 August 1930, container 6, reel 3, Woodson Papers, LC.

35. Carter Woodson to Archibald Grimké, 12 September 1927, box 39-8, folder 145, Archibald H. Grimké Collection, MSRC.

36. Meier and Rudwick, *Black History and the Historical Profession*, 11; Carter Woodson to Rayford Logan, 16 November 1935, box 181-8, folder 7, Rayford W. Logan Papers, MSRC.

37. Eleanor Roberts interview with Miriam Matthews, 14, 16, 17, 22 March 1977, Black Women Oral History Project, 1981, SL, 64–65.

38. Woodson noted particularly successful Negro History Week campaigns in Delaware, North Carolina, and West Virginia. See Carter Woodson to Dorothy Williams, 15 November 1948, mss. 44, box 1, folder 9/1, Center Records, SC; Carter G. Woodson, "Negro History Week," *JNH* 11 (April 1926): 238, 239; letter on Negro History Week in the Baltimore Public Schools, 5 February 1947; "Plans for Negro History Week, 8–15 February 1948"; letter from the Committee on Negro History Week, Elementary Schools, 19 January 1950, box 191-30, folder 17, Vivian Cook Papers, MSRC.

39. "Program of the Association for the Study of Negro Life and History," 1928, box 39-8, folder 145, Archibald H. Grimké Collection, MSRC; John Franklin Hope, "The New Negro," in *Race and History: Selected Essays, 1938–1988* (Baton Rouge: Louisiana State University Press, 1989), 51; Carter Woodson to President John Hope, Atlanta University, 29 October 1935, box 181-1, folder 7, Logan Papers, MSRC; Meier and Rudwick, *Black History and the Historical Profession*, 61–62.

40. Bethune, "Adaptation of the History of the Negro to the Capacity of a Child," 9. In the "Books" section (p. 6) of the October 1938 issue of the *NHB*, for example, seven of nine authors highlighted were women.

41. "Jane D. Shackleford and Her Book" and "Mrs. Helen A. Whiting and the Children," *NHB*, November 1938, 16. In 1940–41 the editorial board members of the *NHB* were Elise Derricotte, Lois Jones, Florence Beatty-Brown, Carol Hayes (Wilhelmina Crosson from 1941 on), and male members Carter Woodson and Albert N. D. Brooks. See the table of contents of the *NHB*, 1940, 1941, 1942.

42. Of the four biographical articles attributed to specific authors, two were about women (Maria Louise Baldwin and Eliza Ann Gardner), and two were about men (Edwin Bannister and George L. Ruffin). See table of contents, *NHB*, October 1941.

43. Carter G. Woodson, "Negro Women Eligible to be Daughters of the American Revolution," *NHB*, November 1943, 36, 39.

44. Woodson, "Negro Historians of Our Times," 159; Helen Boardman, "The Rise of the Negro Historian," *NHB*, April 1945, 148–54, 166.

45. Bethune, "Association for the Study of Negro Life and History," 408, 410.

46. For information on the Negro Book Collectors Exchange, see Elinor Sinnette, Paul Coates, and Thomas C. Battle, eds., *Black Bibliophiles and Collectors: Preservers of Black History* (Washington, D.C.: Howard University Press, 1990), 10. See also Wendy Ball and Tony Martin, *Rare Afro-Americana: A Reconstruction of the Adger Library* (Boston: G. K. Hall, 1981), 21; *The Legacy of Arthur A. Schomburg: A Celebration of the Past, a Vision for the Future*, exhibition at the Schomburg Center for Research in Black Culture, 23 October 1986–28 March 1987 (New York: New York Public Library, Aster, Lenox and Tilden Foundation, 1986), 7–8; Betty M. Culpepper, "Moorland-Spingarn Research Center: A Legacy of Bibliophiles," in Sinnette, Coates, and Battle, *Black Bibliophiles and Collectors*, 103–7; Minnie Clayton, "Special Collections at the Atlanta University Center," in Sinnette, Coates, and Battle, *Black Bibliophiles and Collectors*, 81–87.

47. W. E. B. Du Bois, *A Select Bibliography of the Negro American* (Atlanta: Atlanta

University Studies, 1905); Library of Congress, *Select List of References on the Negro Question*, 2nd ed. (Washington, D.C.: Government Printing Office, 1906); Daniel A. P. Murray, "List of Books and Pamphlets by Negro Authors" (1900). See also *Murray's Historical and Biographical Encyclopedia of the Colored Race Throughout the World: Its Progress and Achievements from the Earliest Period Down to the Present Time, Embracing Twenty-Five Thousand Biographical Sketches of Men and Women of the Colored Race in Every Age* (Chicago: World's Cyclopedia Co., 1912); "Bibliographia-Africana," *Voice of the Negro*, May 1904, 187; "Bibliographer of Afro-American Literature in the Library of Congress," *Colored American Magazine*, October 1902, 432–40; Monroe Work, comp., *The Negro Year Book* (Tuskegee, Ala.: Year Book Pub. Co., 1912); Monroe Work, comp., *A Bibliography of the Negro in Africa and America* (New York: H. W. Wilson, 1928); Jessie (Parkhurst) Guzman, "Monroe Nathan Work and His Accomplishments," *JNH* 34 (October 1949): 428–61.

48. Carl Van Vechten, "The Johnson Collection at Yale," n.d.; card catalog of Elbert's donated books, Gifts—Elbert File, A74-36, 2 of 2 (unprocessed file of the librarian), WCA; "The Elbert Collection in the Wellesley College Library," Elbert Gifts File, Wellesley Special Collections, Wellesley, Mass.

49. Ella Smith Elbert to Blanche Pritchard McCrum, 18 September 1938; Mildred McAfee to Elbert, 4 June 1942; McCrum to Elbert, 14 September 1938, 7 May 1942; Elbert to McCrum, 19 June 1938; McCrum to Elbert, 1 October 1942, 5 June 1941, Gifts—Elbert File, WCA; Terry Pristin, "Rare Book Collection Portrays Alienation of Negro in Society," *Wellesley College News*, 11 March 1965, Ella Smith Elbert biographical file, WCA.

50. Elise J. McDougald, "The Task of New Negro Womanhood," in *The New Negro: An Interpretation*, ed. Alain Locke (New York: Albert and Charles Boni, 1925; reprint, New York: Atheneum Press, 1969), 376, 369–82.

51. Darlene Clark Hine, ed., *Black Women in America: An Historical Encyclopedia*, 2 vols. (Brooklyn: Carlson, 1993), 542–43.

52. Dee Garrison, *Apostles of Culture: The Public Librarian and American Society, 1876–1920* (New York: Free Press, 1979), 224, 173, 178, xiii.

53. A. P. Marshall, "The Search for Identity," in *The Black Librarian in America*, ed. E. J. Josey (Metuchen, N.J.: Scarecrow Press, 1970), 174–79.

54. Marilyn Nelson, "Seven Library Women Whose Human Presence Enlightened Society in the Harlem Renaissance Iconoclastic Ethos" (Ph.D. diss., Graduate School of State University of New York at Buffalo, 1996), 67–73.

55. Virginia L. Jones, "A Dean's Career," in Josey, *Black Librarian in America*, 27–40.

56. Nelson, "Seven Library Women," 2–12, 40; Marshall, "Search for Identity," 178–79; Cuthbert, *Education and Marginality*, 150.

57. Carnegie Institute of Technology, "Negro Graduates of Accredited Library Schools, 1930–1936," in *A Directory of Negro Graduates of Accredited Library Schools, 1900–1936* (Washington, D.C.: Columbia Civic Library Association, 1937), 26–31.

58. Sophonisba Breckinridge, *Women in the Twentieth Century: A Study of their Political, Social, and Economic Activities* (New York: McGraw-Hill, 1933), 203; Elizabeth K. Adams, *Women Professional Workers: A Study Made for the Women's Educational and Industrial Union* (New York: Macmillan, 1921), 358–66; Garrison, *Apostles of Culture*, 226.

59. Nelson, "Seven Library Women," 10.

60. Carnegie Institute of Technology, "Negro Graduates of Accredited Library Schools," 6–25; Eliza A. Gleason, "The Southern Negro and the Public Library: A Study of the Government and Administration of Public Library Service to the Negroes in the South" (Ph.D. diss., University of Chicago, 1940); Roberts interview with Miriam Matthews, Black Women Oral History Project, SL, ii.

61. Garrison, Apostles of Culture, 179–81, 207–8.

62. Augusta Baker, "My Years as a Children's Librarian," in Josey, Black Librarian in America, 117–19; Nelson, "Seven Library Women," 159–62.

63. Before Porter came to Howard in the 1930s, Lula Allen, Edith Brown, Lulu Connar, and Rosa Hershaw processed the Moorland Foundation materials donated to Howard in 1914. See Culpepper, "Moorland-Spingarn Research Center," 104–7; Walter Dyson, Howard University, the Capstone of Negro Education: A History, 1867–1940 (Washington, D.C.: Graduate School of Howard University, 1941), 287–95.

64. Dorothy B. Porter, "Negro Writers before 1830" (master's thesis, Columbia University, 1932); "Dorothy Porter Wesley," in Hine, Black Women in America, 1246–47.

65. Porter's interest in Latin American countries led to the Moorland Foundation's purchase of Arthur Spingarn's private collection of Afro-Brazilian, Haitian, and Cuban literature in 1945. See Dorothy Porter to Rayford Logan, 29 October, 6 November 1943, box 166-19, folder 5; Dorothy B. Porter, "Memorandum: The Syllabus on the Negro in Latin America," to Logan, 1 December 1943, box 181-6, folder 17, Logan Papers, MSRC; Dorothy B. Porter, "Description of the Project: The Contribution of the Negro to the Spanish American and Brazilian Poetry and Fiction: A Bibliographical Essay," n.d., box 94-6, folder 143, Arthur B. Spingarn Papers, MSRC.

66. Kelly Miller to Board of Trustees of Howard University, 20 September 1922; Miller to Dr. Jesse E. Moorland, 3 October 1922, box 126-32, folder 676, Jesse E. Moorland Papers; Dorothy Porter to Miller, 1 June 1938, box 71-1, folder 31, Kelly Miller Papers, MSRC.

67. Dorothy B. Porter, "Report of the Moorland Foundation Carnegie Library, Howard University, Washington, DC," 1933, box 71-1, folder 31, Miller Papers, MSRC; Dorothy Porter to Jesse Moorland, 6 July 1934; Dorothy B. Porter, "Report of Trip to Tuttle Company, Rutland, Vermont," to Emma Murray, acting librarian, Howard University, 9 November 1934, box 126-32, folder 678, Moorland Papers, MSRC.

68. The philosophy behind the New York Public Library branch system is discussed in Legacy of Arthur A. Schomburg, 8–9, and behind the branch library system generally in Garrison, Apostles of Culture, 207–9.

69. Sadie M. P. Delaney, "The Library: A Factor in Negro Education," Messenger, July 1923, 772–73; Nelson, "Seven Library Women," 46–47; biographical sketch; "Sets Goals in Hospital Library Service," n.d., MG 1220, box 1, 1:29, Sadie Delaney Papers, SC.

70. Biography, SCM 87-5, box 1; "Woman Named to Head New York City Public Library Branch," box 7, folder 1, Regina Andrews Papers, SC; Nelson, "Seven Library Women," 124.

71. Ernestine Rose, "Serving New York's Black City," Library Journal, 15 March 1921, 257, box 1, folder 8/1, Center Records, 1921–48, SC.

72. Rose quoted in Arna Bontemps, "The Schomburg Collection of Negro Literature," Library Quarterly 14 (July 1944): 2, mss. 44, box 1, folder 8/1, Center Records, SC.

73. "Report by Ernestine Rose, Librarian," 1936; "Report of Group and Class Visits to the Division of Negro Literature and History," 1939, mss. 44, box 1, folder 8/1; attendance figures in Schomburg Center, 8 May 1925–May 1940, mss. 44, box 3, folder 3/3, Center Records, SC.

74. "Report of Group and Class Visits to the Division of Negro Literature and History," 1939; "Report of the Reference Work in Schomburg Collection," 18 December 1943, mss. 44, box 1, folder 8/1, Center Records, SC.

75. Schomburg was "curator" of the collection from 1932 to 1938, although it is unclear what this meant in terms of his daily interactions with the business and materials of the center. Records indicate that in these years Rose occupied a more hands-on position at the center, writing all of its reports and conducting its day-to-day business. See "Report by Ernestine Rose, Librarian," 1936, mss. 44, box 1, folder 8/1; "Guide to Manuscript Depositories in New York City: Schomburg Collection, NYPL" (reprint prepared by the HRS, New York City, 1941), mss. 44, box 1, folder 6/1, Center Records, SC. Women were also primarily responsible for publicizing the collection. See, for example, Marjorie Shuler, "Exhibit of Negro Achievements," *Christian Science Monitor*, 30 December 1925; Evelyne G. Green, "Those Who Read in Harlem," *Wilson Bulletin for Librarians*, January 1936; Marion Lerou, "Division of Negro Literature, History and Prints, 135th Branch, New York Public Library," *Mission Fields at Home*, February 1934; Rose Henderson, "The Schomburg Collection of Negro History and Literature," *Southern Workman*, November 1934.

76. "Report of Cataloguing for the Schomburg Collection" (August 1940); "Report of Cataloguing for the Schomburg Collection," n.d., mss. 44, box 1, folder 10/1; "Guidelines for Cataloguers of the Schomburg Collection," n.d., box 1, folder 10/1, Center Records, 1921–48, SC.

77. Ernestine Anthony, "Six Months with the Schomburg Collection" (December 1942), mss. 44, box 1, folder 8/1, Center Records, SC.

78. Catherine Latimer, "Where Can I Get Material on the Negro?," *Crisis*, June 1934, 164–65; Dorothy B. Porter, *A Selected List of Books by and about the Negro* (Washington, D.C.: Government Printing Office, 1936); Dorothy B. Porter, "Library Sources for the Study of Negro Life and History," *Journal of Negro Education* 5 (April 1936): 232–44. See also Dorothy B. Porter and Ethel M. Ellis, "Index to the Journal of Negro Life and History," *Journal of Negro Education* 5 (April 1936): 232–44.

79. HRS, *Calendar of the Manuscripts in the Schomburg Collection of Negro Literature* (New York: Andronicus, 1942), vii–viii. The clippings file was continuously updated until 1985 and marketed as the *Ernest D. Kaiser Index to Black Resources*. See Nelson, "Seven Library Women," 113–16.

80. Catherine Latimer to Mr. Bragin, Assistant State Director, HRS, 28 September 1938, mss. 44, box 1, folder 1/1a, Center Records, 1921–48, SC; Jean B. Hutson, "The Schomburg Center for Research in Black Culture," in Sinnette, Coates, and Battle, *Black Bibliophiles and Collectors*, 71; HRS, *Calendar of the Manuscripts in the Schomburg Collection of Negro Literature*. Two years before the Schomburg Calendar, the HRS of Washington also published the *Calendar of the Writings of Frederick Douglass in the Douglass Memorial Home, Anacostia, D.C.* See also *A Catalog of Books in the Moorland Foundation*; Culpepper, "Moorland-Spingarn Research Center," 106; Dorothy Porter to Arthur Spingarn, 27 May 1938, box 94-6, folder 143, Spingarn Papers, MSRC.

81. Virginia Lacey, "United States Government Publications on the American

Negro, 1916–37" (master's thesis, University of Illinois, 1938). See also Miriam Matthews, "The Negro in California, 1781–1910: An Annotated Bibliography" (unpublished).

82. Mollie E. Dunlap, "Special Collections of Negro Literature in the United States," *Journal of Negro Education* 4 (October 1935): 482, 484. See also Mollie E. Dunlap, "An Annotated List of Books by or about the Negro," *Negro College Quarterly*, March 1947.

83. Report by Ernestine Rose, 1936, mss. 44, box 1, folder 8/1, Center Records, SC; Nancy Cunard, comp., *Negro: An Anthology* (London: Wishart, 1934; reprint, New York: F. Ungar, 1970); Vernon Loggins, *The Negro Author, His Development in America* (New York: Columbia University Press, 1931), acknowledgments.

84. Dorothy Porter to Dr. Moorland, 6 July 1934, box 126-32, folder 678, Moorland Papers, MSRC.

85. Darlene Clark Hine, "Rape and the Inner Lives of Black Women in the Middle West: Preliminary Thoughts on the Culture of Dissemblance," in *Unequal Sisters: A Multicultural Reader in U.S. Women's History*, 2nd ed., ed. Ellen C. DuBois and Vicki Ruiz (New York: Routledge, 1994), 342–45; Moira Ferguson, ed., *Nine Black Women: An Anthology of Nineteenth-Century Writers from the United States, Canada, Bermuda, and the Caribbean* (New York: Routledge, 1998), 97; Nell I. Painter, "Soul Murder and Slavery: Toward a Fully Loaded Cost Accounting," in *U.S. History as Women's History: New Feminist Essays*, ed. Linda K. Kerber, Alice Kessler-Harris, and Kathryn Kish Sklar (Chapel Hill: University of North Carolina Press, 1995), 145–46; Carla L. Peterson, *"Doers of the Word": African-American Women Speakers and Writers in the North, 1830–1880* (New York: Oxford University Press, 1995), 20–21; Deborah Gray White, "Private Lives, Public Personae: A Look at Early Twentieth-Century African American Clubwomen," in *Talking Gender: Public Images, Personal Journeys, and Political Critiques*, ed. Nancy Hewitt, Jean O'Barr, and Nancy Rosebaugh (Chapel Hill: University of North Carolina Press, 1996), 107–20. Carla Peterson concludes that figures such as Harriet Wilson, Harriet Jacobs, Frances Ellen Watkins Harper, and others "created fictionalized versions of both self and Other from multiple perspectives, thereby striving to escape the scrutiny of the dominant culture and achieve perspective of omniscience denied them in actual historical moment and place" (*"Doers of the Word,"* 23).

86. Catherine Latimer, comp., *Bibliography on the Contribution of Negro Women to American Civilization* (New York: Schomburg Center, New York Public Library, 1940). The women included in the collection's biographical index were Nannie Burroughs, Henrietta Davis, Alice Dunbar Nelson, Frances Ellen Watkins Harper, Mary Talbert, Harriet Tubman, Ida Wells Barnett, and Phillis Wheatley. See HRS, *Calendar of the Manuscripts in the Schomburg Collection of Negro Literature*; "Guide to Manuscript Depositories in New York City: Schomburg Collection, NYPL" (1941); "Rare Items from the Schomburg Collection Stored for the Duration," n.d., mss. 44, box 1, folder 6/1; List for the Negro Art Exhibit, 1–21 August 1921, mss. 44, box 1, folder 1/1a, Center Records, 1921–48, SC.

87. Latimer believed that Jefferson had shown concern for the welfare of daughters he had with a woman slave, but the details she gave Graham were vague. See Pearl Graham to Dorothy Porter, 22 May 1947, box 117-1, folder 1, TJGC, MSRC.

88. Pearl Graham to Dorothy Porter, 2 July 1949, box 117-1, folder 4; Graham to Porter, 1 August, 17 May 1948, box 117-1, folder 1, TJGC, MSRC.

89. Pearl Graham to Dorothy Porter, 22 May, 24 June 1947; Porter to Graham, 21 May 1948, 3 July, 1 November 1947, box 117-1, folder 1, TJGC, MSRC.

90. Bertha Burnett Sadler to Dorothy Porter, n.d., box 117-1, folder 4, TJGC, MSRC.

91. Pearl Graham to Dorothy Porter, 31 May 1949, box 117-1, folder 1; Lucy C. Williams to Graham, January 1949, box 117-1, folder 4, TJGC, MSRC.

92. Pearl Graham to Dorothy Porter, 6 June 1949, box 117-1, folder 4, TJGC, MSRC.

93. Pearl Graham to Dorothy Porter, 1 November 1947, 1 August 1948, 2 February 1949, box 117-1, folder 1, TJGC, MSRC.

CHAPTER 6

1. Elisabeth Dexter, *Colonial Women of Affairs* (Boston: Houghton Mifflin, 1924); Adelaide Nutting and Lavinia Dock, *A History of Nursing: From Earliest Times to the Present Day*, 4 vols. (New York: Putnam, 1907–12); Adelaide Nutting and Lavinia Dock, *The History of Nursing: The Evolution of Nursing Systems from the Earliest Times to the Foundation of the First English and American Training Schools for Nurses* (New York: Putnam, 1907, 1937). See also Lavinia Dock and Isabel Stewart, *A Short History of Nursing: From the Earliest Times to the Present Day* (New York: Putnam, 1920, 1925, 1931); Dr. Kate Campbell Hurd-Mead, *A History of Women in Medicine* (Haddam, Conn.: Haddam Press, 1938).

2. Paulina W. Davis, *A History of the National Woman's Rights Movement* (New York: Journeymen Printers' Cooperative Association, 1871). Harriot Stanton Blatch recounted the details leading up to the writing of *The History of Woman Suffrage* in Alma Lutz, *Susan B. Anthony: Rebel, Crusader, Humanitarian* (Boston: Beacon Press, 1959), 235–37. Similar accounts are in Ida Harper, *The Life and Work of Susan B. Anthony*, 3 vols. (Indianapolis: Hollenbeck Press, 1899, 1908); Elizabeth Cady Stanton, *Eighty Years and More. Reminiscences of Elizabeth Cady Stanton* (New York: European Publishing, 1898).

3. Harper, *Life and Work*, 2:600–613. See Stanton, *Eighty Years and More*, chap. 19, "Writing 'The History of Woman Suffrage.' "

4. Anthony sent sets of *The History of Woman Suffrage* to over 1,200 libraries in America and Europe, including university libraries, the British Museum, Oxford, and locations in Paris, London, Finland, Edinburgh, Melbourne, Toronto, and Dublin. *The History of Woman Suffrage*, vols. 1 and 2, were published by Fowler and Wells. Susan B. Anthony bought the rights to vol. 3. Vol. 4 was published by Hollenbeck Press, and vols. 5 and 6 were published through the NAWSA and printed by J. J. Little and Ives. All six volumes were reprinted by the Ayer Company, Salem, N.H., in 1985. Vols. 1 through 6 were first published in 1881, 1882, 1886, 1900, 1921, and 1922, respectively. See Harper, *Life and Work*, 2:612–13, 3:1275–78; Harper, *History of Woman Suffrage*, 4:viii.

5. Harper, *Life and Work*, 2:612–13. There is a brief, secondary record of the writing of the *History* in Mari Jo Buhle and Paul Buhle, eds., *The Concise History of Woman Suffrage: Selections from the Classic Work of Stanton, Anthony, Gage, and Harper* (Urbana: University of Illinois Press, 1978), xviii–xxi.

6. Stanton is given credit for the quote in Alma Lutz, *Created Equal: A Biography of Elizabeth Cady Stanton* (New York: John Day, 1940), 248. The quote is attributed to the authors generally in Harper, *Life and Work*, 2:531. See Matilda Joslyn Gage to Lucy

Stone, 4 December 1878, Gage file, container 29, reel 19, NAWSA Collection, LC (microfilm); Lutz, *Created Equal*, 245. The only place in vol. 1 where Stone was more than just named was in the "Massachusetts" chapter, in which her "Protest against Marriage Laws" was mentioned with little additional information.

7. For an overview of NWSA ideology and strategy and AWSA opposition, see Carol E. DuBois, *Elizabeth Cady Stanton and Susan B. Anthony: Correspondence, Writings, and Speeches* (Boston: Northeastern University Press, 1992), 88–103.

8. Harriot Stanton Blatch and Alma Lutz, *Challenging Years: The Memoirs of Harriot Stanton Blatch* (New York: Putnam, 1940), 61–62. Mari Jo and Paul Buhle provide a general overview and critique of the six volumes of *The History of Woman Suffrage* in *Concise History*, xix–xxi.

9. DuBois, *Elizabeth Cady Stanton and Susan B. Anthony*, 172–78.

10. Mary A. Livermore, *The Story of My Life* (Hartford: A. D. Worthington, 1897), vii–x; Julia Ward Howe, *Reminiscences, 1819–1899* (Boston: Houghton Mifflin, 1899). See also Ella G. Ruddy, ed., *The Mother of Clubs Caroline M. Seymour Severance: An Estimate and an Appreciation* (Los Angeles: Baumgardt, 1906); Anna H. Shaw, *The Story of a Pioneer* (New York: Harper and Brothers, 1915); Frances Willard, *Glimpses of Fifty Years: The Autobiography of an American Woman* (Chicago: Woman's Temperance Publication Association, 1889).

11. Ida H. Harper to Carrie C. Catt, 29 October 1938, Ida Husted Harper file, container 13, reel 9, NAWSA Collection, LC; Stanton, *Eighty Years and More*, preface.

12. Alice Stone Blackwell claimed Theodore Tilton wrote "an extravagantly eulogistic biography" of Woodhull before she became the cause of his political demise. See Blackwell, *Lucy Stone: Pioneer of Woman's Rights* (Boston: Little, Brown, 1930), 217.

13. In the biographies of the pioneer suffragists, feminist authors were compelled to explain their subjects' associations with Woodhull or to venerate their subjects for quickly disassociating with her. Biographers of Anthony or Stanton emphasized their rejection of Woodhull in the end. In her 1930 biography of her mother, Lucy Stone, Alice Stone Blackwell criticized Stanton and Anthony for having "a generous but wrong-headed tendency to take up the cudgels for any woman who happened to be under fire, right or wrong." In contrast, she claimed her mother astutely distrusted Woodhull all along and avoided the embarrassment of subscribing to her program. See ibid., 221–25; Harper, *Life and Work*, 3:1478; Lutz, *Created Equal*, 208–21.

14. Harper, *Life and Work*, 3:1210–13.

15. Ida H. Harper to Alice Stone Blackwell, 6 January 1920; to Mary Gray Peck, 13 July 1930; Susan B. Anthony to Harper, 15 February 1903, container 13, reel 9, Harper File, NAWSA Collection, LC; Harper, *Life and Work*, 3:1275–78.

16. Biographical data, Harper File, NAWSA Collection, LC.

17. Harper recounted the reunification of the NWSA and AWSA as a mere detail in a larger discussion of the agenda of the 1890 National-American Convention. Harper did not extrapolate further as to why the original break occurred or on any tensions that remained. See Harper, *History of Woman Suffrage*, 4:164.

18. Buhle and Buhle, *Concise History*, xix–xxi; Ellen C. DuBois, "Making Women's History: Activist Historians of Women's Rights, 1880–1940," in *Intellectuals and Public Life: Between Radicalism and Reform*, ed. Leon Fink, Stephen T. Leonard, and Donald M. Reid (Ithaca: Cornell University Press, 1996), 218; Aileen Kraditor, *The*

Ideas of the Woman Suffrage Movement, 1890–1920 (New York: Columbia University Press, 1965), 227.

19. Between 1896 and 1910 no new states passed suffrage amendments. See Kraditor, *Ideas of Woman Suffrage*, 231, 12.

20. Harper, *Life and Work*, 2:921, 931, 932–33.

21. Some of the "modern" suffrage histories referred to here are Doris Stevens, *Jailed for Freedom* (New York: Boni and Liveright, 1920); Carrie C. Catt and Nettie R. Shuler, *Woman Suffrage and Politics: The Inner Story of the Suffrage Movement* (New York: Charles Scribner's Sons, 1923; reprint, Seattle: University of Washington Press, 1969); Inez H. Irwin, *The Story of the Woman's Party* (New York: Harcourt, Brace, 1921); Rheta Childe Dorr, *Susan B. Anthony: The Woman Who Changed the Mind of a Nation* (New York: F. A. Stokes, 1928). See Kraditor, *Ideas of Woman Suffrage*, 45.

22. Dorr, *Susan B. Anthony*, 289; Stevens, *Jailed for Freedom*, 16.

23. Shaw, *Story of a Pioneer*, 191, 210.

24. Catt and Shuler, *Woman Suffrage and Politics*, 136.

25. Ibid., 107.

26. Ibid., 45. Contract for Harper to compile vol. 5 of *The History of Woman Suffrage*, signed by Carrie Chapman Catt, President of the Leslie Woman Suffrage Commission, 1 January 1919, container 13, reel 9, Harper File, NAWSA Collection, LC.

27. Ida Harper, ed., *The History of Woman Suffrage*, vol. 5 (New York: J. J. Little and Ives, 1922; reprint, Salem, N.H.: Ayer, 1985), v; Ida H. Harper to Alice Stone Blackwell, 23 September, 25 October 1921, 6 January 1920; Harper to Nettie Shuler, 11 October 1920, container 13, reel 9, Harper File, NAWSA Collection, LC.

28. Linda Ford, *Iron-Jawed Angels: The Suffrage Militancy of the National Woman's Party* (New York: University Press of America, 1991), 24; Christine A. Lunardini, *From Equal Suffrage to Equal Rights: Alice Paul and the National Woman's Party, 1910–1928* (New York: University Press of America, 1986), 42–44.

29. Linda Ford and Christine Lunardini describe a large constituency of the NWP as variations of the young "new woman." See Lunardini, *From Equal Suffrage to Equal Rights*, introduction, 1, 17; Ford, *Iron-Jawed Angels*, 3, 253, 26, 91–93.

30. Rheta Childe Dorr, *A Woman of Fifty*, 2nd ed. (New York: Funk and Wagnalls, 1924), 271, 277; Inez Irwin, "Adventures in Yesterday," n.d., unpublished autobiography, Inez Irwin Collection (microfilm), SL, 552, 573–75.

31. Inez Irwin to Maud Wood Park, n.d., container 17, reel 11, Inez Irwin File, NAWSA Collection, LC; Irwin, *Story of the Woman's Party*, 104, 468.

32. Stevens, *Jailed for Freedom*, 3, 4; Dorr, *Susan B. Anthony*, 330–31; Ford, *Iron-Jawed Angels*, 24.

33. Carrie C. Catt to Edna Stantial, October 1941, container 28, reel 19, Edna Stantial File, NAWSA Collection, LC; Stevens, *Jailed for Freedom*, 8, 10, 13.

34. Inez Irwin to Maud Wood Park, 2 December 1912, Irwin File, NAWSA Collection, LC; Irwin, "Adventures in Yesterday," 504.

35. Linda Ford calculates that 87 percent of Congressional Union organizers were between nineteen and twenty-nine years of age in 1917. All the NWP women who wrote feminist histories belonged to this younger cohort of suffragists. See Ford, *Iron-Jawed Angels*, 101; Irwin, *Story of the Woman's Party*, 13, 469.

36. Stevens, *Jailed for Freedom*, vii–viii; Inez Irwin to Maud Wood Park, 29 July

1938, container 17, reel 11, Irwin File, NAWSA Collection, LC; Irwin, *Story of the Woman's Party*, 124–25, 471–72. Doris Stevens maintained that Alice Paul's greatest trait as a leader was her youth, which gave her "concentration" and "indomitable courage" and made her "swift, alert, almost panther-like in her movements" (*Jailed for Freedom*, 10, 17).

37. Stevens, *Jailed for Freedom*, 49; Irwin, *Story of the Woman's Party*, 174, 183, 184.

38. Nancy Cott, *The Grounding of Modern Feminism* (New Haven: Yale University Press, 1987), 86, 95–97. Estelle Freedman discusses the shift from "social" or collective feminism to "individual" or political feminism in the classic essay "Separatism as Strategy: Female Institution Building and American Feminism, 1870–1930," *Feminist Studies* 3 (Fall 1979): 512–29.

39. Rosalind Rosenberg, *Beyond Separate Spheres: Intellectual Roots of Modern Feminism* (New Haven: Yale University Press, 1982), xxii, 208–9, 54; Dorr, *Woman of Fifty*, 101.

40. Ellen DuBois writes, "In all the feminist histories of this period [after 1920], sexual expression, not enfranchisement, was the redeeming goal of women's history" ("Making Women's History," 221–23).

To see changes in depictions of Willard in the pre- and postsuffrage eras, refer to Kate Sanborn, "Frances Willard," in *Our Famous Women. (An authorized and complete record of the lives and deeds of distinguished American women of our times)*, ed. Louisa C. Moulton (Hartford: A. D. Worthington, 1883), 692–714; Anna A. Gordon, *The Life of Frances E. Willard* (Evanston: National Woman's Christian Temperance Union, 1912); Ray Strachey, *Frances Willard: Her Life and Work* (New York: Fleming H. Revell, 1913); Lydia J. Trowbridge, *Frances Willard of Evanston* (Chicago: Willett, Clark, 1938).

41. Sanborn, "Frances Willard." Nineteenth-century biographies of Fuller include Julia Ward Howe, *Margaret Fuller (Marchesa Ossoli)* (Boston: Houghton Mifflin, 1884); T. W. Higginson, "Margaret Fuller," in *Eminent Women of the Age* (Hartford: Betts, 1869), 173–220; text cited from Kate Sanborn, "Margaret Fuller," in Moulton, *Our Famous Women*, 296.

42. Katharine Anthony, *Margaret Fuller: A Psychological Biography* (London: Jonathan Cape, 1920), iii–v, 22.

43. Anthony, *Margaret Fuller*, 80–82, iii–v. See also Katharine Anthony, *The Life of Mercy Otis Warren* (New York: Doubleday, 1958); Katharine Anthony, *Louisa May Alcott* (New York: Knopf, 1938); Katharine Anthony, *Susan B. Anthony: Her Personal History and Her Era* (New York: Doubleday, 1954). Katharine Anthony, coincidentally, was related to Susan B. Anthony, several times removed.

44. Emanie Sachs, *"The Terrible Siren": Victoria Woodhull, 1838–1927* (New York: Harper and Brothers, 1928), xi–xiv, 402, 413.

45. Inez Irwin to Maud Wood Park, 20 June 1929, container 17, reel 11, Irwin File, NAWSA Collection, LC.

46. Kathleen Barry, "Toward a Theory of Women's Biography: From the Life of Susan B. Anthony," in *All Sides of the Subject: Women and Biography*, ed. Teresa Iles (New York: Teachers College, 1992), 23.

47. Florence Kitchelt to Mary Beard, 27 July 1944; Beard to W. K. Jordan, 22 September 1944, box 2, folder 30, Mary Beard Papers, SL; Rosenberg, *Beyond Separate Spheres*, 209.

48. Dorr, *Susan B. Anthony*, 8, 220.

49. Ellen C. DuBois, *Harriot Stanton Blatch and the Winning of Woman Suffrage* (New Haven: Yale University Press, 1997), 246–48; Ford, *Iron-Jawed Angels*, 21.

50. Harper wrote, "Susan B. Anthony has been called the Napoleon of the woman suffrage movement and, in the planning of campaigns and the boldness and daring of carrying them forward, there may be qualities of that famous general, but in character and principles the comparison fails utterly. . . . It has been said that she has been the great Liberator of women, as Lincoln was the negroes. There is indeed something in her countenance and manner which reminds one of Lincoln" (*Life and Work*, 2:952).

51. "Report of the Susan B. Anthony Memorial Committee," n.d., box 1, folder 3, Beard Papers, SL.

52. Rheta Childe Dorr, "Susan B. Anthony Radio Address," 15 February 1935, box 4, folder 144, Jane Norman Smith Papers, SL; "Report of the Susan B. Anthony Memorial Committee," 3–4.

53. It is unclear why the money supposedly allocated by Congress was never put toward the Mount Rushmore project. Despite reports claiming that the monies were secured, Rose Powell tried for another nineteen years to fund Lincoln Borglum's renovation of the memorial. See Rose A. Powell, "Anthony Memorial," *Evening Star*, 1957; press release from Rose Arnold Powell, n.d.; Powell to President Eisenhower, 21 February 1959, box 6, folder 96a, Alma Lutz Papers, SL; Mrs. Robert Adamson, Chairman, "From the Susan B. Anthony Memorial Committee of the National Woman's Party," 20 January 1937, box 4, folder 144, Smith Papers, SL; Carrie C. Catt to Edna Stantial, 9 May 1945, Stantial File, NAWSA Collection, LC; Una Winter to Mary Beard, 28 February 1943; memorandum of the Susan B. Anthony Memorial Committee of California, n.d.; "Report of Susan B. Anthony Memorial Committee," n.d., box 1, folder 3; Memorandum of the "Susan B. Anthony Memorial Library," 1 February 1943; "Los Angeles Public Library Announces an Exhibit honoring the 124th Birthday of Susan B. Anthony," n.d.; "Susan B. Anthony Committee of California," n.d., box 1, folder 3, Beard Papers, SL.

54. This work was published in two volumes. Vol. 1 consisted of a foreword written by Blatch and Theodore Stanton, followed by a version of *Eighty Years and More* that Stanton revised but never published. Vol. 2 opened with Stanton's personal letters covering the period from 1839 to 1880. See Theodore Stanton and Harriot Stanton Blatch, eds., *Elizabeth Cady Stanton as Revealed in Her Letters, Diary, and Reminiscences*, 2 vols. (New York: Harper and Brothers, 1922; reprint, New York: Arno Press, 1969), 1:18, 185.

55. Stanton and Blatch, *Elizabeth Cady Stanton*, 1:11, 13, 15–16, 272–75.

56. Ibid., 272–75; Harper, *Life and Work*, 1:273, 2:600.

57. Blackwell, *Lucy Stone*, 206, 214–17, preface, 266–67, 98–99, 228–31, 226–28.

58. Ibid., 263, preface, 123, 138–41, 240; Marlene D. Merrill, ed., *Growing Up in Boston's Gilded Age: The Journal of Alice Stone Blackwell, 1872–1874* (New Haven: Yale University Press, 1990), 244.

59. That twentieth-century feminists approved of Stone's retention of her maiden name is evident in the establishment of the Lucy Stone League, a group consisting of married radical feminists who kept their maiden names. Heterodoxy member Ruth Hale started it when she married journalist Heywood Broun. Blackwell's and Stone's courtship and love letters are discussed in Blackwell, *Lucy Stone*, 160–61; on Stone's marriage and motherhood, see ibid., 195–204, esp. 198.

60. Maud W. Park, *Lucy Stone: A Chronicle Play* (Boston: Walter H. Baker, 1938); Mary Peck to Maud Wood Park, 8 May 1938, container 24, reel 16, Mary Peck File, NAWSA Collection, LC.

61. Mary G. Peck, *Carrie Chapman Catt: A Biography* (New York: H. W. Wilson, 1944); Mildred Adams to Mary Peck, 10 December 1947; Peck to Edna Stantial, 22 November 1951; Carrie C. Catt to Peck, n.d., container 24, reel 16, Peck File, NAWSA Collection, LC.

62. Stanton and Blatch, *Elizabeth Cady Stanton*, 1:154, 156; DuBois, *Elizabeth Cady Stanton and Susan B. Anthony*, 191.

63. Blatch and Lutz, *Challenging Years*, 13–14, 247–49; Lutz, *Created Equal*, 241–42, 212–21, 233, 161, 317. Lutz's biography vindicated Stanton in the Beecher-Tilton scandal and attributed the breach in confidence that started it indirectly to Anthony. Lutz also challenged Harper's charges that Stanton was the "leisurely member of the woman suffrage group" and even gave credit to Stanton for having an interest in the plight of working-class women, a claim most historians refute today.

64. Blatch and Lutz, *Challenging Years*, 247–49. Ellen DuBois maintains that Blatch was pleased with Lutz's work yet resented its positive attention paid to Anthony. Blatch's "historical vendetta against Anthony," DuBois writes, "created obstacles for Lutz in completing her book." See DuBois, *Harriot Stanton Blatch*, 257, 249–50; Mary Gawthorpe to Alma Lutz, 19 February 1940; Lutz to "Caroline," 26 March 1940, box 3, folder 33, Lutz Papers, SL.

65. The seven women inductees before Anthony were Mary Lyon, Emma Willard, Harriet Beecher Stowe, Maria Mitchell, Charlotte Cushman, Frances Willard, and Alice Freeman Palmer. In 1920 Anthony was only one vote away from induction. The vote tallies for the four suffragists nominated between 1900 and 1945 were as follows: Susan B. Anthony—46 in 1920, 55 in 1935, 40 in 1940, 40 in 1945; Elizabeth Cady Stanton—20 in 1920, 3 in 1935, 3 in 1940; Lucretia Mott—11 in 1900, 33 in 1905, 41 in 1910, 40 in 1915, 46 in 1920, 5 in 1935, 3 in 1940; Lucy Stone—10 in 1905, 7 in 1910, 40 in 1915, 12 in 1920. See Bertha Lyons to Florence Kitchelt, 23 May 1949; Mrs. George Howard to Kitchelt, 9 September 1950; *New York University Hall of Fame Record of the Results of the Ten Quinquennial Elections, 1900–1945, Showing Names Considered and Names Chosen by the Electors with Explanatory Addenda* (New York: Office of the Hall of Fame, n.d.), box 3, folder 60, Florence Kitchelt Papers, SL.

66. The ten women electors for the Hall of Fame in 1950 were Helen Keller, Anne O'Hare McCormick, Edna St. Vincent Millay, Helen Rodgers Reid, Dorothy Thompson, Ruth Bryan Rhode, Sarah Blanding, Berenice Brown Cronkhite, Katharine McBride, and Florence Allen. See Bertha Lyons to Florence Kitchelt, 6 September 1950; Kitchelt to Lyons, 11 August, 2 November 1950; Mrs. George Howard to Kitchelt, 28 August, 29 October 1950; "Copy of a joint letter sent to all Electors of the Hall of Fame by Past Presidents of the National Education Association as an Appeal for the Election of SBA," 19 September 1945; Kitchelt to Alice Clement, 21 August 1950; Kitchelt to Dr. Harry Woodburn Chase, 6 May 1949, box 3, folder 60, Kitchelt Papers, SL.

67. Martha Taylor Howard to the Electors of the Hall of Fame, 12 July 1950, box 3, folder 60, Kitchelt Papers, SL.

68. Florence Kitchelt to Dean Eunice Hilton, 15 August 1950; Bertha Lyons to Kitchelt, 13 November 1950; Mrs. George Howard to Kitchelt, 9 September 1950; "Six

Elected to Hall of Fame," *New York Times*, 2 November 1950, box 3, folder 60, Kitchelt Papers, SL.

69. Anthony, *Susan B. Anthony*, 67, 124, 143, 144.

70. Alma Lutz to Rose Arnold Powell, 26 May 1958, 8 May 1959, box 6, folder 96a, Lutz Papers, SL. Lutz's book was published as *Susan B. Anthony: Rebel, Crusader, and Humanitarian*.

71. Mary Beard to Ethel Adamson, 21 April 1941; Florence Bayard Hilles to Archibald MacLeish, 20 May 1941; Alma Lutz to Jessie Ash Arndt, 6 November 1941, box 3, file 34, Lutz Papers, SL.

72. Patricia M. King, "Forty Years of Collecting on Women: The Arthur and Elizabeth Schlesinger Library on the History of Women in America, Radcliffe College," *Special Collections: Women's Collections, Libraries, Archives, and Consciousness* 3 (Spring/Summer 1986), 76–77; Madeleine B. Perez, " 'Remember the Ladies . . .': The Arthur and Elizabeth Schlesinger Library on the History of Women in America: Its Role in the Collection and Preservation of Women's History Source Materials" (master's thesis, Wake Forest University, 1982 [in Manuscripts Division, SL]), 25–39.

73. Inez Irwin to Maud Wood Park, 29 July 1938, container 17, reel 11; Irwin to Park, 12 August 1943, container 18, reel 11, Irwin File, NAWSA Collection, LC.

74. Carrie C. Catt to W. K. Jordan, 13 November 1944, box 1, folder 10, Beard Papers, SL. Catt's vision for consolidating materials is also described in a letter from Edna Stantial to Mary Peck, 23 October 1951, Peck File, NAWSA Collection, LC.

75. Mary Peck to Edna Stantial, 14 January 1948; Stantial to Carrie C. Catt, 6 October 1941; "M. G. Peck's first draft of a letter suggested as appeal for funds for preservation of Feminist Archives," n.d., Peck File, NAWSA Collection, LC.

76. Edna Stantial to Mary Peck, 19 December 1951; Peck to Eleanor Flexner, n.d. 1956; Stantial to Peck, 13 May 1951; Peck to Stantial, 4 June 1947, 15 May 1949, Peck File, NAWSA Collection, LC.

77. Edna Stantial to Carrie C. Catt, 6 October 1941, Peck File, NAWSA Collection, LC.

78. Edna Stantial to Mary Peck, 13 May 1951, Peck File; Brick Row Book Shop to Stantial, 1 June 1943; Anna Lord Strauss to Stantial, 23 April 1952, Stantial File, NAWSA Collection, LC.

79. Carrie C. Catt to Edna Stantial, October 1941, Stantial File, NAWSA Collection, LC.

80. Mary E. Dillon to Mary Peck, 12 June 1947; Caroline Reilly to Peck, 10 June 1947; Peck to Edna Stantial, 15 May 1949, 4 June 1947, Peck File, NAWSA Collection, LC.

81. Mary Peck to Edna Stantial, 7 August 1952, 28, 14 February 1951, Peck File, NAWSA Collection, LC.

82. Mary Peck to Maud Wood Park and Edna Stantial, 25 March 1950, Peck File; Alice Stone Blackwell to Stantial, 4 October 1940, Stantial File, NAWSA Collection, LC.

83. Edna Stantial to Mary Peck, 18 February 1951, Peck File, NAWSA Collection, LC.

84. Ibid.; Elizabeth Borden, "Report on a conversation with Mrs. Guy W. Stantial," 16 April 1951, Schlesinger Library Office Files, SL; Carrie C. Catt to Edna Stantial, October 1941, Stantial File, NAWSA Collection, LC. Beard convinced Blatch to

deposit her papers in the Library of Congress in 1928. See DuBois, *Harriot Stanton Blatch*, 266.

85. Mary Peck to Maud Wood Park, 12 August 1950, Peck File, NAWSA Collection, LC.

86. Mary Peck to Edna Stantial, 15 May 1949; Stantial to Peck, 23 October 1951, Peck File, NAWSA Collection, LC.

87. Edna Stantial to Mary Peck, 18 February 1951, Peck File, NAWSA Collection, LC.

88. Edna Stantial to Mary Peck, 13 May 1951, 4 June 1947; Peck to Stantial and Maud Wood Park, n.d.; Stantial to Peck, 14 September 1953; Peck to Stantial and Park, 22 August 1947; Peck to Stantial, 28 February, 22 November 1951, Peck File; Margaret Grierson to Stantial, 12 April 1961, container 28, reel 19, Stantial File, NAWSA Collection, LC.

89. Mary Peck to Edna Stantial, 28 October 1951; Stantial to Peck, 14 September 1953; Peck to Stantial, 25 May 1950, Peck File, NAWSA Collection, LC.

90. Stantial's efforts to collect personal papers had been thwarted on multiple occasions by families and executors. Moreover, she and Peck wrote of occasions when they denied researchers, including Alma Lutz, access to documents because they knew they would ignite controversies Catt and other pioneers never wanted disclosed to biographers. See Alma Lutz to Mary Peck, 24 November 1950, container 19, reel 12, Lutz Papers; Peck to Edna Stantial, 28 February 1951; Stantial to Peck, 19 December, 18 February 1951, Peck File, NAWSA Collection, LC.

91. Edna Stantial to Mary Peck, 18 February 1951, 18 March 1952; Peck to Maud Wood Park, 12 August 1950; "M. G. Peck's first draft of letter suggested as appeal for funds for preservation of Feminist Archives"; Stantial to Peck, 23 October 1951, Peck File, NAWSA Collection, LC. See also DuBois, *Harriot Stanton Blatch*, 271.

92. Ida Harper to Mary Peck, 13 July 1938; Peck to Edna Stantial, 28 February 1951, 8 May 1952, Peck File, NAWSA Collection, LC.

93. Edna Stantial to Mary Peck, 18 February 1951, 8 January 1948, 18 March 1952, Peck File; Ronald Schaffer to Stantial, 3 February 1959, container 28, reel 19, Stantial File; Inez Irwin to Stantial, 23 May 1960, container 17, reel 11, Irwin File, NAWSA Collection, LC.

94. Eleanor Flexner, *Century of Struggle: The Woman's Rights Movement in the United States* (Cambridge: Belknap Press, 1959); Eleanor Flexner to Mary Peck, 8 December 1955, Mary Peck Papers, NAWSA Collection, LC. For examples of researchers being unable to locate Catt's papers, see Lola Walker to Mary Peck, 29 November 1948; Edna Stantial to Peck, 2 February 1949; Eleanor Flexner to Peck, 11 November 1955, 2 February 1956, Peck File; Mrs. Maurice Noun to Stantial, 25 May 1961, container 28, reel 19, Stantial File, NAWSA Collection, LC.

95. Edna Stantial to Mary Peck, 14 September 1953, Peck File, NAWSA Collection, LC.

96. Inez Irwin to Maud Wood Park, 15 April 1933; Irwin to Carrie C. Catt, 22 March 1933, Irwin File, NAWSA Collection, LC.

97. Inez Irwin to Maud Wood Park, 15 April 1933, Irwin File, NAWSA Collection, LC.

98. Inez H. Irwin, *Angels and Amazons: A Hundred Years of American Women* (Garden City, N.Y.: Doubleday, Doran, 1933); Inez Irwin to Maud Wood Park, 15 April 1933, Irwin File, NAWSA Collection, LC.

99. Inez Irwin to Carrie C. Catt, 22 March, 8 April 1933; Irwin to Maud Wood Park, 23 March, 8 April 1933, Irwin File, NAWSA Collection, LC.

100. Inez Irwin to Carrie C. Catt, 22 March 1933; Irwin to Maud Wood Park, 15 April 1933, 1 August 1933, Irwin File, NAWSA Collection, LC.

101. Inez Irwin to Carrie C. Catt, 22 March 1933; Irwin to Maud Wood Park, 15 April 1933, Irwin File, NAWSA Collection, LC.

102. Inez Irwin to Carrie C. Catt, 22 March 1933, Irwin File, NAWSA Collection, LC.

103. Ibid., 8 April 1933.

CHAPTER 7

1. Oral History of Viola Barnes, 1972, *Mount Holyoke in the Twentieth Century*, MHASC, 15; Jacqueline Goggin, "Challenging Sexual Discrimination in the Historical Profession: Women Historians and the American Historical Association, 1890–1940," series 6, box 16, Berkshire Conference on the History of Women Collection, SL, 8–9.

2. Louise Fargo Brown, "Brief History of the Berkshire Conference," 1951, box 1, folder 1; Louise Loomis to Vera Brown, 18 February 1931, box 1, folder 2, Berkshire Conference of Women Historians Papers, SL.

3. Viola Barnes, "Early History of Berkshire History Group," Fall 1976, series 4, folder 49, Viola Barnes Papers, MHASC, 1–2; Margaret A. Judson, *Breaking the Barrier: A Professional Autobiography by a Woman Educator and Historian before the Women's Movement* (New Brunswick: Rutgers University Press, 1984), 78, 80–82.

4. Lakeville History Conference Reports of the Secretary, May 1932, 1933, box 1, folder 3, Berkshire Conference Papers, SL; Kathryn Kish Sklar, "American Female Historians in Context, 1770–1930," *Feminist Studies* 3 (Fall 1975): 182; Beatrice Reynolds to Viola Barnes, 14 April 1937, series 4, box 15, folder 47, Barnes Papers, MHASC.

5. Viola Barnes to Beatrice Reynolds, 4 May 1937; Katharine Blunt to Reynolds, 13 May 1937, series 4, box 15, folder 45; Elsie Van Dyck De Witt to Mary Woolley, 21 February 1936, series 4, box 15, folder 47, Barnes Papers, MHASC.

6. Vera Lee Brown, Louise Ropes Loomis, and Louise Fargo Brown to Professor Brown, 16 March 1931, box 1, folder 2, Berkshire Conference Papers, SL.

7. Anne Burlingame's response to "Inquiry Concerning the Proposition to Establish a System of Exchange Professions of Women Teachers in Colleges and Universities," 1931 (unnumbered responses attached to above letter), box 1, folder 2, Berkshire Conference Papers, SL.

8. "Report of the Secretary, Berkshire Historical Conference," 1936–37, series 4, box 15, folder 47, Barnes Papers, MHASC.

9. Sandi Cooper to Helena Lewis, Mildred Campbell, Mary Dunn, Beatrice Hyslop, Jane Ruby, and Emiliana Noether, 14 May 1973, Berkshire Conference Histories, box 1, folder 1; Helen Young and Dorothy Ganfield Fowler to Berkshire Members, 30 May 1941, box 1, folder 4, Berkshire Conference Papers, SL.

10. "The Meeting of the American Historical Association at Cleveland," 25 April 1920, 389–90; Program for the American Historical Association 51st Annual Meeting, Providence, R.I., 29–31 December 1936. Also see the correspondence between Viola Barnes and Kathleen Bruce about the selection process for the Dunning Prize, series 4, box 15, folder 45, Barnes Papers, MHASC. Women's early progress on AHA com-

mittees is also discussed in Jacqueline Goggin, "Challenging Sexual Discrimination in the Historical Profession: Women Historians and the American Historical Association, 1890–1940," *AHR* 97 (June 1992): 788–92.

11. Goggin, "Challenging Sexual Discrimination," Berkshire Conference on the History of Women Collection, SL, 21.

12. Beatrice Reynolds and Emily Hickman to Berkshire Conference members, 9 June 1939, box 1, folder 3; "Report of the Secretary, Berkshire History Conference," 17–19 May 1940; Hickman and Dorothy Fowler to Berkshire Conference members, 23 May 1940; Fowler to Members, 9 June 1940; Fowler to Professor Lawrence Packard, 3 November 1940, box 1, folder 4, Berkshire Conference Papers, SL.

13. In the end the program chair abandoned the plan for a panel on women in ancient civilizations, telling the Berkshire Conference secretary that the papers of Berkshire submitters were "descriptive treatments only," not "interpretive." See Stanley Pargellis to Dorothy Ganfield Fowler, 6, 19, 27 March 1942, box 1, folder 4, Berkshire Conference Papers, SL; Goggin, "Challenging Sex Discrimination," Berkshire Conference on the History of Women Collection, SL, 7–8, 21.

14. Curtis P. Nettels to Dorothy Ganfield Fowler, 19 March 1941; "Report of the Secretary, May 1941–May 1942," box 1, folder 4, Berkshire Conference Papers, SL.

15. Goggin, "Challenging Sexual Discrimination," Berkshire Conference on the History of Women Collection, SL, 15, 21–28.

16. Mary Beard to Dr. Fannie Fern Andrews, 21 April 1940, box 2, folder 19; "World Center for Women's Archives: Archive Projects and their present status," 6 March 1940; "Project Report," WCWA, 13 November 1939; "WCWA Projects for collection of archives," 18 July 1940; "World Center of Women's Archives: Desired Materials"; "A Partial List of Desirable Archives," n.d., box 1, folder 1; "Research Suggestions," n.d., box 2, folder 22, Mary Beard Papers, SL.

17. "Suggestions for Women's Faculty Club, re: Search for Archives," n.d.; "Delta Kappa Gamma Research Project: Outstanding Women who have Rendered Great Service to American Education," n.d.; Sarah A. Marble to Mary Beard, 25 March 1940, box 2, folder 19; "Partial List of Desirable Archives as Types," box 1, folder 1, Beard Papers, SL; Beard to Marjorie White, 25 March 1940, box 26, vol. 150a, Marjorie White Papers, SL.

18. A description of Schwimmer's original collection can be found in "The Schwimmer-Lloyd Collection," *Bulletin of the New York Public Library*, May 1943. (A copy of a reprinted leaflet can be found in box 1, folder 16, Beard Papers, SL.)

19. Rosika Schwimmer to Hannah Clothier Hull, 13 March 1936; Hull to Schwimmer, 19 March 1936, box 1, folder 18; "Some Biographical Data of Rosika Schwimmer," n.d., box 2, folder 23, Beard Papers, SL; Suzanne Hildenbrand and Edyth Wynner, "Women for Peace: The Schwimmer-Lloyd Collection of the New York Public Library," *Special Collections: Women's Collections, Libraries, Archives, and Consciousness* 3 (Spring/Summer 1986): 39–40; Barbara K. Turoff, *Mary Ritter Beard as Force in History* (Dayton, Ohio: Wright State University Monograph Series, 1979), 52–53; Nancy Cott, ed., *A Woman Making History: Mary Ritter Beard* (New Haven: Yale University Press, 1991), 128; "Talk by Mrs. Mary R. Beard at the November Meeting of the World Center for Women's Archives," 14 November 1938, box 26, vol. 150a, White Papers, SL.

20. "World Center for Women's Archives" (outline written by Rosika Schwimmer), enclosure in letter from Mary Beard to Florence Rose, 21 June 1937, box 2,

Florence Rose Papers, SSC; statement of purpose in *Pamphlet for the World Center for Women's Archives*, n.d., container 17, reel 11, Inez Irwin file, NAWSA Collection, LC; *World Center for Women's Archives*, pamphlet, n.d., box 26, vol. 150a, White Papers, SL.

21. Mary Kathleen Trigg, "Four American Feminists, 1910–1940: Inez Haynes Irwin, Mary Ritter Beard, Doris Stevens, and Lorine Pruette" (Ph.D. diss., Brown University, 1989), 289–92; Mary Beard to Margaret Grierson, 15 July 1945, box 1, Mary R. Beard Papers, SSC; Beard to Georgina Hinckley, 30 July 1944, box 2, folder 30; "Call for Papers," n.d., box 1, folder 1, Beard Papers, SL; WCWA pamphlet, Irwin file, NAWSA Collection, LC; Beard to Marjorie White, 23, 27 January 1939, box 26, vol. 150a, White Papers, SL.

22. "World Center for Women's Archives" (outline), Rose Papers, SSC; Barbara Turoff, "An Introduction to Mary Beard: Feminist and Historian" (master's thesis, Wright State University, 1978), 95–99.

23. WCWA, "Desirable Materials," box 1, folder 1, Beard Papers, SL.

24. Mary Beard to Martha Moore, 14 May 1938; Beard to Ellen Glasgow, 7 October 1938, box 2, folder 28; "Directions for State Chairman of the Archives Committee," n.d., box 1, folder 1, Beard Papers, SL.

25. "Call for Private Papers," n.d., box 1, folder 1; WCWA *Bulletin*, February 1940, box 1, folder 2, Beard Papers, SL.

26. Mary Beard, "Directions for State Chairman of the Archives Committee," n.d., box 1, folder 1, Beard Papers, SL; *World Center for Women's Archives*, pamphlet, n.d., box 26, vol. 150a, White Papers, SL; pamphlet for WCWA, n.d., container 17, reel 11, Irwin file, NAWSA Collection, LC.

27. Mary Beard to Nancy Cox-McCormack, 21 April 1940, box 2, Nancy Cox-McCormack Papers, SSC; "Brief Report of World Center for Women's Archives," 13 November 1939, box 1, folder 2; WCWA *Bulletin*, February 1940; "World Center for Women's Archives, Inc., Archives Received," 15 January 1940 to 15 May 1940, box 1, folder 5, Beard Papers, SL.

28. "World Center for Women's Archives, District of Columbia Archives, Committee of the DC State Branch Organization," n.d., box 1, folder 1; "Brief Report of World Center for Women's Archives," 13 November 1939, box 1, folder 2, Beard Papers, SL.

29. Mary Beard to Rosika Schwimmer, 14 February 1936, box 1, part 2, Schwimmer-Lloyd Collection, New York Public Library (reprinted in Cott, *Woman Making History*, 144); "Suggested Activities at Indiana University in Behalf of World Center for Women's Archives," n.d.; "World Center for Women's Archives: Archives Projects and their Present Status," 6 March 1940, box 1, folder 1; "Program for Research Activity Planned by Special Request of Camp Fire Girls," 1939; "Women of Achievement for the Older Camp Fire Girls," Americana Project, 1939, box 2, folder 22, Beard Papers, SL.

30. "Letters Expressing Interest in WCWA," n.d.; Mary H. Burrell to Inez Haynes Irwin, 20 February 1936, box 1, folder 18; Mary Beard to W. K. Jordan, 20 January 1944, box 2, folder 30; Ellen Eastman to WCWA, in "Letters and Newstories Indicating Need for Center" (sec. 5 of "Application from World Center for Women's Archives"), box 1, folder 1; Emma May to Irwin, 20 November 1939, box 1, folder 10, Beard Papers, SL; Beard to Marjorie White, 8 February 1939, box 26, vol. 150a, White Papers, SL.

31. "Projects to procure documents launched by World Center for Women's Ar-

chives," n.d., box 1, folder 1; Isabel Lopez Fages to Mary Beard, 17 April 1940; Beard to Mrs. Alphonse Fages, 1 May 1940, box 2, folder 19, Beard Papers, SL.

32. "Talk by Mrs. Mary R. Beard," 14 November 1938, box 26, vol. 150b, White Papers, SL; "Plan for Building Up the Archives Collection USA," box 1, folder 1, Beard Papers, SL.

33. Mary Beard to Te Ata, 23 June 1939; to Gladys Tantaquidgeon, 6 April 1938, box 2, folder 19, Beard Papers, SL.

34. For a discussion of the distinctions between etic and emic analyses and their application to Indian history, see Peter Novick, *That Noble Dream: The "Objectivity Question" and the American Historical Profession* (New York: Cambridge University Press, 1988), 548–55; Mary Beard to Ella Deloria, 31 August 1938; to Miss Knight, 6 June 1938, box 2, folder 19, Beard Papers, SL.

35. "Projects to procure documents launched by World Center for Women's Archives," n.d.; Ester Boorman Strong to WCWA, 7 December 1937, box 2, folder 22; Julietta Kahn to Ruth Savord, 2 October 1936, box 2, folder 19, Beard Papers, SL.

36. Florence Frank to Mary Beard, 11 May 1939, box 2, folder 19, Beard Papers, SL.

37. Mary Beard, "Women in Long History," n.d., box 26, vol. 150c, White Papers, SL; Mary Beard, "In Pioneer Days," *Independent Woman*, September 1939, 288–90; Mary Beard to W. K. Jordan, 14 January 1944, box 2, folder 30, Beard Papers, SL. Beard used letters of coal mining women in *America through Women's Eyes* to discredit masculine characterizations of mining culture and frontier life. See also "Partial List of Desirable Archives as Types," Beard Papers, SL; Beard to Margaret Grierson, 11 March 1951, box 1, Beard Papers, SSC.

38. Mary Beard to Margaret Grierson, 22 June 194[5?], box 1, Beard Papers, SSC; "WCWA Projects for collection of archives," Beard Papers, SL.

39. Mary Beard to Juanita Mitchell, 1 March 1939; Monroe N. Work to Beard, 17 February 1936; Sadie Daniel St. Clair to Beard, 10 December 1939; Marjorie White to Mary McLeod Bethune, 28 November 1938; Bethune to White, December 1938, box 1, folder 17, Beard Papers, SL. Bettye Collier Thomas notes that although the WCWA had two African American sponsors before 1938, throughout its five-year existence the archive never maintained African American women on its board of directors. See Collier-Thomas, "Towards Black Feminism: The Creation of the Bethune Museum-Archives," *Special Collections: Women's Collections, Libraries, Archives, and Consciousness*, 3 (Spring/Summer 1986): 44.

40. "World Center for Women's Archives: Archive Projects and their present status"; "Plan for Building Up the Archives Collection USA," n.d., box 1, folder 1; Jan Gay to Mary Beard, 18 April 1940; Gay to Eva Hansl, 1 August 1940, box 2, folder 19; Beard Papers, SL; Beard to Marjorie White, 18 March 1939, box 26, vol. 150a, White Papers, SL; Beard to Florence Rose, 21 June 1937, box 2, Rose Papers, SSC.

41. Sec. 3 of "Application from World Center for Women's Archives," box 1, folder 1; "World Center for Women's Archives, Archives Received," 15 January 1940, box 1, folder 5, Beard Papers, SL.

42. Marjorie White, "1940: Corporation of the World Center for Women's Archives Dissolved," n.d., box 26, volume 150a, White Papers, SL.

43. Ibid. Abby Rockefeller agreed to donate $1,000 when the WCWA first opened, provided that the balance of its initial $6,500 budget could be raised. See Abby Rockefeller to Jeanette Nichols, 29 April 1937, box 2, folder 28, Beard Papers, SL.

44. Mary Beard to Marjorie White, 27 January 1939, box 26, vol. 150a, White Papers, SL; "Call for Private Papers," n.d., box 1, folder 1, Beard Papers, SL.

45. Mary Beard to W. K. Jordan, 2 July 1944, box 2, folder 30, Beard Papers, SL.

46. Beard articulated this critique of equal rights feminism in many writings, including *Woman as Force in History* (New York: Macmillan, 1946).

47. Turoff, "Introduction to Mary Beard," 100; Mary Beard to Alice Stone Blackwell, 29 July, 10 December 1938, container 3, reel 2, NAWSA Collection, LC; Beard to Margaret Grierson, 15 July 1945, box 1, Beard Papers, SSC.

48. Dorothy Canfield Fisher to Dr. Fosdick, 16 May 1939, box 2, folder 28, Beard Papers, SL. Beard's separatism is also explored in Anne Lane, ed., *Mary Ritter Beard: A Sourcebook* (Boston: Northeastern University Press, 1988), 35.

49. Mary Beard to Dorothy Porter, 21 February 1940, box 1, folder 17, Beard Papers, SL. The tensions over race in the Washington unit are analyzed more thoroughly in Collier-Thomas, "Towards Black Feminism," 44–53; Turoff, "Introduction to Mary Beard," 112–13; Turoff, *Mary Ritter Beard as Force*, 61–62; Cott, *Woman Making History*, 195–201.

50. Mary Beard to Dr. Stroh, 22 June 1941, box 2, folder 19, Beard Papers, SL.

51. Mary Beard to Harriot Stanton Blatch, 2 January 1937, Alma Lutz Biographical, box 4, Alma Lutz Collection, Vassar College (letter in Cott, *Woman Making History*, 164); Beard to Margaret Grierson, 8 November 1948, 20 October 1945, box 1, Beard Papers, SSC; Beard to Nancy Cushman, 10 August 1945, box 2, Nancy Cushman Papers, SSC.

CHAPTER 8

1. *The Schwimmer-Lloyd Collection*, leaflet (reprinted from *Bulletin of the New York Public Library*, May 1943), box 1, folder 16; Carrie C. Catt to Mary Beard, 10 November 1936, 22 April 1938, box 1, folder 10; Beard to W. K. Jordan, 14 January 1944, box 2, folder 30, Mary Beard Papers, SL.

2. Mary Beard to Margaret Grierson, 15 July 1945, 22 June 194?, 27 June 1945; Eva Hansl to Laura Quinlan, 22 November 1940, box 1, Mary R. Beard Papers, SSC; Beard to Hansl, 12 August 1941, box 1, Eva Hansl Papers, SSC; Beard to Nancy Cushman, 10 August 1945, Nancy Cushman Papers, SSC; Beard to Marjorie White, 24 November 1940, box 26, vol. 150a; "Women Archives Given to Colleges," 24 November 1940; memorandum, WCWA, 25 November 1940, box 26, volume 150b; Beard to Grierson, 18 January 1941, box 27, vol. 154, Marjorie White Papers, SL; Alice Stone Blackwell to Beard, 28 October 1940, box 1, folder 10, Beard Papers, SL. Several of the women's collections that were established in the 1940s are highlighted in *Special Collections: Women's Collections, Libraries, Archives, and Consciousness* 3 (Spring/Summer 1986).

3. Florence Murray, ed., *The Negro Handbook* (New York: Wendell Malliet, 1942), 250; "Negro Women's Archives," *Aframerican Woman's Journal*, Summer/Fall 1940, 29; Bettye Collier-Thomas, "Towards Black Feminism: The Creation of the Bethune Museum-Archives," *Special Collections: Women's Collections, Libraries, Archives, and Consciousness* 3 (Spring/Summer 1986): 52. Examples of the first historical articles in the *Aframerican*, Summer/Fall 1940, include "A Course in Progression with Dates of Achievements," 30–31; "Cameos in Heritage," 33; Mary C. Terrell, "History of the Club Movement," 34–38; "Negro Women's Archives," 29.

4. Dorothy Porter, "Report of the Archives Committee of the National Council of

Negro Women," 17 October 1941, in Linda Henry, "Promoting Historical Consciousness: The Early Archives Committee of the National Council of Negro Women," Linda Henry Articles File, NABWH, 257–58. Henry's article was also printed in *Signs: Journal of Women in Culture and Society* 7 (Autumn 1981): 251–59.

5. Trudi Smith, *Sue Bailey Thurman: Building Bridges to Common Ground* (Boston: Trustees of Boston University, 1995), 12–18; Linda Henry, "Documentation Projects: The National Archives for Black Women's History" (paper delivered at "Black Women: An Historical Perspective," 12 November 1979, in Linda Henry Articles File, NABWH), 2; Henry, "Promoting Historical Consciousness," 252–54; Collier-Thomas, "Towards Black Feminism," 53–56; "Proposed National Archives Day," 2 June 1946, series 5, box 4, folder 2, NABWH.

6. The Fall 1946 issue of *Aframerican* is quoted in Henry, "Documentation Projects," 2.

7. "Proposed National Archives Day."

8. Sue B. Thurman and Lucy Schulte, "On This We Stand," radio script, WWDC, Washington, D.C., 29 June 1946, series 5, box 4, NABWH.

9. "Proposed National Archives Day"; Vivian Mason to Mary McLeod Bethune, 20 May 1946, series 5, box 4, folder 2, NABWH.

10. W. K. Jordan to Mary Beard, 11 December 1943, box 2, folder 30, Beard Papers, SL.

11. Mary Beard to W. K. Jordan, 14 January, 23 June 1944, box 2, folder 30, Beard Papers, SL.

12. Mary Beard attracted to Radcliffe many important collections relating to women and labor, notably materials from the WTUL, Leonora O'Reilly, and the National Consumer's League. See "Gifts of Mrs. Charles A. Beard to Radcliffe Library," 9 June 1944; Mary Beard to W. K. Jordan, 14 January, 23 June 1944, 5 November 1945; Beard to Georgiana Hinckley, 7 June, 2 July 1944; Nancy Cushman to Beard, n.d.; Elizabeth Cotten to Beard, 20 July 1944, box 2, folder 30, Beard Papers, SL.

13. W. K. Jordan to Carrie C. Catt, 7 November 1944, box 1, folder 10; Jordan to Mary Beard, 20 November 1944, box 2, folder 30, Beard Papers, SL; Jordan to Whitney Fund, 16 November 1944, Women's Archive Office, SL; Madeleine B. Perez, " 'Remember the Ladies . . .': The Arthur and Elizabeth Schlesinger Library on the History of Women in America: Its Role in the Collection and Preservation of Women's History Source Materials" (master's thesis, Wake Forest University, 1982 [in Manuscripts Division, SL]), 39; Beard to Nancy Cushman, 10 September 1945, box 2, Cushman Papers, SSC; Beard to Marjorie White, 1 May 1946, box 27, vol. 154, White Papers, SL.

14. Jordan budgeted $60,000 for this research program, with plans to match this sum for the next five years. See W. K. Jordan to Mary Beard, 30 June 1944, box 2, folder 30; "Plan for Advanced Research for Women," n.d., box 2, folder 21, Beard Papers, SL.

15. Mary Beard to Elizabeth Borden, 8 February 1951; to Marine Leland, 8 February 1951, box 1, Beard Papers, SSC; Beard to W. K. Jordan, 25 August 1945, box 2, folder 30, Beard Papers, SL. In *New Viewpoints in American History* (New York: Macmillan, 1922), Arthur Schlesinger criticized academic historians for ignoring women in their histories. He took the *Dictionary of American Biography* to task for its neglect of women in history in a series of articles in the *AHR*, most notably in the July 1937 edition (p. 771). See also Patricia M. King, "Forty Years of Collecting on

Women: The Arthur and Elizabeth Schlesinger Library on the History of Women in America, Radcliffe College," *Special Collections: Women's Collections, Libraries, Archives, and Consciousness* 3 (Spring/Summer 1986): 77.

16. Mary Beard to Margaret Grierson, 20 October 1945; to Marine Leland, 8 February 1951; to Sarah Blanding, 21 November 1950, box 1, Beard Papers, SSC; Beard to Marjorie White, 9 February 1953, box 4, vol. 23, White Papers, SL; "The Historical Approach to Learning about Women," 22 May 1944, box 1, folder 7; Beard to W. K. Jordan, 14 January 1944, box 2, folder 30, Beard Papers, SL.

17. Mary Beard, *A Changing Political Economy as It Affects Women* (Washington, D.C.: AAUW, 1934), 7.

18. Edna Stantial to Edna Slade, 10 April 1943; "Plan for the Woman's Rights Collection at Radcliffe College," container 28, reel 19, Edna Stantial File, NAWSA Collection, LC; Perez, " 'Remember the Ladies,' " 30–34.

19. There were materials in this first section of the Woman's Rights Collection that were older than the Seneca Falls documents, such as personal papers of Anne Hutchinson. Nevertheless, Beard criticized the collection's emphasis on legal status. Beard's "1848 narrative" was thus not a strictly chronological distinction but one of feminist ideology. See Perez, " 'Remember the Ladies,' " 31–32.

20. Mary Beard to W. K. Jordan, 14 January 1944, box 2, folder 30, Beard Papers, SL.

21. Mary Beard to Margery Steer, 5 August 1954, box 2, Marjorie Steer Papers, SSC; Beard to Margaret Grierson, 22 June 194?, box 1, Beard Papers, SSC.

22. Mary E. Murdock, "Exploring Women's Lives: Historical and Contemporary Resources in the College Archives and the Sophia Smith Collection at Smith College," *Special Collections: Women's Collections, Libraries, Archives, and Consciousness* 3 (Spring/Summer 1986): 68–70.

23. Mary Beard to Margaret Grierson, 1 August 1946, 26 March 1950, 14 October 1944, 28 October 1945, 8 February 1948, 12 May, 11 April 1943, 11 March 1951, 28 October, 1 November 1949, box 1, Beard Papers, SSC.

24. Mary Beard to Margaret Grierson, 12 May 1943, 4 May 1951, 26 October 1945, box 1, Beard Papers, SSC.

25. Although Beard wanted Freud's works in the collection, she advised that undergraduates not have access to them. She wrote Grierson, "Here are the volumes I bought in Vienna in 1927 written by psychologists with medical practice, having German titles, and being the books which should certainly be reserved for use only by accredited scholars able to study them in the quest for knowledge of how deep into the mire Freudians could sink." See Mary Beard to Margaret Grierson, 9, 2 February 1950, box 1, Beard Papers, SSC; Beard to Marjorie White, 29 March 1948, box 27, vol. 154, White Papers, SL.

26. Mary Beard to Margaret Grierson, 28 May 1947, box 1, Beard Papers, SSC.

27. Mary Beard to Elizabeth Borden, 8 February 1951, box 1, Beard Papers, SSC.

28. Mary Beard to Margaret Grierson, 24 March 1955, 4 March, 24 April 1951, box 1, Beard Papers, SSC.

29. The titles of some of these papers were "The Status of Women in Business and the Professions in America before 1800" and "Women in Organized Religion, 1860–1900." Lutz also gave several papers on the life of Susan B. Anthony. See Radcliffe College Seminar on Women papers, 1952–59, SL.

30. Edna Stantial to Mary Peck, 23 October 1951, container 24, reel 16, Mary Peck file, NAWSA Collection, LC; Perez, " 'Remember the Ladies,' " 58.

31. Mary Beard to Margaret Grierson, 15 July 1945, 26 March, 5 May 1948, box 1, Beard Papers, SSC. Barbara Turoff analyzes the growing disinterest in Beard's plan for women's education in "An Introduction to Mary Beard: Feminist and Historian" (master's thesis, Wright State University, 1978), 125–27.

32. Mary Beard to Margaret Grierson, 20 October 1945, box 1, Beard Papers, SSC; Mildred McAfee to Glenna Tinnin, 1 June 1938, box 2, folder 28, Beard Papers, SL.

33. Mary Beard to Margaret Grierson, 19 October 1947, 3 February 1948, box 1, Beard Papers, SSC.

34. Mary Beard to Margaret Grierson, 15 July 1945; to Sarah Blanding, 21 November 1950, box 1, Beard Papers, SSC; Beard to W. K. Jordan, 20 January 1944, box 2, folder 30, Beard Papers, SL.

35. Mary Beard to Margaret Grierson, 22 June 194?, box 1, Beard Papers, SSC.

36. Beard quoted in Nancy Cott, ed., *A Woman Making History: Mary Ritter Beard* (New Haven: Yale University Press, 1991), 3–4; Mary Beard to Margaret Grierson, 6 March 1944, box 1, Beard Papers, SSC.

37. Mary Beard and Martha Bensley Bruere, eds., *Laughing Their Way: Women's Humor in America* (New York: Macmillan, 1934); Mary Beard to Marine Leland, 8 April 1950, 17 February 1951; Beard to Margaret Grierson, 28 May 1947, 17 January 1951, box 1, Beard Papers, SSC.

38. Lorine Pruette, "Speaking of Women, She Says 'Tain't So!,'" *New York Herald Tribune Weekly Book Review*, 17 March 1946.

39. Mary Beard, "Feminism as a Social Phenomenon," in *Women Take Stock of Themselves* (New York: Woman's Press, 1940), 6–7.

40. Mary Beard, "Women and Social Crisis," pt. 1, *Independent Woman*, November 1934, 347, 362; pt. 3, January 1935, 8; Mary Beard to Margaret Grierson, 6 August 1947, box 1, Beard Papers, SSC; Beard, *Changing Political Economy as It Affects Women*, 6–7.

41. Ella Winter, "Eve's Numerous Daughters," *Saturday Review*, n.d. 1946, box 26, vol. 150a; James H. Hexter, "The Ladies Were There All the Time," *New York Book Review*, 17 March 1946, box 26, vol. 150e, White Papers, SL.

42. Stephen Peabody, "Fools Gold for Women," publication unknown, 14 April 1946; Hexter, "Ladies Were There All the Time."

43. Mary Beard to Margaret Grierson, 28 May, 11 November 1947, 9 February 1950, 10 February 1953, box 1, Beard Papers, SSC; Beard to Wilbur Jordan, 4 April 1947, box 2, folder 30, Beard Papers, SL. See Ferdinand Lundberg and Marynia Farnham, *Modern Woman: The Lost Sex* (New York: Harper, 1947).

44. Mary Beard to Walter Yust, 3 November 1944, box 27, vol. 154, White Papers, SL; Beard to Wilbur Jordan, 4 April 1947, box 2, folder 30, Beard Papers, SL.

45. Mary Beard to Margaret Grierson, 6 March 1944, box 1, Beard Papers, SSC.

46. Elisabeth Dexter, *Career Women of America* (New York: Jones, 1950); Mary Beard to Marine Leland, 17 February 1951; Beard to Margaret Grierson, 10 December, 13 August 1950, box 1, Beard Papers, SSC.

47. Mary Beard to Margaret Grierson, 27 August 1950, box 1, Beard Papers, SSC.

48. Beard, "Women and Social Crisis," pt. 1, 347, 362. Beard critiqued women's education and institutions of higher learning in several journal articles: "The College and Alumnae in Contemporary Life," *JAAUW* 1 (October 1933): 11–16; "University Discipline for Women: Asset or Handicap?," *JAAUW* 3 (April 1932): 129–33.

49. Mary Beard to Margaret Grierson, 26 March 1948, box 1, Beard Papers, SSC.

50. Mary Beard to Margaret Grierson, 12 December 1945, 18 May 1951, 23 August 1945, 22 June 194?, box 1, Beard Papers, SSC.

51. Mary Beard to President Wright, 23 March 1950; to Margaret Grierson, 18 May 1951, June 1943, 20 October 1945, box 1, Beard Papers, SSC.

52. Mary Beard to Margaret Grierson, 10 November 1944, 22 June 194?, 19 August 1944, 24 April 1951, 10 February 1953, 4 May 1951; to Alice Lachmund, 7 December 1942, box 1, Beard Papers, SSC.

53. Mary Beard to Margaret Grierson, 17 January 1951, box 1, Beard Papers, SSC; Mary Beard, *The Making of Charles Beard: An Interpretation* (New York: Exposition Press, 1955).

54. John Higham, "The Future of American History," *Journal of American History* 80 (March 1994): 1289–1309; Peter Novick, *That Noble Dream: The "Objectivity Question" and the American Historical Profession* (New York: Cambridge University Press, 1988), 304–5, 316–17, 332.

55. Novick discusses the anti-Communist consensus of university history departments in *That Noble Dream*, 323–30.

56. Adlai Stevenson, "A Purpose for Modern Woman" (excerpted from a commencement address, Smith College, 1955), *Woman's Home Companion*, September 1955; Novick, *That Noble Dream*, 306, 310.

57. Novick, *That Noble Dream*, 316–17.

58. John Higham, *History: Professional Scholarship in America* (Baltimore: Johns Hopkins University Press, 1989), 214, 244; Novick, *That Noble Dream*, 316–17.

59. Ellen DuBois and Amy Swerdlow refer to women in left-leaning circles as "left feminists" and argue that they, too, influenced the rise of second-wave feminism in ways that have not been properly acknowledged. See Amy Swerdlow, "The Congress of American Women: Left-Feminist Peace Politics in the Cold War," in *U.S. History as Women's History: New Feminist Essays*, ed. Linda Kerber, Alice Kessler-Harris, and Kathryn Kish Sklar (Chapel Hill: University of North Carolina Press, 1995), 297–98; Daniel Horowitz, *Betty Friedan and the Making of the Feminine Mystique: The American Left, the Cold War, and Modern Feminism* (Amherst: University of Massachusetts Press, 1998), 10, 249.

60. Amy Swerdlow, "Congress of American Women," 306; Horowitz, *Betty Friedan*, 126–27.

61. Flexner is quoted in Horowitz, *Betty Friedan*, 1.

62. Ellen Fitzpatrick, foreword to Eleanor Flexner, *Century of Struggle: The Woman's Rights Movement in the United States* (Cambridge: Harvard University Press, 1996), xvi–xviii.

63. Ibid., xviii–xx.

64. Flexner quoted in ibid., xiv–xv.

65. Swerdlow, "Congress of American Women," 297–98; Horowitz, *Betty Friedan*, 10–12.

66. Joyce Antler, "Between Culture and Politics: The Emma Lazarus Federation of Jewish Women's Clubs and the Promulgation of Women's History, 1944–1989," in Kerber, Kessler-Harris, and Sklar, *U.S. History as Women's History*, 270.

67. Ibid., 276–77, 279.

68. Ibid., 279, 281.

69. Anne Firor Scott, *Making the Invisible Woman Visible* (Urbana: University of Illinois Press, 1984), xv–xvii, xviii–xix, xxi.

70. For a discussion of the historiographical trends in the American university of the 1960s, see Higham, *History*, 240–49; Novick, *That Noble Dream*, 307.

71. Higham, *History*, 236, 260.

72. For a discussion of cultural feminism, see Alice Echols, *Daring to Be Bad: Radical Feminism in America, 1967–1975* (Minneapolis: University of Minnesota Press, 1989); Estelle Freedman, "Separatism as Strategy: Female Institution Building and American Feminism, 1870–1930," *Feminist Studies* 3 (Fall 1979): 512–29; King, "Forty Years of Collecting on Women," 79.

73. Novick, *That Noble Dream*, 366–67.

74. Dolores Barracano Schmidt and Earl Robert Schmidt, "The Invisible Woman: The Historian as Professional Magician," in *Liberating Women's History: Theoretical and Critical Essays*, ed. Berenice Carroll (Urbana: University of Illinois Press, 1976), 42–44.

75. Ann Gordon, Mari Jo Buhle, and Nancy Schrom Dye, "The Problem of Women's History," in Carroll, *Liberating Women's History*, 75.

76. Bonnie Smith, "Seeing Mary Beard," *Feminist Studies* 10 (Fall 1984): 404. See the bibliography for a list of works written in recent years on Mary Beard.

77. Mary Beard, *Changing Political Economy as It Affects Women*, 11, 17–18, 21.

78. Robert Hemenway, *Zora Neale Hurston: A Literary Biography* (Urbana: University of Illinois Press, 1977), 330, 5.

79. Alice Walker is quoted from the foreword of ibid., xi.

80. See, for example, Darlene Clark Hine, *Hine Sight: Black Women and the Reconstruction of American History* (Brooklyn: Carlson, 1994); Jean Fagan Yellin, *The Pen Is Ours: A Listing of Writings by and about African American Women before 1910, with Secondary Bibliography to the Present*, Schomburg Library of Nineteenth Century Black Women Writers (New York: Oxford University Press, 1991).

81. Robert L. Dorman, *Revolt of the Provinces: The Regionalist Movement in America, 1920–1945* (Chapel Hill: University of North Carolina Press, 1993), 235; Nicholas Adams and Bonnie Smith, eds., *History and the Texture of Modern Life: Selected Essays* (Philadelphia: University of Pennsylvania Press, 2001), 1–21.

82. Thomas Dublin, "Caroline F. Ware: Crusader for Social Justice," in *Forgotten Heroes: Inspiring American Portraits from Our Leading Historians*, ed. Susan Ware (New York: Free Press, 1998), 253–54.

83. White and the AHA study are cited from Shirley A. Leckie, *Angie Debo: Pioneering Historian* (Norman: University of Oklahoma Press, 2000), 5.

Bibliography

The works listed here are divided into classifications that are useful for future research. None of the lists is exhaustive, and many of the titles listed could have been placed under more categories than the one chosen. The lists—which reveal genres of history in which women wrote prolifically, as well as the gendered nature of historical production in the late nineteenth and early twentieth centuries—provide mere points of entry into closer investigations of gender and race in historical writing. The bibliography is organized as follows:

Histories and Historical Biographies Written by Women, 1880–1945
    Collective Historical Biographies about Women
    Military, Political, Diplomatic, Economic, and Constitutional Histories
    Race History by White Women
    Historiography and Historical Method and Theory
    Histories of the West, the Frontier, and Native Americans
    Bibliographical and Archival Works
    Colonial and Revolutionary History
    Southern Women Historians and Southern Women's History
    Local/Family Histories
    Collaborations between Man/Woman, Husband/Wife
    Preservationist Publications
    Church/Religious Histories
    Suffrage/Feminist Histories and Biographies
    Historical Education Studies and History Textbooks
    Women's Labor/Immigrant History
    Historical Works by Women Social Scientists
    Histories of Women's Institutions (Patriotic Societies, Temperance, Higher
        Education, etc.)
    Popular Women's History (Nonacademic)
    African American Works of Historical Consciousness/Womanist History
Secondary Sources
    Women Historians and Preservationists in This Study
        Mary Beard
        Other Historians/Collectors/Social Scientists
    History of Women's Professionalization and Higher Education
    Historiography and the History of Social Science/Historical Disciplines
    Historical Memory
    Women's/Race Preservation and the WPA's Historical Record Survey
    Women's Genres
    African American Women/Writers/Historians/Sources
    Archival Collections for Research on Women Historians in This Study.

Histories and Historical Biographies Written by Women, 1880–1945

Collective Historical Biographies about Women

Bolton, Sarah K. *Lives of Poor Boys Who Become Famous*. New York: Crowell, 1885.
——. *Lives of Girls Who Become Famous*. New York: Crowell, 1886.
——. *Famous American Authors*. New York: Crowell, 1887.
——. *Famous American Statesmen*. New York: Crowell, 1888.
——. *Successful Women*. Boston: Lothrop, 1888.
——. *Famous Men of Science*. London: Hodder and Stoughton, 1890.
——. *Famous Types of Womanhood*. New York: Crowell, 1892.
Bradford, Gamaliel. *Portraits of American Women*. Boston: Houghton, 1919.
Brown, Hallie Q. *Pen Pictures of Pioneers of Wilberforce*. Xenia, Ohio: Aldine, 1937.
Cather, Katherine D. *Younger Days of Famous Writers*. New York: Century, 1925.
Dietrick, Ellen B. *Women in the Early Christian Ministry*. Philadelphia: Alfred J. Ferris, 1897.
Ellet, Elizabeth. *The Queens of American Society*. New York: Charles Scribner, 1867.
Griswold, Hattie T. *Sketches of Recent Authors*. Chicago: McClurg, 1898.
Hanaford, Phoebe A. *Daughters of America; or, Women of the Century*. Boston: B. B. Russell, 1883.
Haynes, Elizabeth Ross. *Unsung Heroes*. New York: DuBois and Dill, 1921.
Holloway, Laura C. *The Ladies of the White House*. New York: United States Publishing Co., 1870.
Moulton, Louisa C. *Our Famous Women. (An authorized and complete record of the lives and deeds of distinguished American women of our times)*. Hartford: A. D. Worthington, 1883.
Shorter, Susan L. *Heroines of African Methodism*. Xenia, Ohio: The author, 1891.
Tandy, Mary I. *Living Female Writers of the South*. Philadelphia: Claxton, 1878.
Webb, Mary G., and Edna Lenore. *Famous Living Americans*. Greencastle, Ind.: C. Webb, 1915.
Whiting, Lilian. *Women Who have Ennobled Life*. Philadelphia: Union Press, 1915.
Willard, Frances. *Women in the Pulpit*. Washington, D.C.: Zenger, 1889.
Willard, Frances, and Mary Livermore, eds. *A Woman of the Century: Fourteen Hundred-Seventy Biographical Sketches Accompanied by Portraits of Leading American Women in All Walks of Life*. Buffalo: Charles Wells Moulton, 1893.
Wyman, Lillie Buffum Chace. *American Chivalry*. Boston: W. B. Clarke, 1913.

Military, Political, Diplomatic, Economic, and Constitutional Histories

Abbott, Isabel Ross. "Taxation of Personal Property and of Clerical Incomes, 1399–1402." *Speculum* 17 (October 1942): 471–98.
Barnes, Viola. *The Dominion of New England: A Study in British Colonial Policy*. New Haven: Yale University Press, 1923.
Breckinridge, Sophonisba. *Legal Tender: A Study in English and American Monetary History*. Chicago: University of Chicago Press, 1903.
Brown, Louise Fargo. *Political Activities of the Baptists and Fifth Monarchy Men in England during the Interregnum*. Washington, D.C.: American Historical Association, 1912.

Childs, Frances. *French Refugee Life in the United States*. Baltimore: Johns Hopkins University Press, 1940.

Coman, Katharine. *Industrial History of the United States*. New York: Macmillan, 1905.

——. *Economic Beginnings in the Far West: How We Won the Land beyond the Mississippi*. New York: Macmillan, 1912.

Donnan, Elizabeth. "Early Days of the South Sea Company." *Journal of Economic and Business History* (May 1930): 419–50.

——. "Eighteenth-Century English Merchants: Micajah Perry." *Journal of Economic and Business History* (November 1931): 70–98.

Holmes, Vera. *Anglo-Spanish Relations in America in the Closing Years of the Colonial Era, 1763–1774*. Baltimore: n.p., 1923.

Judson, Margaret A. *The Crisis of the Constitution: An Essay in Constitutional and Political Thought in England, 1603–1616*. New Brunswick: Rutgers University Press, 1949.

Kerr, Clara H. *The Origin and Development of the United States Senate*. Ithaca: Andrus, 1895.

Kimball, Gertrude Selwyn. *The East-India Trade of Providence from 1787–1807*. Providence: Preston and Rounds, 1896.

Manning, Helen Taft. *British Colonial Government after the American Revolution, 1782–1820*. New Haven: Yale University Press, 1933.

Neilson, Nellie. *Economic Conditions on the Manors of Ramsey Abbey*. Philadelphia: Sherman, 1899.

——. *Medieval Agrarian Economy*. New York: H. Holt, 1936.

Putnam, Bertha. *The Enforcement of the Statutes of Labourers during the First Decade after the Black Death, 1349–1359*. New York: Columbia University Press, 1908.

——. "Maximum Wage-Laws for Priests after the Black Death, 1348–1381." *American Historical Review* 21 (October 1915): 12–32.

——. *Proceedings before the Justices of the Peace in the Fourteenth and Fifteenth Centuries*. Cambridge: Ames Foundation, Harvard Law School, 1938.

Robbins, Caroline, ed. *Diary of John Milward, Esq., Member of Parliament for Derbyshire, September 1666–May 1668*. Cambridge: The University Press, 1938.

——. *Eighteenth Century Commonwealthman*. Cambridge: Harvard University Press, 1959.

Tarbell, Ida M. *History of the Standard Oil Company*. New York: McClure, Phillips, 1904.

——. *The Nationalizing of Business, 1878–1898*. New York: Macmillan, 1936.

Tate, Merze. *The Disarmament Illusion: The Movement for a Limitation of Armaments to 1907*. New York: Macmillan, 1942.

Ware, Caroline. *The Early New England Cotton Manufacture*. Boston: Houghton Mifflin, 1931.

White, Laura. "The United States in the 1850s as Seen by British Consuls." *Mississippi Valley Historical Review* 19 (March 1933): 509–36.

Williams, Judith. "The Development of British Commerce with West Africa." *Political Science Quarterly* 174 (July 1934).

——. "The Establishment of British Trade in Argentina." *Hispanic-American Historical Review*, February 1935.

———. *British Commercial Policy and Trade Expansion, 1750–1850*. Oxford: Clarendon Press, 1972.

Williams, Mary Wilhelmine. *Anglo-American Isthmian Diplomacy*. Washington, D.C.: American Historical Association, 1916.

———. *The People and Politics of Latin America: A History*. Boston: Ginn, 1930.

———. *Dom Pedro the Magnanimous: Second Emperor of Brazil*. Chapel Hill: University of North Carolina Press, 1937.

Woolley, Mary E. *The Early History of the Colonial Post-Office*. Providence: n.p., 1894.

Race History by White Women

Adams, Alice Dana. *Neglected Period of Anti-Slavery in America, 1808–1831*. Radcliffe College Monographs, 14. Boston: Ginn, 1908.

Bradford, Sarah H. *Harriet, the Moses of Her People*. New York: G. R. Lockwood and Son, 1886.

Catterall, Helen T. "Some Antecedents of the Dred Scott Case." *American Historical Review* 30 (October 1924): 56–71.

———. *Judicial Cases Concerning American Slavery and the Negro*. Washington, D.C.: Carnegie Institution of Washington, 1929.

———. *Condition of the American Colored Population and of the Colony of Liberia*. Boston: Pierce and Parker, 1933.

Coman, Katharine. "The Negro as Peasant Farmer." *American Statistical Association Publication* 9 (1904–5): 35–54.

Donnan, Elizabeth. *Documents Illustrative of the History of the Slave Trade to America*. 4 vols. Washington, D.C.: Carnegie Institution of Washington, 1926–35.

———. "The Slave Trade into South Carolina." *American Historical Review* 32 (July 1928): 804–28.

———. "New England Slave Trade." *New England Quarterly* 3 (April 1930): 251–78.

Hoggan, Frances. *American Negro Women during Their First Fifty Years of Freedom*. London: Personal Rights Association, 1913.

Locke, Mary Stoughton. *Anti-slavery in America from the Introduction of African Slaves to the Prohibition of the Slave Trade, 1619–1808*. Boston: Ginn, 1901.

Ovington, Mary White. *Half a Man: The Status of the Negro in New York*. New York: Longmans, Green, 1911.

———. *Portraits in Color*. New York: Viking Press, 1927.

Historiography and Historical Method and Theory

Addams, Jane. *The Long Road of Woman's Memory*. New York: Macmillan, 1916.

Barnes, Mary S., ed. *Studies in General History*. Boston: Heath, 1885.

———. *Studies in American History*. Boston: Heath, 1891.

———. *Studies in Historical Method*. Boston: Heath, 1896.

Beard, Mary. "The Historical Approach to Learning about Women." Address to Radcliffe College, 22 May 1944. Copy in Schlesinger Library, Radcliffe College, Cambridge, Mass.

———. "Woman in Long History." Undated paper. Schlesinger Library, Radcliffe College, Cambridge, Mass.

Blythe, Irene T. "The Textbooks and the New Discoveries, Emphases, and

Viewpoints in American History." *Historical Outlook* 23 (December 1932): 395–402.

Boardman, Helen. "The Rise of the Negro Historian." *Negro History Bulletin*, April 1945, 148–49.

Burlingame, Anne E. *The Battle of the Books in Its Historical Setting*. New York: B. W. Huebsch, 1920.

Green, Constance McLaughlin. "The Value of Local History." In *The Cultural Approach to History*, edited by Caroline Ware, 275–86. New York: Columbia University Press, 1940.

Kohler, Anna. "Special Study on the Historic Memory of Children." In *Studies in Historical Method*, edited by Mary S. Barnes, 81–93. Boston: Heath, 1896.

Mason, Hattie. "Special Study on Ballads as Historical Material." In *Studies in Historical Method*, edited by Mary S. Barnes, 28–29. Boston: Heath, 1896.

Patterson, Alma. "Special Study on Children's Sense of Historical Time." In *Studies in Historical Method*, edited by Mary S. Barnes, 94–106. Boston: Heath, 1896.

Rogers, Emma W. "The New Writing of History." *Methodist Review* 87 (January 1905): 44–52.

Salmon, Lucy M. *The Newspaper and the Historian*. New York: Oxford University Press, 1923.

———. *Why Is History Rewritten?* New York: Oxford University Press, 1929.

———. *Historical Material*. New York: Oxford University Press, 1933.

Semple, Ellen C. *American History and Its Geographic Conditions*. Boston: Houghton Mifflin, 1903.

Ware, Caroline F., ed. *The Cultural Approach to History*. New York: Columbia University Press, 1940.

Histories of the West, the Frontier, and Native Americans

Abel, Annie H. "Indian Reservations in Kansas and the Extinguishment of their Title." *Transactions of the Kansas Historical Society* 8 (1903–4): 72–109.

———. "The History of Events Resulting in Indian Consolidation West of the Mississippi." In *Annual Report of the American Historical Association*, 233–450. Washington, D.C.: Government Printing Office, 1908.

———. "Indians of the Civil War." *American Historical Review* 10 (January 1910): 281–96.

———. *The American Indian as Slaveholder and Secessionist: An Omitted Chapter in the Diplomatic History of the Southern Confederacy*. Cleveland: Arthur H. Clark, 1915.

———. "The Cherokee Negotiations of 1822–23." *Smith College Studies in History* 1 (July 1916): 165–221.

———. *The American Indian as Participant in the Civil War*. Cleveland: Arthur H. Clark, 1919.

———. "Trudeau's Description of the Upper Missouri." *Mississippi Valley Historical Review* 8 (June 1921): 148–79.

———. *The American Indian under Reconstruction*. Cleveland: Arthur H. Clark, 1925.

———, ed. *The Official Correspondence of James S. Calhoun While Indian Agent at Santa Fe and Superintendent of Indian Affairs in New Mexico*. Washington, D.C.: Government Printing Office, 1915.

Abel, Annie H., ed. *Chardon's Journal at Fort Clark, 1834–39: Descriptive of Life on the Upper Missouri; of a Fur Trader's Experience among the Mandans, Gros Ventres, and their Neighbors; of the Ravages of the Small Pox Epidemic of 1837*. Pierre, S.D.: Department of History, 1932.

——. *Tabeau's Narrative of Loisel's Expedition to the Upper Missouri*. Norman: University of Oklahoma Press, 1939.

Abel, Annie H., and Frank J. Klingberg. *A Side-Light in Anglo-American Relations, 1839–1858*. Lancaster, Pa.: Association for the Study of Negro Life and History, 1927.

Atherton, Gertrude. *Before the Gringo Came*. New York: J. Selwin Tait, 1894.

——. *The Splendid Idle Forties: Stories of Old California*. New York: F. A. Stokes, 1902.

Austin, Mary. *The Land of Little Rain*. Boston: Houghton Mifflin, 1903.

——. *The American Rhythm*. Boston: Houghton Mifflin, 1913.

——. *Tales of the North American Indian*. Cambridge: Harvard University Press, 1929.

Baldwin, Alice. *An Army Wife on the Frontier: The Memoirs of Alice Blackwood Baldwin, 1867–1877*. Edited by Robert C. Carriker and Eleanor R. Carriker. Salt Lake City: University of Utah Library, 1975.

Barr, Amelia. *Remember the Alamo*. New York: Dodd, Mead, 1888.

Beach, Cora, ed. *Women of Wyoming*. Casper, Wyo.: S. E. Boyer, 1927.

Berry, Jane M. "Indian Policy of Spain in the Southwest." *Mississippi Valley Historical Review* 3 (March 1917): 462–77.

Blair, Emma Helen. *The Indian Tribes of the Upper Mississippi Valley and Region of the Great Lakes as Described by Nicholas Perrot, French Commandant in the Northwest; Bacqueville de la Potherie, French Royal Commissioner to Canada; Morrell Marston, American Army Officer; and Thomas Forsyth, United States Agent at Fort Armstrong*. Cleveland: Arthur H. Clark, 1911.

Brooks, Juanita. "Indian Relations of the Mormon Frontier." *Utah Historical Quarterly* 12 (January–April 1944): 1–48.

——. "The First One Hundred Years of Southern Utah History." *Proceedings of the Utah Academy of Sciences, Arts, and Letters* 24 (1946–47): 71–79.

——. "Let's Preserve Our Records." *Utah Humanities Review* 2 (July 1948): 259–63.

——. *The Mountain Meadows Massacre*. Stanford: Stanford University Press, 1950.

Broshar, Helen. "First Push Westward of Albany Traders." *Mississippi Valley Historical Review* 7 (December 1920): 228–41.

Cleveland, Catharine C. *The Great Revival in the West, 1797–1805*. Chicago: University of Chicago Press, 1916.

Custer, Elizabeth. *"Boots and Saddles," or, Life in Dakota with General Custer, 1885*. 1885. Reprint, Norman: University of Oklahoma Press, 1961.

Debo, Angie. *The Rise and Fall of the Choctaw Republic*. Norman: University of Oklahoma Press, 1934.

——. *And Still the Waters Run: The Betrayal of the Five Civilized Tribes*. Princeton: Princeton University Press, 1940.

——. *The Road to Disappearance*. Norman: University of Oklahoma Press, 1941.

——. *Tulsa: From Creek Town to Oil Capital*. Norman: University of Oklahoma Press, 1943.

——. *Prairie City: The Story of an American Community*. New York: Knopf, 1944.

——. *Oklahoma: Foot-loose and Fancy-free*. Norman: University of Oklahoma Press, 1949.

Debo, Angie, and James Fred Rippy. "The Historical Background of the American Policy of Isolation." Smith College, *Studies in History* 3–4 (April–July 1924): 71–165.

Dondore, Dorothy. "Points of Contact between History and Literature in the Mississippi Valley." *Mississippi Valley Historical Review* 11 (September 1924): 227–36.

Duniway, Abigail Scott. *Path Breaking: An Autobiographical History of the Equal Suffrage Movement in Pacific Coast States.* Portland, Ore.: James, Kerns and Abbott, 1914.

Eaton, Rachel. *John Ross and the Cherokee Indians.* Menasha, Wis.: George Banta, 1914.

Ellet, Elizabeth. *Pioneer Women of the West.* Philadelphia: Porter and Coates, 1873.

Farmer, Hallie. "The Economic Background of Frontier Populism." *Mississippi Valley Historical Review* 10 (March 1924): 406–27.

———. "Railroads and Frontier Populism." *Mississippi Valley Historical Review* 13 (December 1926): 387–97.

Fletcher, Alice. *A Study of Omaha Music.* Boston: Peabody Museum, 1893.

———. *Indian Story and Song from North America.* Boston: Small and Maynard, 1900.

Fletcher, Alice, and Francis LaFlesche. *The Omaha Tribe.* 1911. Reprint, New York: Johnson, 1970.

Fuller, Mrs. Marcus B. *The Wrongs of Indian Womanhood.* New York: Revell, 1900.

Gerould, Katherine Fullerton. *The Aristocratic West.* New York: Harper and Brothers, 1925.

Hallock, Mary Foote. *A Victorian Gentlewoman in the Far West: The Reminiscences of Mary Hallock Foote.* Edited by Rodman W. Paul. San Marino: Huntington Library, 1972.

Hebard, Grace R. "Pilot of the First White Men to Cross the American Continent." *Journal of American History* 1 (1907): 467–84.

———. *The Pathbreakers from River to Ocean: The Story of the Great West from the Time of Coronado to the Present.* Chicago: Lakeside Press, 1911.

———. "The First White Women in Wyoming." *Washington Historical Quarterly* 8 (January 1917): 29–31.

———. *Washakie.* Cleveland: Arthur H. Clark, 1930.

———. *Sacajawea: A Guide and interpreter of the Lewis and Clark Expedition, with an account of the travels of Toussaint Charbonneau, and of Jean Baptiste, the expedition papoose.* Glendale: Arthur H. Clark, 1933.

Hebard, Grace R., and E. A. Brinistool. *The Bozeman Trail.* 2 vols. Cleveland: Arthur H. Clark, 1922.

Higginson, Ella. *From the Land of the Snow-Pearls: Tales from Puget Sound.* New York: Macmillan, 1902.

Kellogg, Louise Phelps. *Documentary History of Dunmore's War, 1774.* Madison: Wisconsin Historical Society, 1905.

———. *The Revolution of the Upper Ohio, 1775–1777.* Madison: Wisconsin Historical Society, 1908.

———. *Journal of a Voyage to North America.* Chicago: Caxton Club, 1923.

———. *The French Regime in Wisconsin and the Northwest.* Madison: State Historical Society of Wisconsin, 1925.

———, ed. *Early Narratives of the Northwest, 1634–1699.* New York: Charles Scribner's Sons, 1917.

——. *Wau-bun and Early Days in the Northwest.* Menasha, Wis.: George Banta, 1930.

Laut, Agnes C. *Pathfinders of the West.* New York: Macmillan, 1904.

——. *Conquest of the Great Northwest.* New York: Doubleday, Doran, 1919.

Mitchell, Mary. "Reminiscences of the Early Northwest." *Proceedings of the Wisconsin State Historical Society* (1903): 173–89.

Roe, Mrs. Elizabeth A. *Recollections of Frontier Life.* Rockford, Ill.: Gazette Publishing, 1885.

Sandoz, Mari. *Old Jules.* Boston: Little, Brown, 1935.

——. *Crazy Horse.* New York: Knopf, 1942.

——. *Cheyenne Autumn.* New York: McGraw-Hill, 1953.

——. *The Battle of Little Bighorn.* Philadelphia: Lippincott, 1966.

Seymour, Flora W. *The Story of the Red Man.* New York: Longmans, Green, 1929.

Skinner, Constance Lindsay. *Adventurers of Oregon: A Chronicle of the Fur Trade.* New Haven: Yale University Press, 1921.

——. *Pioneers of the Old Southwest: A Chronicle of the Dark and Bloody Ground.* New Haven: Yale University Press, 1921.

——. *Adventures in the Wilderness.* New Haven: Yale University Press, 1925.

——. *Becky Landers, Frontier Warrior.* New York: Macmillan, 1927.

——. *Beaver, Kings, and Cabins.* New York: Macmillan, 1933.

Victor, Frances F. *The River of the West.* Hartford: Columbian Book Co., 1870.

——. *The Women's War with Whiskey; or, Crusading in Portland.* Portland, Ore.: George H. Himes, SteamBook and Job, 1874.

——. *History of the Pacific States.* Edited by Hubert Howe Bancroft. San Francisco: History Company, 1884–1990 (California, Colorado, Nevada, Wyoming, Oregon).

——. *The Early Indian Wars of Oregon.* Salem, Ore.: F. C. Baker, 1894.

Bibliographical and Archival Works

Dunlap, Mollie E. "Special Collections of Negro Literature in the United States." *Journal of Negro Education* 4 (October 1935): 482–89.

Fisher, Ruth A. *Extracts from the Records of the African Companies.* Washington, D.C.: Association for the Study of Negro Life and History, 1930.

Fries, Adelaide L., ed. *Records of the Moravians in North Carolina, 1752–1783.* 4 vols. Raleigh: North Carolina Historical Commission, 1922–1930.

Gallagher, Katharine. "Elisha W. Keyes Papers." *Bulletin of State Historical Society of Wisconsin,* 1916.

——. "Kemper Manuscript Collections." *Bulletin of State Historical Society of Wisconsin,* 1916.

Gilmer, Gertrude C. *Checklist of Southern Periodicals to 1861.* Boston: F. W. Faxon, 1934.

Griffin, Grace G. *Writings on American History.* Washington, D.C.: Carnegie Institution of Washington, 1903.

Guzman, Jessie Parkhurst. *The Negro Yearbook.* Tuskegee, Ala.: Tuskegee Institute, 1947.

Hasse, Adelaide R. *Index to Economic Material in Documents of the States.* Washington, D.C.: Carnegie Institution of Washington, 1907–19.

——. *Index to United States Documents Relating to Foreign Affairs, 1828–1861.* Washington, D.C.: American Historical Association, 1914–21.

Lacey, Virginia. "United States Government Publications on the American Negro, 1916–37." Master's thesis, University of Illinois, 1938.

Latimer, Catherine. "Where Can I Get Material on the Negro?" *Crisis*, June 1934, 164–65.

——, comp. *Bibliography on the Contribution of Negro Women to American Civilization.* New York: Schomburg Center, New York Public Library, 1940.

Matthews, Miriam. "The Negro in California from 1781 to 1916: An Annotated Bibliography." Master's thesis, University of Southern California, 1927.

Murray, Florence, ed. *The Negro Handbook.* New York: Wendell Malliet, 1942.

Noyes, Gertrude. *Bibliography of Courtesy and Conduct Books in Seventeenth Century England.* New Haven: Tuttle, Morehouse, and Taylor, 1937.

Phelps, Edith M., comp. *Selected Articles of Woman Suffrage.* New York: Wilson, 1916.

Porter, Dorothy B. "Negro Writers before 1830." Master's thesis, Columbia University, 1932.

——. "Library Sources for the Study of Negro Life and History." *Journal of Negro Education* 5 (April 1936): 232–44.

——. "Early American Negro Writings: A Bibliographical Study." *Papers of the Bibliographical Society of America* 39 (1945): 192–268.

——. "Bibliography and Research in Afro-American Familiar and Less Familiar Sources." *African Studies Bulletin* 12 (December 1969): 293–303.

——. *Negro Protest Pamphlets.* New York: Arno Press, 1969.

——. *Afro-Braziliana: A Working Bibliography.* Boston: G. K. Hall, 1978.

——. "Black Antiquarians and Bibliophiles Revisited, with a Glance at Today's Lovers of Books and Memorabilia." In *Black Bibliophiles and Collectors: Preservers of Black History*, edited by Elinor Sinnette, Paul Coates, and Thomas C. Battle, 5–15. Washington, D.C.: Howard University Press, 1990.

——, ed. *Early Negro Writing, 1760–1840.* Boston: Beacon Press, 1970.

Porter, Dorothy B., and Ethel M. Ellis. "Index to the Journal of Negro Life and History." *Journal of Negro Education* 5 (April 1936): 232–44.

——. *Index to the Journal of Negro Education.* 31 vols. Washington, D.C.: Howard University Press, 1953.

Theobald, Ruth. "A Suggested List for School Libraries of Books about the Negro." *Children's Library Yearbook* (1932).

Thornton, Mary Lindsay. *North Carolina: A Classified List of Books.* Raleigh: Library Commission of North Carolina, 1929.

Williams, Judith. *A Guide to Printed Materials for English Social and Economic History, 1750–1850.* New York: Columbia University Press, 1926.

Colonial and Revolutionary History

Baldwin, Alice. *New England Clergy in the American Revolution.* Durham, N.C.: Duke University Press, 1928.

Bittenger, Lucy Forney. *The Germans in Colonial Times.* Philadelphia: Lippincott, 1901.

Earle, Alice Morse. "The New England Meeting House." *Atlantic Monthly*, February 1891, 191–204.

——. *The Sabbath in Puritan New England*. New York: Charles Scribner's Sons, 1891.

——. *China Collecting in America*. New York: Charles Scribner's Sons, 1892.

——. *Customs and Fashions in Old New England*. New York: Charles Scribner's Sons, 1893.

——. "The Oldest Episcopal Church in New England." *New England Magazine*, January 1893, 577–93.

——. "Old-Time Church Music in New England." *Outlook*, November 1893, 933–34.

——. "Old-Time Marriage Customs in New England." *Journal of American Folklore* 6 (April–June 1893): 97–102.

——. *Costumes of Colonial Times*. New York: Charles Scribner's Sons, 1894.

——. *Diary of Anna Green Winslow: A Boston School Girl of 1771*. Boston: Houghton Mifflin, 1894.

——. *Colonial Dames and Good Wives*. Boston: Houghton Mifflin, 1895.

——. *Margaret Winthrop*. New York: Charles Scribner's Sons, 1895.

——. *Colonial Days in Old New York*. New York: Charles Scribner's Sons, 1896.

——. *Curious Punishments of Bygone Days*. Chicago: Herbert S. Stone, 1896.

——. *In Old Narragansett*. New York: Charles Scribner's Sons, 1897.

——. "Colonial Household Industries." *Chautauquan* 26 (February 1898): 475–79.

——. *Home Life in Colonial Days*. New York: Macmillan, 1898.

——. "Schools and Education in American Colonies." *Chautauquan* 26 (January 1898): 362–66.

——. *Child Life in Colonial Days*. New York: Macmillan, 1899.

——. *Stage Coach and Tavern Days*. New York: Macmillan, 1899.

——. *Old-Time Gardens, Newly Set Forth*. New York: Macmillan, 1901.

——. *Sun Dials and Roses of Yesterday*. New York: Macmillan, 1902.

——. *Two Centuries of American Costume in America*. New York: Macmillan, 1903.

Mathews, Lois Kimball. *The Expansion of New England: The Spread of New England Settlements and Institutions to the Mississippi River, 1620–1865*. Boston: Houghton Mifflin, 1909.

Singleton, Esther. *Furniture of Our Forefathers*. Garden City, N.Y.: Doubleday Page, 1900.

Stanard, Mary N. *Colonial Virginia: Its People and Customs*. Philadelphia: Lippincott, 1917.

Sterns, Bertha. "Early New England Magazines for Ladies." *New England Quarterly* 2 (July 1929).

Ware, Caroline. *The Early New England Cotton Manufacture*. New York: Russell and Russell, 1966.

Wharton, Anne H. *Through Colonial Doorways*. Philadelphia: Lippincott, 1893.

——. *Colonial Days and Dames*. Philadelphia: Lippincott, 1898.

Southern Women Historians and Southern Women's History

Ames, Susie. "The Reunion of Two Virginia Counties." *Journal of Southern History* 8 (November 1942): 536–48.

Benedict, Mary. *The Higher Education of Women in the Southern States*. Richmond: Southern Historical Publication Society, 1909.

Blandin, Mrs. I. M. E. *History of Higher Education of Women in the South, Prior to 1860*. New York: Neale, 1909.

Craig, Marjorie. "Survivals of the Chivalric Tournament in Southern Life and Literature." Master's thesis, University of North Carolina, 1935.

Flisch, Julia. "The Common People of the Old South." In *Annual Report of the American Historical Association*, 133–422. Washington, D.C.: Government Printing Office, 1908.

Gearhart, Virginia. "The Southern Woman, 1840–1860." Ph.D. diss., University of Wisconsin, 1927.

Goodwin, Maud W. *The Colonial Cavalier; or, Southern Life before the Revolution*. New York: Lovell, Coryell, 1894.

Johnson, Guion Griffis. *Ante-Bellum North Carolina: A Social History*. Chapel Hill: University of North Carolina Press, 1937.

——. "My Exploration of the Southern Experience." *North Carolina Historical Review* 57 (April 1980): 192–207.

Lonn, Ella. *Reconstruction in Louisiana after 1868*. New York: Putnam, 1918.

——. *Desertion during the Civil War*. New York: Century, 1928.

——. *Salt as a Factor in the Confederacy*. New York: Neale, 1933.

——. *Foreigners in the Confederacy*. Chapel Hill: University of North Carolina Press, 1940.

——. *The Colonial Agents of the Southern Colonies*. Chapel Hill: University of North Carolina Press, 1945.

——. "Reconciliation between North and South." *Journal of Southern History* 13 (February 1947): 3–26.

——. *Foreigners in the Union Army and Navy*. Baton Rouge: Louisiana State University Press, 1951.

Looney, Louisa P. "The Southern Planter of the Fifties." *Southern History Association Publications* 4 (1900): 248–53.

McMillan, Genevieve. "History of Higher Education of Women in the South." Master's thesis, University of North Carolina, 1923.

Smith, Mary Phlegar. "Special Legal Relations of Married Women in North Carolina as to Property, Contracts, and Guardianship." *University of North Carolina Extension Bulletin* 7 (1928).

——. "Municipal Development in North Carolina, 1665–1930." Ph.D. diss., University of North Carolina, 1930.

Spruill, Julia Cherry. *Women's Life and Work in the Southern Colonies*. Chapel Hill: University of North Carolina Press, 1938.

Stearns, Bertha. "Southern Magazines for Ladies, 1819–1860." *South Atlantic Quarterly* 31 (January 1932).

Local/Family Histories

Atherton, Gertrude. *California: An Intimate History*. New York: Harper, 1914.

Booth, Mary Louise. *History of the City of New York, From Its Earliest Settlement to the Present Time*. New York: W. R. C. Clark and Meeker, 1859.

Caldwell, Bettie D., ed. *Founders and Builders of Greensboro, 1808–1908*. Greensboro, N.C.: J. J. Stone, 1925.

Crawford, Mary C. *Famous Families of Boston*. 2 vols. Boston: Little, Brown, 1930.

Croughton, Amy H. *Antislavery Days in Rochester*. Rochester, N.Y.: n.p., 1936.

Early, Ruth H. *By-Ways of Virginia History*. Richmond: Everett Waddey, 1907.

Hemenway, Abby Maria, ed. *The Local History of Andover, VT*. 1886. Reprint, Perth Amboy, N.J.: C. F. Heartman, 1922.

Hillhouse, Margaret P. *Historical and Genealogical Collections Relating to the Descendants of Reverend James Hillhouse*. New York: n.p., 1924.

Hurn, Ethel. *Wisconsin Women in the War between the States*. Madison, Wis.: State Printer, 1911.

Knight, Kate B. *History of the Work of Connecticut Women at the World's Columbian Exposition, Chicago, 1893*. Hartford: Hartford Press, 1898.

Lamb, Elizabeth, comp. *Historical Sketch of Hay St. Methodist Episcopal Church, South, Fayetteville, NC, 1808–1934*. Fayetteville: n.p., 1934.

Lamb, Martha J. *The Homes of America*. New York: Appleton, 1879.

Levi, Kate Asaphine (Everest). *How Wisconsin Came by its Large German Element*. Madison: State Historical Society of Wisconsin, 1892.

Mathews, Lois Kimball. "The Erie Canal and the Settlement of the West." *Buffalo Historical Society Publications* 14 (1910): 189–203.

McIlvaine, Mabel, ed. *Reminiscences of Early Chicago*. Chicago: R. R. Donnelley and Sons, 1912.

Montgomery, Lizzie Wilson. *Sketches of Old Warrenton, North Carolina: Traditions and Reminiscences of the Town and People Who Made It*. Raleigh: North Carolina Historical Commission, 1924.

Pierce, Bessie. *A History of Chicago*. 3 vols. New York: Knopf, 1937.

Pritchard, Louise G. "A History of the Chicago Public Library." Master's thesis, University of Illinois, 1928.

Putnam, Ruth, Alice Carrington Royce, and Maud Wilder Goodwin. *Historic New York*. New York: Putnam, 1899.

Richards, Caroline Cowles. *Village Life in America*. New York: Holt, 1912.

Sewall, Harriet. "Geographic Factors in the Development of Chicago." Master's thesis, University of Chicago, 1910.

Shapiro, Dena Evelyn. "Indian Tribes and Trails of the Chicago Region." Master's thesis, University of Chicago, 1929.

Stockard, Sallie Walker. *The History of Alamance County*. Raleigh: Capital Printing, 1900.

Tapley, Harriet S. *Salem Imprints, 1768–1825: History of the First Fifty Years of Printing in Salem, 1768–1825*. Salem, Mass.: Essex Institute, 1927.

Collaborations between Man/Woman, Husband/Wife

Albjerg, Marguerite Hall, and Victor Lincoln Albjerg. *From Seddan to Stresa: Europe since 1870*. New York: D. Van Nostrand, 1937.

Beard, Mary, and Charles Beard. *American Citizenship*. New York: Macmillan, 1914.

——. *History of the United States*. New York: Macmillan, 1921. Later editions are titled *A Study in American Civilization*.

——. *The Rise of American Civilization*. 2 vols. New York: Macmillan, 1927.

——. *The Making of American Civilization*. New York: Macmillan, 1937.

——. *America in Midpassage*. 2 vols. New York: Macmillan, 1939.

——. *The American Spirit: A Study of the Idea of Civilization in the United States.* New York: Macmillan, 1942.

——. *A Basic History of the United States.* New York: Doubleday, 1944.

Beekman, Katharine M., and Norman Isham. *The Story of Van Cortlandt.* New York: National Society of Colonial Dames of New York, 1917.

Berry, Margaret K., and Samuel B. Howe. *Actual Democracy.* New York: Prentice Hall, 1923.

Goebel, Dorothy, and Julius Goebel. *Generals in the White House.* Garden City, N.Y.: Doubleday, Doran, 1945.

Scott, Anne Firor, and Andrew Scott. *Political Thought in America.* New York: Rinehart, 1959.

——. *The Southern Lady: From Pedestal to Politics, 1830–1930.* Chicago: University of Chicago Press, 1970.

——. *One Half the People: The Fight for Woman Suffrage.* Urbana: University of Illinois Press, 1982. (Andrew Scott is not an official author but assisted.)

Shackleton, Elizabeth, and Robert Shackleton. *The Quest of the Colonial.* Philadelphia: Century, 1907.

Wolcott, Mary, and Harry C. Green. *Pioneer Mothers.* 3 vols. New York: Putnam, 1912.

Preservationist Publications

Bangs, Ella M. *An Historic Mansion: The Wadsworth-Longfellow House.* Portland, Maine: Lamson Studio, 1902.

Bush, Celeste, E. *The Old Lee House, East Lyme, Connecticut.* N.p.: East Lyme Historical Society, 1917.

Coleman, Emma L. *Frary House, Deerfield, 1685.* Deerfield, Mass.: Pocumtuck Valley Memorial Association, 1940.

Coles, Elizabeth. *Historical Sketch of the Washington Headquarters, Prepared under the Auspices of the White Plains Chapter, Daughters of the American Revolution.* White Plains, N.Y.: Daughters of the American Revolution, 1917.

Curtis, Nathalie. "An Historic House on the Hudson: The Silent Witness of the Growth of American Freedom." *Craftsman* 17 (October 1909): 3–11.

Dorris, Mary C. *Preservation of the Hermitage, 1889–1915.* Nashville: Ladies' Hermitage Association, 1915.

Downing, Antoinette F. *Early Homes of Rhode Island.* Richmond: Garrett and Massie, 1937.

Emmerton, Caroline O. *The Chronicles of Three Old Houses.* Boston: Thomas Todd, 1935.

Keith, Eliza D. *Report of the Historical Landmarks Committee of the Native Daughters of the Golden West.* San Francisco: n.p., 1902.

Littleton, Maud. *Monticello.* New York: n.p., 1912.

Longyear, Mary B. *The History of a House, Its Founder, Family, and Guests.* Boston: Longyear Foundation, 1925.

Muir, Dorothy T. *Presence of a Lady, Mount Vernon, 1861–1868.* Washington, D.C.: Mount Vernon Publishing, 1946.

Newton, Mary M. P. "The Association for the Preservation of Virginia Antiquities." *American Historical Register* 1 (September 1894): 11–21.

Peck, Mamie D. *Thomas Jefferson and His Home, Monticello*. Corsicana, Tex.: Marr, 1928.

Pryor, Mrs. Roger A. "The Mount Vernon Association." *American Historical Register* 1 (January 1895): 407–20.

Roof, Katharine M. *The Story of the Abigail Adams Smith Mansion and the Mount Vernon Estate*. New York: Colonial Dames of America, 1949.

Schuyler, Georgina. *The Schuyler Mansion at Albany*. New York: De Vinne Press, 1911.

Sears, Clara E. *Bronson Alcott's Fruitlands*. Boston: Houghton Mifflin, 1915.

Smith, Emma A. F. *Historical Sketch of Washington's Headquarters*. New York: Washington Headquarters Association, 1908.

Stevens, Maud L. *The Vernon House, Newport, RI, 1758–1915*. Newport, R.I.: Charity Organization Society of Newport, 1915.

Tilley, Edith M. "The Newport Historical Society in Its Earlier Days." *Bulletin of the Newport Historical Society* 12 (April 1914): 1–16.

Tower, Elizabeth A. *The John Hancock House*. Ticonderoga: New York State Historical Association, 1926.

Trowbridge, Bertha C., ed. *Old Houses of Connecticut*. New Haven: Yale University Press, 1923.

Tutt, Hannah. *The Lee Mansion, What It Was, and What It Is*. Marblehead, Mass.: Marblehead Historical Society, 1911.

Weaver, Addie G. *The Story of Our Flag, Colonial and National, with Historical Sketch of The Quakeress Betsy Ross*. Chicago: A. G. Weaver, 1898.

Church/Religious Histories

Babcock, Florence. "Pioneer Women in the Universalist Church." *Christian Leader*, 9 August 1930.

Baldwin, Alice. *New England Clergy in the American Revolution*. Durham, N.C.: Duke University Press, 1928.

Bennett, Helen C. *American Women in Civic Work*. New York: Dodd, Mead, 1915.

Bowles, Ada C. "Woman in the Ministry." In *Woman's Work in America*, edited by Annie Nathan Meyer, 206–17. New York: H. Holt, 1891.

Brodie, Fawn M. *No Man Knows My History: The Life of Joseph Smith, the Mormon Prophet*. New York: Knopf, 1945.

Brown, Annie E. *Religious Works and Travels*. Chester, Pa.: Olin T. Pancost, 1909.

Brown, Sue M. Wilson. *The History of the Order of the Eastern Star among Colored People*. Des Moines: Bystander Press, 1925.

Edwards, Martha. "Religious Forces in the U.S." *Mississippi Valley Historical Review* 5 (March 1919): 434–49.

Evans, Aurora. "Origins and Work of the Daughters of Conference and Kindred Societies." *A.M.E. Zion Quarterly Review*, January 1898.

McAfee, Sarah. *History of the Women's Missionary Society in the Colored Methodist Episcopal Church, Comprising Its Founders, Organizations, Pathfinders, Subsequent Developments, and Present Status*. Phenix City, Ala.: Phenix City Herald, 1945.

Meyer, Lucy R. *Deaconesses, Biblical, Early Church, European, American*. Cincinnati: Cranston and Stowe, 1889.

Parsons, Ellen C. "History of Women's Organized Missionary Work as Promoted by

American Women." In *Women in Missions*, edited by E. M. Wherry. New York: n.p., 1894.

Ray, Emma J. Smith. *Twice Sold, Twice Ransomed: An Autobiography of Mr. and Mrs. L. P. Ray*. Chicago: Free Methodist Publishing House, 1926.

Stenhouse, Mrs. T. B. H. *"Tell it All": The Story of a Life's Experience in Mormonism. An Autobiography*. Hartford: A. D. Worthington, 1874.

Suffrage/Feminist Histories and Biographies

Algeo, Sara M. *The Story of a Sub-Pioneer*. Providence, R.I.: Snow and Farnham, 1925.

Anthony, Katharine. *Feminism in Germany and Scandinavia*. New York: H. Holt, 1915.

———. *Margaret Fuller: A Psychological Biography*. London: Jonathan Cape, 1920.

———. *Susan B. Anthony: Her Personal History and Her Era*. New York: Doubleday, 1954.

Blackwell, Alice Stone. "Woman's Seventy-five-Year Fight." *Nation*, 18 July 1923, 53–55.

———. *Lucy Stone: Pioneer of Woman's Rights*. Boston: Little, Brown, 1930.

Blatch, Harriot Stanton. *A Sketch of the Life of Elizabeth Cady Stanton by Her Daughter*. New York: n.p., 1915.

Blatch, Harriot Stanton, and Alma Lutz. *Challenging Years: The Memoirs of Harriet Stanton Blatch*. New York: Putnam, 1940.

Catt, Carrie C., and Nettie R. Shuler. *Woman Suffrage and Politics: The Inner Study of the Suffrage Movement*. New York: Charles Scribner's Sons, 1923.

Clarke, Ida Clyde, comp. *Suffrage in the Southern States: A Brief History of the Progress of the Movement in Fourteen States*. Nashville: Williams Printing, 1914.

Davis, Paulina W. *A History of the National Woman's Rights Movement*. New York: Journeymen Printers' Cooperative Association, 1871.

Dorr, Rheta Childe. *What Eight Million Women Want*. Boston: Small and Maynard, 1910.

———. *Susan B. Anthony: The Woman Who Changed the Mind of a Nation*. New York: F. A. Stokes, 1928.

Hall, Florence H. *Julia Ward Howe and the Woman Suffrage Movement*. Boston: Dana Estes and Co., 1913.

Hallowell, Anna Davis. *James and Lucretia Mott*. Boston: Houghton Mifflin, 1884.

Harper, Ida. *The Life and Work of Susan B. Anthony*. 3 vols. Indianapolis: Bobbs-Merrill, 1898, 1908.

———. *Story of the National Amendment for Woman Suffrage*. New York: National Woman Suffrage Publishing Co., 1919.

———, ed. *History of Woman Suffrage*. Vol. 4. Indianapolis: Hollenbeck Press, 1902.

———. *History of Woman Suffrage*. Vols. 5–6. New York: J. J. Little and Ives, 1922.

Irwin, Inez H. *The Story of the Woman's Party*. New York: Harcourt, Brace, 1921.

———. *Angels and Amazons: A Hundred Years of American Women*. Garden City, N.Y.: Doubleday, Doran, 1933.

Lutz, Alma. *Created Equal: A Biography of Elizabeth Cady Stanton*. New York: John Day, 1940.

———. *Susan B. Anthony: Rebel, Crusader, Humanitarian*. Boston: Beacon Press, 1959.

Park, Maud W. *Lucy Stone: A Chronicle Play*. Boston: Walter H. Baker, 1938.

Peck, Mary G. *Carrie Chapman Catt: A Biography*. New York: H. W. Wilson, 1944.

Sachs, Emanie. *"The Terrible Siren": Victoria Woodhull, 1838–1927*. New York: Harper and Brothers, 1928.

Shuler, Marjorie. *For Rent: One Pedestal*. New York: National American Woman Suffrage Association Publishing Co., 1917.

Squire, Belle. *The Woman Movement in America*. Chicago: McClurg, 1911.

Stanton, Elizabeth Cady. *Eighty Years and More, 1815–1897: Reminiscences*. New York: Harper, 1898.

Stanton, Elizabeth Cady, Susan B. Anthony, and Matilda J. Gage, eds. *History of Woman Suffrage*. Vols. 1–3. New York: Fowler and Wells, 1881.

Stanton, Theodore, and Harriot Stanton Blatch, eds. *Elizabeth Cady Stanton as Revealed in Her Letters, Diary, and Reminiscences*. 2 vols. New York: Harper and Brothers, 1922.

Stevens, Doris. *Jailed for Freedom*. New York: Boni and Liveright, 1920.

Historical Education Studies and History Textbooks

Andrews, Regina. "The Library's Responsibility for Better Human Relations." *Wilson Library Bulletin* 23 (February 1949): 433.

Barnes, Mary S. *Aids for Teaching General History, including a List of Books Recommended for a Working School Library*. Boston: Heath, 1888.

——. *Studies in General History Teachers' Manual*. Boston: Heath, 1891.

——. "The Teaching of Local History." *Educational Review* 10 (December 1895): 481–88.

Carpenter, Marie Elizabeth Ruffin. *The Treatment of the Negro in American History School Textbooks: A Comparison of Changing Textbook Content, 1826 to 1939, with Developing Scholarship in the History of the Negro in the United States*. Menasha, Wis.: George Banta, 1941.

Colson, Edna. "An Analysis of the Specific References to Negroes in Selected Curricula for Teachers." Ph.D. diss., New York Teachers College, Columbia University, 1940.

Coman, Katharine, and Elizabeth Kendall. *A History of England for High School Academies*. New York: Macmillan, 1899.

——. *A Short History of England for School Use*. New York: Macmillan, 1902.

Compton, Miriam A. "An Evaluation of History Texts." *Historical Outlook* 23 (October 1932).

Delany, Sadie M. P. "The Library: A Factor in Negro Education." *Messenger*, July 1923, 772–73.

Gallagher, Katharine. "Teaching of Contemporary History in the Colleges." *Proceedings of the Historical Society of Colleges and Preparatory Schools of Middle States and Maryland* (1917).

Hebard, Grace R. *Teaching Wyoming History by Counties*. Department of Education, State of Wyoming, 1922.

——. *The History and Government of Wyoming: The History, Constitution, and Administration of Affairs*. San Francisco: C. F. Weber, 1923.

Lawson, Elizabeth. *Study Outline History of the American Negro People, 1619–1918*. New York: Workers Book Shop, 1939.

Lee, Susan Pendleton. *New School History of the United States*. Richmond: B. F. Johnson, 1899.

Lonn, Ella. "A Course in Methods of Teaching the Social Studies in High Schools." *Historical Outlook* 15 (December 1924).

———. "Making Geography Attractive to History Students." *Proceedings of the Association of History Teachers of the Middle States and Maryland* 29 (1931).

Pierce, Bessie L. *Public Opinion and the Teaching of History in the United States*. New York: Knopf, 1926.

———. *Civic Attitudes in American School Textbooks*. Chicago: University of Chicago Press, 1930.

———. *Citizens' Organizations and the Civic Training of Youth*. New York: Charles Scribner's Sons, 1933.

Salmon, Lucy. "The Teaching of History in Academies and Colleges." *Academy* 5 (1890): 283–92.

———. "The Teaching of History in Elementary Schools." *Educational Review* 1 (1891): 438–52.

———. "The Teaching of History in Academies and Colleges." In *Woman and the Higher Education*, edited by Anna C. Brackett. New York: Harper, 1893.

Smith, Emma P. "The Evolution of the Textbook in High School History." Master's thesis, Teachers College, Columbia University, 1909.

Thompson, Anna Boynton. "Suggestions to Teachers." In *Students' History of the United States*. New York: Macmillan, 1898.

Williams, Mary. "The Lecture Method: An Indictment." *Historical Outlook* 9 (June 1918).

———. "Outline for the Incidental Teaching of Hispanic-American History in the Secondary School." *Historical Outlook* 9 (June 1918).

Wright, Marion M. T. *Education of Negroes in New Jersey*. New York: Columbia University Teachers College, 1941.

Women's Labor/Immigrant History

Abbott, Edith. *Wages of Unskilled Labor, 1850–1900*. Chicago: University of Chicago Publications, 1905.

———. *Women in Industry: A Study in American Economic History*. New York: Appleton, 1910.

———. *Historical Aspects of the Immigration Problem*. Chicago: University of Chicago Press, 1926.

Adams, Elizabeth K. *Women Professional Workers: A Study Made for the Women's Educational and Industrial Union*. New York: Macmillan, 1921.

Beard, Mary. *Woman's Work in Municipalities*. New York: Appleton, 1915.

———. *A Short History of the American Labor Movement*. New York: Worker's Education Bureau of America, 1920.

Blackwell, Elizabeth. *Pioneer Work in Opening the Medical Profession to Women: Autobiographical Sketches*. London: Longmans, Green, 1895.

———. *Pioneer Work for Women*. New York: Dutton, 1914.

Campbell, Helen. *Prisoners of Poverty: Women wage-workers, their trades, and their lives*. Boston: Little, Brown, 1887.

——. *Women Wage-Earners: Their Past, their Present and their Future*. Boston: Roberts, 1893.

Clark, Alice. *The Working Life of Women in the Seventeenth Century*. New York: Harcourt Brace, 1920.

Coman, Katharine. *The History of Contract Labor in the Hawaiian Islands*. New York: Macmillan, 1903.

——. "A Sweated Industry." *Life and Labor*, January 1911, 13–15.

Eaton, Isabel. "Special report on Negro domestic service in the seventh ward, Philadelphia." In *The Philadelphia Negro: A Social Study*, edited by W. E. B. Du Bois, 425–509. Philadelphia: Publications of the University of Pennsylvania, 1899.

Gallagher, Katharine. "Problems of the Former German Colonies." *Current History Magazine* (February 1927).

——. "Women and the Guilds in Florence." Paper presented at the American Historical Association Annual Meeting, Minneapolis, Minn., 29 December 1931.

Hebard, Grace R. "Americanization and the Immigrant." *General Federation of Women's Clubs Magazine*, February 1917.

——. "Americanization of Alien Women." *Vanguard*, March 1918, 8–9.

Henry, Alice. *The Trade Union Woman*. New York: Appleton, 1915.

——. *Women and the Labor Movement*. New York: George Doran, 1923.

Jansen, Florence E. *The Background of Swedish Immigration, 1840–1930*. Chicago: University of Chicago Press, 1931.

Lebeson, Anita L. *Jewish Pioneers in America, 1492–1848*. New York: Brentano, 1931.

Lonn, Ella. "Problems of Americanization." *Bulletin of Goucher College*, April 1920.

——. *Problems in Americanization: A Course of Suggested Readings for Native Born Americans*. Baltimore: Women's Civic League, 1920.

Neff, Wanda. *Victorian Working Women*. New York: Columbia University Press, 1929.

Rhine, Alice H. "Women in Industry." In *Women's Work in America*, edited by Annie Nathan Meyer. New York: H. Holt, 1891.

Robinson, Harriet H. *Early Factory Labor in New England*. Boston: Wright and Potter, 1883.

——. *Loom and Spindle; or, life among the early mill girls*. New York: Crowell, 1898.

Salmon, Lucy M. *Domestic Service*. New York: Macmillan, 1897.

——. *Progress in the Household*. Boston: Houghton Mifflin, 1906.

Woodbury, Helen L. Sumner. "History of Women in Industry in the United States." In *Report on Conditions of Women and Child Wage Earners*. Vol. 9. Washington, D.C.: U.S. Bureau of Labor, 1910.

——. "The Historical Development of Women's Work in the United States." *Proceedings of the Academy of Political Science in the City of New York*. New York, 1929.

Woodbury, Helen L. Sumner, and Thomas Sewall Adams. *Labor Problems: A Textbook*. 4th ed. New York: Macmillan, 1905.

Woodbury, Helen L. Sumner, and J. R. Commons. *The Causes of the Union-Shop Policy*. N.p.: American Economics Association Publications, 1905.

Woodbury, Helen L. Sumner, John R. Commons, Ulrich Phillips, Eugene A. Gilmore, and John Andrews, eds. *A Documentary History of American Industrial Society*. Cleveland: Arthur H. Clark, 1910–11.

Woodbury, Helen L. Sumner, John R. Commons, David J. Saposs, E. B. Mittelman, H. E. Hoagland, and John B. Andrews, eds. *History of Labor in the United States.* New York: Macmillan, 1921–35.

Historical Works by Women Social Scientists

Blauvelt, Mary Taylor. "The Race Problem: As Discussed by Negro Women." *American Journal of Sociology* 6 (March 1901): 662–72.

Breckinridge, Sophonisba P. *Women in the Twentieth Century: A Study of their Political, Social, and Economic Activities.* New York: McGraw-Hill, 1933.

Campbell, Helen. *Household Economics.* New York: Putnam, 1897.

Coman, Katharine, and Katherine L. Bates. *English History Told by English Poets.* New York: Macmillan, 1902.

Gilman, Charlotte P. *Women and Economics.* Boston: Small, Maynard, 1898.

———. *The Man-Made World; or, Our Androcentric Culture.* New York: Charlton, 1911.

Hurston, Zora Neale. "Characteristics of Negro Expression." In *Negro: An Anthology*, compiled by Nancy Cunard. London: Wishart, 1934.

———. *Tell My Horse.* Philadelphia: Lippincott, 1938.

MacGill, Caroline E. *History of Transportation in the United States before 1860.* Washington, D.C.: Carnegie Institution of Washington, 1917.

Parkhurst, Jessie. "The Role of the Black Mammy in the Plantation Household." *Journal of Negro History* 23 (July 1938): 349–69.

Parsons, Elsie Clews. *The Family: An Ethnographical and Historical Outline with descriptive Notes, Planned as a Textbook.* New York: Putnam, 1906.

———. *The Old-Fashioned Woman: Primitive Fancies about Sex.* New York: Putnam, 1913.

———. *Fear and Conventionality.* New York: Putnam, 1914.

Spencer, Anna G. *Woman's Share in Social Culture.* New York: Mitchell Kennerley, 1913.

———. *The Family and Its Members.* Philadelphia: Lippincott, 1923.

Thompson, Helen B. *The Mental Traits of Sex.* Chicago: University of Chicago Press, 1903.

———. *Psychological Norms in Men and Women.* Chicago: University of Chicago Press, 1903.

Histories of Women's Institutions
(Patriotic Societies, Temperance, Higher Education, etc.)

Addams, Jane. *Women at The Hague.* New York: Macmillan, 1915.

Baker, Juliette Boyer, ed. *West Virginia State History of the Daughters of the American Revolution.* N.p., 1928.

Brackett, Anna C., ed. *Woman and the Higher Education.* New York: Harper, 1893.

Clarke, Ida C. *American Women and the World War.* New York: Appleton, 1918.

Cole, Marion S. *The Women's College in Brown University, Its Progress and Expansion.* Providence, R.I.: n.p., 1917.

Colonial Dames of America. *The Colonial Dames of America, 1890–1904.* New York: Irving Press, 1904.

———. *Patriotic and Historical Record of the Colonial Dames of America, 1890–1926.* New York: Colonial Dames of America, 1926.

Converse, Florence. *The Story of Wellesley*. Boston: Little, Brown, 1915.

Croly, Jennie C. *The History of the Woman's Club Movement in America*. New York: Henry G. Allen, 1898.

Degnan, Mary L. *The History of the Women's Peace Party*. Baltimore: Johns Hopkins University Press, 1939.

Dock, Lavinia L., Sarah Elizabeth Pickett, Clara D. Noyes, Fannie F. Clement, Elizabeth G. Fox, and Anna R. Van Meter. *History of American Red Cross Nursing*. New York: Macmillan, 1922.

Hurd-Mead, Dr. Kate Campbell. *A History of Women in Medicine*. Haddam, Conn.: Haddam Press, 1938.

Jacobi, Mary Putnam. "Women in Medicine." In *Women's Work in America*, edited by Annie Nathan Meyer. New York: H. Holt, 1891. ,

Lamar, Mrs. Joseph Rucker. *The National Society of Colonial Dames of America: Its Beginnings, Its Purpose, and a Record of Its Work, 1891–1913*. Washington, D.C.: The Society, 1913.

———. *A History of the National Society of the Colonial Dames of America, from 1891 to 1933*. Atlanta: Walter W. Brown, 1934.

Marshall, Clara. *The Woman's Medical College of Pennsylvania*. Philadelphia: P. Blakiston, Son, and Co., 1897.

McConnell, Dorothy. *Women, War, and Fascism*. New York: American League against War and Fascism, 1935.

Nutting, Adelaide, and Lavinia Dock. *A History of Nursing: From Earliest Times to the Present Day*. 4 vols. New York: Putnam, 1907–12.

———. *The History of Nursing: The Evolution of Nursing Systems from the Earliest Times to the Foundation of the First English and American Training Schools for Nurses*. New York: Putnam, 1937.

Pryor, Mrs. Roger A. *Reminiscences of Peace and War*. New York: Macmillan, 1905.

Seymour, Lucy Ridgely. *A General History of Nursing*. New York: Macmillan, 1933.

Stow, Sarah D. *History of Mount Holyoke Seminary, 1834–87*. Springfield, Mass.: Springfield Printing Co., 1887.

Talbot, Marion, and Lois Matthews Rosenberry. *The History of the American Association of University Women, 1881–1931*. Boston: Houghton Mifflin, 1931.

Terrell, Mary C. "The History of the Club Women's Movement." *Aframerican Women's Journal* 1 (Summer/Fall 1940): 34–38.

Thomas, Adam B. *Pathfinders: A History of Progress of Colored Graduate Nurses*. New York: Kay Printing House, 1929.

Victor, Frances F. *The Women's War with Whiskey; or, Crusading in Portland*. Portland, Ore.: George H. Himes, Steam Book and Job, 1874.

Walworth, Ellen H. "Principle of Organization of the National Society of the Daughters of the American Revolution." *American Monthly Magazine* 1 (1892): 8–11.

Ward, May. *The Influence of Women's Clubs in New England and the Middle-Eastern States*. Philadelphia: American Academy of Political and Social Science, 1906.

Weeden, Anne T. *The Women's College in Brown University, Its Origins and Development*. Providence, R.l.: n.p., 1912.

Willard, Frances. *Glimpses of Fifty Years: The Autobiography of an American Woman*. Chicago: Woman's Temperance Publication Association, 1889.

Wittenmyer, Annie. *History of the Woman's Temperance Crusade. A Complete Official History of the Wonderful Uprising of the Christian Woman of the United States*

Against the Liquor Traffic, Which Culminated in the Gospel Temperance Movement. Philadelphia: Office of the Christian Woman, 1878.
——. *History of the Woman's Temperance Crusade.* Boston: J. H. Earle, 1882.
Wood, Frances A. *Earliest Years at Vassar.* Poughkeepsie, N.Y.: Vassar College Press, 1909.
Wood, Mary I. *The History of the General Federation of Women's Clubs.* New York: General Federation of Women's Clubs, 1912.

Popular Women's History (Nonacademic)

Atkeson, Mary M. *The Woman on the Farm.* New York: Century, 1924.
Beard, Mary. *On Understanding Women.* New York: Grosset and Dunlap, 1931.
——. *Woman as Force in History: A Study in Traditions and Realities.* New York: Macmillan, 1946.
——, ed. *America through Women's Eyes.* New York: Macmillan, 1933.
Beard, Mary, and Martha Bruere, eds. *Laughing Their Way: Women's Humor in America.* New York: Macmillan, 1934.
Bennett Helen C. *American Women in Civic Work.* New York: Dodd, Mead, 1915.
Benson, Mary Sumner. *Women in Eighteenth Century America.* New York: Columbia University Press, 1935.
Brooks, Geraldine. *Dames and Daughters of Colonial Days.* New York: Crowell, 1901.
Cavert, Inez M. *Women in American Church Life.* New York: Friendship Press, 1948.
Creevey, Mrs. C. A. S. *A Daughter of the Puritans.* New York: Putnam, 1916.
Dexter, Elisabeth. *Colonial Women of Affairs.* Boston: Houghton Mifflin, 1924.
Dietrick, Ellen B. *Women in the Early Christian Ministry.* Philadelphia: Alfred J. Ferris, 1897.
Froiseth, Jennie Anderson, ed. *The Women of Mormonism; or, The Story of Polygamy as Told By the Victims Themselves.* Detroit: C. G. G. Paine, 1882.
Gamble, Eliza R. *The Sexes in Science and History.* New York: Putnam, 1916.
Heck, Fannie, E. S. *In Royal Service: The Mission Work of Southern Baptist Women.* Richmond: Education Department, Foreign Mission Board, Southern Baptist Convention, 1926.
Humphrey, Grace. *Women in American History.* Indianapolis: Bobbs-Merrill, 1919.
Ingpen, Ada M. *Women as Letter Writers.* New York: Baker and Taylor, 1909.
Logan, Mrs. John A. *The Part Taken by Women in American History.* Wilmington, Del.: Perry-Nalle, 1912.
Marble, Annie R. *The Women Who Came in the Mayflower.* Boston: Pilgrim Press, 1920.
Meyer, Annie Nathan, ed. *Woman's Work in America.* New York: H. Holt, 1891.
Neely, Ruth. *Women of Ohio: A Record of Their Achievements in the History of the State.* Chicago: S. J. Clarke, 1939.
Noyes, J. R. C. *The Women of the Mayflower.* Plymouth, Mass.: Memorial Press, 1921.
Putnam, Emily J. *The Lady: Studies of Certain Significant Phases of Her History.* New York: Sturgis and Walton, 1910.
Tandy, Mary I. *Living Female Writers of the South.* Philadelphia: Claxton, 1878.
Tillson, Christiana. *Woman's Story of Pioneer Illinois.* Chicago: R. R. Donnelley and Sons, 1919.

White, Sarah P. *A Moral History of Women*. New York: Doubleday, Doran, 1937.

Winter, Alice A. *The Heritage of Women*. New York: Minton, Balch, 1927.

African American Works of Historical Consciousness/Womanist History

Brown, Hallie Q., ed. *Homespun Heroines and Other Women of Distinction*. Xenia, Ohio: Aldine, 1926.

———. *Our Women Past, Present, and Future*. Xenia, Ohio: Eckerle, 1940.

Burroughs, Nannie. "Not Color but Character." *Voice of the Negro*, July 1904, 277–79.

Burton, Annie L. Campbell. *Memories of Childhood Slavery Days*. Boston: Ross, 1909.

Cooper, Anna J. *A Voice from the South*. Xenia, Ohio: Aldine, 1892.

Coppin, Fanny M. Jackson. *Reminiscences of School Life, and Hints on Teaching*. Philadelphia: AME Book Concern, 1913.

Curtis, Mary. *The Black Soldier: The Colored Boys of the United States Army*. Washington: A. D. Morris, 1915.

Cuthbert, Marion. *Education and Marginality: A Study of the Negro Woman College Graduate*. New York: Columbia University Press, 1942.

Daniel, Sadie I. *Women Builders*. Washington, D.C.: Associated Publishers, 1931.

Davis, Elizabeth L. *Lifting as They Climb*. Washington, D.C.: National Association of Colored Women, 1933.

Dunbar-Nelson, Alice Ruth. "Negro Women in War Work." In *Scott's Official History of the American Negro in the World War*, edited by Emmett J. Scott. Chicago: Homewood Press, 1919.

Evans, Aurora. "Origins and Work of the Daughters of Conference and Kindred Societies." *A.M.E. Zion Quarterly Review*, January 1898.

Fleming, Beatrice J. "America's First Woman Bank President." *Negro History Bulletin*, January 1942, 75.

———. *Distinguished Negroes Abroad*. Washington, D.C.: Associated Publishers, 1946.

Green, Elizabeth Lay. *The Negro in Contemporary American Literature*. Chapel Hill: University of North Carolina Press, 1928.

Harris, Meriah. "Women in the Pioneer Work of the Church." *A.M.E. Zion Quarterly Review*, April 1899.

Harris, Mrs. L. H. "Negro Womanhood." *Independent*, June 1899, 1687–90.

Haynes, Elizabeth R. "Negroes in Domestic Service in the United States." *Journal of Negro History* 8 (October 1923): 384–89.

Houston, Drusilla D. *Wonderful Ethiopians of the Ancient Cushite Empire*. Oklahoma City: Universal Publishing, 1926.

Hunter, Jane E. H. *A Nickel and a Prayer*. Cleveland: Elli Kani, 1940.

Hunton, Addie W. "Negro Womanhood Defended." *Voice of the Negro*, July 1904, 280–82.

Hunton, Addie W., and Kathryn M. Johnson. *Two Colored Women with the American Expeditionary Forces*. Brooklyn: Eagle Press, 1920.

Hurston, Zora Neale. *Dust Tracks on a Road: An Autobiography*. Philadelphia: Lippincott, 1942.

Isabelle, Lizzie. "The Women of Our Race Worthy of Imitation." *Christian Recorder*, 3 October 1889, 3.

Jenness, Mary. *Twelve Negro Americans.* New York: Friendship Press, 1936.

Johnson, Kathryn M. *The Dark Race in the Dawn: Proof of Black African Civilization, in the Americas before Columbus.* New York: William-Frederick Press, 1948.

Jones, Anna H. "A Century's Progress of the American Colored Woman." *Voice of the Negro,* August 1905, 631–33.

Mossell, Mrs. N. F. *The Work of the Afro-American Woman.* Philadelphia: George S. Ferguson, 1894.

Shackleford, Jane D. *The Child's Story of the Negro.* Washington, D.C.: Associated Publishers, 1938.

——. *My Happy Days.* Washington, D.C.: Associated Publishers, 1944.

Taylor, Mrs. G. E. "Woman's Work and Influence in Home and Church." *A.M.E. Church Review,* July 1906.

Taylor, Susan King. *Reminiscences of My Life in Camp with the 33rd United States Colored Troops, Late 1st S.C. Volunteers.* Boston: The author, 1902.

Terrell, Mary C. *A Colored Woman in a White World.* Washington, D.C.: Ransdell, 1940.

Thurman, Sue Bailey. *Pioneers of Negro Origin in California.* San Francisco: Acme, 1949.

Veney, Bethany. *The Narrative of Bethany Veney: A Slave Woman.* Worcester, Mass.: A. P. Bickness Press, 1889.

Wilkes, Laura. *Missing pages in American History, revealing the services of Negroes in the early wars in the United States of America, 1641–1815.* Washington, D.C.: R. I. Pendleton, 1919.

Secondary Sources

Women Historians and Preservationists in This Study

MARY BEARD

Carroll, Berenice. "Mary Beard's *Woman as Force in History*: A Critique." In *Liberating Women's History: Theoretical and Critical Essays,* edited by Berenice Carroll, 26–41. Urbana: University of Illinois Press, 1976.

Cott, Nancy. "Two Beards: Coauthorship and the Concept of Civilization." *American Quarterly* 42 (1990): 274–300.

——, ed. *A Woman Making History: Mary Ritter Beard.* New Haven: Yale University Press, 1991.

Degler, Carl N. "*Woman as Force in History* by Mary Beard." *Daedalus* 103 (1974): 71–72.

Lane, Ann, ed. *Mary Ritter Beard: A Sourcebook.* Boston: Northeastern University Press, 1988.

Lebsock, Suzanne. "Reading Mary Beard." *Reviews in American History* 17 (June 1989): 324–39.

Smith, Bonnie. "Seeing Mary Beard." *Feminist Studies* 10 (Fall 1984): 399–416.

Trigg, Mary Kathleen. "Four American Feminists, 1910–1940: Inez Haynes Irwin, Mary Ritter Beard, Doris Stevens, and Lorine Pruette." Ph.D. diss., Brown University, 1989.

Turoff, Barbara K. *Mary Ritter Beard as Force in History.* Dayton, Ohio: Wright State University Monograph Series, 1979.

Zimmerman, Loretta. "Mary Ritter Beard: An Activist of the Progressive Era." *University of Portland Review* 26 (Spring 1974): 18–36.

OTHER HISTORIANS/COLLECTORS/SOCIAL SCIENTISTS

Adams, Nicholas, and Bonnie Smith, eds. *History and the Texture of Modern Life: Selected Essays.* Philadelphia: University of Pennsylvania Press, 2001.

Antler, Joyce. "Between Culture and Politics: The Emma Lazarus Federation of Jewish Women's Clubs and the Promulgation of Women's History, 1944–1989." In *U.S. History as Women's History: New Feminist Essays*, edited by Linda K. Kerber, Alice Kessler-Harris, and Kathryn Kish Sklar, 267–95. Chapel Hill: University of North Carolina Press, 1995.

Averill, Esther C. "Alice Morse Earle, a Writer Who Popularized Old New England." *Old-Time New England* 37 (January 1947): 73–78.

Barry, Kathleen. *Susan B. Anthony: A Biography of a Singular Feminist.* New York: New York University Press, 1988.

Berg, Maxine. "The First Women Economic Historians." *Economic History Review* 45 (1992): 308–26.

Bleser, Carol K. "The Three Women Presidents of the Southern Historical Association: Ella Lonn, Kathryn Abby Hanna, and Mary Elizabeth Massey." *Southern Studies* 20 (Summer 1981): 101–21.

Brady, Kathleen. *Ida Tarbell: Portrait of a Muckraker.* New York: Seaview/Putnam, 1984.

Brown, Louise Fargo. *Apostle of Democracy: The Life of Lucy Maynard Salmon.* New York: Harper and Brothers, 1943.

Buhle, Mari Jo, and Paul Buhle, eds. *The Concise History of Woman Suffrage: Selections from the Classic Work of Stanton, Anthony, Gage, and Harper.* Urbana: University of Illinois Press, 1978.

College of Arts and Sciences, Department of History. *Angie Debo: An Autobiographical Sketch, Eulogy, and Biography.* Stillwater: Oklahoma State University, 1988.

Costin, Lela. *Two Sisters for Social Justice: A Biography of Grace and Edith Abbott.* Urbana: University of Illinois Press, 1983.

Daniels, Elizabeth A. "Lucy Maynard Salmon and James Baldwin: A Forgotten Episode." Paper prepared for the Evelyn A. Clark Conference, Vassar College, 12–13 October 1984.

French, Hanna D. "Ella L. Elbert." In "Slave Narratives from the Collection of Robert Mara Adger." Unpublished exhibition notes, Rare Book Room, Wellesley College, 1977.

Goggin, Jacqueline. "Mary Wilhelmine Williams: Feminist, Activist, and Historian." Paper presented at the Eighth Berkshire Conference on the History of Women, Douglas College, 9 June 1990, and at the Bunting Institute Colloquium Series, Radcliffe College, January 1991. Berkshire Conference of Women Historians Papers, Schlesinger Library, Radcliffe College.

———. "Challenging Sexual Discrimination in the Historical Profession: Women Historians and the American Historical Association, 1890–1940." *American Historical Review* 97 (June 1992): 769–802.

———. "Bessie L. Pierce and the Creation of *Public Opinion and the Teaching of History*." Vassar College, 1993. Berkshire Conference of Women Historians Papers, Schlesinger Library, Radcliffe College.

Hastings, Margaret, and Elisabeth G. Kimball. "Two Distinguished Medievalists: Nellie Neilson and Bertha Haven Putnam." *Journal of British Studies* 18 (Summer 1979): 142–59.

Holt, Rackham. *Mary McLeod Bethune: A Biography*. New York: Doubleday, 1964.

Indians, Outlaws, and Angie Debo. Video transcript. Boston: WGBH, 1988.

James, Janet W. "History and Women at Harvard: The Schlesinger Library." *Harvard Library Bulletin* 16 (October 1968): 385–99.

Jones, Beverly W. *Quest for Equality: The Life and Writings of Mary Eliza Church Terrell, 1863–1954*. Brooklyn: Carlson, 1990.

Judson, Margaret A. *Breaking the Barrier: A Professional Autobiography by a Woman Educator and Historian before the Women's Movement*. New Brunswick: Rutgers University Press, 1984.

Kammen, Michael. *In the Past Lane: Historical Perspectives on American Culture*. New York: Oxford University Press, 1997.

Kaplan, Carla, ed. *Zora Neale Hurston: A Life in Letters*. New York: Doubleday, 2002.

Kelsey, Harry. "A Dedication to the Memory of Annie Heloise Abel-Henderson, 1873–1947." In *Arizona and the West*, 1–2. Tucson: University of Arizona Press, 1973.

Leckie, Shirley A. *Angie Debo: Pioneer Historian*. Norman: University of Oklahoma Press, 2000.

Lerner, Gerda. *Fireweed: A Political Autobiography*. Philadelphia: Temple University Press, 2002.

Mark, Joan. *A Stranger in Her Native Land: Alice Fletcher and the American Indians*. Lincoln: University of Nebraska Press, 1989.

Martin, Jim. *A Bit of Blue: The Life and Work of Frances Fuller Victor*. Salem, Ore.: Deep Well, 1992.

Mathes, Valerie S. *Helen Hunt Jackson and Her Indian Reform Legacy*. Austin: University of Texas Press, 1990.

Matthews, Glenna, and Gloria Valencia-Weber. "Against Great Odds: The Life of Angie Debo." *Organization of American Historians' Newsletter* 13 (May 1985): 8–11.

Merrill, Marlene D., ed. *Growing Up in Boston's Gilded Age: The Journal of Alice Stone Blackwell, 1872–1874*. New Haven: Yale University Press, 1990.

Mills, Hazel E. "The Emergence of Frances Fuller Victor, Historian." *Oregon Historical Quarterly* 62 (December 1961): 309–36.

Morris, William A. "Historian of the Northwest." *Quarterly of the Oregon Historical Society* 3 (December 1902): 429–34.

Peterson, Levi S. *Juanita Brooks: Mormon Woman Historian*. Salt Lake City: University of Utah Press, 1988.

Scanlon, Jennifer, and Sharon Cosner, eds. *American Women Historians, 1700s–1900s: A Biographical Dictionary*. Westport, Conn.: Greenwood Press, 1996.

Scott, Anne Firor. *Making the Invisible Woman Visible*. Urbana: University of Illinois Press, 1984.

——. *Unheard Voices: The First Historians of Southern Women*. Charlottesville: University Press of Virginia, 1993.

Scott, Joan W. "American Women Historians, 1884–1984." In *Gender and the Politics of History*, 178–98. New York: Columbia University Press, 1988.

Sklar, Kathryn Kish. "American Female Historians in Context, 1770–1930." *Feminist Studies* 3 (Fall 1975): 171–84.

Smith, Bonnie. "The Contribution of Women to Modern Historiography in Great Britain, France, and the United States, 1750–1940." *American Historical Review* 89 (June 1984): 709–32.

———. "History Written and Professed: Women Inside and Outside the Academy, 1880–1930." Unpublished paper presented at the meeting of the American Historical Association, San Francisco, December 1989.

———. *The Gender of History: Men, Women, and Historical Practice*. Cambridge: Harvard University Press, 1998.

Smith, Trudi. *Sue Bailey Thurman: Building Bridges to Common Ground*. Boston: Trustees of Boston University, 1995.

Tibbets, Celeste. *Ernestine Rose and the Origins of the Schomburg Center*. New York: Schomburg Center for Research in Black Culture, 1989.

Washington, Mary Helen. "Anna Julia Cooper: The Black Feminist Voice of the 1890s." *Legacy*, Fall 1987, 3–15.

Wenzel, Janell M. "Dr. Grace Raymond Hebard as Western Historian." Master's thesis, University of Wyoming, 1960.

Whitaker, Rosemary. *Helen Hunt Jackson*. Boise: Boise State University Western Writers, 1987.

Williams, Susan R. "In the Garden of New England: Alice Morse Earle and the History of Domestic Life." Ph.D. diss., University of Delaware, 1992.

"The Woman Historian: Interesting Passages in the Life of Frances Fuller Victor." *San Francisco Call*, 7 July 1895, 20.

History of Women's Professionalization and Higher Education

Aisenberg, Nadya, and Mona Harrington. *Women of Academe: Outsiders in the Sacred Grove*. Amherst: University of Massachusetts Press, 1988.

Antler, Joyce. *The Educated Woman and Professionalization: The Struggle for a New Feminine Identity, 1890–1920*. New York: Garland, 1987.

Beard, Mary. "University Discipline for Women: Asset or Handicap?" *Journal of the American Association of University Women* 25 (April 1932): 129–33.

———. *A Changing Political Economy as It Affects Women*. Washington, D.C.: American Association of University Women, 1934.

Brumberg, Joan Jacobs, and Nancy Tomes. "Women in the Professions: A Research Agenda for American Historians." *Reviews in American History* 10 (June 1982): 275–96.

Carter, Susan B. "Academic Women Revisited: An Empirical Study of Changing Patterns in Women's Employment as College and University Faculty, 1890–1963." *Journal of Social History* 14 (Summer 1981): 675–99.

Caswell, Ellis. "Preliminary Report of Committee W, on the Status of Women in College and University Faculties." *American Association of University Professors Bulletin* 7 (October 1921): 21–32.

Clifford, Geraldine J., ed. *Lone Voyagers: Academic Women in Coeducational Universities, 1870–1937*. New York: Feminist Press, 1989.

Conway, Jill. "Perspectives on the History of Women's Education in the United States." *History of Education Quarterly* 14 (Spring 1974): 1–12.

Fitzpatrick, Ellen. *Endless Crusade: Women Social Scientists and Progressive Reform*. New York: Oxford University Press, 1990.

Freeman, Jo. "Women on the Social Science Faculties since 1892, University of Chicago." Transcript of speech delivered at the minority workshop of the Political Science Association Conference, the University Panel on the status of women at Chicago, Winter 1969.

Garrison, Dee. *Apostles of Culture: The Public Librarian and American Society, 1876–1920*. New York: Free Press, 1979.

Glazer, Penina, and Miriam Slater. *Unequal Colleagues: The Entrance of Women into the Professions, 1890–1940*. New Brunswick: Rutgers University Press, 1987.

Gordon, Lynn. "Coeducation on Two Campuses: Berkeley and Chicago, 1890–1912." In *Women's Being, Women's Place: Female Identity and Vocation in American History*, edited by Mary Kelley, 171–93. Boston: G. K. Hall, 1979.

——. *Gender and Higher Education in the Progressive Era*. New Haven: Yale University Press, 1990.

Graham, Patricia Albjerg. "Expansion and Exclusion: A History of Women in American Higher Education." *Signs* 3 (Summer 1978): 759–73.

Hesseltine, William B., and Louis Kaplan. "Women Doctors of Philosophy in History." *Journal of Higher Education* 14 (May 1943): 235–59.

Hoffman, Nancy. *"Women's True Profession": Voices from the History of Teaching*. Old Westbury, N.Y.: Feminist Press, 1981.

Holmes, Lulu. *A History of the Position of the Dean of Women in a Selected Group of Co-Educational Colleges and Universities in the United States*. New York: Teachers College, Columbia University Contributions to Education, 1939.

Horowitz, Helen L. *Alma Mater: Design and Experience in the Women's Colleges from Their Nineteenth Century Beginnings to the 1930s*. New York: Knopf, 1984.

——. "Does Gender Bend the History of Higher Education?" *American Literary History* 7 (Summer 1995): 344–49.

Hummer, Patricia M. *The Decade of Elusive Promise: Professional Women in the United States, 1920–1930*. Ann Arbor: UMI Research Premise, 1976.

Hutchinson, Emilie J. "The Vocational Interest of College Women." *Columbia University Quarterly*, June 1915, 227–32.

——. *Women and the Ph.D.: Facts from the Experiences of 1,025 Women Who Have Taken the Degree of Doctor of Philosophy since 1877*. Greensboro: Institutes of Women's Professional Relations at North Carolina College for Women, 1930.

Jones, Jane L. *A Personnel Study of Women Deans in Colleges and Universities*. New York: Teachers College, Columbia University Contributions to Education, 1928.

Lonn, Ella. "Academic Status of Women on University Faculties." *Journal of the American Association of University Women* 17 (January 1924): 5–11.

——. "The Work of Recognition." *Journal of the American Association of University Women* 20 (January 1927): 33–36.

Lurie, Nancy O. "Women in Early American Anthropology." In *Pioneers of American Anthropology*, edited by June Helm, 29–81. Seattle: University of Washington Press, 1966.

Mathew, Lois Kimball. *The Dean of Women*. Boston: Houghton Mifflin, 1915.

Muncy, Robyn. *Creating a Female Dominion in American Reform, 1890–1935*. New York: Oxford University Press, 1991.

Newcomer, Mabel. *A Century of Women's Higher Education*. New York: Harper and Brothers, 1959.

Olin, Helen. *The Women of a State University*. New York: Putnam, 1910.

Palmieri, Patricia. *In Adamless Eden: The Community of Women Faculty at Wellesley*. New Haven: Yale University Press, 1995.

Pollard, Lucille A. *Women on College and University Faculties: A Historical Survey and a Study of Their Present Academic Status*. New York: Arno Press, 1977.

Robinson, Mabel L. *The Curriculum of the Woman's College*. Washington, D.C.: Government Printing Office, 1918.

Rosenberg, Rosalind. *Beyond Separate Spheres: Intellectual Roots of Modern Feminism*. New Haven: Yale University Press, 1982.

Rossiter, Margaret W. *Women Scientists in America: Struggle and Strategies to 1940*. Baltimore: Johns Hopkins University Press, 1982.

Silverberg, Helene, ed. *Gender and American Social Science: The Formative Years*. Princeton: Princeton University Press, 1998.

Solomon, Barbara. *In the Company of Educated Women: A History of Women and Higher Education in America*. New Haven: Yale University Press, 1985.

"A Statistical Report on the Participation of Women in the Southern Historical Association, 1935–1985." *Journal of Southern History* 52 (May 1986): 282–88.

Sturtevant, Sarah, and Ruth Strang. *Personnel Study of Deans of Women in Teachers Colleges and Normal Schools*. New York: Teachers College, 1928.

Talbot, Marion. *The Education of Women*. Chicago: University of Chicago Press, 1910.

Woody, Thomas. *A History of Women's Education in the United States*. New York: Science Press, 1929.

Historiography and the History of Social Science/Historical Disciplines

Adams, Herbert B. *The Study and Teaching of History*. Richmond: Whittet and Shepperson, 1898.

——. *Leopold von Ranke*. Boston: American Academy of the Arts and Sciences, n.d.

Appleby, Joyce, Lynn Hunt, and Margaret Jacob. *Telling the Truth about History*. New York: Norton, 1994.

Bassett, John Spencer. *The Middle Group of American Historians*. New York: Macmillan, 1917.

Beard, Charles. "Written History as an Act of Faith." *American Historical Review* 39 (January 1934): 219–31.

Bender, Thomas. "The New History—Then and Now." *Reviews in American History* 12 (December 1984): 612–22.

Breisach, Ernst A. *American Progressive History: An Experiment in Modernization*. Chicago: University of Chicago Press, 1993.

Channing, Edward, Frederick Jackson Turner, and Albert Bushnell Hart. *Guide to the Study and Reading of American History*. Boston: Ginn, 1896.

Fitzgerald, Frances. *America Revised: History Schoolbooks in the Twentieth Century*. Boston: Little, Brown, 1979.

Furner, Mary O. *Advocacy and Objectivity: A Crisis in the Professionalization of American Social Science, 1865–1905*. Lexington: University Press of Kentucky, 1975.

Haines, Deborah L. "Scientific History as a Teaching Method: The Formative Years." *Journal of American History* 63 (1976–77): 892–912.

Hall, G. Stanley, ed. *Methods of Teaching History*. Boston: Heath, 1883.

Haskell, Thomas L. *The Emergence of Professional Social Science: the American Social*

Science Association and the Nineteenth Century Crisis of Authority. Urbana: University of Illinois Press, 1977.

———, ed. *The Authority of Experts: Studies in History and Theory.* Bloomington: Indiana University Press, 1984.

Hauptman, Laurence M. "Mythologizing Westward Expansion: Schoolbooks and the Image of the American Frontier before Turner." *Western Historical Quarterly* 8 (July 1977): 269–82.

Higham, John. *History: Professional Scholarship in America.* Baltimore: Johns Hopkins University Press, 1989.

Higham, John, Leonard Krieger, and Felix Gilbert. *History: The Development of Historical Studies in the United States.* Englewood Cliffs, N.J.: Prentice-Hall, 1965.

Hofstadter, Richard. *The Progressive Historians: Turner, Beard, Parrington.* New York: Knopf, 1968.

Hollinger, David. "Inquiry and Uplift: Late Nineteenth-Century American Academics and the Moral Efficiency of Scientific Practice." In *The Authority of Experts: Studies in History and Theory,* edited by Thomas L. Haskell, 144–51. Bloomington: Indiana University Press, 1984.

Jameson, Franklin. *The History of Historical Writing in America.* Boston: Houghton Mifflin, 1891.

———. "The American Historical Association, 1884–1909." *American Historical Review* 15 (October 1909): 1–20.

———. "The American Historical Review, 1895–1920." *American Historical Review* 26 (October 1920): 6.

———. "Early Days of the American Historical Association, 1884–1895." *American Historical Review* 40 (October 1934): 1–9.

Larson, Magali S. *The Rise of Professionalism: A Sociological Analysis.* Berkeley: University of California Press, 1977.

Link, Arthur. "The American Historical Association, 1884–1984: Retrospect and Prospect." *American Historical Review* 90 (February 1985): 1–17.

Mahan, Harold E. *Benson J. Lossing and Historical Writing in the United States, 1830–1890.* Westport, Conn.: Greenwood Press, 1996.

Noble, David. *Historians against History: The Frontier Thesis and the National Covenant in American Historical Writing since 1830.* Minneapolis: University of Minnesota Press, 1965.

Novick, Peter. *That Noble Dream: The "Objectivity Question" and the American Historical Profession.* New York: Cambridge University Press, 1988.

Ogg, Frederick A. "On the Literary Decline of History." *Dial,* 1 April 1902, 233–35.

Ross, Dorothy. "American Social Science and the Idea of Progress." In *The Authority of Experts: Studies in History and Theory,* edited by Thomas Haskell, 157–70. Bloomington: Indiana University Press, 1984.

———. "Historical Consciousness in Nineteenth-Century America." *American Historical Review* 89 (October 1984): 909–28.

Rothberg, Morey D. "Servant to History: A Study of John Franklin Jameson, 1859–1937." Ph.D. diss., Brown University, 1982.

Shotwell, J. T. *An Introduction to the History of History.* New York: Columbia University Press, 1922.

Turner, Frederick Jackson. *The Frontier in American History.* New York: H. Holt, 1920.

Van Tassell, David. "The American Historical Association and the South." *Journal of Southern History* 23 (November 1957): 465–82.

———. "From Learned Society to Professional Organization: The American Historical Association, 1884–1900." *American Historical Review* 89 (October 1984): 929–56.

Vitzthum, Richard. *The American Compromise: Theme and Method in the Histories of Bancroft, Parkman, and Adams.* Norman: University of Oklahoma Press, 1974.

Winsor, Justin. "The Perils of Historical Narrative." *Atlantic*, September 1890, 289–97.

Historical Memory

Axelrod, Allan, ed. *The Colonial Revival in America.* New York: Norton, 1985.

Beard, Mary. "Memory and Human Relations." *Key of Kappa Kappa Gamma*, 1 December 1936, 308–11.

Benson, Susan Porter, Steven Brier, and Roy Rosenzweig, eds. *Presenting the Past: Essays on History and the Public.* Philadelphia: Temple University Press, 1986.

Blatti, Jo, ed. *Past Meets Present: Essay about Historic Interpretation and Public Audiences.* Washington, D.C.: Smithsonian Institution Press, 1995.

Bodnar, John. *Remaking America: Public Memory, Commemoration, and Patriotism in the Twentieth Century.* Princeton: Princeton University Press, 1992.

Glassberg, David. *American Historical Pageantry: The Uses of Tradition in the Early Twentieth Century.* Chapel Hill: University of North Carolina Press, 1990.

———. "Public History and the Study of Memory." *Public Historian* 18 (Spring 1996): 7–24.

Kammen, Michael. *Selvages and Biases: The Fabric of History in American Culture.* Ithaca: Cornell University Press, 1987.

———. *Mystic Chords of Memory: The Transformation of Tradition in American Culture.* New York: Knopf, 1991.

Lowenthal, David. *The Past Is a Foreign Country.* New York: Cambridge University Press, 1985.

Marling, Karal Ann. *George Washington Slept Here: Colonial Revivals and American Culture.* Cambridge: Harvard University Press, 1988.

May, Bridget A. "Progressivism and the Colonial Revival: The Modern Colonial House, 1900–1920." *Winterthur Portfolio* 26 (1991): 108–22.

Rhodes, William B. *The Colonial Revival.* New York: Garland, 1977.

Riley, Glenda. "Frederick Jackson Turner Overlooked the Ladies." *Journal of the Early Republic* 13 (Summer 1993): 216–30.

Van Howe, Annette. "Remembering the Women of History." *Humanist*, September/October 1996, 27–28.

Women's/Race Preservation and the WPA's Historical Record Survey

Ball, Wendy, and Tony Martin. *Rare Afro-Americana: A Reconstruction of the Adger Library.* Boston: G. K. Hall, 1981.

Battle, Thomas. "Research Centers Document the Black Experience." *History News* 36 (February 1981): 8–11.

Collier-Thomas, Bettye. "Towards Black Feminism: The Creation of the Bethune Museum Archives." *Special Collections: Women's Collections, Libraries, Archives, and Consciousness* 3 (Spring/Summer 1986): 43–63.

Davies, Wallace Evans. *Patriotism on Parade: The Story of Veterans' and Hereditary Organizations in America, 1783–1900.* Cambridge: Harvard University Press, 1955.

Evans, Luther H. *The Historical Records Survey: A Statement on Its Program and Accomplishments Presented to the Sub-Committee of the Senate Committee on Education and Labor, in Connection with the Bill to Create a Permanent Bureau of Fine Arts.* Washington, D.C.: Historical Records Survey Division of Women's and Professional Projects, WPA, 1938.

Glaser, Jane R., and Artemis A. Zenetou, eds. *Gender Perspectives: Essays on Women in Museums.* Washington, D.C.: Smithsonian Institution Press, 1994.

Goggin, Jacqueline. "Politics, Patriotism, and Professionalism: American Women Historians and the Preservation of Southern Culture, 1890–1940." Paper presented at the American Historical Association Annual Meeting, San Francisco, December 1989.

Gold, Renee. "A Room of One's Own: Radcliffe's Schlesinger Library." *Wilson Library Bulletin* 55 (June 1981): 750–55.

Hicks, Ellen C., ed. *Women's Changing Roles in Museums.* Washington, D.C.: Smithsonian Institution Press, 1986.

Hildenbrand, Suzanne. "Women's Collections Today." *Special Collections: Women's Collections, Libraries, Archives, and Consciousness* 3 (Spring/Summer 1986): 1–4.

Hildenbrand, Suzanne, and Edyth Wynner. "Women for Peace: The Schwimmer-Lloyd Collection of the New York Public Library." *Special Collections: Women's Collections, Libraries, Archives, and Consciousness* 3 (Spring/Summer 1986): 37–42.

Hosmer, Charles B., Jr. *Presence of the Past: A History of the Preservation Movement in the United States before Williamsburg.* New York: Putnam, 1965.

Howe, Barbara J. "Women in Historic Preservation: The Legacy of Ann Pamela Cunningham." *Public Historian* 12 (Winter 1990): 31–61.

Kellock, Katherine. "The WPA Writers: Portraitists of the United States." *American Scholar* 9 (Autumn 1940): 474.

King, Patricia M. "Forty Years of Collecting on Women: The Arthur and Elizabeth Schlesinger Library on the History of Women in America, Radcliffe College." *Special Collections: Women's Collections, Libraries, Archives, and Consciousness* 3 (Spring/Summer 1986): 75–100.

Leffler, Phyllis K., and Joseph Brent. *Public and Academic History: A Philosophy and Paradigm.* Malabar, Fla.: R. E. Krieger, 1990.

Lindgren, James. *Preserving the Old Dominion: Historic Preservation and Virginia Traditionalism.* Charlottesville: University Press of Virginia, 1993.

———. "'A New Departure in Historic, Patriotic Work': Personalism, Professionalism, and Conflicting Concepts of Material Culture in the Late Nineteenth and Early Twentieth Centuries." *Public Historian* 18 (Spring 1996): 42–60.

Moseley, Eva. "Women's Archives: Documenting the History of Women in America." *American Archivist* 36 (April 1973): 215–22.

Murdock, Mary-Elizabeth. "Exploring Women's Lives: Historical and Contemporary Resources in the College Archives and the Sophia Smith Collection at Smith College." *Special Collections: Women's Collections, Libraries, Archives, and Consciousness* 3 (Spring/Summer 1986): 67–74.

Perez, Madeleine B. "'Remember the Ladies . . .': The Arthur and Elizabeth Schlesinger Library on the History of Women in America: Its Role in the

Collection and Preservation of Women's History Source Materials." Master's thesis, Wake Forest University, 1982.

Pritchard, Sarah. "Library of Congress Resources for the Study of Women." *Special Collections: Women's Collections, Libraries, Archives, and Consciousness* 3 (Spring/Summer 1986): 13–36.

Ruffins, Fath D. "The Historic House Museum as History Text: The Frederick Douglass Home at Cedar Hill." Paper delivered to Museum Education Program, George Washington University, 9 October 1984.

Sinnette, Elinor. "Arthur Alfonso Schomburg, Black Bibliophile and Curator: His Contribution to the Collection and Dissemination of Materials about Africans and People of African Descent." Ph.D. diss., Columbia University, 1977.

Smith, Margaret S. "Beyond the Domestic Sphere . . . Barely: Early Women Preservationists and Historic Preservation." Paper presented at National Trust for Historic Preservation Annual Meeting, Washington, D.C., October 1987.

Somerville, Mollie. *Historic and Memorial Buildings of the Daughters of the American Revolution.* Washington, D.C.: National Society of the Daughters of the American Revolution, 1979.

Spady, James. "The Afro-American Historical Society: The Nucleus of Black Bibliophiles, 1897–1923." *Negro History Bulletin,* June/July 1974, 254–57.

Stewart, Jeffrey C., and Fath Davis Ruffins. "A Faithful Witness: Afro-American Public History in Historical Perspective, 1828–1984." In *Presenting the Past: Essays on History and the Public,* edited by Susan Porter Benson, Steven Brier, and Roy Rosenzweig, 310–35. Philadelphia: Temple University Press, 1986.

Strayer, Martha. *The D.A.R.: An Informal History.* Westport, Conn.: Greenwood Press, 1958.

Women's Genres

Anderson, Linda. *Women and Autobiography in the Twentieth Century: Remembered Futures.* New York: Prentice Hall/Harvester Wheatsheaf, 1997.

Armitage, Susan, and Elizabeth Jameson, eds. *The Women's West.* Norman: University of Oklahoma Press, 1987.

Baym, Nina. "Mercy Otis Warren's Gendered Melodrama of Revolution." *South Atlantic Quarterly* 90 (Summer 1991): 531–54.

———. "Between Enlightenment and Victorian: Toward a Narrative of American Women Writers Writing History." *Critical Inquiry* 18 (Autumn 1991): 22–41.

———. *American Women Writers and the Work of History, 1790–1860.* New Brunswick: Rutgers University Press, 1995.

Bennion, Sherilyn C. *Equal to the Occasion: Women Editors of the Nineteenth Century West.* Reno: University of Nevada Press, 1990.

Coultrap-McQuin, Susan. *Doing Literary Business: American Women Writers in the Nineteenth Century.* Chapel Hill: University of North Carolina Press, 1990.

Donovan, Josephine. *New England Local Color Literature: A Woman's Tradition.* New York: Ungar, 1983.

Douglas, Ann. "The Literature of Impoverishment: The Women Local Colorists in America, 1865–1914." *Women's Studies* 1 (1972): 3–45.

DuBois, Ellen C. "Making Women's History: Active Historians of Women's Rights, 1880–1940." In *Intellectuals and Public Life: Between Radicalism and Reform,* edited by Leon Fink, Stephen T. Leonard, and Donald M. Reid, 214–27. Ithaca: Cornell University Press, 1996.

Egli, Ida R. *No Rooms of Their Own: Women Writers of Early California*. Berkeley: Heyday Books, 1992.

Fetterley, Judith, and Marjorie Pryse, eds. *American Women Regionalists, 1850–1910*. New York: Norton, 1992.

Fischer, Christiane, ed. *Let Them Speak for Themselves: Women in the American West, 1849–1900*. Hamden, Conn.: Shoe String Press, 1977.

Georgi-Findlay, Brigitte. *The Frontiers of Women's Writing: Women's Narratives and the Rhetoric of Westward Expansion*. Tucson: University of Arizona Press, 1996.

Harris, Sharon. "Whose Past Is It? Women Writers in Early America." *Early American Literature* 30 (1995): 175–81.

Heatherinton, Madelon E. "Romance without Women: The Sterile Fiction of the American West." *Georgia Review* 33 (1979): 643–56.

Kelley, Mary. *Private Woman, Public Stage: Literary Domesticity in Nineteenth-Century America*. New York: Oxford University Press, 1984.

Knight, Denise D. *Nineteenth-Century American Women Writers: A Bio-Bibliographical Critical Sourcebook*. Westport, Conn.: Greenwood Press, 1997.

Lee, L. L., and Merrill Lewis, eds. *Women, Women Writers, and the West*. Troy, N.Y.: Whitson, 1979.

Mainiero, Lina, ed. *American Women Writers*. New York: Ungar, 1979.

Maitzen, Rohan. "This Feminine Preserve: Historical Biographies by Victorian Women." *Victorian Studies* 38 (Spring 1995): 371–93.

Mills, Sara. *Discourses of Difference: An Analysis of Women's Travel Writing and Colonialism*. New York: Routledge, 1991.

Mulder, William, and Russell Mortensen, eds. *Among the Mormons: Historic Accounts by Contemporary Observers*. New York: Knopf, 1958.

Myres, Sandra L. "Army Women's Narratives as Documents of Social History: Some Examples from the Western Frontier, 1840–1900." *New Mexico Historical Review* 65 (April 1990): 175–98.

Showalter, Elaine, ed. *These Modern Women: Autobiographical Essays from the Twenties*. Old Westbury, N.Y.: Feminist Press, 1978.

Stauffer, Helen Winter, and Susan J. Rosowski. *Women and Western American Literature*. Troy, N.Y.: Whitson, 1982.

African American Women/Writers/Historians/Sources

African American Women: A Biographical Dictionary. Vol. 2 of *Biographical Dictionaries of Minority Women*. New York: Garland, 1993.

Afro-American Women Writers, 1746–1933: An Anthology and Critical Guide. Boston: G. K. Hall, 1988.

Alfred, Mary V. "Outsiders-Within: The Professional Development History of Black Tenured Female Faculty in the White Research Academy." Ph.D. diss., University of Texas at Austin, 1995.

Berkeley, Kathleen C. " 'Colored Ladies Also Contributed': Black Women's Activities from Benevolence to Social Welfare, 1866–1896." *Black Book Publishers in the United States: A Historical Dictionary of the Presses, 1917–1990*. Westport, Conn.: Greenwood Press, 1991.

Braxton, Joanne M. *Black Women Writing Autobiography: A Tradition within a Tradition*. Philadelphia: Temple University Press, 1989.

Brignano, Russel C. *Black Americans in Autobiography: An Annotated Bibliography of Autobiographies and Autobiographical Books Written since the Civil War*. Durham, N.C.: Duke University Press, 1984.

Bullock, Penelope. *The Afro-American Periodical Press, 1838–1909*. Baton Rouge: Louisiana State University Press, 1981.

Carby, Hazel. *Reconstructing Womanhood: The Emergence of the Afro-American Woman Novelist*. New York: Oxford University Press, 1987.

Christian, Barbara. *Black Women Novelists: The Development of a Tradition, 1892–1976*. Westport, Conn.: Greenwood Press, 1980.

Collected Black Women Narratives. The Schomburg Library of Nineteenth-Century Black Women Writers. New York: Oxford University Press, 1988.

Dann, Martin E., comp. *The Black Press, 1827–1890: The Quest for National Identity*. New York: Putnam, 1971.

Davis, Charles, and Henry Louis Gates Jr., eds. *The Slave's Narrative*. 2nd ed. New York: Oxford University Press, 1985.

DuMont, Rosemary R. "The Education of Black Librarians: An Historical Perspective." *Journal of Education for Library and Information Science* 26 (1985–86): 233–48.

Ferguson, Moira, ed. *Nine Black Women: An Anthology of Nineteenth-Century Writers from the United States, Canada, Bermuda, and the Caribbean*. New York: Routledge, 1998.

Foster, Frances S. *Witnessing Slavery: The Development of Ante-bellum Slave Narratives*. Westport, Conn.: Greenwood Press, 1979.

——. *Written by Herself: Literary Production by African American Women, 1746–1892*. Bloomington: Indiana University Press, 1993.

Gates, Henry Louis, and K. A. Appiah, eds. *Zora Neale Hurston: Critical Perspectives Past and Present*. New York: Amistad Press, 1993.

Glikin, Ronda. *Black American Women in Literature: A Bibliography, 1976–1987*. Jefferson, N.C.: McFarland, 1989.

Goggin, Jacqueline. "Countering White Racist Scholarship: Carter G. Woodson and the *Journal of Negro History*." *Journal of Negro History* 68 (Fall 1983): 355–75.

——. "Carter G. Woodson and the Movement to Promote Black History." Ph.D. diss., University of Rochester, 1984.

Gubert, Betty K. *Black Bibliographies, 1863–1918*. New York: Garland, 1982.

Guy-Sheftall, Beverly. *Daughters of Sorrow: Attitudes toward Black Women, 1880–1920*. Brooklyn: Carlson, 1990.

Harris, Robert L., Jr. "Daniel Murray and *The Encyclopedia of the Colored Race*." *Phylon* 37 (Fall 1976): 281.

Hemenway, Robert E. *Zora Neale Hurston: A Literary Biography*. Urbana: University of Illinois Press, 1977.

Henry, Linda. " 'Promoting Historical Consciousness': The Early Archives Committee of the National Council of Negro Women." *Signs* 7 (Autumn 1981): 251–59.

Hine, Darlene Clark. *Black Women in American History: Theory and Practice*. Vols. 9–10. Brooklyn: Carlson, 1990.

——. *Hine Sight: Black Women and the Reconstruction of American History.* Brooklyn: Carlson, 1994.

——, ed. *Black Women in America: An Historical Encyclopedia.* 2 vols. Brooklyn: Carlson, 1993.

Hull, Gloria. *Color, Sex, Poetry: Three Women Writers of the Harlem Renaissance.* Bloomington: Indiana University Press, 1987.

Jordan, Casper L. *A Bibliographical Guide to African-American Women Writers: Bibliographies and Indexes in Afro-American and African Studies.* Westport, Conn.: Greenwood Press, 1993.

Joyce, Donald. *Gatekeepers of Black Culture: Black-Owned Book Publishing in the United States, 1817–1981.* Westport, Conn.: Greenwood Press, 1983.

Kaiser, Ernest. "The History of Negro History." *Negro Digest* 17 (February 1968): 64–80.

Lowenberg, Bert, and Ruth Bogin, eds. *Black Women in Nineteenth Century Life: Their Thoughts, Their Words, Their Feelings.* University Park: Pennsylvania State University Press, 1976.

McMurray, Linda O. *Recorder of the Black Experience: A Biography of Monroe Nathan Work.* Baton Rouge: Louisiana State University Press, 1985.

Meier, August, and Elliott M. Rudwick. "J. Franklin Jameson, Carter G. Woodson, and the Foundations of Black Historiography." *American History Review* 89 (October 1984): 1005–15.

——. *Black History and the Historical Profession, 1915–1980.* Urbana: University of Illinois Press, 1986.

Morton, Patricia. *Disfigured Images: The Historical Assault on Afro-American Women.* Westport, Conn.: Greenwood Press, 1991.

Neverdon-Morton, Cynthia. *Afro-American Women of the South and the Advancement of the Race, 1895–1925.* Knoxville: Knoxville University Press, 1989.

Newman, Richard, comp. *Black Index: Afro-Americana in Selected Periodicals, 1907–1949.* New York: Garland, 1981.

Notable Black American Women. Detroit: Gale Research, 1992.

Peterson, Carla L. *"Doers of the Word": African-American Women Speakers and Writers in the North, 1830–1880.* New York: Oxford University Press, 1995.

Redfern, Bernice. *Women of Color in the United States: A Guide to the Literature.* New York: Garland, 1989.

Richardson, Marilyn. *Black Women and Religion: A Bibliography.* Boston: G. K. Hall, 1980.

Robinson, Wilhelmina S. *Historical Negro Biographies.* International Library of Negro Life and History. New York: New York Publishers Co., 1967.

Roses, Lorraine E., and Ruth E. Randolph, eds. *Harlem Renaissance and Beyond: Literary Biographies of One Hundred Black Women Writers, 1900–1945.* Boston: G. K. Hall, 1990.

Salem, Dorothy. *To Better Our World: Black Women in Organized Reform, 1890–1920.* Brooklyn: Carlson, 1990.

Shaw, Stephanie. *What a Woman Ought to Be and Do: Black Professional Women Workers during the Jim Crow Era.* Chicago: University of Chicago Press, 1996.

Shockley, Ann Allen. *Afro-American Women Writers, 1746–1933: An Anthology and Critical Guide.* Boston: G. K. Hall, 1988.

Smith, Valerie, ed. *African American Writers*. New York: Charles Scribner's Sons, 1991.

Starling, Marion W. *The Slave Narrative: Its Place in History*. 2nd ed. Washington, D.C.: Howard University Press, 1988.

Streitmatter, Rodger. *Raising Her Voice: African American Women Journalists Who Changed History*. Lexington: University Press of Kentucky, 1994.

Tate, Claudia. *Domestic Allegories of Political Desire: The Black Heroine's Text at the Turn of the Century*. New York: Oxford University Press, 1992.

Turner, Darwin T., comp. *Afro-American Writers*. New York: Appleton-Century Crofts, 1970.

Von Salis, Susan J. *Revealing Documents: A Guide to African American Manuscript Sources in the Schlesinger Library and the Radcliffe College Archive*. Boston: G. K. Hall, 1993.

Washington, Mary H. *Invented Lives: Narratives of Black Women, 1860–1960*. Garden City, N.Y.: Doubleday, 1987.

Wesley, Charles. *The History of the National Association of Colored Women's Clubs, Inc*. Washington, D.C.: National Association of Colored Women, 1984.

West, Earl H. *A Bibliography of Doctoral Research in the Negro, 1933–1966*. Washington, D.C.: Xerox, 1969.

White, Deborah Gray. "Private Lives, Public Personae: A Look at Early Twentieth-Century African American Clubwomen." In *Talking Gender: Public Images, Personal Journeys, and Political Critiques*, edited by Nancy Hewitt, Jean O'Barr, and Nancy Rosebaugh, 107–20. Chapel Hill: University of North Carolina Press, 1996.

Williams, Ora. *American Black Women in the Arts and Social Sciences: A Bibliographic Survey*. Metuchen, N.J.: Scarecrow Press, 1978.

Wilson, Greta S., comp. *Guide to Processed Collections in the Manuscript Division of the Moorland-Spingarn Research Center*. Washington, D.C.: Howard University Press, 1983.

Yellin, Jean Fagan. *The Pen Is Ours: A Listing of Writings by and about African American Women before 1910, with Secondary Bibliography to the Present*. New York: Oxford University Press, 1991.

Archival Collections for Research on Women Historians in This Study

Baltimore, Md.
  Goucher College Archives
    Annie Heloise Abel Papers
    Katharine Gallagher Papers
    History Department Papers
    Ella Lonn Papers
    President's File
    Dorothy Stimson Collection
    Mary Wilhelmine Williams Papers
Boston, Mass.
  Rare Book Department, Boston Public Library
    Alice Morse Earle Letters

Cambridge, Mass.
 Schlesinger Library, Radcliffe College
  Mary Beard Papers/World Center for Women's Archives materials
  Berkshire Conference of Women Historians Papers
  Berkshire Conference on the History of Women Collection
  Sarah K. Bolton Papers
  Jane Cunningham Croly Papers
  Charlotte Perkins Gilman Papers
  Inez Irwin Papers
  Florence Kitchelt Papers
  Alma Lutz Papers
  Jane Norman Smith Papers
  Woman's Rights Collection Papers
  Women's Archive Records
  Marjorie White Papers
Chicago, Ill.
 University of Chicago Archives
  Marion Talbot Papers
Greencastle, Ind.
 DePauw University Archives
  Mary Beard Papers
Hyde Park, N.Y.
 Franklin D. Roosevelt Library
  Caroline Farrar Ware Collection
Laramie, Wyo.
 American Heritage Center, Coe Library, University of Wyoming
  Grace Raymond Hebard Papers
 Department of Archives, University of Wyoming
  Grace Raymond Hebard Files
Madison, Wis.
 State Historical Society of Wisconsin
  Merle Curti Papers
  Louise Phelps Kellogg Papers
Minneapolis, Minn.
 Minnesota Historical Society
  Maria Sanford Papers
Mount Vernon, Va.
 Archives of the Mount Vernon Ladies' Association of the Union
  Mount Vernon Ladies' Association Records
Newark, N.J.
 New Jersey Historical Society
  WPA-Women's Archives Collection
New York, N.Y.
 New York Public Library Annex, Manuscript Division
  Carrie Chapman Catt Papers
  Macmillan Company Papers
  Schwimmer/Lloyd Collection

Schomburg Center for Research in Black Culture
    Regina Andrews Papers
    Center Records
    Sadie Delaney Papers
    Jean Blackwell Hutson Papers
    Schomburg Clipping File
Northampton, Mass.
    Sophia Smith Collection, Smith College
        Mary Sheldon Barnes Papers
        Mary R. Beard Papers
        Elisabeth Williams Anthony Dexter Papers
        Alice Morse Earle Letters
        Martha J. Lamb Papers
        Sorosis Papers
        Ida Tarbell Papers
Palo Alto, Calif.
    Stanford Cecil Green Library
        Mary Wilhelmine Williams Papers
Philadelphia, Pa.
    Betsy Ross House
        American Flag House and Betsy Ross Association Files
    Historical Society of Pennsylvania
        Alice Morse Earle Papers
        Anne Hollingsworth Wharton Papers
Portland, Ore.
    Oregon Historical Society
        Frances Victor Letters
Poughkeepsie, N.Y.
    Vassar College Archives
        Alma Lutz Papers
        Lucy Maynard Salmon Collection
Princeton, N.J.
    Firestone Library, Princeton University
        Charles Scribner's Sons Papers
Providence, R.I.
    Brown University Library
        Isabel Abbott Papers
        J. Franklin Jameson Historical Seminar Minutes
        J. Franklin Jameson Papers
    John Hay Library, Brown University
        American Historical Association programs
        Elisabeth Dexter Papers
San Marino, Calif.
    Henry E. Huntington Library
        Ida Harper Papers
        Caroline Severance Papers
South Hadley, Mass.
    Mount Holyoke College Archives and Special Collections

Viola Barnes Papers
History Department Records
Annah Soule Papers
Washington, D.C.
Bethune Council House
National Archive of Black Women's History Papers
Bethune Foundation Collection (microfilm). John Bracey and August Meier, eds. University Publications of America, 1996.
Mary McLeod Bethune Papers
Library of Congress Manuscripts Division
American Historical Association Papers
Blackwell Family Papers
Carrie Chapman Catt Papers
National American Woman Suffrage Association Collection
National Woman's Party Collection
Mary Church Terrell Papers
Carter G. Woodson Papers
Moorland-Spingarn Research Center, Howard University
Bethel Literary and Historical Association Collection
Anna J. Cooper Papers
Frederick Douglass Collection
Archibald H. Grimké Collection
Angelina Weld Grimké Papers
Thomas Jefferson Genealogical Collection
Kelly Miller Papers
Lucy D. Slowe Papers
Joel Spingarn Papers
Mary Church Terrell Papers
National Society of the Daughters of the American Revolution Library
Wellesley, Mass.
Wellesley College Archive
Biographical Files
Katharine Coman
Elizabeth Donnan
Ella Smith Elbert
Elizabeth Kendall
Edna Moffett
Julia Orvis
Alice Freeman Palmer
History and Political Science Department, Annual Reports
Wellesley College Special Collections
Elbert Gifts File
Worcester, Mass.
American Antiquarian Society
Alice Morse Earle Papers

Index

Ku Klux Klan, 147
"Kulturgeschichte," 79

Labor history/historians, 60–64, 73,
234–35
Lacey, Virginia: "United States Govern-
ment Publications on the American
Negro, 1916–1937" (1938), 171
Ladies' Hermitage Association, 3
Lakeville Conference. *See* Berkshire
Conference of Women Historians
Lamb, Martha J., 16, 22, 29, 38, 40, 274
(n. 29); as editor of *Magazine of
American History*, 13, 29, 30, 46;
eulogies for, 14–15; *History of the
City of New York: Its Origins, Rise,
and Progress* (1877–1881), 13, 14, 29;
Wall Street History (1883), 14; *Homes
of America* (1897), 14
Lamprecht, Karl, 79
Lane, Ann, 266
Larsen, Nella, 163
Latimer, Catherine, 169, 170, 171, 172, 173,
174, 306 (n. 87); "Where Can I Get
Material on the Negro" (1934), 170;
*Bibliography on the Contribution of
Negro Women to American Civiliza-
tion* (1940), 172
Laut, Agnes: *Pathfinders of the West*
(1904), 104
League of Women Voters (LWV), 192,
196, 201, 210, 249, 263
Lears, T. J. Jackson, 67
Lebsock, Suzanne, 266
Leckie, Shirley: *Angie Debo: Pioneering
Historian* (2000), 270
Lee, Jerena, 135, 161
"Left feminism," 259, 323 (n. 59)
Lemlich (Shavelson), Clara, 262
Lerner, Gerda, 259, 261; "The Lady and
the Mill Girl" (1949), 260
Levi, Kate Everest, 34
Lewis, Helen, 229
Liberating Women's History (1976), 265,
266
Librarianship, 160–62; women in, 162–
64. *See also* African American
women: librarians

Library of Congress, 64, 163, 170, 203,
207, 241
Livermore, Mary, 127, 181, 182; *My Story
of the War* (1887), 126; *Women of the
Century* (1893), 17; *The Story of My
Life* (1897), 126
Lloyd, Lola Maverick, 241
Locke, Alain, 122, 133, 151, 297 (n. 48);
The New Negro (1925), 132, 162,
163
Lockwood, Mary, 219
Logan, Rayford, 166
Loggins, Vernon: *The Negro Author, His
Development in America* (1931), 171
Lonn, Ella, 41, 42, 44, 57, 87, 96, 97, 150,
289 (n. 17); *Reconstruction in Loui-
siana* (1918), 150
Loomis, Louise, 43, 219
Lowell Mill girls, 260
Lundberg, Ferdinand: *Modern Woman:
The Lost Sex* (1947), 254
Lutz, Alma, 201, 202, 209, 217, 224, 250,
255, 314 (n. 90); *Challenging Years*
(1940), 201; *Created Equal* (1940),
201, 255

MacLeish, Archibald, 241
Magazine of American History, 13, 14, 40
Majors, Alphus: *Noted Negro Women*
(1893), 127, 128
Mann, Horace, 2
Martineau, Harriet: *Retrospect of West-
ern Travel* (1838), 249
Mathes, Valerie, 108
Mathews, Lois, 39, 45
Matthews, Miriam, 158; "Library
Activities in the Field of Race Rela-
tions" (1927), 165; "The Negro in
California, 1781–1910: An Annotated
Bibliography," 171
Maynor, Dorothy, 242
McAfee, Mildred, 251
McDougald, Elise Johnson: "The Task
of New Negro Womanhood" (1925),
162, 163
McMillan, Genevieve: "History of
Higher Education of Women in the
South" (1923), 94

Mead, Kate. *See* Hurd-Mead, Kate

Mead, Margaret, 78, 114, 250, 255; *Sex and Temperament in Three Primitive Societies* (1935), 79

Medieval Academy, 32

Mendenhall, Marjorie: "History of Agriculture in South Carolina, 1790–1860," 96

Merritt, Emma, 123–24

Meyer, Annie, 118; *Woman's Work in America* (1891), 128

Milholland, Inez, 191

Militant feminism, 189–91

Miller, Kelly, 133, 161

Mississippi Valley Historical Association, 97

Mississippi Valley Historical Review (*MVHR*), 97–98, 154. See also *Journal of American History*

Modernism, 268

Monticello-Jefferson Memorial Association, 3

Moorland, Jesse, 155, 161

Moorland Foundation. *See* Moorland-Spingarn Research Center

Moorland-Spingarn Research Center (MSRC), 161, 165–67; Moorland collection, 166, 170, 172, 260; *A Catalogue of Books in the Moorland Foundation* (1938), 170

Morgan, Madeline, 160

Morriss, Margaret, 48; "Maryland under the Royal Government," 34

Morrow, Elizabeth Cutter, 248

Mossell, Gertrude Bustill, 122, 123, 135, 157; *The Work of the Afro-American Woman* (1894), 128

Mossell, Nathan, 123

Mossell (Alexander), Sadie, 131

Mott, Lucretia, 190, 201, 205, 247, 260

Moulton, Louisa: *Our Famous Women* (1883), 17

Mount Rushmore, 198, 311 (n. 53)

Mount Vernon Ladies' Association, 3

Multiculturalism, 267

Murray, Daniel, 123, 161, 163; wife of, 173

Murray, Pauli, 269

National American Woman Suffrage Association (NAWSA), 82, 183, 185, 192, 212, 227, 237, 249; archive, 187; congressional committee, 188, 309 (n. 35); Collection, 207–9, 210, 241, 247

National Archive of Black Women's History, 244

National Association for the Advancement of Colored People, 167, 243

National Association of Colored Women (NACW), 123, 124–25, 138, 157

National Consumer's League, 63, 245

National Council of Catholic Women, 243

National Council of Jewish Women, 233, 243

National Council of Negro Women (NCNW), 167, 243; Negro Archive Committee, 235, 238, 242–44; Archives Museum Department, 242–44; National Archives Day, 243

National Cyclopedia of the Colored Race (1919), 161

National Hall of Fame, 201–2, 312 (nn. 65, 66)

National Woman's Party (NWP), 57, 188, 192, 196, 211, 227, 249; party historians, 188–91, 237; memorial committee, 197–98; Anthony Hall of Fame campaign, 201–2; feminist collection, 203

National Woman Suffrage Association (NWSA), 181, 183, 184, 196, 211

Native American history, 64–66, 106–17, 232–33

Native Daughters of the Golden West, 3

Native Sons of the Golden West, 106

Negro Book Collectors Exchange, 160

Negro History Bulletin (*NHB*), 159–60

Negro History Week, 157–59, 263, 302 (n. 38)

Negro Society for Historical Research (NSHR), 133, 153, 160

Neilson, Nellie, 32, 33, 39, 42, 51, 276 (n. 58), 281 (n. 115); in AHA, 49, 223–25; "Boon Services on the Estates of Ramsey Abbey" (1897), 41

Nell, William C.: *Colored Patriots of the American Revolution* (1855), 121
Nelson, Marilyn, 164
Neo-Malthusian League, 227
New England History Teachers Association, 221
New Historians, 58–59, 80
New Indian History, 270
New Left, 261, 263
New Masses, 261
New Negro History Movement, 122, 142, 146, 147–76, 213, 243, 262
New School of Social Research, 80
"New Woman," 19, 24, 192, 273 (n. 21), 309 (n. 29); depictions of in feminist history, 192–202, 263
New York Training School for Public Service, 80
Nichols, Jeanette, 224
Nineteenth Amendment, 178, 188, 190, 196, 201, 203, 265
Novick, Peter, 6, 56, 58, 79–80, 258, 259, 277 (n. 66)
Nutting, Adelaide: *A History of Nursing* (1907), 178, 250

Odum, Howard, 94–95, 105, 118
Oral history, 100, 101, 111, 152, 172–74, 233
O'Reilly, Leonora, 234
Organized feminism. *See* Woman's rights movement
Orvis, Julia, 50, 76, 223

Page, Zelia, 127
Palmer, Alice Freeman, 35, 45; Fellowship, 50
Papers of the American Historical Association, 38, 40, 223
Park, Maud Wood, 195, 203–4, 210, 211–12, 247
Park, Robert E., 148
Parkhurst (Guzman), Jessie, 151, 153, 158, 171; "The Role of the Black Mammy in the Plantation Household" (1938), 152
Parkman, Francis, 16, 22
Parsons, Elise Clews, 78, 113, 151; *The Old-Fashioned Woman* (1913), 79

Pascoe, Peggy, 102, 289 (n. 5). *See also* "Intercultural brokers"
Paul, Alice, 188, 190, 196, 200, 203, 212, 253, 310 (n. 36)
Paxson, Frederic, 47
Peabody Museum, 108
Peck, Mary Gray, 205, 206, 208, 209; *Carrie Chapman Catt: A Biography* (1944), 200
Pendleton, Leila Amos, 154
Perkins, Frances, 228
Peterson, Carla, 119, 121, 306 (n. 85)
Peterson, Dorothy, 161
Phillips, Ulrich Bonnell, 134
Pierce, Bessie, 42, 45, 47, 145, 223; *Public Opinion and the Teaching of History* (1926), 69–70, 71
Pinckney, Eliza, 18
Popper, Karl, 20
Porter, Dorothy, 151, 152, 153, 171, 172, 173, 174; as director of Moorland collection, 166–67, 260; and American Negro Exposition, 217; WCWA work of, 238; on NCNW archives committee, 242; "Negro Writers before 1830" (1932), 166; "Library Sources for the Study of Negro Life and History" (1936), 170; *A Selected List of Books by and about the Negro* (1936), 170
Positivism, historical, 21, 266
Postmodernism, 266
Powley, Margaret Nelson, 141
Prince, Nancy, 135
Professionalization, historical, 6, 7, 24–30
Progressive Era, 5, 88, 118, 163, 266
Progressive history/historians, 59–63, 71–72, 94, 105, 134, 139, 148, 258–59
Public libraries, 162–65, 204, 241; 135th Street branch of New York Public Library (*See* Schomburg Center); George Cleveland Hall branch (Chicago), 162, 171; Countee Cullen Branch (New York), 165; Vernon and Watts branches (Los Angeles), 165
Puckett, Newell Niles: *Folk Beliefs of the Southern Negro* (1926), 118

Black Culture), 167–70, 260; collection, 170, 172; Historic Honor Roll, 242; *Calendar of the Manuscripts in the Schomburg Collection of Negro Literature* (1942), 170

Schreiner, Olive, 87

Schuyler, Catherine, 18

Schwimmer, Rosika, 227, 228, 235, 241

Scientific history, 6, 7, 186, 233; gendering of, 21–66

Scott, Anne Firor, 94, 95, 263; *The Southern Lady* (1970), 263

Scott, Margaret Gale, 44

Scribner's Publishers, 275 (n. 39); Women of Colonial and Revolutionary Times series, 18, 19, 26

Scruggs, Lawson A.: *Women of Distinction* (1893), 127

Sears, Clara Endicott, 3

Second-wave feminism, 213, 259, 261, 265

Separatism, feminist, 237–38, 265

Severance, Caroline, 182

Seymour, Flora: *The Story of the Red Man* (1929), 110, 112

Shackleford, Jane, 158, 160; *Child's Story of the Negro* (1938), 159

Shaw, Anna Howard, 182, 185, 190; *Story of a Pioneer* (1915), 186

Shorter, Susan: *Heroines of African Methodism* (1891), 127

Shouler, James, 134

Shuler, Nettie, 186

Singleton, Esther: *Dutch New York* (1909), 13

Slaughter, Henry, 161

Slave narratives, 100, 126, 135, 140–41, 161, 172

Slowe, Lucy Diggs, 130, 145, 235

Smith, Anna Bustill, 154

Smith, Bonnie, 5, 6, 25, 28, 80, 266, 269

Smith, Mary Roberts: *Chinese Immigration* (1909), 63

Smith, William, 13

Social Science Research Council, 49

Society of Colonial Dames (SCD), 3, 20, 66–69, 70, 105, 124, 125

Society of the Descendants of Early New England Negroes, 125, 157

Sophia Smith Collection, 249–51, 252, 321 (n. 25)

Sorosis, 14

Southern Historical Association, 97, 263

Spaulding, Eliza, 110

Spear, Chloe, 161

Speculum, 32, 48

Spencer, Anna, 83, 85; *Woman's Share in Social Culture* (1913), 84

Spingarn, Amy, 161

Spingarn, Arthur, 161

Spruill, Julia Cherry, 93, 231, 263; *Women's Life and Work in the Southern Colonies* (1938), 91, 94, 95

Stantial, Edna, 203–10 passim, 247, 314 (n. 90)

Stanton, Elizabeth Cady, 202, 207, 211, 247; as leader of NWSA, 181; brand of suffragism/feminism, 181, 183, 185, 189, 196; as depicted in suffrage history, 198–99, 255, 312 (n. 63); as NAWSA president, 201; *History of Woman Suffrage*, 179–80, 182; *Eighty Years and More*, 182, 198, 200

Stanton, Theodore, 198, 199

Stauffer, Helen, 115

Stephenson, Jean, 98

Stevens, Doris, 188, 189, 191, 203, 228; *Jailed for Freedom* (1920), 186, 189, 190, 191

Stevenson, Adlai, 258

Stevenson, Matilda, 79

Still, William: Underground Railroad Collection, 122

Stimson, Dorothy, 42, 45–46, 49, 50, 57, 76, 87; "The Gradual Acceptance of the Copernican Theory of the Universe," 87; *Scientists and Amateurs: A History of the Royal Society* (1947), 46

Stone, Lucy, 181, 182, 183, 185, 196, 199–200, 311 (n. 59)

Stowe, Harriet Beecher, 125, 172

Suffrage movement. *See* Woman's rights movement

Summerhayes, Martha, 102

Wilkes, Laura, 150; *The Story of Frederick Douglass* (1899), 124; *Missing Pages in American History* (1919), 121, 150
Willard, Emma, 2
Willard, Frances, 17, 127, 182, 193, 310 (n. 40); *Women in the Pulpit* (1889), 17; *Women of the Century* (1893), 17
Williams, E. C., 153
Williams, Fannie Barrier, 171
Williams, Judith Blow, 224
Williams, Lucy, 174, 175
Williams, Mary: in AHA, 39, 41, 283 (n. 10); as academic historian, 42, 44, 46, 49, 50; pedagogy of, 53, 55, 87; as scholar/advocate, 57, 219, 224; "History of the Latin American People and Their Politics," 49
Williams, Susan, 24
Wilson, Woodrow, 38
Winnemucca, Sarah: *Life among the Paiutes* (1883), 110
Wittenmyer, Annie: *History of the Woman's Temperance Crusade* (1878), 126; *Under the Guns: A Woman's Reminiscence of the Civil War* (1895), 126
Wollstonecraft, Mary, 205
Woman Citizen, 207, 247
Womanism, 136–37, 146, 164, 268
Woman's Christian Temperance Union (WCTU), 57, 202
Woman's Institute, 256–57, 265
Woman's International League for Peace and Freedom (WILPF), 57, 288 (n. 80)
Woman's Journal, 207, 245, 247
Woman's Rights Collection, 204–7, 217, 247, 321 (n. 19)
Woman's rights movement, 177–213, 265; history of, 177–213
Women anthropologists. *See* Anthropology: women in
Women pedagogues, 44–46, 53–55, 87, 221
Women's Bureau, U.S., 63

Women's Centennial Congress (1940), 57
Women's collections, 203–10, 241–51, 252
Women's Colleges (Sister Schools), 35, 50–51, 223, 246–47, 251–52
—history departments at: Bryn Mawr, 31; Mount Holyoke, 31–33
Women's liberation movement. *See* Second-wave feminism
Women's National Indian Association (WNIA), 103–4, 105, 108
Women's National Liberal Union, 196
Women's Trade Union League (WTUL), 61, 82, 234
Woodbury, Helen Sumner, 56, 73; "History of Women in Industry in the United States" (1910), 63
Woodhull, Victoria, 183, 193, 194–95, 207, 308 (n. 13)
Woodhull and Claflin Weekly, 207
Woodson, Carter G., 131, 139, 145, 171, 239; as director of ASNLH, 146–60 passim; "The Negro Washerwoman: A Vanishing Figure" (1930), 153; "Negro Women Eligible to be Daughters of the American Revolution" (1943), 159; "The Negro Historian of Our Times" (1945), 160
Woolley, Helen Thompson, 56
Woolley, Mary, 32, 41, 50, 276 (n. 57), 277 (n. 70); "The Development of the Love of Romantic Scenery in America" (1897), 41
Work, Monroe: *Negro Year Book* (1912), 161; *A Bibliography of the Negro in Africa and America* (1928), 161
Works Projects Administration (WPA), 66, 98, 100, 139, 170, 172. *See also* Federal Writers' Project
World Center for Women's Archives (WCWA), 218, 225–40, 243, 244, 262, 265; auxiliaries, 230; Negro Women's Committee, 235, 238, 242; and pan-women's history, 235–36; demise of, 236–39, 241, 251; feminist debates within, 237–38
World's Fair (New York, 1940), 242

Index 379

Wright, Frances, 182
Wright, Irene, 149
Wright, Marion Thompson, 145
Wright, Richard, 162
Wylie, Philip, 254

Young Women's Christian Association, 243

Zimmerman, Loretta, 266
Zinga, Anna, 128

GENDER & AMERICAN CULTURE

Toward an Intellectual History of Women: Essays by Linda K. Kerber (1997)

Gender and Jim Crow: Women and the Politics of White Supremacy in North Carolina,
  1896–1920, by Glenda Elizabeth Gilmore (1996)

Delinquent Daughters: Protecting and Policing Adolescent Female Sexuality in the
  United States, 1885–1920, by Mary E. Odem (1995)

U.S. History as Women's History: New Feminist Essays,
  edited by Linda K. Kerber, Alice Kessler-Harris, and Kathryn Kish Sklar (1995)

Common Sense and a Little Fire: Women and Working-Class Politics in the United States,
  1900–1965, by Annelise Orleck (1995)

How Am I to Be Heard?: Letters of Lillian Smith, edited by Margaret Rose Gladney (1993)

Entitled to Power: Farm Women and Technology, 1913–1963, by Katherine Jellison (1993)

Revising Life: Sylvia Plath's Ariel Poems, by Susan R. Van Dyne (1993)

Made From This Earth: American Women and Nature, by Vera Norwood (1993)

Unruly Women: The Politics of Social and Sexual Control in the Old South,
  by Victoria E. Bynum (1992)

The Work of Self-Representation: Lyric Poetry in Colonial New England,
  by Ivy Schweitzer (1991)

Labor and Desire: Women's Revolutionary Fiction in Depression America,
  by Paula Rabinowitz (1991)

Community of Suffering and Struggle: Women, Men, and the Labor Movement in
  Minneapolis, 1915–1945, by Elizabeth Faue (1991)

All That Hollywood Allows: Re-reading Gender in 1950s Melodrama, by Jackie Byars (1991)

Doing Literary Business: American Women Writers in the Nineteenth Century,
  by Susan Coultrap-McQuin (1990)

Ladies, Women, and Wenches: Choice and Constraint in Antebellum Charleston and
  Boston, by Jane H. Pease and William H. Pease (1990)

The Secret Eye: The Journal of Ella Gertrude Clanton Thomas, 1848–1889,
  edited by Virginia Ingraham Burr, with an introduction by Nell Irvin Painter (1990)

Second Stories: The Politics of Language, Form, and Gender in Early American Fictions,
  by Cynthia S. Jordan (1989)

Within the Plantation Household: Black and White Women of the Old South,
  by Elizabeth Fox-Genovese (1988)

The Limits of Sisterhood: The Beecher Sisters on Women's Rights and Woman's Sphere,
  by Jeanne Boydston, Mary Kelley, and Anne Margolis (1988)